THE CLASSICS
OF WESTERN
SPIRITUALITY

THE CLASSICS OF WESTERN SPIRITUALITY
A Library of the Great Spiritual Masters

Ephrem the Syrian
HYMNS

TRANSLATED AND INTRODUCED BY
KATHLEEN E. McVEY

PREFACE BY
JOHN MEYENDORFF

PAULIST PRESS
NEW YORK • MAHWAH

Cover art: The Icon of Saint Ephrem the Syrian was written by ANDRIJ MADAY, an Iconographer of the Holy Orthodox Church. He has been involved in Iconography for a number of years now, independently studying the craft as well as the scripture which Icons portray. Andrij's desire is "to live and work for the glory of Our Lord and Savior Jesus Christ, which is a difficult struggle, a struggle toward the complete surrender to His Holy Will." Andrij asks only that the readers remember Iconographers in their prayers.

The preparation of this volume was made possible by a grant from the Translations Program of the National Endowment for the Humanities, an independent Federal agency.

Copyright © 1989 by
Kathleen E. McVey

Library of Congress Cataloging-in-Publication Data

Ephraem, Syrus, Saint, 303–373.
    [Hymns. English. Selections]
    Ephrem the Syrian : hymns / [translated] by Kathleen E. McVey.
       p.   cm.—(Classics of Western spirituality)
    Includes bibliographical references.
    Contents: Hymns on the Nativity—Hymns against Julian—The hymns on virginity and on the symbols of the Lord.
    ISBN 0-8091-0429-6 : $17.95 (est.).—ISBN 0-8091-3093-9 (pbk.) : $14.95 (est.)
    1. Hymns, English—Translations from Syriac. 2. Hymns, Syriac—Translations into English. I. McVey, Kathleen E., 1944–
II. Title. III. Series.
BR65.E362E5 1989
264′.01402—dc20

Published by Paulist Press
997 Macarthur Boulevard
Mahwah, New Jersey 07430

Printed and bound in the United States of America

Contents

For my parents

Translator of This Volume

KATHLEEN E. McVEY is associate professor of early and eastern church history at Princeton Theological Seminary. She is a graduate of Radcliffe College (A.B. 1966), where she majored in Russian history and literature and wrote her senior thesis on Georges Florovsky. She has studied church history at Harvard, and Syriac and Coptic at the Catholic University of America, and she has excavated with the American School of Oriental Research at Carthage in Tunisia and at Idalion in Cyprus. After receiving the doctorate at Harvard in 1977, she was awarded a visiting fellowship at Dumbarton Oaks Center for Byzantine Studies in Washington, D.C. In the capacity of Catholic Biblical Association visiting professor she taught at the École Biblique et Archéologique Française in Jerusalem for one year before joining the faculty at Princeton in 1979. Her previous publications include articles in *Dumbarton Oaks Papers* and in *Orientalia Christiana Analecta* as well as several reviews in *Theology Today*, the *Catholic Biblical Quarterly* and the *Journal of the American Academy of Religion*. She has been a member of the Council of the American Society of Church History, is presently a member of the board of directors of the North American Patristic Society, and is a member of the the editorial board of the *Fathers of the Church* series. She lives with her husband and two children in Princeton, New Jersey, where she is presently working on a book on George, Bishop of the Arabs, the subject of her doctoral dissertation.

Author of the Preface

JOHN MEYENDORFF is professor of history at Fordham University and professor and dean at St. Vladimir's Orthodox Theological Seminary in Crestwood, New York. He received the degree of *Docteur èslettres* at the Sorbonne, Paris, in 1958 and has been on the faculty of Harvard University, Center for Byzantine Studies, Dumbarton Oaks (1960–67) where he also served as acting director of studies (1978). Father

Meyendorff is an internationally esteemed authority on Eastern Christian history, theology and spirituality and a corresponding Fellow, The British Academy. His books include *St. Gregory Palamas and Orthodox Spirituality* (1959), *Christ in Eastern Christian Thought* (1969) and *Byzantium and the Rise of Russia* (1981).

Foreword

The production of this book has occupied a larger segment of my life than I could have imagined when I began. As a consequence it is simply impossible to name all those to whom I am indebted for professional insight or personal support in this project. Before attempting to enumerate some of them, however, I would like to make a few remarks about the picture of Ephrem on the cover and its relation to the contents of the book.

The artist's representation is based on the Greek Orthodox iconographic tradition for the portrayal of St. Ephrem. Garbed in a monastic habit, he holds a scroll on which is inscribed an admonition against mixing seriousness with laughter. This is quite consistent with the literary and theological themes of the corpus of writings in Greek attributed to him. The accuracy of these attributions, however, is doubtful at best. Although the transitoriness of life and the consequent need for penitence figure in the Syriac hymns, especially in the *Hymns on Paradise*, the *Carmina Nisibena* and the *Hymns against Julian*, they are not Ephrem's predominant themes. A very different icon of the saint emerges if only the authentic Syriac writings are mixed on our palette: a symbolic-poet-theologian entranced with the paradox of the Incarnation of the ineffable God and with the Divine presence in Nature and Scripture. During the last years of his life, moreover, Ephrem was a deacon of the Church at Edessa; he was never a monk. Neither a member of a monastic community nor a hermit, he was instead an ascetic of a peculiarly Syrian sort, an *yḥydy'*, a solitary or "single" one, a celibate living in the ordinary Christian congregation as the special representative of Christ, the "Only-begotten." In the *Hymns on Virginity and the Symbols of the Lord* he draws out the theological implications of this understanding of the ascetic life and clarifies its relation to his symbolic theology. Unfortunately practical concerns prevented the production of a cover more consistent with the Syriac traditions and thus with the content of the hymns translated here.

Many people have provided me with vital encouragement and useful criticism in the production of this book. First I wish to thank John Meyendorff for suggesting I might make a contribution from the Syriac Christian tradition to the Classics of Western Spirituality series. Thanks to a translation grant from the National Endowment for the Humanities, matched by funds from Princeton Theological Seminary, I was able to work exclusively on this project in the spring semester of 1984. From Sebastian Brock, Robert Murray and Hans J.W. Drijvers I received useful initial advice on methods and style of translation. I am appreciative of conversations about Ephrem, Judaism and Julian the Apostate with David Levenson, Martha Himmelfarb, Robert Kraft and other members of the Philadelphia Seminar on Christian Origins. I am especially indebted to Sidney Griffith, as well as to Glen Bowersock, David Bundy, Luisa Abramowski, John Strugnell and Corby Finney, for reading earlier drafts of portions of the manuscript and for offering both encouragement and constructive criticism. John Gager and Elizabeth Clark generously agreed to read through the completed manuscript. Of course any remaining flaws are solely my responsibility. For conscientious typing and word-processing of portions of the manuscript I am grateful to Elizabeth Meirs, Maude Farrow and Helaine Randerson. For encouragement to plunge into the wordprocessing world with this translation project and for correctly diagnosing my ailing computer I am indebted to Charles Willard and James Armstrong respectively. The editors of the Classics of Western Spirituality series, John Farina and Bernard McGinn, and the editorial staff of Paulist Press, especially Pat Egan and Georgia Christo, have been graciously helpful.

I am thankful for the interest and support of my colleagues at Princeton Theological Seminary, especially, although not exclusively, Karlfried Froehlich, Chris Beker, Betty Edwards, Freda Gardner, Lois Livezey, Kathie Sakenfeld, Jean-Loup Seban and the other members of the history department. Other friends have provided personal support, sometimes from afar, especially Faine McMullen, Kate Skrebutenas, Joan Biella, Kathryn Nichols, Maurice Phillips, and my sister Elizabeth McVey. All the members of my family—my mother and sisters as well as my husband and children—have graciously admitted Ephrem to their midst for many years.

FOREWORD

In the preparation of this translation I have relied on the critical texts by Edmund Beck. His German translations, notes and cross references have often been useful as well. Nevertheless I have translated from the Syriac text, have made my own judgments about the relevance of biblical citations and cross references, and have added some discussion of the secondary literature. Since the principal dialogue in technical matters is with Beck, and since I have followed his numbering of hymns and strophes, I have not used page numbers in referring to his work; the reader will find the relevant passage by consulting the corresponding hymn, strophe and line of his edition in the *Corpus Scriptorum Christianorum Orientalium*.

In rendering Ephrem's Syriac into English I have tried to be as literal as possible without sacrificing grace and fluidity. In the interest of eloquence, I have routinely omitted "behold" and the otiose "and" and have freely transformed relative clauses and genitive phrases into participles or adjectives where appropriate. As much as possible I have preserved the structure of Ephrem's thought by leaving his lines and half-lines of poetry intact. At times when this obscured the meaning or awkwardly halted the flow of words, especially in the *casus pendens* construction, however, I have changed the word order or cut the lines to suit aesthetic rather than scholarly criteria. My intention has been to use a single English word to render a given Syriac word except where a significant change of nuance dictated a different choice. In at least two instances, however, I have discovered unintended inconsistencies too late in the publication process to correct them: Syriac *knr'* is rendered variously as "lyre" or "harp," and *'m'* and its plural are translated in some hymns as "the People" and "the peoples" and in others as "the [Jewish] people" and "the Gentiles." Words in brackets have been supplied by me. Ellipses indicate a lacuna in the Syriac text. Since scientifically correct transliteration poses some difficulties for the general reader and especially for the typesetter, I have tried to follow a course of moderate compromise, being consistent in my inconsistencies! Conventional spellings of proper names, grammatical terms, letters of the Syriac alphabet and months of the year have been used. All other Syriac words have been more precisely transliterated using the equivalents in T. Nöldeke's *Kurzgefasste Syrische Grammatik* (Leipzig, 1898; rep. Darmstadt, 1966), p. 2, without indicating softening or doubling of consonants and without vocalization except when a pun is dependent on differing vocalizations.

Preface

The idea that the early Christian tradition was limited to its Greek and Latin expressions is still widespread. This assumption distorts historical reality and weakens greatly our understanding of the roots of Christian theology and spirituality. In the third and fourth centuries Syriac was the third international language of the church. It served as the major means of communication in the Roman diocese of the "East," which included Syria, Palestine, and Mesopotamia. It was the vehicle of Christian missionary expansion in Persia, Armenia, Georgia, India, and even Ethiopia. Furthermore, and most important, Syriac was a dialect of Aramean, the language spoken by Jesus and his immediate disciples. Jewish communities existed in Syriac-speaking countries at the time of Christ, and it is possible to assume a very early Christian presence in their midst. Although direct evidence is lacking, spiritual, theological and personal contacts between the Judeo-Christians in Palestine and early Syrian Christianity are probable. The legend of the correspondence between Jesus and King Abgar of Edessa, and the story of the image of Christ "not-made-with-hands" received by the king, might be a later reflection of such contacts, preserved in the memory of Syrian Christians.

St. Ephrem is the only Syrian writer who—for the historical reasons described by Dr. McVey in her Introduction—was well-known and admired among his Greek and Latin contemporaries. His name entered the lists of venerated saints in the East and in the West, and his writings influenced liturgical hymnography. Whether or not one is able to read him in the original Syriac, one has to acknowledge that he is the greatest Christian poet of his age. One can only regret that there seems to be no way of restoring the musical melodies, which he doubtlessly composed also, and which were an integral part of his meditation on the mysteries of the faith.

PREFACE

An orthodox Nicean Christian living in the midst of doctrinal controversies involving Arianism, Manicheism, Marcionism, as well as the still powerful pagan tradition and Judeo-Christian polemics, Ephrem is always able to transcend frozen formulas and to maintain that extraordinary biblical freshness that gives the early Syriac Christian tradition a flavor of true universality. This is particularly true of Ephrem's theology of the incarnation, his sacramental typology and his understanding of ethical issues.

There are numerous translations of Ephrem into German and French, but he remains relatively inaccessible to those who read only English. In this volume Dr. McVey offers three large collections of Ephrem's *Hymns*, translated in a smooth and highly readable English.

As a Syriac specialist, concerned not only with erudition in a difficult field but also with making the tradition of the Fathers a living source of Christian thought for many, Dr. McVey joins the increasing group of scholars who—following the lead of Robert Murray and Sebastian Brock—are making the Syriac Christian writers better-known to English-speaking readers.

John Meyendorff

Introduction

I   Ephrem the Syrian and His Importance for Christian History and Theology

Ephrem the Syrian, the foremost writer in the Syriac tradition of Christianity, was born in Nisibis near the beginning of the fourth century C.E. and spent his early life there, teaching and writing hymns, homilies and commentaries, with the approval of a succession of orthodox bishops. The Roman loss to Persia in 363 C.E. forced him, along with the rest of the citizenry, to abandon his native city and move westward in order to remain within the Roman Empire. He continued his rich literary production in Edessa, where he is said to have established both a school of biblical and theological studies and women's choirs to sing his hymns. Ordained to the diaconate, he died while ministering to victims of the plague in 373 C.E.[1]

Ephrem's importance for the history of Syriac literature and for the history of Christianity in the Syriac-speaking context is immense. His hymns, incorporated early into the liturgy, have remained central in both the East and West Syrian liturgical traditions. From this paramount position they have exerted a formative influence on all aspects of ecclesiastical life. The literary and hymnic forms that he used, some of which he may have invented, became the standard forms of all subsequent Syriac literature and hymnography. Although his works incorporate many of the themes found in the Jewish-Christian or Gnostic writings of the earliest Syriac Christianity, Ephrem's commitment to Nicene orthodoxy set the subsequent direction of the Syriac Church. In his own lifetime and for a half-century thereafter his method of biblical interpretation was the sole

---

1. Soz. HE 3.16; Pall. H. Laus. 40.

standard among Syriac writers. Even after the formal introduction of Greek hermeneutical methods in the fifth century, Ephrem's interpretations continued to be studied and held in esteem. Despite uncertainty over the precise lines of his contact with Greek culture, not only a concept of orthodoxy but also many philosophical presuppositions and literary forms analogous to those of Greek Christian theological literature are to be found in his work, and through him they descend in the Syriac heritage.

Appreciation of Ephrem's hymns was not limited to those who spoke Syriac. Among the Eastern traditions most closely allied with the Syriac— Greek, Coptic, Ethiopic, Armenian, and, later, Arabic—he found a place almost as central as in his own tradition. Writing within decades of his death Jerome attests to his fame in the Latin church as well.[2] At about the same time and with an enthusiasm perhaps predictable in a man named after the feast, Epiphanius cites with approval the Syrian poet's association of Christ and the Twelve with the Epiphany, the thirteenth day after the winter solstice.[3] The fifth-century Greek ecclesiastical writers Palladius, Theodoret and Sozomen include him in their histories, where he is not only portrayed as a model of the ascetic life—a role he shared with many others—but also readily appreciated for his extraordinary poetic gift.[4] Both Jerome and Sozomen assert that even in translation they were able to appreciate his eloquence.[5] According to Sozomen the translation of his works into Greek had begun even during his lifetime, and in the following centuries they were translated into virtually every language known to Christianity.[6] Although study of the nature and extent of his influence on

---

2. Hier. de vir. ill. 115.
3. Nat. 5.13, cf. Epiph. Pan. 52.22.7; noted by Beck, Lobgesang, 11.
4. Theod. HE 4.26; Soz. loc. cit.; Pall. loc. cit.
5. Hier. loc. cit; Soz. loc. cit.
6. Soz. loc. cit. Like other illustrious writers Ephrem was also frequently credited with the compositions of others. The task of sorting the authentic works from the spurious is often complex. For an overview of the editions of his Syriac corpus and a thorough discussion of the criteria of authenticity used by Burkitt, Vööbus and Beck, cf. J. Melki, "Saint Éphrem: Bilan de l'Édition Critique," PdO 11 (1983), 3–88. The task of sorting authentic from pseudo-Ephrem in the translation traditions is even more difficult; for a survey of the texts and secondary literature, cf. D. Hemmerdinger-Iliadou and Jean Kirchmeyer, "Éphrem (Les versions)," Dictionnaire de Spiritualité 4 (1960), 800–22; further, on the Arabic versions, Kh. Samir, "L'Éphrem arabe. État des travaux," OCA 205 (1978), 229–42; on the Latin, M. Schmidt, "Ephraem Latinus," ZDMG suppl. 4 (1980), 181–84; on the Armenian and Georgian, B. Outtier, "Les recueils georgiens d'oeuvres attribuées à S. Éphrem le Syrien," BK 32 (1974), 118–25; idem, "Les recueils arméniens et georgiens d'oeuvres attribuées à S. Éphrem le Syrien," Actes 29e congrès international des orientalistes, Orient chrètien (1975), 53–58; in Greek, M. Geerard, "Ephraem Graecus" in Clavis Patrum Graecorum II (Turnhout, 1974), 366–468.

later Western Christianity is still in a fairly rudimentary stage, it is clear that he played a significant role in the development of both Byzantine hymnography and Western medieval religious drama.[7]

II Ephrem's Life in Political and Social Context

A Nisibis and Its Christians

Nisibis, the birthplace of Ephrem Syrus, was a major commercial and political center in northeastern Mesopotamia.[8] Situated on a fertile plain adjacent to the River Mygdonius, the city had been an urban center for well over a millennium before his time.[9] Its population was a conglomeration of Arameans, Arabs, Greeks, Jews, Parthians, Romans, and Iranians. The culture, and consequently the pre-Christian religion, consisted of a complex mixture of elements distilled from the several civilizations that had held sway there through the prior centuries.[10] The pagan deities

---

7. For his influence on Romanos the Melode, cf. William L. Petersen, *The Diatesseron and Ephrem Syrus as Sources of Romanos the Melodist*, (CSCO v. 466, subsidia 73; Louvain, 1986), with a summary and discussion of the earlier literature on this subject, pp. 1–13. For the influence of Romanos on western medieval drama, cf. G. La Piana, *Le Rappresentazioni Sacre nelle Letteratura Bizantina dalle Origini al sec. 9*, (Grottaferrata, 1912); M. Carpenter, "Romanos and the Mystery Play of the East," in *Philological Studies in Honor of Walter Miller*, University of Missouri Studies 11.3 (1936), 21–51; and W. Greisenegger, *Die Realität im Religiösen Theater des mittelalters*, (Wien, 1978), 18, n. 32. For the evidence of direct influence of Ephrem on the development of western medieval drama cf. Margot Schmidt, "Orientalischer Einfluss auf die deutsche Literatur. Quellengeschichliche Studien zum 'Abraham' der Hrotsvit von Ganderheim," *Colloquia Germanica* 1/2 (1968), 152–87; a condensed French version of this article appears as "Influence de saint Éphrem sur la littérature latine et allemande du début du moyen-age," PdO 4 (1973), 325–41; also cf. August C. Mahr, *Relations of Passion Plays to St. Ephrem the Syrian* (Columbus, 1942).

8. On Nisibis as the birthplace of Ephrem, cf. Sozomen, HE 3.16. Although several "lives" of Ephrem exist in Greek and Syriac, some of them claiming Ephrem's own authorship, none can be traced to him or to his contemporaries. The most trustworthy data for Ephrem's life are incidental remarks in his writings; next are the Greek accounts of Palladius, Socrates, Sozomen and Theodoret; among Syriac sources the most reliable are Jacob of Sarug and Barhadbshabba, cf. B. Outtier, O.S.B., "Saint Éphrem d'après ses biographies et ses oeuvres," PdO 4 (1973), 11–34. For enumeration and examination of the hagiographic sources and a less critical assessment of certain of them, cf. A. Vööbus, *Literal Critical and Historical Studies in Ephrem the Syrian*, Papers of the Estonian Theological Society in Exile 10, (Stockholm, 1958).

9. On Nisibis, cf. J. Sturm, RE 17, 714–57. Especially on the history of the Christian community of Nisibis, cf. J. M. Fiey, *Nisibe: metropole syriaque orientale et ses suffragants des origines à nos jours*, CSCO 388, subsidia 54 (Louvain, 1977), on the early period, esp. 16–39.

10. There is no study of the religion of Nisibis itself in the relevant time period. Studies of the religion of the area as an aspect of the culture include works cited in Drijvers, Persistence, 41, nn.1,2. The work of Drijvers with regard to other Mesopotamian cities, viz. Hatra, Palmyra and Edessa, is relevant; cf. idem, Cults and idem, Hatra.

still worshipped in the fourth-century Mesopotamian cities included Babylonian gods, such as Bel and Nebo, and Aramean *baalim* and their consorts, more remotely derived from Phoenician religion. Subsequent to the Hellenistic and Roman dominations these deities were likely to have donned the name or characteristics of their counterparts from the Greco-Roman pantheon. Arab religious influence was to be found in the cults of the *djinni* and *gads*, as well as in a plethora of other gods and goddesses of whom the most frequently attested are Azizos, Monimos and Sams.

As speakers of Syriac, an east Aramean dialect, Ephrem and the Christian community to which he belonged were probably among the Aramean portion of the city's populace.[11] Evidence about the Christians there before his time is quite sparse. Only the epitaph of Bishop Aberkios of Hierapolis directly attests the existence of a Christian community at Nisibis among others in Mesopotamia in the late second century:

And I saw the plain of Syria and all the cities, even Nisibis,
having crossed the Euphrates. And everywhere I had associates.
Having Paul as a companion, everywhere faith led the way
and set before me for food the fish from the spring
mighty and pure, whom a spotless Virgin caught,
and gave this to friends to eat, always
having sweet wine and giving the mixed cup with bread.[12]

Although it is impossible to say with certainty what sort of community this was, it was probably a Syriac-speaking community evangelized either by Gnostic Christians from Edessa or by Jewish-Christian merchants travelling to Adiabene.[13] Later legends with some claim to cre-

---

11. On the relation of Syriac to the other Aramaic dialects, cf. Sebastian Brock, "An Introduction to Syriac Studies," in *Horizons in Semitic Studies: Articles for the Student*, ed. J. H. Eaton (Birmingham, England, 1980), viii, 1–38, esp. 11–13.

12. On the Aberkios inscription, cf. Quasten, *Patrology*, (Utrecht, 1975), I, 171–73. W. M. Calder, *Anatolian Studies* 5 (1955), 25f. Wolfgang Wischmeyer, "Die Aberkiosinschrift als Grabepigramm," JAC 23 (1980), 22–47. J. M. Fiey, *Nisibe*, 19.

13. Every aspect of the question is controversial. If, on the basis of their common Syriac language, the Christian community at Nisibis is assumed to have originated from the slightly better-known church at Edessa, the earliest Syriac literature is the primary basis for its characterization. In Murray's estimation the prominent features of the literature are asceticism, artful prose in the Hellenistic style, and a rich symbolic imagination; cf. R. Murray, "The Characteristics of the Earliest Syriac Christianity," *East of Byzantium: Syria and Armenia in the Formative Period*, ed. N. G. Garsoian, T. F. Mathews and R. W. Thomson (Washington, D.C., 1982), 3–16. These features have been variously interpreted as indicative of a Christian community with

dence identify Addai or his disciples Ahha and Mari as the apostle(s) of Nisibis.[14]

As the Christians of Mesopotamia emerge into the clearer light of history, their fate is closely intertwined with political events. Throughout the second and third centuries Nisibis had been a valuable prize in the struggle for control of Mesopotamia—first between the Parthians and Romans, then among the Sassanid Persians, Palmyrenes and Romans. In 298 A.D., after twelve years of campaigns in the East, the Roman Emperor Diocletian signed a treaty with Narses of Persia by which Roman control of the area was firmly reasserted. Thus after a half-century of Sassanid and Palmyrene control Nisibis was reestablished as the military and administrative center of Roman Mesopotamia and, in addition, as the sole point of commercial exchange between Romans and Persians.[15] The first recorded consequence of this political transformation for Christians

---

Gnostic or Jewish-Christian leanings. For the view that the earliest Syriac-speaking Christian community subscribed to a Gnostic form of Christianity, cf. W. Bauer, *Orthodoxy and Heresy in the Earliest Christianity*, trans. from the second German edition by R. Kraft, G. Krodel et al. (Philadelphia, 1971); this view was forcefully reiterated for the city of Edessa itself by H.J.W. Drijvers in "Edessa und das jüdische Christentum," VC 24 (1970), 4–33. For the major opposing view, that early Syriac Christianity was a form of Jewish-Christianity derived from sectarian Judaism, cf. A. Vööbus, *A History of Asceticism in the Syrian Orient*, I, CSCO 184, subs. 14 (Louvain, 1958), 3–108, and G. Quispel, "The Discussion of Judaic Christianity," VC 22 (1968), 81–93. Accepting a Gnostic origin of Christianity for Edessa but a Jewish-Christian origin in Adiabene is R. Murray, *Symbols of Church and Kingdom: A Study in Early Syriac Tradition* (Cambridge, England, 1975), 4–24. A thorny problem with any claim for a distinctive Jewish-Christian heritage in Adiabene is that its principal evidence, the Chronicle of Arbela, is probably a forgery; cf. J. Assfalg, "Zur Textüberlieferung der Chronik von Arbela, Beobachtungen zu Ms. or. fol. 3126," OC (1966), 19–36, and J. M. Fiey, "Auteur et date de la Chronique d'Arbèles," OS 12 (1967), 265–302. Although this view has been modified or challenged by others, there is no consensus; cf. S. Brock, "Alphonse Mingana and the letter of Philoxenus to Abu 'Afr," BJRL 50 (1967), 199–206, esp. 200; and W. Hage, "Early Christianity in Mesopotamia: Some Remarks Concerning Authenticity of the Chronicle of Arbela" *The Harp* I.2–3 (1988), 39–46.

14. Fiey, Nisibe, 19.

15. Ibid. 19. Ephrem's contemporary, the unknown author of the *Expositio totius mundi et gentium*, described Nisibis' unique status:

Even Mesopotamia has numerous and varied cities, of which I want to mention the excellent ones. They are, then, Nisibis and Edessa [read Amida rather than Edessa, as Fiey suggests], which have the best men of all, both especially wise in business and good hunters. Above all they are both rich and adorned with all goods. For, receiving from the Persians, they themselves cross over into all the land of the Romans, selling and buying again, except for bronze and iron, because it is not permitted to give bronze or iron to enemies. These cities, moreover, still standing by the wisdom of the gods and emperor, since they have famous walls, in war always dissipate the strength of the Persians; seething with business and transacting well with the entire province.

Expositio XXII (J. Rougé, ed. trans., SC 124, Paris, 1966, 156; quoted in French by Fiey, Nisibe, 32).

there was an unhappy one. Lists of the victims of the Diocletian persecution include several from Nisibis: the confessor, Hermas; a soldier, Adelphos; and Gaios; a group of three women, Olivia, Eutropia, and Leonis; and finally Febronia, to whom a basilica was later dedicated.[16]

B Ephrem's Early Years: ca. 306–37

Ephrem, born ca. 306, only a few years after the persecution, is the most important witness to the life of Christians in Nisibis in the early fourth century. His *Carmina Nisibena* describe the personalities and accomplishments of the first bishops whose names enter into the historical record there: Jacob, Babu, Vologeses and Abraham.[17] When Jacob was appointed the first bishop of Nisibis in 308/9, it is probable that his appointment was made through the hierarchy within the Roman Empire rather than in Persia—an indirect consequence of the reestablishment of Roman Imperial control in the region.[18] Perhaps for the first time, then, the church of Nisibis was brought into substantial contact with the churches of the West and with Western notions of orthodoxy and heresy. Ephrem portrays Jacob as a stern but loving parent, firmly leading the people from their immature ways:

> by his simple [words] he gave milk to his infants . . .
> [The Nisbene Church] was childlike with [him].
> As with a child, he loved her and threatened her. . . .
> The womb of him who gave birth to the flock bore her infancy. . . .
> The first priest gave milk to her infancy. . . .
> The wealthy father, laid up treasures for her childhood.[19]

During his thirty-year episcopacy major changes took place. Of the first importance was Constantine's rise to power and his subsequent adop-

---

16. For details and discussion of the evidence, cf. Fiey, Nisibe, 20f.

17. For analysis of the materials in Ephrem's CNis 13–21 on these bishops, cf. J. M. Fiey, "Les évêques de Nisibe au temps de saint Éphrem," PdO 4 (1973), 123–36; idem, Nisibe 21–38; also J. Martikainen, "Some Remarks About the Carmina Nisibena as a Literary and a Theological Source," OCA 197 (1974), 345–52; and I. Ortiz de Urbina, "L'évêque et son rôle d'après saint Éphrem," PdO 4 (1973), 137–46. For a discussion of other materials on Jacob's life, cf. P. Peeters, "La légende de St. Jacques de Nisibe," AB 38 (1920), 285–373, esp. 295–312.

18. Fiey, Nisibe, 23.

19. CNis 14.16–22; cf. Fiey, Nisibe, 22f.

tion with Licinius of measures not only ending the persecutions of Christians in the Roman Empire but also restoring their confiscated property and even suggesting that the policy of persecution was wrong.[20] No doubt as a consequence of the new freedom enjoyed by Christians throughout the Roman Empire, the bishop undertook the construction of a church building at Nisibis between 313 and 320.[21] The Council of Nicea in 325 C.E. intensified the relatively new focus on orthodox doctrine in general and on Trinitarian theology in particular. Perhaps Bishop Jacob availed himself of the emperor's offer of the use of the Imperial post to travel to Nicea for this first ecumenical council, since his presence there is well-attested.[22]

Meanwhile Ephrem had spent his early years in this newly prospering church. On the basis of his own words in the *Hymns Against Heresies* we may deduce that his parents were members of the Christian community and that he was baptized in his youth after a period of study and reflection, perhaps in the context of a formal catechumenate:

By our Lord stand both:
[the time] when I was to enter into the creation
and when it would be good to leave it.
In the way of truth was I born
even though I as a child did not yet perceive it.
Examining, I acquired it for myself, as I perceived it.
My faith despised the confusing paths that came toward me.[23]

20. T. D. Barnes, *Constantine and Eusebius* (Cambridge, MA, 1981), 62–65 and 318 n.4.
21. Fiey, Nisibe, 23.
22. On Constantine's offer, cf. Eusebius' *Vita Constantini* 3.6.1,9, cited by Barnes, 214, 379, n.49. Jacob of Nisibis is listed among the signatories of the Council, cf. Honigmann, Liste, p. 46 #74 and p. 62 #74; further, cf. Fiey, Nisibe, 23, n.51.
23. CH 26.10. So Edmund Beck argues in his *Ephräm der Syrer: Lobgesang aus der Wüste*, Sophia 7 (Freiburg im Breisgau, 1967), 18. This reference to his birth in the orthodox Christian faith, admittedly vague, nevertheless outweighs the later hagiographic tradition that Ephrem's parents were a pagan priest and a Christian woman. As further evidence of youthful (but not infant) baptism and of a period of catechetical instruction, respectively, Beck adduces the following two excerpts from Ephrem's hymns:

Your truth [was] in my youth; Your truth [is] in my old age.
I rejected and expelled the party of the crucifiers;
I scorned graven images and the metal of strangers
and the new fraud that would be contrived to deceive us.

Virg. 37.10.1–4

I was taught and believed in You
Who are the only One.

INTRODUCTION

Upon his return from Nicea, Jacob appointed Ephrem interpreter or exegete of Nisibis. Two centuries later the official historian of the School of Nisibis would look back to this event as constituting its birth.[24]

We may safely assume that Ephrem's production of hymns and prose works began in this period.[25] While some of these works may have been addressed to clergy in training, at least the hymns must have been written for a broader audience. Beginning characteristically with the unique Syriac type of ante-Nicene Christianity, its encratism,[26] Gnosticism and special relationship to Judaism, Ephrem introduced these features into an orthodox Christian framework, often through polemics. Although he freely and adeptly used the imagery of the non-canonical biblical literature, his work is self-consciously orthodox. He wrote commentaries not only on the canonical scripture but also on Tatian's *Diatesseron*, the most widespread version of the New Testament among the earliest Syriac-speaking Christians.[27] Like the *Odes of Solomon*, Ephrem's hymns sometimes use graphic feminine imagery for God.[28] His *Hymns on the Pearl* take

---

Through Your being I heard and held You as true,
You Who are Father through your Only-begotten.
I was three times baptized,
also in the name of the Holy Spirit.
I learned that it is all true,
that Your treasure remains impossible to investigate
although Your wealth is widespread.

CH 3.13

The view that Ephrem was baptized as a young adult is confirmed by the general practice as attested by early baptismal commentaries, which do not mention infant baptisands, cf. S. Brock, "Some Early Syriac Baptismal Commentaries," OCP 46 (1980), 20–61, esp. 30f.

24. Barhadbshabba 'Arbaya, *Cause de la Fondation des Écoles*, Texte Syriaque publié et traduit par A. Scher, PO 4.4 (1907), 327–97, cf. esp. 377. The office to which Ephrem was appointed was *mpšqn'*. On the interpretation of this office cf. A. Vööbus, *School of Nisibis*, 8f.; Outtier, Ephrem, PdO (1973), 25f.; Fiey, Nisibe, 24; Neusner, HJB III, 195–200.

25. Ephrem's works are difficult to date; for the sequence presumed here I have depended mainly on the proposals of Beck, presented in summary form in his Lobgesang, 14–18, and more systematically by Kronholm, Motifs, 20–25.

26. On the meaning of encratism and its importance for the ascetic, but not necessarily monastic, emphasis in early Syriac Christianity, cf. Murray, Characteristics, 6–9 and Brock, Luminous, 107–17.

27. For Ephrem's commentary, cf. Comm. Diat. On Tatian's gospel harmony and its place among the early Syriac biblical versions, cf. B. M. Metzger, *The Early Versions of the New Testament: Their Origin, Transmission and Limitations* (Oxford, 1977), 3–98, esp. 10–36.

28. Ephrem uses feminine imagery for each of the persons of the Trinity. For the Father's or the Divinity's womb, cf. Nat. 13.7, 21.7, 27.15 and 27.19; for the Son as mother through the incarnation, Nat. 149–54, cf. Nat. 23.5; and for the related concept of Christ as a bird, cf. Nat.

up and develop the image of salvation as a precious pearl, an image which has roots not only in the New Testament but also in the Gnostic Hymn of the Pearl in the *Acts of Thomas*.[29] Yet his *Hymns Against Heresies* are polemical, attacking Mani, Marcion, Bardaisan and the astrologers.[30]

Likewise with respect to Judaism he is unusually well-informed yet often strongly polemical. His *Hymns on Paradise* and his commentary on

---

17.1, 26.13, and Virg. 12.7 and 41.2; for references to the Holy Spirit using feminine pronouns, cf. Nat. 5.10 and Virg. 7.6; for God as weaver, the archetypal occupation of women in antiquity, cf. Nat. 21.5 (Father) and Virg. 37.6 (Christ); God as housekeeper, cf. CJ 2.11; for some suggestions of Ephrem's place among patristic writers on this subject, cf. esp. Nat. 17.1 and note *ad loc.*

For the feminine theological imagery in the Odes, cf. H.J.W. Drijvers, "The 19th Ode of Solomon: Its Interpretation and Place in Syrian Christianity," JTS n.s. 31 (1980), 337–55, esp. 352–55.

There is no consensus on the date, original language and theological orientation of the *Odes of Solomon*. For the text with English translation and bibliography to 1971, cf. J. Charlesworth, SBLTT 13 (Missoula, Montana, 1977). Charlesworth has argued for a Jewish-Christian rather than Gnostic context and an early second-century date for the Odes, cf. idem, "The Odes of Solomon—not Gnostic," CBQ 31 (1969), 357–69, and "The Odes of Solomon and the Gospel of John," CBQ 35 (1973), 298–322. For the argument that the Odes are an anti-Marcionite polemic and therefore to be dated ca. 200 c.e., cf. Drijvers, "Die Oden Salomos und die Polemik mit den Markioniten im syrischen Christentum," OCA 205 (1978), 39–55; more recently he has argued for a later date, first half of the third century, in "Kerygma und Logos in den Oden Salomos dargestellt am Beispiel der 23. Ode," im *Kerygma und Logos*, Festschrift C. Andresen (Göttingen, 1979), 153–72, and in "19th Ode," cited above, esp. 353; subsequently he argued a date of 275 c.e., in "Odes of Solomon and Psalms of Mani: Christians and Manichaeans in Third-century Syria," in *Studies in Gnosticism and Hellenistic Religions*, G. Quispel Festschrift, Études préliminaires aux religions orientales dans l'Empire Romain 91 (Leiden, 1981), 117–30, esp. 129. His argument is rejected by L. Abramowski, in "Sprache und Abfassungszeit der Oden Salomos" OC 68 (1984), 80–90; although in agreement with Drijvers' philosophical and apologetic parallels, she disputes the dependencies he derives from them. For recent bibliography (1971–85) and a survey of the scholarship on the Odes, cf. G. R. Blaszczak, *A Formcritical Study of Selected Odes of Solomon*, Harvard Semitic Monographs 36 (Atlanta, 1985), esp. 1–8, 137–55.

29. Ephrem's *Hymns on the Pearl* are numbers 81–87 of his *Hymns on Faith*; for the Syriac text with German translation, cf. E. Beck HdF; for French translation with comments, cf. F. Graffin, Hymnes de saint Éphrem sur la perle, L'OS 12 (1967), 129–50; for HdF 82 in English with comments, cf. Brock, Harp, 31–33; for a less satisfactory English version of all seven by J. B. Morris, cf. NPNF 13, 293–301. Ephrem explores the image of the pearl in other contexts as well, cf. Nat. 16.12 and Virg. 11.9.

As is the case for most of the early Syriac literature, the date, place, original language and theological provenience of the *Acts of Thomas* are disputed. For an English translation and discussion of the Syriac version with an argument for its priority over the Greek as well as its Jewish-Christian encratite rather than Gnostic character, cf. A.F.J. Klijn, *The Acts of Thomas*, Supplements to Novum Testamentum V (Leiden, 1962). For English translation of the Greek text, an argument for its priority and hence its originally Gnostic character, cf. G. Bornkamm in E. Hennecke, *New Testament Apocrypha*, ed. W. Schneemelcher, English translation and edition by R. McL. Wilson, (Philadelphia, 1963–65), II, 425–531.

30. For the hymns, cf. CH. Although Kronholm dates this entire collection to Ephrem's Nisibene period, some must be from the Edessene period; cf. n. 109 below. To my knowledge Beck does not offer a dating of this group of hymns.

Genesis and Exodus are permeated with non-canonical Jewish traditions.[31] The *Carmina Nisibena* represent an appropriation of the prophetic tradition of the Old Testament.[32] On the other hand, the *Sermons on Faith* combine opposition to Judaizing with anti-Arian arguments, the *Paschal Hymns* combine polemics on the proper understanding of Jewish scripture and custom with a positive theology of the crucifixion and resurrection, and the *Nativity Hymns* present a developed theology of the incarnation and mariology in the context of a strong anti-Jewish polemic.

C Nisibis Under Siege: 337–50

From the political standpoint Ephrem's early years in the service of the church of Nisibis were relatively secure. Constantine's reign brought peace and even patronage for the Christians of the Roman Empire. The Christians of a border garrison like Nisibis might participate in this sense of well-being as long as relations between the two empires remained peaceful. Even when Shapur II reached his majority and began to consolidate his power in 325, he turned first to internal affairs and then to the East. Not until 335, when he had finished the task of bringing order to the eastern and central portions of his empire, did he turn toward his western frontier to begin the enterprise that would occupy the remainder of his long reign, the reconquest of Mesopotamia. When, as a first step he raided Armenia, he was quickly rebuffed by Constantine, who sent an army at the request of the Armenian nobility. Constantine's letter to Shapur, preserved in Eusebius' *Vita Constantini* may have been written at this time.[33] In the letter he asserts his faith in God, the providential nature of his own rule, and the certainty of Divine vengeance on the persecutors of Christians. His wishes that both Shapur and the Christians in the Persian realm prosper would probably have been overshadowed in

---

31. For Ephrem's hymns, cf. HdP. For his use of Jewish exegetical themes, cf. Séd, hymnes sur paradis; also cf. Levene, Early Syrian Fathers, and S. Hidal, *Interpretatio Syriaca. Die Kommentare des heiligen Ephräm des Syrers zu Genesis und Exodus mit besonderer Berücksichtigung ihrer Auslegungsgeschichtlichen Stellung*, Lund, 1974; Nabil El-Khoury, *Die Interpretation der Welt bei Ephraem dem Syrer* (Mainz, 1976); Kronholm, Motifs; S. Brock, "Jewish Traditions in Syriac Soures," JJS 30 (1979), 212–32; and Drijvers, Jews, esp. 100–1.

32. Cf. Martikainen, Remarks.

33. For a recent discussion of this correspondence, its authenticity and date, with references to earlier studies, cf. S. Brock, "Christians in the Sassanian Empire: A Case of Divided Loyalties," *Studies in Church History* 18 (1982), 1–19; also cf. Neusner, HJB IV, 21ff.; and Barnes, *Constantine and Eusebius*, 258f., who thinks the letter may be "as early as 324/5," p. 397, n.144.

INTRODUCTION

Shapur's mind by the audacity of his *interpretatio christiana* of recent history, virtually an assertion that in a conflict between Persia and Rome, the latter would surely be victorious. Still more presumptuous is the Roman emperor's commendation of the Persian Christians to the Sassanid ruler's care, a veiled threat that they would be loyal to him rather than to their own sovereign in the event of war. Whether or not it was this letter that provoked Shapur's hostility to the Christians within his realm, he took advantage of Constantine's death in 337 to undertake a military campaign in Mesopotamia the following spring. In the course of this conflict Christians in the Persian Empire were treated as potential or actual traitors.

The Christians of Persia had themselves contributed to the mixing of religious interpretations with political and military events. Aphrahat, writing in an unknown location within the Persian Empire, was disposed to view the conflict in apocalyptic terms as a battle between the forces of good and evil with virtually no room for nuance or compromise.[34] Upon returning from his first Mesopotamian campaign Shapur imposed a double head-tax on the Christians of his empire. Many either refused or were simply unable to pay. Simeon bar Sabba'e, bishop of Seleucia-Ctesiphon and thereby representative of the Persian Christian community to the Sassanid government, informed the emperor that his people could not pay the double tax. As a consequence he and several of his associates met their deaths, and a lengthy and brutal persecution of Christians in the Persian Empire began.[35]

The worsened relations between Christians and their Persian ruler could be expected to have an immediate effect on the determination of the Roman cities of Mesopotamia to resist capture. A second effect, less immediately obvious, was the deterioration of relations between Chris-

---

34. For the Syriac text, cf. Parisot, PS I, i (Paris, 1894), and PS I, ii (Paris, 1907). For an English translation of homilies 1,5,6,8,10,17,21,22, cf. J. Gwynn, NPNF 13.2, 345–412; for a more recent translation of homilies 11–13, 15–19, 21, and excerpts of 23, cf. J. Neusner, *Aphrahat and Judaism: The Christian-Jewish Argument in Fourth-Century Iran*, Studia Post Biblica 19 (Leiden, 1971). For bibliography and a resume of earlier scholarship, cf. Neusner, Aphrahat, 7–13. On Aphrahat's interpretation of the political situation, cf. especially the fifth homily, and Brock, Christians, 7f.

35. Accounts of the persecution are in J. Labourt, *Le christianisme dans l'empire perse sous la dynastie sassanide 224–632* (Paris, 1904), 43–82; A. Christensen, *L'Iran sous les sassanides* (Copenhagen, 1936), 258–68; Vööbus, *History of Asceticism*, I, 209–58; an important recent study of the *acta martyrum* is G. Wiessner, *Zur Märtyrerüberlieferung aus der Christenverfolgung Schapurs II*, Untersuchungen zur syrischen Literaturgeschichte I, Abh. Ak. Wiss. Göttingen (Göttingen, 1967); reviewed by S. Brock, JTS 19 (1968), 300–9.

tians and Jews. The Jewish community had constituted a substantial minority throughout the region for nearly a millennium.[36] Nisibis itself had long been the center for the collection and transmission of the Temple offering from the Jews of northern Mesopotamia.[37] Since the early second century C.E. there had been a rabbinic school there, and the city had become a major center for rabbinic Judaism.[38] Although the Jewish community had been the object of some political and religious intolerance under the early Sassanid rulers, their lot had improved steadily just as the Christians' situation was declining.[39] Certain of the acts of the Persian Christian martyrs accuse the Jews of inciting the persecution by suggesting that the Christians were potentially disloyal to the Persian government. Whether or not this accusation is true, Jews were never more than minor characters in the Persian state persecution.[40] Yet the dramatic disparity between the conditions of the two communities in the Persian territories gave an apologetic advantage to the Jews, who apparently exploited the opportunity to recoup some of their losses in the competition for converts.[41] Under the circumstances relations between the two religious communities were bound to be strained.

The restoration of Nisibis to the Roman Empire and Constantine's endorsement of Christianity had suddenly reversed the prospects of the Jews and Christians, but the reversal would last only as long as the city resisted Persian attack. Political and religious issues were tightly interwoven, and Ephrem was necessarily deeply involved in the conflicts. At least part of his task as the exegete of the Christian school of Nisibis must have been the elaboration of a Christian interpretation of the Old Testament—one that could compete with the growing sophistication of the rabbinic schools and attract to Christianity the uncertain, whether of Aramean pagan or Jewish background. In gathering *testimonia* that Jesus had fulfilled the Jewish expectations of a messiah and that he was anticipated in virtually every word and symbol of the Old Testament, Ephrem was not

36. J. Neusner, *A History of the Jews in Babylonia* (=HJB), I, 10–15.
37. Ibid. 13f. 43–50.
38. Ibid. 113–63.
39. Ibid. II, 27–91.
40. For a thorough discussion and overview of previous work on this issue, cf. J. Neusner, "Babylonian Jewry and Shapur II's Persecution of Christianity from 339 to 379," *Hebrew Union College Annual* 43 (1972), 77–102 (rep. in TJSB, 150–77).
41. According to Neusner, HJB III, 12–16, rabbinic sources of the late third century have more to say than earlier sources against the "minim."

engaged in a novel enterprise. The debate with Judaism is as old as Christianity; it is well-attested and has been studied in Greek and Latin sources prior to and contemporary with him.[42] The uniqueness of his endeavor lay in the fact that he taught in a city where the rabbinic traditions were well-established and sophisticated and where the Jewish community may have been more prosperous and numerous than its Christian counterpart.[43] Political developments in this border garrison in the mid-fourth century, moreover, had intensified this disparity. These conditions partially account for Ephrem's extraordinary bitterness toward the Jews, to whom he often refers as "slanderers," "crucifiers," or "murderers."[44]

One of the cities unsuccessfully besieged by Shapur in his first Mesopotamian campaign was Nisibis. In his *Carmina Nisibena* Ephrem credited Bishop Jacob with the salvation of the city from this first siege, and later tradition was to magnify his role considerably.[45] Ephrem's mentor died soon after the successful rebuff of Shapur in 338. His successor, Babu, cared for a church beset with the problems of wartime.[46] The hymnodist praises him for his almsgiving and for his efforts at ransoming captives.[47] Although he also lauds his "plain teaching," his "interpretation [of scripture]," his orthodoxy and eucharistic ministry, the hymns give few clues as to the specific social or ecclesiastical issues of this episcopacy other than the ongoing warfare and its accompanying hardships.[48] The

---

42. M. Simon, *Verus Israel: Étude sur les Rélations entre Chrétiens et Juifs dans l'Empire Romain (135–425)* (Paris, 1947; 2 ed. 1964) remains an important study; more recently, cf. R. Ruether, *Faith and Fratricide* (New York, 1969); A. T. Davies, ed., *Antisemitism and the Foundations of Christianity* (New York, 1979); J. Gager, *The Origins of Christian Anti-Semitism* (Oxford, 1983); and R. Wilken, *John Chrysostom and the Jews: Rhetoric and Reality in the Late 4th Century*, The Transformation of the Classical Heritage IV (Berkeley, 1983). In the Syriac context, cf. S. Kazan, "Isaac of Antioch's Homily against the Jews," OC 45 (1961), 30–53, 46 (1962), 87–98; 47 (1963), 89–97; 49(1965), 57–78; A. M. Hayman, *The Disputation of Sergius the Stylite against a Jew*, CSCO 338–39 (Louvain, 1973); M. Albert, *Jacques de Saroug, Homélies contre les juifs*, PO 38.1 (1976); A. P. Hayman, "The Image of the Jew in the Syriac Anti-Jewish Polemical Literature," in *"To See Ourselves as Others See Us": Christians, Jews "Others" in Late Antiquity*, ed. J. Neusner and E. S. Frerichs (Chico, California, 1985), 423–41; and Drijvers, Jews.

43. Radically disparate circumstances for the two communities are assumed by Murray, Symbols, 19.

44. For other possible sources of his strong antagonism, cf. comments on Ephrem's mariology and on the *Hymns against Julian*.

45. The siege lasted sixty-three days, cf. RE ser.I, v. 4, col. 1047f. On the role attributed to Jacob and confusions of the three sieges, cf. Peeters, Legende, 295–312.

46. Cf. CNis 13.4.2, 13.5.2, 13.6.2, 13.7.2, 13.14.2.

47. CNis 14.4.2 and 14.24.

48. CNis 14.15.2, 14.16.2, 14.13.2, 14.2.2. Martikainen concludes on the basis of the references to Babu in the CNis that conditions of social, economic and legal collapse prevailed during his episcopacy, cf. Martikainen, Remarks, 351.

INTRODUCTION

Emperor Constantius stationed a larger army in Mesopotamia and personally visited the fortresses to add force to Roman claims to the area.[49] Yet his preoccupation with difficulties in the West allowed Shapur to make inroads into the area, besieging Nisibis for three months in 346 and again for four months in 350.[50]

In his *Carmina Nisibena* Ephrem contemplated all three sieges of his native city, but it was the third siege that fascinated him, as it did the future Emperor Julian and Ammianus Marcellinus.[51] This siege was marked by Shapur's bold attempt to undermine the city's fortifications by diverting the River Mygdonius to engulf them. Although he succeeded in breaching the wall, the intrepid Nisibenes quickly rebuilt it, while Shapur's elephants, under attack from insects, floundered in mud. Whereas their valiant efforts inspired Julian to Homeric comparisons,[52] Ephrem was reminded of Noah's ark as well as of the resurrection of Christ after three days in the tomb:

> [Nisibis speaks]
> Hear and weigh my likeness with Noah,
> and since my pain is less than his,
> may Your grace be equal to our salvation,
> for my children stand like Noah
> between the wrathful and the destroyers.
> Make peace, my Lord, with the besieged,
> and cast down before me the besiegers,
> to double my victory.
> Since the killer three times [expressed] his anger,
> [express] three times the mercy of Your Third One.
> Grant not victory over Your beloved to the Evil One
> whose avarice You [defeated] twice and three times.
> Allow my victory to fly over the whole world
> to acquire glory for You in the whole world.

---

49. Constantius came to Edessa in 340, to Nisibis in May 345, stationed the army at Edessa in the summer of 346, and visited Hierapolis in 347; cf. Fiey, Nisibe, 27 and RE ser. I, v. 4, col. 1055, 1060f.

50. Ibid. 1060, 1063f. A major battle fought at Singara in 348 was a significant victory for Rome, but the truce concluded was immediately broken by Shapur; ibid. 1061f.

51. Jul. Imp. Orat. 1.27B–28D, Orat. 2, 62B–67A, and Amm. Mar. 25.8.13f. Later hagiographers also contributed their descriptions of the famous siege, cf. Peeters, Legende, 300f.

52. Jul. Imp. Orat. 2, 67A–73C.

O He Who was revived the third [day],
put me not to death in the third [trial]![53]

This dramatic incident inspired in the hymnodist not only the discernment of these intricate typological patterns but also a pure paean to faith and grace:

He saved us without a wall and taught that He is our wall.
He saved us without a king and made known that He is our king.
He saved us in all from all and showed He is all.
He saved us by His grace and again revealed
that He is freely gracious and life-giving. From each who boasts
He takes away the boast and gives to him His grace.[54]

D   Ephrem's Last Years in Nisibis: 350–63

When Shapur abandoned the siege in the fall of 350 to attend to troubles farther east near the Caspian Sea, the Armenians re-allied themselves with Rome while the Nisibenes celebrated the freeing of their city and began the task of restoring her to her former status as queen of Mesopotamia. Apparently Bishop Babu did not live to enjoy the happier decade that followed. His successor, Vologeses, constructed the city's first baptistery in 359.[55] At this time as well, Ephrem looked back over the previous history of the city and wrote his hymns characterizing the first three episcopacies as three phases in the growth of the Christian city: childhood, adolescence and adulthood. He portrays each of the three prelates, Jacob, Babu and Vologeses, as uniquely suited to the ruling of the Christian community at the time appointed. Whereas the first two bishops administered a combination of love and discipline appropriate to childhood and youth, Vologeses' gentleness and humility are better suited to the mature community he shepherded.[56] Despite the fact that heresies,

---

53. CNis 1.11; cf. also CNis 3.11–12. On Christ as the "third" one, cf. Beck's remarks ad loc.
54. CNis 2.2.
55. On the building, its inscription and sculptures, cf. Fiey, Nisibe, 29f.
56. Cf. CNis 14.17–19, 15.13–20, and 16.6–22.

INTRODUCTION

especially Arianism, divided the Nisibene Christians, Ephrem defended
his bishop against critics who demanded a more severe approach.[57]

Within a decade Shapur had restored his position in the East and
turned his attention once again to Armenia and Mesopotamia. Negotia-
tions had come to a halt when Shapur's determination to recover his
"forefathers' empire" encountered Constantius' insistence that it would be
"absurd and silly to surrender what we have long preserved unmo-
lested."[58] In 359 Shapur "armed with the help of savage tribes which he
had subdued, and burning with superhuman desire of extending his do-
main, was preparing arms, forces, and supplies, embroiling his plans
with infernal powers and consulting all superstitions about the future. . . . He planned with the first mildness of spring to overrun everything."[59] A combination of betrayal and ill-preparedness led the Romans
to destroy the north Mesopotamian countryside to deprive Shapur of
fodder during the anticipated invasion.[60] Ephrem portrays the city seeking divine assistance on behalf of the population both within and without
her walls:

My Lord, my children have fled like chicks
pursued by an eagle. They are hidden in a refuge!
Let Your Peace return to them![61]

I have lifted up my eyes to all the squares; they are deserted.
Ten are left from a hundred and a thousand from ten thousand.
Grant peace, let the clamor of my inhabitants fill my squares.
Return those outside and make those inside rejoice.
Great enough is Your grace to extend inside and outside.
Let the wings of Your grace gather my chicks.
Let the prayer of my just ones preserve my fleeing ones.
The unbelievers broke me, but the believers sustained me.
By the believers deprive the unbelievers![62]

---

57. Cf. CNis 15.1–4, but, citing CNis 7.9–13, Fiey suggests the malcontents were the
heretics themselves, probably Arians, cf. Fiey, Nisibe, 31f.
58. Amm. Mar. 17.5.1–15.
59. Amm. Mar. 18.4.1.
60. Amm. Mar. 18.4–7.
61. CNis 4.23.
62. CNis 6.27–29. Further cf. CNis 4–7 passim.

18

INTRODUCTION

In the spring of 359 the Persian army arrived in Mesopotamia. Bypassing Nisibis, Shapur first attempted to strike more deeply into Roman territory while Constantius was occupied in Gaul. Frustrated in this attempt, he turned back to fight the Roman army in Mesopotamia and to attempt once more the capture of the major fortresses there. When he had besieged and captured Amida, Shapur ordered all its citizens to be killed or enslaved as punishment for their refusal to surrender and for their provocative behavior.[63] After wintering across the Tigris, Shapur returned, captured Singara and deported its people.[64] Again bypassing Nisibis, guarded by the Roman army, he besieged and captured Bezabde, slaughtered its inhabitants and rebuilt its fortifications.[65] At last Constantius arrived. Having passed through Edessa and mourned over the ashes of Amida, he attempted to retake Bezabde but abandoned the enterprise as winter approached.[66]

The emperor's defense of Roman Mesopotamia was hampered by the refusal of his Gallic troops to come to his aid in the East and their acclamation instead of the young Caesar Julian as a rival Augustus. While Shapur and Constantius faced off across Mesopotamia in the spring of 361, Julian openly stepped forth as a rival augustus. As he set out against his rebellious cousin, Constantius died, thus leaving the way clear for the young apostate emperor to define his own policies. Initially content to promote the public practice of pagan religions and to defend its intellectual integrity, Julian expected that internecine rivalry among Christians would suffice to undermine the church. In time, however, his measures became more directly anti-Christian. These developments coincide more or less with his movement toward the East. Arriving at Antioch in 362, Julian engaged in a prolonged struggle with its population over religious and social mores as he attempted to impose his ascetic and philosophically-interpreted version of paganism on the city. The emperor's religious policies were closely related to his Persian military campaign.[67] Like most of his contemporaries, including Ephrem, Julian believed that military victory would go to those who had offered suitable worship to the correct God or gods. Much of his time in Antioch had been spent in the offering of sacrifices and the consultation

---

63. Amm. Mar. 19.8.
64. Amm. Mar. 20.6.7.
65. Amm. Mar. 20.6.9, 20.7.15.
66. Amm. Mar. 20.11.
67. Cf. Amm. Mar. 22 and 23.

of oracles and auguries.[68] At the outset of his Mesopotamian campaign, he stopped at Harran to worship its celestial deities.[69] While in Constantinople in the spring of 362, Julian had hastily composed a hymn to the Great Mother of the gods, in which he displayed his strongly neo-Platonic interpretation of her cult, and he had visited her shrine at Pessinus en route from Constantinople to Antioch.[70] Now he led his army to Hierapolis, the Mesopotamian city particularly identified with her cult in its syncretistic form, Cybele having been identified with the Semitic Atargatis-Anahitha-Astarte as well as the Greek Hera.[71] Finally, Julian paused in his march down the Euphrates to celebrate her feast on March 27.[72] Ephrem recorded the emperor's celebration with angry disgust:

> Agreeable to him was the feast of the detestable idol
> on whose feast-day women and men rave,
> virgins fornicate and wives become lascivious,
> vomit out [and] speak words of shame.[73]

As a part of his program of restoration of traditional temples, and possibly also as an anti-Christian measure, Julian had undertaken to rebuild the Jewish Temple in Jerusalem.[74] At about the same time he had issued a new coin displaying the image of a bull with two stars. From Ephrem's perspective these two measures were linked not only to each other but also to the emperor's general promotion of paganism:

> Perhaps because of that money on which the bull was portrayed,
> the Jews were overjoyed that [Julian] carried it in his heart
> and also in his purse and in his hand
> as a type of that calf of the wilderness

---

68. Cf. esp. Amm. Mar. 22.12.6–13.

69. Amm. Mar. 23.3, cf. Bowersock, Julian, 109, and Segal, Edessa, 104f.

70. For the hymn, cf. Jul. Imp. Orat. 5, Bowersock, Julian 82f. and Malley, Hellenism, 65–67 et passim. For the visits to Pessinus cf. Amm. Mar. 22.9.5.

71. The most important source on her cult at Hierapolis is Lucian's satire, cf. Luc. Sam. de Syr. Dea; it is discussed by Segal, Edessa, 46–48 and Drijvers, Cults, 76–121. Although he mentions Julian's visit to Hierapolis, Ammianus does not mention any religious devotions conducted there, Amm. Mar. 23.2.6.

72. The visit to Hierapolis was 5 March, Amm. Mar. 23.2.6, celebration of the feast, Amm. Mar. 23.3.1.

73. CJ 2.6.1–4.

74. On the rebuilding as anti-Christian propaganda, cf. Wilken, Chrysostom, esp. 130–48.

that was before his eye and heart and mind;
and probably in his dreams he used to see the calf![75]

At the same time Julian's attitude toward the Christians of Mesopotamia had worsened. He had pointedly refrained from visiting Edessa, well-known by this time as a center of Christianity. In a letter sent from Antioch he had ironically informed the Christian citizens of his intention to confiscate their property to help them to conform more closely to the ascetic ideal of their religion.[76] Ephrem claims further that Julian sent a threatening letter to the Christians of Mesopotamia, or perhaps of Nisibis itself:

For he foretold and promised and wrote and sent to us
that he would come down and trample it; Persia he would disperse.
Singara he would rebuild. [This was] the threat of his letter.[77]

The poet responded with a hymn of encouragement to the Christians of Nisibis to persevere under conditions of duress, following the example of Elijah and Daniel in rebuking idolatrous rulers.[78] Nevertheless, an idol was set up in the city with an accompanying public cult, and the Christians of Nisibis did nothing to eliminate it.[79]

Julian's choice of a route through Roman Mesopotamia was not dictated solely by religious motives, however. After feigning an intent to proceed across the north to Adiabene, he abruptly changed direction and, taking part of his troops with his navy, proceeded boldly down the Euphrates directly toward the Persian capital, Seleucia-Ctesiphon. Shapur meanwhile followed a tactic of withdrawal, allowing the Romans to penetrate into Persian territory so that retreat would be difficult in the event that they overextended their campaign. This Julian did. He found himself at the gates of the Persian capital without the forces to take the city. Shapur's army was lying in wait just to the east; the Roman reinforcements had not yet arrived from the north. Following the advice of a

---

75. CJ 1.19, cf. also CJ 1.16–18.
76. Jul. Imp. Letter 115, cf. Bowersock, Julian, 92.
77. CJ 2.15.
78. HdEccl. 1.
79. CJ 2.20–22. Since a variety of pagan cults had remained in existence there, the particularly offensive character of this cult for Ephrem must have been the public imperial endorsement of paganism after two generations of rule by Christian emperors.

supposed traitor, who was in fact a Persian agent, Julian destroyed his own fleet. Then, as he retreated through Mesopotamia with the Sassanid forces destroying the crops in his path, he was killed in battle. In Ephrem's view Julian's death was virtually a suicide in the face of a hopeless situation:

> When he saw that his gods were confuted and exposed
> and that he could neither gain victory nor flee,
> [that] between fear and disgrace he was prostrate and beaten,
> cunningly he stripped off his armor in order to be wounded,
> in order to die so that the Galileans would not see his shame.[80]

Sometime during all these upheavals, Vologeses, the bishop of Nisibis, had died and had been succeeded by a much younger man, his protegé Abraham. Ephrem composed several hymns, including one upon the new bishop's installation, filled with advice. Now in his fifties, the hymnodist had not only passed from childhood to adulthood with respect to his bishops, he was now ready to assume the role of the wise parent.[81] In addition to the advice that he be firm and imitate his worthy predecessors, Ephrem adds the hope that the episcopal power will work effectively with the imperial power. For after the death of Julian, the Roman army had chosen a new emperor, Jovian, an orthodox Christian.

Seeing no alternative to surrender under the disadvantageous terms offered him by Shapur, Jovian accepted them. These terms included cession to Persia of the city of Nisibis without its inhabitants. The city was, in Ephrem's eyes, the sacrificial lamb that saved the Roman army.[82] Unlike Ammianus Marcellinus, however, who portrays the fate of Nisibis in exclusively negative terms,[83] Ephrem stresses that, although the city itself was ceded to Persia, the Persian ruler showed respect for its Christian churches and permitted its citizens to depart for Roman territory rather than executing them, enslaving them or exiling them into the eastern reaches of the Persian Empire, as had been the fate of the inhabitants of other recalcitrant Mesopotamian cities.[84] To celebrate his victory

---

80. CJ 3.16; cf. note ad loc.
81. Cf. CNis 17.
82. Cf. CJ 2.15.6.
83. Cf. Amm. Mar. 25.7.11, 25.8.13–14, 25.8.17, 25.9.1–12.
84. Cf. CJ 2.22–27.

and show appropriate disdain for the religion of the Roman army that had attacked his empire, the Persian king was apparently satisfied to destroy the pagan temples associated specifically with Julian.[85]

Still the entire Christian population of this fortress city migrated within a short time to the adjacent cities of the Roman Empire. Ephrem was among those who went first to Amida, then to Edessa, where he would spend his last ten years. Thus the heroic struggle of his native city, a symbol of Rome and of Christianity, against the mighty Persian Empire, a struggle which had occupied most of his adult life, ended in defeat and disgrace. The "constant, unwearying herald" was surrendered to the Persians.[86] As he meditates on these events in his *Carmina Nisibena* and in his *Hymns against Julian*, Ephrem shows himself to be a genuine heir to the Jewish prophetic tradition, interpreting historical events as directed by divine Providence toward the attainment of justice in this world.[87] There must be a reason for God's allowing Nisibis to be taken. For him that reason is clear: the apostasy of the Christian Roman emperor and of those who followed him in reinstating pagan worship:

> Who else has so multiplied altars?
> Who else has so honored all the evil spirits?
> Who else has so pleased all the demons?
> He angered only the One, and he was broken.
> In him was confuted the entire faction of wrong,
> a force unable to support its worshippers![88]

E   Ephrem at Edessa: 363–73

Ephrem arrived in Edessa in 363 to find a city that retained much of its unique cultural and religious heritage.[89] The city had been ruled by a dynasty of Nabatean kings who had deftly navigated the political strug-

---

85. CJ 2.22.
86. CJ 2.16.6.
87. Martikainen, Remarks. The Babylonian Jewish community, by contrast, was alienated from this tradition of historical interpretation, according to Neusner: "It is as if the biblical genius at interpreting the theological substance of historical forms had been lost, or abandoned so the rabbis no longer seriously cared about history" (TJSB, 39).
88. CJ 4.6.
89. The lost Nisibene Hymns, 22–25, probably deal with the period of Ephrem's journey from Nisibis to Edessa via Amida; cf. Beck, Lobgesang, 15.

gles of the Hellenistic and early Roman periods until it was incorporated into the Roman Empire in the early third century.[90] Like Nisibis, Edessa had been the object of the Roman struggles with Parthia, Sassanid Persia and Palmyra and had been definitively recovered for Rome by Diocletian. Likewise as at Nisibis, the population, its culture and religion were mixed. Pagan worship of several varieties is clearly attested: From the ancient Mesopotamian pantheon, Bel and Nebo are found, often associated as father and son. Bel is Bel Marduk, the chief god of Babylonian religion, "kosmokrator, lord of planets and stars who guided the world and gave it fertility."[91] From his function as cosmic ruler, astrology had come to be associated with Bel. A major New Year's festival, which took place in his honor in April, continued to flourish. Nebo, son of Bel, was the "Babylonian god of wisdom and human fate," who had become the patron of wisdom and of the art of writing as well as a powerful mediator between his father and humankind.[92] From the native Aramean culture came Hadad, Baal Shamin, lord of the heavens in the sense of master of the weather, storms, rain and fertility, who was symbolized by both the bull and the eagle. His consort, Atargatis, a female fertility goddess associated with fish and water, had surpassed him in importance in the Hellenistic and Roman periods when she had acquired the characteristics of Cybele, the Great Mother of Asia Minor. Her cult, as described by Lucian of Samosata in *On the Syrian Goddess*, with its castrated priests, the *galli*, and raucous musical processions, was centered at neighboring Hierapolis. It was clearly important at Edessa as well, where large ponds containing sacred fish were associated with her worship.[93] The moon god, Sin, and the Arabian deities, Azizos and Monimos, received homage here.[94] Also clearly attested is the presence of a substantial and prosperous Jewish community associated with the silk trade and with their co-religionists in Nisibis.[95]

---

90. Segal, Edessa, 13–16.
91. Drijvers, Persistence, 37; cf. also idem, Cults, 40–75; but some of Bel's functions may have been taken over from Bol, a local Semitic deity, cf. J. Starcky, *Palmyréniens, Nabatéens et Arabes du Nord avant l'Islam*, in *Histoire des Religions* 4, ed. M. Brillant and R. Aigrain (Tournai, Belgium, 1957), 206.
92. Drijvers, Persistence, 37; cf. also J. Teixidor, *The Pantheon of Palmyra* (Leiden, 1979), 107.
93. Segal, Edessa, 46–49; Drijvers, Cults, 76–121.
94. Drijvers, Cults, 122–74.
95. Segal, Edessa, 41–43, 100–2, 108–9, 136f.; cf. also Drijvers, Jews.

INTRODUCTION

Fourth-century Edessa was a proud center of Christianity with legends and associations sufficient to capture the imaginations of such Western Christians as Eusebius and Egeria.[96] According to the *Doctrine of Addai*, an early version of which Eusebius had read in the city's archives, Jesus himself had corresponded with King Abgar of Edessa. In response to the king's recognition of his messianic role and his offer of refuge, Jesus had assured him that an apostle would be sent to teach him and to heal him of an illness. By the end of the fourth century it was held that Jesus' letter had the capacity to protect the city, and that Jesus had also sent his portrait to Abgar, and within a few more decades that portrait was proudly functioning as the palladium of the city.[97] Although the non-canonical *Acts of Thomas* associate their protagonist not with Edessa, but with India, both they and the gospel attributed to him may have originated in Edessa.[98] Although the *Doctrine of Addai* claims only that Addai, or Thaddeus, one of the seventy, was sent to the city by the apostle Thomas, by Ephrem's time the bones of Thomas himself were venerated there. Aware of a conflict between this development and the tradition of the apostle's death in India according to the *Acts of Thomas*, the hymnodist alludes to a transferral of the bones:

> The evil one wails, "Where then
> can I flee from the righteous?
> I incited Death to kill the apostles
> as if to escape from their scourges
> by their death. More than ever now
> I am scourged harshly. The apostle I killed in India
> [has come] to Edessa before me. Here is he and also there.
> I went there, there he is.
> Here and there I found him, and I am gloomy.
> Did that merchant carry the bones?
> Or perhaps, indeed, they carried him!"[99]

---

96. Cf. Euseb.HE 1.13 and Eger. Itin. 17–19.
97. The essential work on the legend and its development is E. von Dobschütz, *Christusbilder: Untersuchungen zur Christlicher Legende*, TU, ser. 2, III (Leipzig, 1899); for the argument that Egeria's is the original version, cf. P. Devos, "Égérie à Édesse. S. Thomas L'Apôtre: Le Roi Abgar," AB 85 (1967), 381–400; also, cf. Cameron, Shroud.
98. Cf. nn. 13 and 28 above.
99. CNis 42.1.1–2.2 and cf. CNis 27.62 and 49.9–40; vs. Acta Thomae 1–2 and 159–170.

INTRODUCTION

A decade or two later Egeria would come to the Syrian city expressly to see the martyrium of Thomas, whom she believed to be the apostle sent to Abgar by Jesus.[100]

In addition to their claim to apostolic foundation and royal endorsement, the Christians of Edessa could lay claim to most of the earliest Syriac literature.[101] The first Syriac author whose name has been preserved, Bardaisan composed his one hundred fifty hymns there in the second century. His work consists of a unique blend of ideas and imagery drawn from Christianity, Aramaean paganism, astrology and later Platonism.[102] Bardaisan was the originator of the *madrāšâ*, a hymn composed in isosyllabic verse, which uses parallelism, rhyme, alliteration and a variety of word play to achieve its effects.[103] Composing hymns in the same form to combat the heretic's views, Ephrem became the unquestioned master of the genre.[104]

Edessa also had its Diocletianic martyrs, Shamona, Gurya and Habbib, as well as less reliable legends of earlier martyrs.[105] Despite its early apostolic traditions, its literature and martyrs, the city's succession of bishops is problematic until 313, when Bishop Qona is said to have undertaken the construction of a new cathedral church, just coinciding with the new status of the church under Constantine.[106] The city was also

---

100. Eger. Itin. 17.1; cf. Devos, Egerie, 381f.

101. For enumeration of the works to be included under this rubric, their characteristic features and problems involved in their interpretation, cf. Murray, Characteristics; further, cf. n. 13, above.

102. For a general introduction to Bardaisan, cf. Drijvers, Bardaisan of Edessa; for additional bibliography, cf. Kronholm, Motifs, 29, n.99, and add Drijvers, "Bardaisan of Edessa and the Hermetica: The Aramaic Philosopher and the Philosophy of His Time," *Jaarbericht Ex Oriente Lux* 21 (1969–70), 190–210.

103. Although Ephrem mentions only Bardaisan himself, Sozomen credits his putative son Harmonius with the invention of the genre; cf. Outtier 21. The Greek and overly appropriate name of Harmonious coupled with the prevalent chauvinism of Greek Christian writers have made some suspicious of this datum. Yet it is difficult to see why the hagiographic tradition surrounding Ephrem would maintain Bardaisan's priority here without reason. On this question and on Syriac poetic forms in brief, cf. Brock, Introduction, esp. 5–6.

104. For a careful analysis of Ephrem's poetic technique, cf. S. Brock, "The Poetic Artistry of St. Ephrem: An Analysis of H. Azym. III," PdO 6 (1975), 21–28; also, P. Robson, "Ephrem as Poet," in J.H. Eaton, *Horizons*, 34–38, analyzes a short section from the first two Hymns against Julian.

105. For the text and translation of the acts of Shamona and Gurya, cf. F. C. Burkitt, *Euphemia and the Goth with the Acts of Martyrdom of the Confessors of Edessa* (London, 1913); on their authenticity, cf. H. Achelis, *Die Martyrologien*, Abh. der Gesellschaft der Wiss. zu Göttingen, 3.3 (1900), 30–71; for a general discussion, cf. Segal, Edessa, 82–86.

106. Bauer, Orthodoxy, esp. 14–43.

represented at the Council of Nicea.[107] Even more clearly than in the case of Nisibis, however, the concept of orthodoxy was of more recent vintage than the presence of a Christian community. For when Ephrem arrived in 363 C.E. he found a city in which the orthodox were identified by the name of a predecessor of Qona, Palut, who had been ordained by the bishop of Antioch. Likewise the Marcionites, Bardaisanites, Manichaeans, Arians and all other Christians were identified by the epithet of their group to distinguish them among the larger group of Christians.[108] Such identifications could not be accepted by orthodox Christians, Ephrem argued. They and they alone had the right to be called by the name of Christ. Just as the image of the emperor for the manufacture of coins is strictly controlled, so is the image of the Lord not to be used by just anybody. Indeed, all the heretics should be designated by the names of their founders, but orthodox should be known simply as "Christians," not as "Palutians."[109]

Clearly the Gnostic and Manichaean forms of Christianity, and Arianism as well, had substantial followings in Edessa, and just as in Nisibis Ephrem did not hesitate to enter the polemical fray. Many of his *Hymns against Heresies*, composed in Nisibis, were refutations of the doctrines of Mani, Marcion and Bardaisan; in his new home he supplemented these polemics with more hymns as well as prose refutations.[110] Likewise Ephrem had already written his *Sermons on Faith* against Arianism in Nisibis, but this struggle assumed a larger role in his Edessene period.[111] In the later historical *Carmina Nisibena* and in the *Hymns on Faith*, he

---

107. Although the lists of signatories include a bishop of Edessa, the name varies; cf. Honigmann, Liste, p. 46 #73 Aethalas of Edessa and p. 62 #73 Abšelma of Urha (Edessa), and Honigmann's Remarks p. 63.

108. We cannot discuss fully the complex question whether Bauer has demonstrated that the Marcionites of Edessa were known simply by the name of Christian, cf. Bauer, Orthodoxy, 22–29. Suffice it to say that Ephrem does not so state in the passages Bauer cites, and that his discussion needs to be evaluated in the light of a full analysis of Ephrem's polemical works; for a useful overview of the polemical works, cf. Kronholm, Motifs, 28–33.

109. CH 22, esp. 22.1–10.

110. Although Kronholm ascribes the *Hymns against Heresies* "in all probability" to the Nisibene period, cf. Kronholm, Motifs, 20, surely CH 22–24, with the clear references to Palut in 22.5–6, come from the Edessene period. Beck has not, I think, expressed a view on the dating of that collection. His remarks on the philosophical arguments in the prose refutations suggest the later period, cf. Eph. Hypat., esp. 119f., n.135, and Eph. Domnus, esp. 67f.

111. For dating of the SdF, cf. Beck, Lobgesang, 17.

defends not only the orthodox doctrine but also the anti-Arian bishops, Barsai and Vitus of Harran, against the machinations of their episcopal and imperial opponents.[112] In a less polemical vein are the collections entitled *Hymns on the Church* and *Hymns on Virginity*, which set forth most fully his symbolic theology in the context of scriptural interpretation and ecclesiology.[113] As at Nisibis Ephrem probably taught in a school, perhaps one he himself founded.[114] Here, too, Ephrem is said to have founded choirs of women whom he personally instructed in the singing of his hymns.[115] Ephrem's admiration of the ascetic life and his enthusiasm for Christian virginity are evident throughout his writings in his descriptions of bishops he admired as well as in more general treatments.[116] There is no indication, however, in the clearly authentic writings that he personally embraced the monastic life either as a hermit or as a member of a community.[117] Ephrem was ordained to the diaconate at Edessa, and in the course of caring for the sick in an outbreak of the plague, he died there on 9 June 373 C.E.[118]

---

112. Cf. CNis 26–34, esp. 26–27, and Beck, Lobgesang 15. For the dating and contents of the HdF, cf. Beck, Theologie; also Beck, Lobgesang, 15, and Kronholm, Motifs, 28, n.95. As Griffith has argued at length, however, for Ephrem it is the bishops, rather than the emperors who bear the major responsibility for these problems, cf. Griffith, Ephraem, esp. 37–47.

113. On the basis of Virg. 37.10, the similarity of themes in the two collections, and their fully developed symbolic theology, Beck places them late in Ephrem's life; cf. Beck, Lobgesang, 16.

114. Barhadbshabba claims Ephrem as the founder of this school, just as he claimed his appointment by Jacob of Nisibis as the beginning of that school; cf. n. 24 above, *loc. cit.* Hayes' view that Ephrem taught in an institution that antedated his arrival in Edessa is based on the unsubstantiated presumption that "partout où le christianisme prenait pied, on créait une école pour l'instruction de la jeunesse et pour celle des clercs." Cf. E. R. Hayes *L'École d'Édesse* (Paris, 1930), 39–40. Whereas Vööbus is sceptical of both claims, cf. *History of the School of Nisibis*, CSCO subs. p.9, Outtier credits Barhadbshabba, cf. Outtier, Saint Ephrem, 20f., 25f.

115. Jacob of Serug's homily on Ephrem is the source of this notion, cf. P. Bedjan, *Acta martyrum et Sanctorum Syriace*, 6 vols. (Paris-Leipzig, 1892; rep. Hildesheim, 1968), 3, 665–78; again, Outtier finds it creditable, loc. cit.

116. Cf. for example CNis 26–34, on the one hand, and de Virg 1–3, on the other.

117. Kronholm, Motifs, 24f., nn. 65f. and 70f., for the literature, and add Outtier, Saint Ephrem, 14–16.

118. The most important testimony to his ordination is Ephrem's own, cf. CH 56.10; Palladius, Jerome and Sozomen also refer to him as a deacon; the Chronicle of Edessa is the source for the date of his death, and Palladius and Sozomen for his service in the plague; cf. Outtier, Saint Ephrem, esp. 14f. and 19.

INTRODUCTION

III Hymns Chosen for This Volume

A The Hymns on the Nativity

1 The Manuscript Collections

The core of the collection of *Hymns on the Nativity* is a collection of sixteen hymns (Hymns 5–20 of the present translation), probably gathered together and entitled "lullabyes" by Ephrem himself.[119] The designation is appropriate since most of the hymns are sung by Mary to her son. Ephrem probably composed the collection of hymns for liturgical use at the feast of Christ's birth and manifestation to the world, celebrated in his time on 6 January.[120]

A sixth-century compiler of Ephrem's hymns supplemented this collection with four authentic hymns on the same subject (hymns 1–4 of the present translation).[121] In the manuscript collections of Ephrem's hymns subsequently made for liturgical use, the sixth-century collection of twenty hymns is supplemented with eight more on the birth of Christ. All except the last of these additional hymns (hymns 21–27 of the present translation) are surely authentic; even the last hymn (hymn 28) is probably a later compilation of strophes from authentic hymns.[122] The entire collection, therefore, has been included in the present translation. Many of the Nativity Hymns have appeared previously in English, but this is the first English translation of the full collection of twenty-eight hymns based on Beck's edition.[123]

---

119. Hymns 5–20 of the present collection all have the same melody and are grouped under the title "Hymns on the Nativity" in the oldest manuscript, BM Add 14571; the second-oldest manuscript, Vat. Syr. 112, dated 551 A.D., adds the designation *nwṣrt'* for this core group and supplements it with hymns 1–4; cf. E. Beck, in CSCO 187, v. Further on the development of the collection, cf. A. de Halleux, "La transmission des Hymnes d'Éphrem d'après les ms. Sinai Syr. 10, f. 165v–178r.," OCA 197 (1974), 21–63, esp. 38f.

120. Cf. Nat. 5.13–14 and Beck, CSCO 186, v–vi.

121. Contrary to the view expressed in Kronholm (in Motifs, 21), Beck considers these four unquestionably authentic, cf. Beck, CSCO 187, v–vi.

122. The manuscripts in question date from the eighth to thirteenth centuries. For the detailed discussion of the authenticity of Nat. 21–28, cf. Beck, CSCO 187, v–viii.

123. An excellent translation of Nat. 11 appears in Brock, Harp, 34–36. An earlier version of thirteen hymns based on the edition of Assemani was published by J. B. Morris, *Select Works of S. Ephrem the Syrian* (Oxford, 1847), 1–60; it was supplemented by J. Gwynn with six additional hymns from Lamy's edition (hymns 21–26 of the present translation) and republished in NPNF XIII, 221–62. Hymns 2, 12, 19, 20, 27 and 28 appear here for the first time in English. In the rest of the collection many lesser changes in translation and arrangement have been made thanks to Beck's edition.

Later the Syriac church brought its celebration of the nativity into conformity with the Roman tradition, celebrating Christmas on 25 December and the Epiphany on 6 January. The latter date, now understood as the feast of the baptism of Christ, became the occasion for the baptism of catechumens.[124] In conformity with this later tradition the liturgical manuscripts add a collection of *Hymns on the Epiphany*, which concern the sacrament of baptism. Although several of the *Hymns on Epiphany* are genuinely Ephrem's work, they are not included here since they were not linked with the Nativity Hymns in Ephrem's time.[125] Given the limitations of space I preferred to present other texts which have not been previously translated into English.[126]

2   Theological and Literary Themes of the *Hymns on the Nativity*
    The central theological theme of the *Hymns on the Nativity* is Ephrem's understanding of the incarnation as the miraculous and paradoxical self-abasement of God out of love for humankind. It is a theological concept that evokes profound questions: How can the Ruler of the universe, whom the entire created order is unable to contain, have been contained in a single, small human womb?

The Power that governs all dwelt in a small womb.
While dwelling there, He was holding the reins of the universe.
His Parent was ready for His will to be fulfilled.
The heavens and all the creation were filled by Him.
The Sun entered the womb, and in the height and depth
His rays were dwelling.

He dwelt in the vast wombs of all creation.
They were too small to contain the greatness of the Firstborn.
How indeed did that small womb of Mary suffice for Him?
It is a wonder if [anything] sufficed for Him.

---

124. In conformity with the rest of the early church, the Syriac church of Ephrem's time had baptized catechumens at Easter. That this was the custom in Ephrem's time is confirmed by Virg 7 as well as by Aphrahat, Dem. 12 and 13, cf. Beck, CSCO 186, v ff., 187, vi ff.

125. For a more extensive discussion of the authenticity of the Epiphany Hymns and of the *swgyt'* also appended to the later manuscripts, cf. Beck, CSCO 186, vii-viii, 187, viii–xiii.

126. The Epiphany Hymns were translated by A. E. Johnston, in NPNF ser. 2, XIII, 265–89.

INTRODUCTION

Of all the wombs that contained Him, one womb sufficed:
[the womb] of the Great One Who begot Him.

The womb that contained Him, if it contained all of Him,
is equal to the wonderful womb
that is greater than [the womb] of His birth.
But who will dare to say that a small womb,
weak and despised, is equal to [the womb] of the Great Being.
He dwelt [there] because of His compassion,
and since His nature is great,
He was not limited in anything.[127]

Not only the bare fact of the incarnation but also of its specific circumstances are miraculous and paradoxical: "[God] deprived the married womb; He made fruitful the virgin womb."[128] Far from showing a weakness, these apparent contradictions show the majesty of the Creator, the "Lord of natures." Yet these are not pointless displays of might; instead they are the concessions of a loving God to human frailty:

God had seen that we worshipped creatures.
He put on a created body to catch us by our habit.
Behold by this fashioned one our Fashioner healed us,
and by this creature our Creator revived us.[129]

The divine condescension to humankind in the incarnation has brought about a permanent change in the relationship between human beings and their Creator:

the Deity imprinted Itself on humanity, so that humanity might
also be cut into the seal of the Deity.[130]

In addition to this language of seals and stamps, which he shares with the Logos theology of Greek Christianity, Ephrem expresses the intimate union of divine and human with the language of painting, likening it to the artist's blending of pigments:

---

127. Nat. 21.6–8.
128. Nat. 21.17.
129. Nat. 21.12; cf. Nat. 22.4 and 22.16–18.
130. Nat. 1.99.

INTRODUCTION

Glorious is the Wise One Who allied and joined
Divinity with humanity,
One from the height and the other from below.
He mingled the natures like pigments,
and an image came into being: the God-man![131]

Although this grand concession to human frailty took place uniquely in the incarnation, it also continues to take place in every time and place for each individual human being. God is revealed to each according to his or her capacity to perceive:

He was cheerful among the infants as a baby;
awesome was He among the Watchers as a commander.
Too awesome was He for John to loosen His sandals;
accessible was He for sinners who kissed His feet.
The Watchers as Watchers saw Him;
according to the degree of his knowledge each person saw Him.
Everyone according to the measure of his discernment thus perceived Him, that One greater than all.[132]

These hymns are also an extraordinarily rich source of early Christian typological exegesis. In conformity with the incarnational emphasis of the hymns, the central figures of this typology are Jesus and Mary. Especially in the first two hymns Ephrem presents a rich variety of Old Testament types for Christ. In the second hymn he systematically presents Jesus as the prophet, priest and king. Throughout the hymns he uses many of the usual Old Testament figures as forerunners of Christ, but he adds unexpected interpretations as well. For example, Jesus is anticipated not only by Isaac, Melchizedek, Moses and David, but also by Jacob, who is kicked by Esau but does not retaliate. Above all, the wealth of his typology for Mary sets Ephrem's effort apart from the other early Christian examples of typological exegesis. Mary is not only the second Eve, but she is also a second Sarah, Rachel and Anna; she is even compared

---

131. Nat. 8.2, cf. also Nat. 21.12.5–6. For the same imagery vis-à-vis baptism, cf. Virg. 7.5–6, and for a radical mingling of the natures without the painting imagery, Virg. 37.2.
132. Nat. 4.197–200. On "Watchers" cf. CJ 1.8.3–6 and note *ad loc.*

with Tamar, Ruth and Rahab.[133] Indeed she is the Tablet of the Law and the Ark of the Covenant.[134]

Ephrem's choice of types for Mary and his argument on her behalf are motivated in part by a desire to defend the virgin birth from criticism or ridicule. In the sixth hymn Mary sings to her infant son:

> . . . With Your pure conception
> evil men have slandered me. O Holy One,
> be Your mother's defender. Show miracles
> to convince them whence is Your conception.[135]

In response Ephrem has crafted an intricate typology of sealed tombs and sealed wombs:

> Sealed was the grave which they entrusted
> with keeping the dead man. Virginal was the womb
> that no man knew. The virginal womb
> and the sealed grave like trumpets
> for a deaf people, shouted in its ear.[136]

Ephrem adds a menacing dimension to his typology directed at the Jewish authorities to whom he attributes the attacks on Mary's virtue.[137] Just as the daughter of Saul was punished for her criticism and ridicule of David's dance, so also the "daughter of Sion" will be punished if these attacks do not cease.[138]

Despite the polemical overtones of these hymns, their mariology has important positive dimensions as well. Ephrem's mariology is central to his understanding of the incarnation. Mary was chosen because she was most pleasing to God.[139] Yet she who gave birth to the Son of the Most High was given birth by him in baptism.[140] Paradoxically, Mary gave

---

133. Cf. Nat. 8. 13, 13. 2–5; 9. 7–16, 15.8, 16.12.
134. Cf. Nat. 16.16–17.
135. Nat. 6.3.
136. Nat. 10.8; further cf. Nat. 10.2–10, 12.2–3.
137. Further on the place of these hymns in Jewish-Christian polemics of the fourth century, cf. K. McVey, "Ephrem the Syrian's Hymns on the Nativity and the Tol'dot Yeshu'," (to appear).
138. Cf. Nat. 14. 7–19, 15. 7–8.
139. Cf. Nat. 2.7.
140. Cf. Nat. 16. 9–11.

birth to and nourished and cared for the Incarnate One who gave life, nourishment and care to her. In this she represents all humans and indeed all creation:

> By power from Him Mary's womb became able
> to bear the One Who bears all.
> From the great treasury of all creation
> Mary gave to Him every thing that she gave.
> She gave Him milk from what He made exist.
> She gave Him food from what He had created.
> As God, He gave milk to Mary.
> In turn, as man, He was given suck by her.[141]

The radical identification of God with creation and especially with humankind is a result of the incarnation. In the incarnation the God who utterly transcends his creation has imprinted himself onto his creation like a seal.[142] He has done this not out of any limitation or need, but out of passionate love for humankind.[143] By assenting to the incarnation at the moment of the annunciation, Mary has made this possible, because God willed to be dependent on humans even in this.[144]

B   The Hymns Against Julian

The five hymns concerning the apostate emperor are surely authentic. They follow the fifteen *Hymns on Paradise* in one of the earliest manuscripts, apparently because both collections have the same melody.[145] Whereas the *Hymns on Paradise* were probably composed in Ephrem's earliest years in Nisibis, he did not begin the *Hymns against Julian* until the final weeks of Julian's reign, during the Mesopotamian campaign undertaken in the spring of 363 from Antioch. The hymns were completed

---

141. Nat. 4. 182–185; cf. also Nat. 4. 143–213 and Nat. 11.
142. Cf. Nat. 1. 97–99; also 2.21, 3.5, 3.17.
143. Cf. Nat. 13.12–14.
144. Cf. Nat. 5.20.
145. Cf. E. Beck, CSCO 174, i–ii. That manuscript, B.M.Add. 14571, includes the hymn "de Ecclesia" between the *Hymns on Paradise* and the four hymns explicitly against Julian. Its colophon, which refers to "five hymns against Emperor Julian the pagan," confirms that the hymn ought to be considered together with the other four against Julian.

INTRODUCTION

after the emperor's death, since Ephrem mentions having seen his body carried in state past Nisibis.[146]

1 Editions and Translations of the *Hymns against Julian*

The *Hymns against Julian* were edited by Overbeck in 1865.[147] Overbeck's text has been translated into German by Bickell, Euringer and Beck.[148] Excerpts have been quoted in English translation by Bowersock, Browning, Levenson and Griffith; a first complete English translation was recently published by Samuel N. C. Lieu.[149]

2 The Hymns As a Historical Source

In these four hymns, which Bowersock has called "four astonishingly vivid and intense invectives," Ephrem shows himself to be far from dispassionate. Since he is nevertheless an eyewitness to the events he describes, his words constitute a significant historical source for the last weeks of the emperor's life and for the circumstances of his death.[150] Ephrem is the only ancient author to mention the coinage issued just before the ill-fated campaign in Mesopotamia. His claim that its image of a bull with two stars represents the Golden Calf of Sinai, however, is problematic.[151] The hymns also help to clarify the circumstances that led to Julian's orders to burn his own fleet. Ephrem's claim that the emperor was deceived by Easterners and that "his idols and diviners were entangled in a snare" corroborate the report of Ammianus Marcellinus that a betrayal led to the

---

146. CJ 3.1. On the dating of the final four hymns, cf. Glen W. Bowersock, *Julian the Apostate* (Cambridge, Mass., 1978), 10.

147. J.J. Overbeck, *S. Ephraemi Syri, Rabulae Episcopi Edesseni, Balaci Aliorumque Opera Selecta*, (Oxford, 1865), 3–20.

148. G. Bickell, ZKT II, 335–56; S. Euringer, BKV (Kempten-Muenchen, 1919), 197–233; E. Beck, CSCO 174–75, scr. syr. 78–79 (Louvain, 1957). For Beck's discussion of the previous work and his relation to it, cf. Beck, CSCO 174, scr. syr. 78, i–ii and CSCO 175, scr. syr. 79, ii.

149. Glen W. Bowersock, *Julian the Apostate* (Cambridge, Mass., 1978), 114, 116; Robert Browning, *The Emperor Julian* (London, 1975), 217; David B. Levenson, *A Source- and Tradition-Critical Study of the Stories of Julian's Attempt to Rebuild the Jerusalem Temple* (Harvard diss., 1980); Sidney H. Griffith, "Ephraem the Syrian's Hymns 'Against Julian': Meditations on History and Imperial Power," *Vigiliae Christianae* 41 (1987), 238–66; Samuel N.C. Lieu, ed., *The Emperor Julian: Panegyric and Polemic*, Claudius Mamertinus, John Chrysostom, Ephrem the Syrian, (Liverpool, 1986).

150. Although he sounds a cautionary note on the historical value of Ephrem's information, Beck enumerates several points on which he offers information, CSCO 175, 1f. Bowersock especially emphasizes the importance of these hymns as a historical source, cf. Julian, 10, 104, 114ff.; Browning also uses them, cf. Emperor, 192, 213–17.

151. Cf. CJ 1.16–19 and notes ad loc.

35

emperor's action as opposed to Libanius' claim that Julian formulated this plan for his own tactical reasons. Moreover, Ephrem's remarks are consistent with Gregory Nazianzen's contention that a treacherous Persian nobleman was the source of the emperor's faulty strategy.[152] Further, unlike Libanius, Gregory and Sozomen, Ephrem shows no interest in the identity of Julian's assailant,[153] asserting instead that the emperor virtually committed suicide.[154] The fact that Ammianus is silent on this point probably indicates that any Christian plot to eliminate the pagan emperor is strictly the product of later imagination.[155] Finally, although the city itself was ceded to Persia, the settlement of Jovian with Shapur must have included respecting the Christian churches of the city and allowing the citizens of Nisibis to leave for Roman territory rather than executing them, enslaving them or exiling them into the eastern reaches of the Persian Empire, as Shapur had done with the inhabitants of other recalcitrant Mesopotamian cities.[156]

3 Literary and Theological Themes

The *Hymns against Julian*, along with the *Carmina Nisibena*, display Ephrem's kinship with the Jewish prophets.[157] Like them, he contemplates the political and military events of his time in the light of his ethical and theological tenets, looking for evidence of divine activity, rewards, punishments and edifying moral lessons. Warnings against idolatry and encouragement in adversity are as prominent in these hymns as in the pronouncements of Jeremiah and Isaiah. In Ephrem's view God made the apostate emperor the representative and symbol of all who hold erroneous views— not only pagans but also heretics and Jews. His defeat is a sign to all nations of the ultimate fate of those who oppose God.

The first of these five hymns stands apart from the rest since it was written prior to Julian's death. Here the poet offers a message of hope and perseverance to the people of Nisibis, threatened with persecution. The

---

152. Cf. CJ 2.18 and note ad loc., also CJ 3.15.
153. Cf. CJ 3.14.1 and note ad loc.
154. CJ 3.16; cf. note ad loc.
155. So Bowersock correctly argues, cf. idem, Julian, 116.
156. Cf. CJ 2.22–27.
157. I am grateful to Sidney Griffith for drawing my attention to the importance of the theological themes of these hymns. There is considerable congruence between motifs here set forth and those Griffith has presented in his recent article in the context of a persuasive argument that as *madrāšê* these hymns should be seen not as invectives but rather as "biblically oriented meditations on history" (cf. Griffith, Julian, esp. 244).

other four hymns reiterate and develop that message in the light of subsequent events. Rather than focussing on the loss of their city to the Persians, a catastrophe caused by Nisibene acquiescence to Julian's reestablishment of paganism there, Ephrem emphasizes that the claims of paganism have been proved false by the fate of the apostate emperor. The political events provide a larger-than-life drama of the cosmic conflict between good and evil. God's partisans, the true members of the church of Nisibis, with the encouragement of the watching angels, withstood the onslaughts of Satan in the form of imperial persecution and Persian military attacks.

Using a favorite metaphor, the mirror as the instrument of divine ethical lessons, Ephrem takes the apostate emperor as the model of human pride as well as of political promotion of religious error. His policies unmasked the false Christians within the church; his ignomious death demonstrates the folly of his pride as well as the falsity of his beliefs. The divine purpose in the defeat and death of the Roman emperor was to present to all people a model of the vanity of idolatry. At the same time the fidelity of Christians has been tested and many have been found wanting during the pagan emperor's brief reign. Weak or false Christians have returned openly to paganism, or they have attacked their Creator in the contentious error of the Arian heresy. The Jewish people have also returned to idolatrous worship. On the other hand, the city of Nisibis presents, again as if in a mirror, a model for fidelity to God, its rewards, and the consequences of its lapse. Reinforcing this primary imagery is the symbol of the church as the true vine, beneficially pruned by the rigors of persecution:

> Rely on the truth, my brothers, and be not afraid
> for our Lord is not so weak as to fail us in the test.
> He is the power on which the world and its inhabitants depend.
> The hope of His church depends on Him.
> Who is able to sever its heavenly roots?[158]

> Although the branch is living, on it are dead fruits
> blooming only outwardly.
> The wind tried them and cast off the wild grapes.[159]

---

158. CJ 1.1.
159. CJ 1.5; cf. 1.10–11.

INTRODUCTION

Several other metaphors serve to teach the same lesson: separation of the wheat from the tares,[160] the purification of gold in the furnace,[161] and separation of the curds and whey in cheesemaking.[162]

To these symbols current in both biblical and general Hellenistic contexts, Ephrem adds biblical examples of faithless sovereigns and the consequences of their erroneous ways: Nebuchadnezzar, Jeroboam, Ahab, Jotham, Manasseh, Jezebel, Athaliah and Saul provide precedents for Julian's errors as well as his fate.[163] The attendant notions of true and false prophecy provide a context for his contention that in this case the church has followed the course of Daniel, confronting the pagan ruler, whereas the Jewish people have followed the precedent of the Israelites under Jeroboam, worshipping the golden calf.[164] While this general approach, aptly named "prophetic anti-Judaism" by Ruether, is typical of patristic writers,[165] Ephrem pursues his view with tenacious originality, accompanied, one suspects, by a modicum of perverse mis-representation. In support of the parallel with the Israelite worship of the golden calf, for example, he associates Julian's bull coinage with his attempt to rebuild the Temple in Jerusalem as well as claiming that the music and sacrifice of traditional Jewish worship resemble pagan wor-ship in its raucousness.[166] Likewise, to the established argument that Daniel prophesied the permanent destruction of the Jewish Temple, he adds the claim implicit in Constantine's building program but not gener-ally stated in theological polemics that Christian pilgrimage functions as a substitute for the Jewish cult of Jerusalem.[167]

Throughout the hymns, he exploits an extensive variety of animal imagery. The Orphic and broadly Hellenistic notion of a philanthropic shepherd king, already well-established as a model for Christ, is pre-sented as a foil for Julian, the bad king.[168] Rather than a good shepherd, he is a wolf in sheep's clothing, or a he-goat, favoring the goats rather than

---

160. CJ 1.10–13, 2.10–11.
161. CJ 1.13, 2.24, 4.1.
162. CJ 4.2.
163. CJ 1.8, 1.20, 2.2, 4.5, 4.8.
164. CJ 1.16–20, 2.2.
165. Ruether, Fratricide, 117–82.
166. CJ 1.16.
167. CJ 4.23–25.
168. CJ 1.1–2. On Orpheus in Edessa, cf. Segal, Edessa, 52. On Christ-Orpheus in Ephrem and in other early Christian writers, cf. Nat. 3.7.3–6 and notes ad loc.

38

the sheep.[169] The latter image has the added punch of alluding to Julian's unpopular beard as well as intimating lasciviousness.[170] Ephrem's almost apocalyptic description of the conflict between the forces of good and evil is enhanced by his association of the pagans with vermin, dragons and the primal chaos as well as with the more mundane insults of association with hogs and filth.[171]

Finally, Ephrem's symbolic imagination provides several examples of the ironic outcome of Julian's efforts. Considering it suitable that "the punishment should fit the crime," he finds numerous coincidences to confirm this view. For example, the emperor's death near Babylon in conjunction with his "denial" of Daniel's prophecy cements the parallel of Julian with Nebuchadnezzar.[172] Moreover, Ephrem spins out in elaborate detail the inherent contradiction of Julian's attempt to use Chaldean religion to defeat Persians,[173] and the paradox that he was misled by the oracles to become himself the sacrificial goat.[174] The coincidental features of his Uncle Julian's fate should have astonished the apostate emperor as they did Ephrem.[175] Likewise heavy with significance is the similarity of Julian's death by a lance to the death of his sacrificial animals, both of which are implicitly contrasted with the death of the True Lamb who, being pierced, released humankind from the curse of the lance that barred the gate to Paradise.[176]

C   The Hymns on Virginity and on the Symbols of Our Lord

1   The Contents of the Collection

This collection of hymns is in reality a compilation of several smaller collections, each identifiable by unity of subject matter as well as by the use of a single melody. A few single hymns, usually related in subject matter, are interspersed with the smaller collections, which range in size from two to eighteen hymns. The largest of the sub-collections, hymns

---

169. CJ 2.1–4.
170. CJ 2.6–9, and cf. notes ad loc.
171. CJ 1.3, 1.5, 2.13.
172. CJ 1.18–20.
173. Cf. CJ 2.14, 4.5–14.
174. CJ 2.4–15.
175. Cf. CJ 4.3 and note ad loc. on Julian's uncle Julian.
176. CJ 3.14.

thirteen to thirty, ends with three hymns on the "three harps of God," the Old and New Testaments and Nature. These hymns set forth the central theme of the entire collection, an idea that is the basis of Ephrem's symbolic theology: the presence of God in scripture and in nature. Hymns twenty-seven to thirty may, therefore, serve as a guide to the rest of the hymns in this collection and, indeed, to his entire hymnological production.

The theme of the first three hymns, from which the entire collection has received its name, is the consecrated virginity of the "daughters of the covenant." Through the baptismal anointing this group is linked to the following sub-collection of four hymns (hymns 4–7) "on oil [or ointment], the olive and the symbols of the Lord," which illustrate especially well Ephrem's intertwining of various types of symbols: linguistic, scriptural, natural and sacramental. The next sub-collection is a group of three hymns (hymns 8–10) defending the Christian claim that Jesus is the messiah promised by the Jewish scripture. The theme of messianism links this group to the previous sub-collection. The next two sub-collections (hymns 13–30 and hymns 32–37) offer interpretations of a series of New Testament passages, treated in roughly chronological order. In both these groups of hymns Ephrem displays a marked interest in places associated with Jesus' ministry. In the latter collection women are unusually prominent. The last of the sub-collections is a group of hymns on the prophet Jonah (hymns 42–50).

Considered in its entirety this collection of hymns contains a variety of polemics closely related to Ephrem's fundamental theological insight. The pagans err in worshipping the works of God rather than God their Creator. Conversely the Marcionites err in claiming to worship God while denying the goodness and beauty of God's creation. Both Judaism and Marcionism are pointedly rejected because they deny the presence of Christ in the Jewish scripture and in nature. The only correct path is through nature to the revelation of God in scripture. Some polemics against Manichaeism and Arianism appear here as well, particularly in the last two hymns.

To emphasize the polemical aspect of Ephrem's work perhaps creates too harsh an impression. The set of hymns on Jonah contains a sharp anti-Jewish polemic reproaching Jonah as a Jewish prophet reluctant to be sent to the Gentiles of Nineveh and contrasting the Ninevites' willingness to repent with Jonah's unwillingness to preach repentance to them. Yet

INTRODUCTION

throughout these hymns Ephrem plays on a variety of paradoxes, ranging from fairly strong polemics to playful musings, such as that a fish swallowed a human whereas fish were meant to be swallowed by humans, or that a rational human being gave birth to an irrational infant whereas an irrational fish brought forth a rational adult. In short, it would be virtually impossible to separate the serious and sustained arguments from the light and occasionally entertaining asides, but that, of course, was precisely Ephrem's intent.

2 The Symbolic Theology of the Hymns on Virginity

Ephrem's poetry is based upon a vision of the world as a vast system of symbols or mysteries.[177] No person, thing or event in the world exists without a mysterious relation to the whole. History and nature constitute the warp and woof of reality. To divorce an individual from its context in either direction would destroy the handiwork of God in time and space. Each moment of life is governed by the Lord of life and is an opportunity to see oneself and the community in relation to that Lord. So not only the events described in scripture but all historical events must have profound religious significance, as we have seen in Ephrem's *Hymns against Julian*. Nature, too, is replete with intimations of the presence of God. In creating the world God deliberately presented us not only with examples of beauty and order but also with symbols that allude more richly to the identity of their Creator:

> In every place, if you look, His symbol is there,
> and when you read, you will find His prototypes.
> For by Him were created all creatures,

---

177. On Ephrem's use of symbols, cf. E. Beck, "Symbolum-Mysterium bei Aphraat und Ephraem," OC 42 (1958), 19–40; idem, "Das Bild vom Spiegel bei Ephraem, OCP 19 (1953), 1–24; F. Graffin, "L'Eucharistie chez Saint Éphrem," PdO 4 (1973), 93–121; L. Leloir, "Symbolisme et Parallélisme chez Éphrem," *À la recontre de Dieu*, Mem. A. Gélin (Lyons, 1961), 364–73; R. Murray, "The Lance Which Reopened Paradise," OCP 39 (1973), 224–34, 491; idem, "The Theory of Symbolism in St. Ephrem's Theology," PdO 6 (1975), 1–20; idem, *Symbols of Church and Kingdom* (Cambridge, 1975); P. Yousif, "La Croix de Jésus et le Paradis d'Eden dans la typologie biblique de Saint Éphrem," PdO 6 (1975), 29–48; idem, "Le symbolisme de la croix dans la nature chez Saint Éphrem de Nisibe," OCA 205 (1978), Symposium Syriacum 1976, 207–27; idem, "Symbolisme christologique dans la Bible et dans la nature chez Saint Éphrem, de Nisibe," PdO 8 (1977–78), 5–66; idem, "St. Ephrem on symbols in nature: Faith, the Trinity and the Cross (Hymns on Faith no. 18)," ECR 10 (1978), 52–60; idem, "Histoire et temps dans la pensée de saint Éphrem de Nisibe," PdO 10 (1981–82), 3–35; S. Brock, *The Luminous Eye: The Spiritual World Vision of St. Ephrem* (Rome, 1985).

41

and He imprinted His symbols upon His possessions.
When He created the world,
He gazed at it and adorned it with His images.
Streams of His symbols opened, flowed and poured forth
His symbols on its members.[178]

Biblical Symbols

Among the historical symbols biblical typology plays the central role.
The events in Jewish history narrated in Hebrew scripture have religious
significance for all people. Like most early Christian writers, however,
Ephrem saw the Hebrew scripture as preliminary sketches, as shadows,
when compared with the realities of the New Testament:

[Christ's] power perfected the types,
and His truth the mysteries,
His interpretation the similes,
His explanations the sayings,
and His assurances the difficulties.

By His sacrifice He abolished sacrifices,
and libations by His incense,
and the [passover] lambs by His slaughter,
the unleavened [bread] by His bread,
and the bitter [herbs] by His Passion.

By His healthy meal
He weaned [and] took away the milk.
By His baptism were abolished
the bathing and sprinkling
that the elders of the People taught.[179]

Despite the intrinsic importance of the events and persons of the "Old
Testament," they are only "anteteypes," which were fulfilled in the
"types" of the New Testament. On the one hand, the Passover Lamb is an
anticipation of Christ and of the salvation gained through him. To at-

---

178. Virg. 20.12.
179. Virg. 8.8–10.

tempt to understand Christ without knowing about the Passover would be to deprive oneself of the depth and richness of meaning placed in human history by God himself. Yet conversely, in Ephrem's view, to stop with the Passover Lamb rather than interpreting it as a symbol of Christ would mean missing the fullness of God's revelation and accepting a truncated version of the meaning of history.[180]

The Role of the Incarnation and Humankind

At the center of all is Jesus Christ, the incarnate Word, who is at once the apex of history and the metaphysical Mediator between the ineffable Creator and the creation. Ephrem sets forth this notion most succinctly in the *Hymns on Virginity* 28–30, where he speaks of the three harps of God:

> The Word of the Most High came down and put on
> a weak body with hands,
> and He took two harps [Old and New Testaments]
> in His right and left hands.
> The third [nature] He set before Himself
> to be a witness to the [other] two,
> for the middle harp taught
> that their Lord is playing them.[181]

This strophe shows clearly that the lynchpin of his theological system is the paradox of the incarnation, through which God has revealed the relation of the two Testaments to one another and to nature.

As we have seen, the major theme of the nativity hymns is the wonder of the incarnation, conceived not only as a singular historical event but also as an ongoing availability of God to each human being. In the *Hymns on Virginity* Ephrem explores and refines these ideas. Jesus' encounter with the Samaritan woman at the well is especially symbolic of God's personal relation to each human being:

> The glorious fount of Him Who was sitting
> at the well as Giver of drink to all,
> flows to each according to His will:

---

180. Cf. Virg. 10.
181. Virg. 29.1.

> different springs according to those who drink.
> From the well a single undifferentiated drink
> came up each time for those who drank.
> The Living Fount lets distinct blessings
> flow to distinct people.[182]

But, not satisfied merely to meet each of us at our present level of spiritual discernment, God leads each of us step by step to higher levels of understanding. Again, the Samaritan woman is paradigmatic of this process:

> Because she in her love said, "The Messiah will come,"
> he revealed to her with love, "I am He."
> That He was a prophet she believed already,
> soon after, that He was the Messiah . . .
> . . . she is a type of our humanity
> that He leads step by step.[183]

Mary, the mother of Jesus, and the Beloved Disciple are also especially significant in Ephrem's understanding of the ongoing process of the incarnation in sanctification, the full restoration in each human being of the lost *imago dei*. Mary and John see in one another the complementary mysteries of God's condescending love for us and the bold access to divine love now open to human beings.[184] Through them we, too, may see this twofold mystery of our Savior:

> You, Lord, . . . they saw . . .
> while observing one another:
> Your mother saw You in Your disciple,
> and he saw You in Your mother.
> The seers who at every moment
> see You, Lord in a mirror

---

182. Virg. 23.3. For further exploration of this theme, cf. K. E. McVey, "St. Ephrem's Understanding of Spiritual Progress: Some Points of Comparison with Origen of Alexandria," *The Harp* I.2–3 (1988), 117–28.

183. Virg. 22.21.

184. Cf. Virg. 25.8.

manifest a type so that we, too, in one another
may see You, Our Savior.[185]

John is placed in this exemplary role not only because he was literally
given to Mary by Jesus as her son, but because his love of his Lord led
him to imitate Jesus, thus bringing into higher relief that *imago dei* engraved on each human being:

> The youth who loved our Lord very much,
> who portrayed [and] put Him on and resembled Him,
> was zealous in all these matters to resemble Him,
> in his speech, his aspect and his ways.
> The creature put on his Creator,
> and he resembled Him although indeed he did not resemble what He
>   was!
> It was amazing how much the clay is able to be imprinted
> with the beauty of its Sculptor.[186]

For Ephrem, the virgin exemplifies most perfectly the concentration
on the inner presence of Christ that leads to the full restoration of the
imago dei:

> [Mary Magdalen] turned her face away from everything
> to gaze on one beauty alone.
> Blessed is her love that was intoxicated, not sober,
> so that she sat at His feet to gaze at Him.
> Let you also portray the Messiah in your heart
> and love Him in your mind.[187]

Likewise it is the virgin who has most fully stripped off the old Adam to
put on the new at baptism.[188] Her body is clothed in a new garment; it is
the temple of God and his royal palace. However strongly Ephrem ad-

---

185. Virg. 25.9.
186. Virg. 25.4; cf. John 19.26.
187. Virg. 24.7.3–8; cf. also the remainder of Virg. 24, esp. Virg. 24.5. This hymn links
the themes of the larger collection of the initial hymns, from which the collection gained its
name.
188. Cf. Virg. 1.1–8.

monishes the virgin to preserve her sexual innocence, it is clear that this is not an end in itself, but rather it is symbolic of the full dedication of self to God, which is the goal of every Christian life:

> Let chastity be portrayed in your eyes and in your ears the sound of
>   truth.
> Imprint your tongue with the word of life and upon your hands
>   [imprint] all alms.
> Stamp your footsteps with visiting the sick,
> and let the image of your Lord be portrayed in your heart.
> Tablets are honored because of the image of kings.
> How much more will one be honored who portrayed the Lord in all
>   the senses.[189]

The Role of Things

Although it is clear that human beings with the *imago dei* enjoy a unique position in the world, certain material things enjoy a privileged place because they link the world of nature to the world of scripture. That privileged place is rooted in nature, in their physical properties and their names. So oil is symbolic of Christ and the salvation brought by him, not only because he is literally "the Anointed One" who fulfills the roles of priest, prophet and king, but also due to the natural properties of oil: its healing and strengthening properties, its capacity to provide light, its use with pigments for painting an image, its ability to ease forces in conflict, and even its property of floating on water, as Jesus walked on the water![190] All these properties resonate in the baptismal anointing in which the *imago dei* is restored to us:

> The lamp returned our lost things, and the Anointed also [returned]
>   our treasures.
> The lamp found the coin, and the Anointed [found] the image of
>   Adam.[191]

---

189. Virg. 2.15. On the importance of celibacy and virginity in the Syriac tradition of Christianity and its relation to "single-mindedness," cf. Vööbus, Celibacy; Murray, Symbols, 11–17, and idem Characteristics, 6–9, and A.F.J. Klijn, "The 'Single One' in the Gospel of Thomas," JBL 81 (1962), 271–78.

190. Cf. Virg. 4–7.

191. Virg. 5.8.5–6; cf. Virg. 7.5–7, where it is also clear that a last anointing performs a similar function, Virg. 7.7.1–2.

INTRODUCTION

The bread and wine of the Eucharist, although they provide a less fertile field for Ephrem's imagination, play a similar role.[192] Not only the elements of the sacraments, however, but other material things and concepts are symbolic of Christ. So Satan's temptations of Jesus have ironic appropriateness: He tempted with bread the "Sustainer of all"; with stones the perfect Stone, with kingship, the true King.[193] Even things without a symbolic tradition in scripture may be seen as representative of Christ's altruistic suffering.[194] Finally, every beauty of daily life is a tangible reminder of the graciousness of our God:

> But remaining are all those things the Gracious One made in His
>   mercy.
> Let us see those things that He does for us every day!
> How many tastes for the mouth! How many beauties for the eye!
> How many melodies for the ear! How many scents for the nostrils!
> Who is sufficient in comparison to the goodness
> of these little things![195]

IV Suggestions for Further Study of St. Ephrem

Interest in the literary and hymnographic corpus of Ephrem the Syrian has grown considerably in recent years. Several major monographs and many more scholarly articles on various aspects of Ephrem's life, literary corpus and theology have appeared in the past thirty years. The pace has accelerated in the past decade. Likewise the interest in Syriac Christianity has grown considerably. As is often the case with areas of intensive scholarly work, it is difficult for the general reader to obtain a picture of the overall trends and to gain access to these subjects. There are two reasons for this problem: (1) much of the literature is in scholarly periodicals rather than in books; (2) the majority of the literature is in French or German. Further, a significant amount is in European languages other than English, or it is in Arabic or modern Syriac.

The English reader may wish to begin with Robert Murray's *Symbols*

---

192. Virg. 16.2,4,5 and 31.13–14; cf. also Graffin, Eucharistie.
193. Virg. 14; cf. also, Virg. 31.
194. Cf. Virg. 11.
195. Virg. 31.16.

INTRODUCTION

of Church and Kingdom: A Study in Early Syriac Tradition (Cambridge, England, 1975) or with Sebastian Brock's forthcoming translation of the *Hymns on Paradise*, or with his selection of translations entitled *the Harp of the Spirit: Eighteen Poems of St. Ephrem* (Studies Supplemental to Sobornost 4, 2nd enlarged edition. Fellowship of St. Alban and St. Sergius, 1983), or with the same author's monograph entitled *The Luminous Eye: The Spiritual World Vision of St. Ephrem* (Rome, 1985). The latter two works contain further bibliographic suggestions. Sidney Griffith and others at the Institute of Christian Oriental Research, The Catholic University of America, promise an English translation of Ephrem's *Paschal Hymns* in the near future. The articles by Sidney Griffith listed in the abbreviations below will also be helpful.

The reader of French may wish to begin with the *Hymnes sur Paradis*, translated by R. Lavenant (Sources Chrétiennes 137, Paris, 1968), or the *Commentaire de L'Évangile Concordant ou Diatessaron*, translated by L. Leloir (SC 121, Paris, 1966). Several important studies by P. Yousif of Ephrem's system of symbolism may be found in the pages of *Parôle de l'Orient*, nos. 6–10 (1975–82). Many other translations of individual hymns as well as articles are in *L'Orient Syrien* and *Parôle de l'Orient*.

The German reader has the advantage of Beck's full set of translations of the authentic corpus of Ephrem accompanying the critical texts in the Corpus Scriptorum Christianorum Orientalium. They are listed in the first section of abbreviations on page 49. Equally important are Beck's monographs and articles, which are also listed with the other abbreviations, in the third section under his name.

It would be superfluous to attempt to present a full bibliography of the secondary literature on Ephrem since others have accomplished this task. They are:

M. P. Roncaglia, "Essai de bibliographie sur saint Éphrem," PdO 4 (1973), 343–70.

Samir Khalil, "Compléments de bibliographie éphrémienne," PdO 4 (1973), 371–92.

S. Brock, "Syriac studies 1971–1980, a classified Bibliography," PdO 10 (1981–82), 291–412; esp. 320–27.

Abbreviations

I The Works of Ephrem the Syrian

		CSCO vol.	scr. syr.
HdF	Hymns on Faith	154–55	73–74
CH	Hymns against Heresies	169–70	76–77
HdP	Hymns on Paradise	174–75	78–79
CJ	Hymns against Julian	"	"
Nat.	Hymns on the Nativity	186–87	82–83
Epiph.	Hymns on the Epiphany	"	"
Eccl.	Hymns on the Church	198–99	84–85
CNis	Hymns on Nisibis	218–19	92–93
	(=Carmina Nisibena)	240–41	102–3
Virg.	Hymns on Virginity	223–24	94–95
Ieiun.	Hymns on Fasting	246–47	106–7
Azym.	Hymns on Unleavened bread	248–9	108–9
Cruc.	Hymns on the Crucifixion	"	"
Res.	Hymns on the Resurrection	"	"
Abr.	Hymns on Abraham Qidunaya	322–23	140–41
Jul. Sab.	Hymns on Juliana Saba	"	"
SdF	Mêmrê on Faith	212–13	88–89
de Dom. nos.	Sermon on Our Lord	270–71	116–17
	Mêmrê I	305–6	130–31
	Mêmrê II	311–12	134–35
	Mêmrê III	320–21	138–39
	Mêmrê IV	334–35	148–49
Supplementary Hymns and Homilies		363–64	156–57
Homilies on Holy Week		412–13	181–82

ABBREVIATIONS

Comm. Diat. = Ephrem, Commentary on the Diatesseron: *Commentaire de l'Évangile Concordant, Texte syriaque*, ed. L. Leloir, Chester Beatty Monographs 8 (Dublin, 1963; French trans. L. Leloir, SC 121 [Paris, 1966]).

Eph. Domnus = "Ephräms Rede gegen eine philosophische Schrift des Bardaisan," übersetzt und erklärt von E. Beck, OC 60 (1976), 24–68.

Eph. Hypat. = "Ephraems Brief an Hypatios," übersetzt und erklärt von E. Beck, OC 58 (1974), 76–120.

Eph. Pr. Ref. I = *S. Ephraim's Prose Refutations of Mani, Marcion and Bardaisan*, I, ed. and trans. C. W. Mitchell (London, 1912).

Eph. Pr. Ref. II = Ibid. II, ed. and trans. E. A. Bevan and F. C. Burkitt (London, 1921).

Tonneau, Gen/Exod = R.-M. Tonneau. *Sancti Ephraem Syri in Genesim et in Exodum Commentarii*, CSCO 152–53, scr. syr. 71–72 (Louvain, 1955).

II Primary Sources other than Ephrem

Amm. Mar. = Ammianus Marcellinus, *rerum gestarum libri*

Aph. Dem. = Aphraates, *demonstrationes*

Ath. de inc. = Athanasius Alexandrinus, *de incarnatione*

Ath. gent. = Athanasius Alexandrinus, *contra gentes*

Ath. adv. Ar. = Athanasius Alexandrinus, *orationes tres adversus Arianos*

Bord. = *Itinerarium burdigalense*

Clem. prot. = Clemens Alexandrinus, *protrepticus*

Clem. paed. = Clemens Alexandrinus, *paedagogus*

Clem. str. = Clemens Alexandrinus, *stromateis*

Cod. Theod. = Theodosius II Imperator, *Codex Theodosianus*

Didache = *Didache XII Apostolorum*

Eger. Itin. = Egeria, *itinerarium Egeriae*

Epiph. Pan. = *anakephalaioses seu recapitulatio brevis panarii*

Eusebius EH = Eusebius Caesariensis, *historia ecclesiastica*

Greg. Naz. orat. = Gregorius Nazianzenus, *orationes*

Greg. Nys. vit. Mos. = Gregorius Nyssenus, *de vita Mosis*

Greg. Nys. de virg. = Gregorius Nyssenus, *de virginitate*

Hier. epis. = Hieronymus Stridonensis, *epistulae*

ABBREVIATIONS

Hier. de vir. ill. = Hieronymus Stridonensis, *de viris illustribus*
Hipp. Apos. Trad. = Hippolytus Romanus, *traditio apostolica*
Ign. Eph. = Ignatius Antiochenus, *epistula ad Ephesios*
Iren. A.H. = Irenaeus Lugdunensis, *adversus haereses*
Iren. Demonstr. = Irenaeus Lugdunensis, *demonstratio*
Jo. Chrys. de virg. = Joannes Chrysostomus, *de virginitate*
Jul. Imp. Galil. = Julianus Imperator, *oratio adversus Galilaeos*
Jul. Imp. Misop. = Julianus Imperator, *Misopogon*
Jul. Imp. orat. = Julianus Imperator, *orationes*
Just. apol. = Justinus Martyr, Philosophus, *apologiae*
Just. dial. = Justinus Martyr, Philosophus, *dialogus cum Tryphone Judaeo*
Lib. orat. = Libanius Antiochenus, *orationes*
Luc. Sam. de Syr. Dea = Lucianus Samosatensis, *de Syria Dea*
Meth. symp. = Methodius Olympius, *symposium*
Min. Fel. Oct. = Marcius Minucius Felix, *Octavius*
Od. Sol. = *Odes of Solomon*
Or. c. Cels. = Origenes, *contra Celsum*
Or. de prin. = Origenes, *de principiis*
Or. Comm. Jn. = Origenes, *commentarii in Joannem*
Or. dial.c.Her. = Origenes, *dialogus cum Heraclide*
Pall. H. Laus. = Palladius Monachus, *historia Lausiaca*
Prot. = *Evangelia Apocrypha, Protevangelium Jacobi*
Soz. HE = Sozomenus Salaminus, historia ecclesiastica
Tert. adv. Marc. = Q.S.F. Tertullianus, *adversus Marcionem*
Tert. de idol. = Q.S.F. Tertullianus, *de idololatria*
Tert. exh. ad cast. = Q.S.F. Tertullianus, *exhortatio ad castitatem*
Theod. HE = Theodoretus Cyrrhensis, *historia ecclesiastica*
Thphl. Ant. Autol. = Theophilus Antiochenus, *ad Autolycum*

III Journals, Series and Secondary Literature

AB = Analecta Bollandiana
AC = Antike und Christentum
ACW = Ancient Christian Writers
ANRW = Aufstieg und Niedergang der Römischen Welt
Bauer, Orthodoxy = Walter Bauer, *Orthodoxy and Heresy in the Earliest*

Christianity, trans. from the second German edition by R. Kraft, G. Krodel et al. (Philadelphia, 1971).

Beck, Asketentum = Asketentum und Mönchtum bei Ephräm, OCA 153, 341–62.

idem, Baptême = idem, "Le baptême chez Saint Éphrem," OS 2 (1956) 111–30.

idem, Bildtheologie = "Zur Terminologie von Ephräms Bildtheologie," in Schmidt and Geyer, Typus, 239–77.

idem, Eucharistie = "Die Eucharistie bei Ephräm," OC 38 (1954), 41–67.

idem, Lobgesang = *Ephräm der Syrer: Lobgesang aus der Wüste*, Sophia 7, (Freiburg im Breisgau, 1967).

idem, Mariologie = "Die Mariologie der echten Schriften Ephräms," OC 40 (1956), 29–34.

idem, Paradies = *Ephräms Hymnen über das Paradies*, SA 26 (Rome, 1951).

idem, Polemik = *Ephräms Polemik gegen Mani und die Manichäer*. CSCO 391 = Subs. 55 (Louvain, 1978).

idem, Psychologie = *Ephräms des Syrers Psychologie und Erkenntnislehre*, CSCO 419, Subs. 58 (Louvain, 1980).

idem, Reden = *Ephräms Reden über den Glauben, ihr theologischer Lehrgehalt und ihr geschichtliche Rahmen*, SA 33 (Rome, 1953).

idem, Spiegel = "Das Bild vom Spiegel bei Ephräm" OCP 19 (1953), 1–24.

idem, Symbolum-Mysterium = "Symbolum-Mysterium bei Aphraat und Ephräm," OC 42 (1958), 19–40.

idem, TEXNH = "TEXNH und TEXNITHΣ bei dem Syrer Ephräm," OCP 47 (1981), 295–331.

idem, Theologie = *Die Theologie des heiligen Ephraem in seinen Hymnen über den Glauben*, SA 21 (Vatican City, 1949).

Bertrand, Mystique = Frederick Bertrand, *Mystique de Jésus chez Origène*, Théologie 23 (Paris, 1951).

Biblia Patristica = *Biblia Patristica. Index des citations et allusions bibliques dans la littérature patristique*. A. Benoit et al., eds., Centre d'Analyse et de Documentation patristiques, 3 vols. (Paris, 1975–80).

BJRL = Bulletin of the John Rylands Library

BKV = Bibliothek der Kirchnväter

Boak and Sinnigen = A.E.R. Boak and William Sinnigen, *A History of Rome to A.D. 565*, 5th ed. (New York, 1965).

ABBREVIATIONS

Bowersock, Julian = Glen W. Bowersock, *Julian the Apostate*, (Cambridge, Mass., 1978).

Bradley, Background = Ritamary Bradley, "The Patristic Background of the Motherhood Similitude in Julian of Norwich," *Christian Scholar's Review* 1978, 101–13.

Brock, Christians = "Christians in the Sassanian Empire: A Case of Divided Loyalties," *Studies in Church History* 18 (1982), 1–19.

idem, Clothing = "Clothing Metaphors As a Means of Theological Expression in Syriac Tradition," in Schmidt and Geyer, Typus, 11–40.

idem, Harp = *The Harp of the Spirit: Eighteen Poems of Saint Ephrem*, 2d ed., Studies Supplementary to Sobornost 4 (London, 1983).

idem, Introduction = "An Introduction to Syriac Studies," in Eaton, Horizons, 1–33.

idem, Luminous = *The Luminous Eye: The Spiritual World Vision of St. Ephrem* (Rome, 1985).

idem, Temple = "A Letter Attributed to Cyril of Jerusalem on the Rebuilding of the Temple," BSOAS 40 (1977), 267–86.

Brown, Gospel According to John = Raymond E. Brown, *The Gospel According to John*, 2 vols., The Anchor Bible (New York, 1966).

idem, Messiah = *The Birth of the Messiah: A Commentary on the Infancy Narratives in Matthew and Luke* (New York, 1977).

Browning, Emperor = Robert Browning, *The Emperor Julian* (London 1975).

BSOAS = Bulletin of the School of Oriental and African Studies

Cameron, Shroud = Averil Cameron, "The Sceptic and the Shroud," Inaugural Lecture, Departments of Classics and History, King's College (London, 29 April 1980).

CBQ = Catholic Biblical Quarterly

CE = The Catholic Encyclopedia

CHR = The Catholic Historical Review

Cramer, Engelvorstellungen = Winfrid Cramer, *Die Engelvorstellungen bei Ephräm dem Syrer*, OCA 173 (Rome, 1965).

CSCO = Corpus Scriptorum Christianorum Orientalium

DACL = *Dictionnaire d'Archéologie Chrétienne et de Liturgie*, ed. F. Cabrol and H. Leclerq (Paris, 1907–1953).

Davies, Anti-Semitism = A.T. Davies, *Anti-Semitism and the Foundations of Christianity* (New York, 1979).

ABBREVIATIONS

de Halleux, Mar Éphrem = André de Halleux, "Mar Éphrem Théologien," PdO 4 (1973), 35–54.

Devos, Egerie = P. Devos, "Égérie à Édesse. S. Thomas L'Apôtre: Le Roi Abgar," AB 85 (1967), 381–400.

Dillon, Platonists = John Dillon, *The Middle Platonists: 80 B.C. to A.D. 220* (Ithaca, New York, 1977).

Dölger, AC = F.J. Dölger, Antike und Christentum, Münster.

idem, Ichthus = *Ichthus. Das Fisch-Symbol in Frühchristlicher Zeit*, 5 vols., (Münster, 1928–32).

idem, Sphragis = *Sphragis: Eine altchristliche Taufbezeichnung in ihren Beziehungen zur profanen und religiösen Kultur des Altertums*, Studien zur Geschichte u. Kultur des Altertums 5 (Paderborn, 1911; rep. 1967).

DOP = Dumbarton Oaks Papers

Drijvers, Bardaisan = H.J.W. Drijvers, *Bardaisan of Edessa*, Studia Semitica Neerlandica 6 (Assen, 1966).

idem, Book = *The Book of the Laws of the Countries: The Dialogue on Fate of Bardaisan of Edessa* (Assen, 1965).

idem, Cults = *Cults and Beliefs at Edessa* (Leiden, 1980).

idem, Hatra = "Hatra Palmyra und Edessa. Die Städte der syrisch-mesopotamischen Wüste in politischer, kulturgeschichtlicher und religionsgeschichtlicher Beleuchtung," ANRW II, 8 (1977), 799–906.

idem, Jews = "Jews and Christians at Edessa," JJS 36 (1985), 88–102.

idem, Persistence = "The Persistence of Pagan Cults and Practices in Christian Syria," in Garsoian et al., East of Byzantium, 35–43.

Eaton, Horizons = *Horizons in Semitics Studies: Articles for the Student*, ed. J. H. Eaton (Birmingham, 1980).

ECR = Eastern Churches Review

EJ = *Encyclopedia Judaica*, 16 vols. (Jerusalem, 1971).

Fiey, Évêques = J. M. Fiey, "Les évêques de Nisibe au temps de saint Éphrem," PdO 4 (1973), 123–36.

idem, Nisibe = *Nisibe: metropole syriaque orientale et ses suffragants des origines à nos jours*, CSCO 388, subsidia 54 (Louvain, 1977).

Garsoian, et al. East of Byzantium = N. G. Garsoian, T. F. Mathews and R. W. Thomson, eds., *East of Byzantium: Syria and Armenia in the Formative Period* (Washington, D.C., 1982).

GCS = Die griechischen chrislichen Schriftsteller

Ginzberg, Legends = Louis Ginzberg, *The Legends of the Jews*, 7 vols. (Philadelphia, 1939–42).

ABBREVIATIONS

Graef, Mary = Graef, Hilda, *Mary: A History of Doctrine and Devotion*, 2 vols. (New York, 1965).

Graffin, Cherubin = F. Graffin, "La soghita du cherubin et du larron," OS 12 (1967), 481–90.

idem, Eucharistie = "L'Eucharistie chez Saint Éphrem," PdO 4 (1973), 93–116.

Griffith, Ephraem = Griffith, Sidney H., "Ephraem, the Deacon of Edessa, and the Church of the Empire," in *Diakonia: Studies in Honor of Robert T. Meyer*, ed. Thomas Halton and J. P. Williman (Washington, D.C., 1986), 25–52.

idem, Julian = "Ephraem the Syrian's Hymns 'Against Julian': Meditations on History and Imperial Power," *Vigiliae Christianae* 41 (1987), 238–66.

Hausherr, Noms = I. Hausherr, *Noms de Jésus et voies d'oraison*, OCA 157 (Rome, 1960).

Hayman, Image = A. P. Hayman, "The Image of the Jew in the Syriac Anti-Jewish Polemical Literature," in *To See Ourselves as Others See Us: Christians, Jews, "Others" in Late Antiquity*, ed. J. Neusner and E. S. Frerichs, Scholar's Press Studies in the Humanities (Chico, California, 1986), 423–42.

Hennecke, NT Apocrypha = E. Hennecke, *New Testament Apocrypha*, ed. by W. Schneemelcher, 2 vols. (Tübingen, 1959), English trans. by R. McL. Wilson, (Philadelphia, 1963).

Honigmann, Liste = E. Honigmann, "La Liste originale des Pères de Nicée," *Byzantion* 14 (1939), 17–76.

JAC = Jahrbuch für Antike und Christentum

JE = *The Jewish Encyclopedia*, I. Singer, et al., 12 vols (New York, 1901–1907)

JJA = Journal of Jewish Art

JRS = Journal of Roman Studies

Jones, Social and Economic History = A.H.M. Jones, *The Later Roman Empire 284–602: A Social Economic and Administrative Survey*, 2 vols. (Oxford, 1964).

King, Julian = C. W. King, *Julian the Emperor, Containing Gregory Nazianzens's Two Invectives and Libanius' Monody with Julian's Extant Theosophical Works* (London, 1888).

Kraeling, Final Report = *The Excavations at Dura-Europos, Conducted by Yale University and the French Academy of Inscriptions and Letters*, ed. M.

55

ABBREVIATIONS

I. Rostovtzeff, et al.; C. H. Kraeling, *Final report 8: The Synagogue, Mithraeum and Christian Chapel* (New Haven, 1956).

Kronholm, Motifs = Tryggve Kronholm, *Motifs from Genesis 1–11 in the Genuine Hymns of Ephrem the Syrian with Particular Reference to the Influence of Jewish Exegetical Tradition*, Coniectanea Biblica, Old Testament series 11 (Uppsala, 1978).

Levene, Early Syrian Fathers = A. Levene, *The Early Syrian Fathers on Genesis* (London, 1951).

Levenson, Attempt = David B. Levenson, *A Source- and Tradition- Critical Study of the Stories of Julian's Attempt to Rebuild the Jerusalem Temple* (Harvard diss., 1980).

Lewy, Sobria ebrietas = H. Lewy, *Sobria ebrietas. Untersuchungen zur Geschichte der antiken Mystik*, Beihefte zur Zeitschrift zur neutestamentiliche Wissenschaft und die Kunde der älteren Kirche 9 (Giessen, 1929).

Malley, Hellenism = William Malley. *Hellenism and Christianity: The Conflict Between Hellenic and Christian Wisdom in the (Contra Galileos) of Julian the Apostate and the (Contra Julianum) of S. Cyril of Alexandria*, (Diss. P. Universita Gregoriana; Roma, 1978).

Mansour, Liberté = T. B. Mansour, "La défense éphrémienne de la liberté contre les doctrines marcionite, bardesanite et manichéenne" OCP 50 (1984), 331–46.

Margoliouth = *A Compendious Syriac Dictionary Founded upon the Thesaurus Syriacus of R. Payne Smith*, ed. by J. Payne Smith (Mrs. Margoliouth) (Oxford, 1903; rep. 1967).

Martikainen, Böse = Jouko Martikainen, *Das Böse und der Teufel in der Theologie Ephraems des Syrers* (Åbo, 1978).

idem, Gerechtigkeit = *Gerechtigkeit und Güte Gottes: Studien zur Theologie von Ephraem dem Syrer und Philoxenos von Mabbug*, Göttinger Orientforschungen 20 (Wiesbaden, 1981).

idem, Remarks = "Some Remarks about the Carmina Nisibena as a Literary and a Theological Source," OCA 197 (1974), 345–52.

McVey, Microcosm = Kathleen McVey, "The Domed Church as Microcosm: Literary Roots of an Architectural Symbol," DOP 37 (1983), 91–121.

idem, Singing = "Jacob of Sarug on Ephrem and the Singing of Women" (to appear).

ABBREVIATIONS

idem, Tol'dot = "Ephrem the Syrian's Hymns on the Nativity and the Tol'dot Yeshu'" (to appear).

Moore, Judaism = George Foot Moore, *Judaism in the First Centuries of the Christian Era: The Age of the Tannaim*, 3 vols. (Cambridge, Mass., 1929; rep. 1966).

Morris = J.B. Morris, *Select Works of S. Ephrem the Syrian* (Oxford, 1847).

Murray, Characteristics = Robert Murray, "The Characteristics of the Earliest Syriac Christianity," in Garsoian, et al., East of Byzantium, 3–16.

idem, Exhortation = "The Exhortation to Candidates for Ascetical Vows at Baptism in the Ancient Syriac Church," NTS 21 (1974–75), 59–80.

idem, Lance = "The Lance Which Re-opened Paradise" OCP 39 (1973), 224–34.

idem, Mary = "Mary, the Second Eve in the Early Syrian Fathers," ECR 3.4 (1971), 372–84.

idem, Symbols = *Symbols of Church and Kingdom: A Study in Early Syriac Tradition* (Cambridge, England, 1975).

idem, Theory = "The Theory of Symbolism in St. Ephrem's Theology," PdO 6–7 (1975–76), 1–28.

Neusner, HJB = Jacob Neusner, *History of the Jews in Babylonia*, 5 vols. (Leiden, 1965–70).

idem, TJSB = *Talmudic Judaism in Sasanian Babylonia: essays and studies* (Leiden, 1976).

Nöldeke = Theodor Nöldeke, *Kurzgefasste Syrische Grammatik* (Leipzig, 1898; rep. 1966).

NPNF = The Nicene and Post-Nicene Fathers of the Christian Church

NTS = New Testament Studies

OC = Oriens Christianus

OCA = Orientalia Christiana Analecta

OCP = Orientalia Christiana Periodica

Ortiz de Urbina, Vergine = I. Ortiz de Urbina, "La Vergine Maria nella Teologia di S. Efrem," OCA 197 (1972), 65–104.

OS = L'Orient Syrien

Ouspensky, Icons = L. Ouspensky and V. Lossky, *The Meaning of Icons*, rev. ed. (Crestwood, New York, 1982).

ABBREVIATIONS

Outtier, Saint Éphrem = B. Outtier, "Saint Éphrem d'après ses biographies et ses oeuvres," PdO 4 (1973), 11–33.

PdO = Parôle de l'Orient

Payne-Smith = *Thesaurus syriacus*, collegerunt Stephanus M. Quatremere, Georgius Henricus Bernstein et allii; auxit, digessit, exposuit, edidit Robert Payne Smith, 2 vols. (Oxford, 1879–1901).

Peeters, Legende = P. Peeters, "La légende de St. Jacques de Nisibe," AB 38 (1920), 285–373.

Petersen, Diatesseron = William L. Petersen, *The Diatesseron and Ephrem Syrus as Sources of Romanos the Melodist*, CSCO 466, subsidia 73 (Louvain, 1986).

PS = Patrologia Syriaca

Quasten, Musik = J. Quasten, *Musik und Gesang in den Kulten der Heidnischen Antike und Christlichen Frühzeit*, Liturgiewissenschaftliche Quellen und Forschungen 25 (Maria-Laach, 1930; rep. Münster, 1973, with additional notes, 275–84).

idem, Singing = "The Liturgical Singing of Women in Christian Antiquity," CHR 27 (1941), 149–65.

RE = Pauly, August, *Realencyclopädie der classischen Altertumswissenschaft*, Neue Bearbeitung hrsg. von Georg Wissowa (Stuttgart, Serie I: vol. 1–24 [A–Q]: 1894–1963; Serie II: vol. 1–10 [R–Z]: 1920–1972; Suppl.: Vol. 1–15: 1903–1978).

Robinson, NHL = *The Nag Hammadi Library in English*, translated by members of the Coptic Gnostic Library Project of the Institute for Antiquity and Christianity, James M. Robinson, Director (New York, 1977).

Ruether, Fratricide = Rosemary Ruether, *Faith and Fratricide* (New York, 1974).

SA = Studia Anselmiana

Saber, Théologie = P. Georges Saber, *La théologie baptismale de Saint Éphrem, Essai de théologie historique*, Bibliothèque de l'Université Saint Esprit 8 (Kaslik, 1974).

idem, Typologie = "La typologie sacramentaire et baptismale de saint Éphrem," PdO 4 (1973), 73–92.

SBL = Society of Biblical Literature

SBLTT = Society of Biblical Literature Texts and Translations Series

SC = Sources Chrétiennes

Scholer, NHB = David Scholer, *Nag Hammadi Bibliography*, Nag

ABBREVIATIONS

Hammadi Studies 1 (Leiden, 1971), with annual supplements in NT 13 (1971ff.)

Séd, Hymnes sur Paradis = M. Séd, "Les hymnes sur le Paradis de saint Éphrem et les traditions juives," *Le Museón* 81 (1968), 455–501.

Segal, Edessa = J.B. Segal, *Edessa the "Blessed City"* (Oxford, 1970).

Schmidt and Geyer, Typus = *Typus, Symbol, Allegorie bei den ostlichen Vätern und ihre Parallelen im Mittelalter,* ed. M. Schmidt with C. F. Geyer (Regensburg, 1982).

Scholem, Major Trends = Gershom Scholem, *Major Trends in Jewish Mysticism* (New York, 1941).

SPCK = Society for Promoting Christian Knowledge

Teixidor, Déscente = J. Teixidor, "Le thème de la déscente aux enfers chez Saint Éphrem," OS 6 (1961), 25–40.

idem, Muerte = "Muerte, Cielo y Seol en san Efren," OCP 27 (1961), 82–114.

TU = Texte und Untersuchungen

Van Buren, Discerning the Way = Paul Van Buren, *Discerning the Way: A Theology of the Jewish-Christian Reality* (New York, 1980).

Vielhauer, Oikodome = P. Vielhauer, *Oikodome: das Bild von Bau in der christlichen Literatur vom Neuen Testament bis Clemens Alexandrinus* (diss. Heidelberg; Karlsruhe-Durlach, 1940).

Vööbus, Celibacy = Arthur Vööbus, *Celibacy, A Requirement for Admission to Baptism in the Early Syrian Church*, Papers of the Estonian Theological Society in Exile (Stockholm, 1951).

ZKT = Zeitschrift für Katolische Theologie

Westermann, Slave Systems = William Linn Westermann, *The Slave Systems of Greek and Roman antiquity*, Memoirs of the American Philosophical Society 40, (Philadelphia, 1955).

Wilken, Christians = Robert L. Wilken, *The Christians as the Romans Saw Them* (New Haven, 1984).

idem, Chrysostom = *John Chrysostom and the Jews: Rhetoric and Reality in the Late Fourth Century*, The Transformation of the Classical Heritage IV (Berkeley, 1983).

Wilkinson, Pilgrims = John Wilkinson, *Jerusalem Pilgrims Before the Crusades* (Warminster, England, 1977).

Yousif, Croix = P. Yousif, "La croix de Jésus et le Paradis d'Éden dans la typologie biblique de saint Éphrem," PdO 6 (1975), 29–48.

ZKT = Zeitschrift für Katolische Theologie

Hymns on the Nativity

1

This hymn presents an array of testimonies by the kings, priests and prophets to Jesus' messianic office (str. 1). Ephrem begins with some of the citations that even within the New Testament had been claimed as messianic prophecies by David and Solomon as well as Isaiah, Micah, Balaam and Zechariah (str. 2–9). The worm provides an intimation from the world of nature of the wonders of the incarnation and virgin birth, also anticipated by the creation of Adam and Eve and the sprouting of Aaron's staff (str. 10–19). Using an argument known in rabbinic sources, that Ruth was guided in her behavior by the anticipation of the Messiah (str. 13), he applies it to Tamar as well (str. 12). Then he applies it to a line of personages from the Old Testament, beginning with Seth and his descendants and reaching to Elijah (str. 20–38). He reiterates the idea that the righteous of the Old Testament "saw" the Messiah, recapitulating with a line from Adam, Abel and Eve, through Noah, Enoch, Abraham and Isaac (str. 39–60). The angelic Watchers provide a transition to the theme of watchfulness, keeping vigil—on the one hand, urging its importance (str. 61–75), on the other, arguing the greater necessity of moral rectitude (str. 76–81). The final strophes (82–99), a series of moral exhortations explicitly related to the liturgical theme, show that the hymn was composed for the vigil of Christmas-Epiphany.

1

To the melody, "The confessors."[1]

1 My Lord, this day gladdens kings, priests and prophets,
for on it were fulfilled and realized all their words.

---

1. Although the melodies to which these hymns were sung are no longer known, the manuscript tradition identified each tune by the first few words of what was evidently a well-known hymn. Further, cf. Beck, CSCO 186 (scr. syr. 82), xx–xxii.

Refrain: Glory to You, Son of our Creator!

2 Since today the Virgin has given birth to Emmanuel[2] in Bethlehem,
the word Isaiah spoke was accomplished today.

3 He Who registers the peoples[3] was born there;
the psalm that David sang has been fulfilled today.

4 The word that Micah spoke was realized today,
for a shepherd went out from Ephrata, and his staff herded souls.[4]

5 "Behold, a star shone forth from Jacob, and a prince arose from
Israel."[5]
The prophecy that Balaam spoke found its meaning today.

6 The hidden light descended, and its beauty shone forth from a
body;
the dawn of which Zechariah spoke lights up Bethlehem today.[6]

7 The light of kingship glorifies him in Ephrata, the city of kings;
the blessing that Jacob pronounced found its fulfillment today.[7]

8 "The tree of life brings hope" to the dying;[8]
the hidden saying of Solomon found its explanation today.

9 Today a child was born, and he was called "wonder,"[9]
for it is a wonder that God reveals Himself as an infant.

10 The Spirit spoke a parable in the worm, for it reproduces without
sexual union;
the type the Holy Spirit fashioned receives its meaning today.[10]

---

2. Isa. 7.14.

3. Ps. 87.6. In the Peshitta this verse reads, "The Lord registers the peoples; this one was born there." By changing almost nothing except the word order, Ephrem gives the verse a Christian interpretation.

4. Mic. 5.2 (5.1 Pes.).

5. Num. 24.17 (Pes.).

6. Zech. 2.5 The dawn, *dnḥ'*, and the corresponding symbolism of light shining out of darkness, are important to Ephrem's notion of the Nativity. Light symbolism is inextricably tied to Epiphany since the same word, *dnḥ'*, means epiphany, manifestation. Further, cf. H. Usener, *Das Weinachtfest*, Religionsgeschichtliche Untersuchungen (Bonn, 1911; rep. Hildesheim, 1972), 202–8.

7 Gen. 49.8–12.

8. Prov. 12.13 (Pes.). The tree of life is an important symbol for Ephrem, cf. Yousif, Croix, esp. 42ff.; Kronholm, Motifs, 73f. For Ephrem's use of the image in the context of other Syriac authors and earlier Near Eastern traditions, cf. Murray, Symbols, 114–30, 320–24 et passim.

9. Isa. 9.6.

10. Ephrem sees the unusual reproductive system of the worm (*twl'*), as foreshadowing the virginal conception of Christ. In the anti-Arian HdF 41.1.4 Ephrem cites the "solitary" reproduction of the same animal (*yḥyd'yt nb'*) as analogous to the Father's begetting of the Son. "Type" here translates Syriac *ṭwps'*, which is approximately equivalent to Greek τύπος from which it derives; further, cf. Beck, Bildtheologie, 240–44.

11   He rose up like a shoot before Him, a shoot from the parched
          earth;[11]
      something spoken secretly occurred openly today.

12   Since the King was hidden in Judah, Tamar stole Him from his
          loins;
      today shone forth the splendor of the beauty whose hidden form she
          loved.[12]

13   Ruth lay down with Boaz because she saw hidden in him the
          medicine of life;[13]
      today her vow is fulfilled since from her seed arose the Giver of all
          life.[14]

14   Man imposed corruption on woman when she came forth from him;
      today she has repaid him—she who bore for him the Savior.[15]

15   He gave birth to the Mother, Eve—he, the man who never was
          born;
      how worthy of faith is the daughter of Eve, who without a man
          bore a child![16]

16   The virgin earth gave birth to that Adam, head of the earth;
      the Virgin today gave birth to [second] Adam, head of heaven.

17   The staff of Aaron sprouted, and the dry wood brought forth;
      his symbol has been explained today—it is the virgin womb that
          gave birth.[17]

18   Put to shame is the people that holds the prophets to be true,
      for if our Savior had not come, their words would have become
          lies.[18]

---

11. Isa. 53.2 (Pes.).

12. Gen. 38.12–19; Matt. 1.3.

13. Cf. Ruth 3.7; Matt. 1.5. For a rabbinic parallel, cf. Kronholm, Motifs, 153, n.6; for the same argument with regard to the Matthean genealogy, cf. Nat. 9.7–16.

14. Cf. Ruth 1.16f., 4.17.

15. Cf. Gen. 1.12. Here and in the following two verses it is important to note that "Adam" is the same Syriac word as "man" and it may be used in a generic sense. Also, *ḥwbl'* is used in two distinct senses here, "corruption" and "recompense." For discussion of this passage, cf. Murray, Symbols, 145.

16. For Eve, mother of the living, cf. Gen. 3.20. Ephrem is fond of the paradox elaborated here and in the following verse; cf. Nat. 2.12 and Kronholm, Motifs, 54–56.

17. Cf. Num. 17.23. "Symbol" (*r'z'*), sometimes better rendered in English as "mystery," is a technical term central to Ephrem's symbolic theology and generally equivalent to *twps'*; cf. Beck, Bildtheologie, 240–44.

18. "The people" (*'mm'*) is Ephrem's usual term for the Jewish people over against "the peoples," the Gentiles. Ephrem clearly states here the polemical aspect of Christian typological interpretation of the Jewish scripture: if Jews do not accept Christian interpretation of the

19   Blessed is the True One Who comes from the True Father.[19]
He fulfilled the words[20] of the true [prophets], and they are
        complete in their truth.

20   From Your treasury, my Lord, let us fetch from the treasures of
        Your scriptures
the names of the just men of old who said they saw Your coming.

21   That Seth who took the place of Abel resembled the murdered son
to dull the sword that Cain brought into the creation.[21]

22   Noah saw the sons of God, the holy ones, who were suddenly made
        wanton,
and he anticipated the Holy Son by Whom fornicators would be
        made chaste.[22]

23   The two brothers who hid Noah looked for the Only-Begotten of
        God
to come and hide the nakedness of man,[23] intoxicated with pride.

24   Shem and Japheth, as compassionate [men] anticipated the
        compassionate Son
Who would come and free Canaan from the servitude of sin.

25   Melchizedek anticipated Him; he the vicar was watching
to see priesthood's Lord Whose hyssop cleanses creation.[24]

---

prophets (and typological interpretation of even the Torah), their own scripture is invalidated. Of course, Ephrem ignores the possibility that the messianic prophecies would be fulfilled at a later date.

19. Or "Father of Truth." Ephrem often uses *šrr'*, "truth" or "reality" rather than the roughly synonymous *qwšt'* to denote the fulfillment of the types or symbols, both scriptural and natural. The term Father of Truth also occurs in Marcionite and Valentinian Gnostic texts. Ephrem may have deliberately chosen their term here with ironic intent since he stresses the fulfillment of the Old Testament prophecies by the Son of the Father of Truth.

20. A pun in Syriac, *wmly ml'*.

21. Gen. 4.25 states that Seth took the place of Abel since he had been killed by Cain. Both in Jewish legends and in certain forms of Gnosticism Seth was considered to be the ancestor of the Messiah and to resemble Adam or God in a particular way; cf. Ginzberg, Legends, I, 121, n.52, V, 149; Robinson, NHL s.v. "Seth." Ephrem shares these notions, but for him they, not the angels, are the "sons of God" of Gen. 6.1–4, who are degraded by intercourse with the daughters of Cain, cf. str. 22 and 48 below, and Kronholm, Motifs, 154, 163–71, 220–23.

22. On chastity as righteousness, cf. ibid. 159.

23. "man" = *'dm* = Adam; cf. Gen. 9.23.

24. Cf. Gen. 14.18–20. Melchizedek's offering of bread and wine was commonly seen by early Christian writers as a type of the Eucharist. Although Ephrem uses his sacrifice as a type of the Eucharist, cf. Azym 2.8, Melchizedek is less important to his eucharistic doctrine than to his baptismal theology (for his more important eucharistic types, cf. Graffin, Eucharistie). He frequently alludes to the hyssop of Melchizedek, the symbol of the cleansing and forgiving power of the priesthood, which other writers normally associate with Aaron or the levitical priesthood. He seems deliberately to emphasize Melchizedek as a priest who antedates the

26   Lot saw the Sodomites who perverted nature;
      he looked for the Lord of natures Who gave chastity beyond
         nature.[25]

27   Aaron anticipated Him—he who saw that if his staff swallowed
         reptiles,
      His cross would swallow the Reptile that swallowed Adam and
         Eve.[26]

28   Moses saw the fixed serpent that healed the stings of basilisks,
      and he anticipated he would see the Healer of the first Serpent's
         wound.[27]

29   Moses saw that he alone received the brightness of God,
      and he anticipated the One to come—by His teaching, the
         Multiplier of the godlike.[28]

30   Kaleb, the scout, came carrying the cluster on a pole;
      he anticipated seeing the Grape Whose wine would console
         creation.[29]

31   Joshua bar Nun anticipated Him—he who represents the power of
      His name;[30]

Mosaic covenant. He thus anticipates the sacrament of baptism as well as the Eucharist; cf. Saber, Typologie, esp. 87–89.

25. Cf. Gen. 19. Chastity (*qdšwt'*) might also be translated as "holiness." For Ephrem, as for other early Syriac authors, however, the term acquired a technical significance specifying chastity within marriage. Throughout the present translation this word and related words on the root *qdš* are rendered in this encratite sense.

26. On Aaron's staff, cf. Exod. 7.8–13. The word rendered "reptile" (*tnyn'*), used in Pes. Exod. 7.11f., may also mean dragon, as in the Pes. supplements to Daniel; i.e., Bel and the Dragon. The latter sense is more appropriate for the creature that "swallowed" Adam and Eve. Further, cf. Nat. 4.117f. and 8.3. On the reference to Eve, cf. Yousif, Croix, 44.

27. Cf. Num. 21.4–9.

28. Cf. Exod. 34.29–35. This passage was of considerable interest to Greek Christians of a Platonic bent; cf. Greg. Nys. vit. Mos. For Ephrem, light and fire are especially associated with the presence of the Holy Spirit and hence play a role in both baptism and the Eucharist; cf. Nat. 4.88.

29. Cf. Num. 13.23f. The cluster (*sgwl'*) and the Grape (*twtyt'*, also a cluster, but smaller than the *sgwl'*) are important Christological symbols in both Ephrem and Aphrahat. They are closely associated with the True Vine and the Tree of Life, cf. Murray, Symbols, 95–130. On this specific passage and its relation to iconography, cf. ibid. 119, nn. 3f.

30. Joshua and Jesus are identical names in Syriac, as in Hebrew. Ephrem assumes that both proper names and the designations of objects in the natural world may have innate symbolic significance. A more complex example of Ephrem's association of Joshua and Jesus is in his polemic against astrology in CH 4.18, where Josh. 10.12–15 is invoked typologically to show Christ's power over the heavenly bodies. Further on the name of Jesus, cf. HdF 6.17 and the discussion in Hausherr, Noms, 64–72. On the relation of language to Ephrem's general theory of symbolism, cf. Murray, Theory, 9–14; on the relation of name to nature or substance, cf. Noujaim, Essai, esp. 30f.

if by His name he is thus magnified, how much more would he be
exalted by His birth!

32 That Joshua who also plucked and carried with him some of the
fruits

anticipated the Tree of Life Who would give His all life-giving fruit
to taste.[31]

33 Rahab beheld Him; for if the scarlet thread
saved her by a symbol from [divine] wrath, by a symbol she tasted
the truth.[32]

34 Elijah yearned for Him and without having seen the Son on earth,
he believed and increased his prayers that he might ascend and see
Him in heaven.[33]

35 Moses and Elijah looked for Him; the humble one[34] ascended from
the depth,

and the zealous one came down from the height, and they saw the
Son in the middle.[35]

36 They represented a symbol of His coming: Moses was a type for the
dead,

and Elijah a type for the living who will fly to meet Him when He
comes.

37 Because the dead have tasted death, He will repair them first,
but those not yet buried will be snatched up to meet Him at the
end.[36]

38 Who will bring me to the end of enumerating the just men who
anticipated the Son, whose number cannot be encompassed by our
weak mouth?

39 Pray for me, my friends, that I may be strengthened once more
to set forth their qualities again in another account as much as I am
able.

40 Who is able to glorify the true Son Who rises for us,
Whom just men yearned to see in their lifetimes?

---

31. Cf. Num. 13. 1–24; Deut. 1.22–25.
32. Josh. 2.18–21, 6. 17–25.
33. 2 Kgs. 2.1–18.
34. I.e., Moses, cf. Num. 12.3.
35. At the transfiguration, Mark 9.2–8 et par., Moses comes up from Sheol while Elijah descends from on high to meet Jesus "in the middle," i.e., on the mountain on earth, cf. Teixidor, Muerte, 98f.
36. 1 Thess. 4.16f. (Pes. 4.17).

41   Adam anticipated Him Who is the Lord of the Cherubim[37]
     and was able to have him enter and dwell near the boughs of the
        Tree of Life.

42   Abel yearned for him to come in his days,
     so that instead of the lamb he sacrificed, he might see the Lamb of
        God.[38]

43   Eve looked for Him, for the shame of women was great,
     but He would be able to clothe them not in leaves but rather in the
        glory they had shed.[39]

44   The symbol of the tower that many built envisages One Who would
     come down and build upon the earth a Tower that goes up to
        heaven.[40]

45   Even the type of the ark of animals envisages our Lord,
     Who would build the holy church in which souls take refuge.[41]

46   In the days of Peleg the earth was divided into seventy tongues;[42]
     he anticipated that One Who would divide the earth by tongues for
        His apostles.[43]

47   The earth that the Flood drowned called her Lord silently;
     He came down and opened baptism by which people were drawn
        out to heaven.

48   Seth and Enosh and Kenan were named sons of God;[44]
     they anticipated the Son of God, for they were brothers to Him in
        mercy.

49   Slightly less than one thousand years Methuselah lived;
     he anticipated the Son Who gives eternal life as an inheritance.[45]

---

37. The Cherubim posted at the gate of Eden to keep Adam from the Tree of Life, Gen. 3.24, is subject to Christ. Further on this theme, cf. Graffin, Cherubim.

38. Cf. Gen. 4.4. Abel provides a eucharistic type as one who sacrifices a lamb. Elsewhere, Cruc. 2.8.9, he is a double type since he is also a victim, cf. Graffin, Eucharistie, 97f.

39. The Syriac word "shame" (*pwrsy*) also means "nakedness." The fig leaves are a garment of shame woven by Eve; cf. Gen. 3.7. Only the new garment woven by Mary, i.e., the body of Jesus, will be adequate; cf. HdP 2.7, 4.5, Nat. 4.187f.

40. Cf. Gen. 11.1–9, Virg 40.11–13, Murray, Symbols, 222ff. and Kronholm, Motifs, 210–14.

41. Cf. HdF 49.4; Christ builds the church of which Noah's ark is the type; the dove and olive branch are symbols of baptism. For Noah as a type of Christ, cf. Kronholm, Motifs, 172–214.

42. Cf. Gen. 10.25. In Syriac as in Hebrew the root *plg* means "to divide."

43. Cf. Acts 2.

44. Cf. Gen. 5.6–14.

45. Gen. 5.27. Literally the Syriac has "unceasing life from everlasting" here rendered "eternal life."

50   For their sake by a hidden symbol, grace was asking
      their Lord to come in their lifetimes to fill their needs.

51   For it is the Holy Spirit, Who for their sake by quiet contemplation
          in them
      stirs them up to see by Her the Savior for whom they yearned.[46]

52   The soul of just men perceived the Son, the Medicine of life,
      and she[47] eagerly desired that in her days He would come and she
          would taste His sweetness.

53   Enoch yearned for Him, and without having seen the Son on earth,
      he increased his faith and was made righteous so that he ascended to
          see Him in heaven.[48]

54   Who will refuse grace? For this gift that the ancients
      did not acquire [even] with great effort has come freely to the people
          of today.

55   Even Lamech looked for the Compassionate One to come and
          console him
      from his labor and the work of his hands and from the earth that the
          Just One cursed.[49]

56   But Lamech saw his son Noah in whom the symbols of the Son are
          portrayed;
      instead of this distant Lord the nearby symbol consoled him.

57   Even Noah yearned to see Him, for he tasted of his benefits:
      if [even] His type preserved the animals, how much [more] does He
          save souls.[50]

58   Noah anticipated Him—Noah who surmised that by Him the ark
          stood still;
      if His type saved in this way, how much more will He save in His
          reality.[51]

---

46. Cf. Rom. 8.26. Based on the grammatical convention that "spirit" (rwḥ) is feminine in Syriac, early Syriac Christian literature developed a rich feminine imagery for the Holy Spirit. Glimpses of this tradition survive in Ephrem; cf. Murray, Symbols, 312–20.

47. I.e., the soul.

48. Gen. 5.24.

49. Gen. 5.29.

50. Ephrem's interpretative technique here, typified by the phrase "how much more" is analogous to the Rabbinic method of "qal w homer"—from light to heavy—an argument proceeding from a lesser to a greater example; cf. H. L. Strack, *Introduction to the Talmud and Midrash* (Philadelphia, 1945), 93–98.

51. Cf. Gen. 8.4. The word here rendered "reality" (qnwm') may be used to render the Greek ὑπόστγοις. It is used by Ephrem as a technical term with several different senses; cf.

59 By the Spirit Abraham perceived that the birth of the Son was
distant;

for his own sake he eagerly desired even in his day to see Him.[52]

60 Isaac who tasted of His salvation yearned to see Him;

if His sign is saved in this way, how much more will He be saved in
His truth.[53]

61 Today the Watchers[54] were rejoicing that the Awakener came to
awaken us;

who will go to sleep on this night on which all Creation is awake?

62 Since by sins Adam let the sleep of death enter Creation,[55]

the Awakener came down to awaken us from the slumber of sin.

63 Let us keep vigil as do the greedy who contemplate money lent on
interest,

who stay awake often at night to calculate principal and interest.

64 Awake and thinking is the thief who dug a hiding place in the
ground for his sleep;[56]

his wakefulness is all [for] this: to increase lamentation for those who
sleep.

65 Keeping vigil also is the glutton in order to eat more and to suffer
agony;

his vigil was torment for him since he did not eat with moderation.

66 Keeping vigil also is the merchant; at night he wearies his fingers

to calculate how much [interest] came [in on] his mina and whether
he doubled and tripled his obol.

67 Keeping vigil also is the rich [man] whose sleep mammon pursues;

his dogs are sleeping, but he is keeping his treasure from thieves.

68 Keeping vigil also is the worrier whose sleep has been swallowed up
by his worries,

Beck, Theologie, 13–18; idem, Reden, 4–8; and Noujaim, "Essai." In this instance it is simply
synonymous with *b-šrr'*, "in truth, in reality."

52. Cf. John 8.56. The Syriac reads "even if" rather than "even."

53. Here rather than "type" and "reality" (*twps'* and *qnwym'*) as in strophe 58, Ephrem uses
"sign" and "truth" (*nyš'* and *šrr'*) with essentially the same meaning. On *nyš'*, cf. Beck,
Bildtheologie, esp. 256–60.

54. I.e., the angels, cf. CJ1.8 and note ad loc.

55. Beck retains the plural, "sins," with the earlier mss. and interprets this as an indication
of Ephrem's undeveloped notion of Original Sin. Further on Ephrem's doctrine of the Fall, cf.
Saber, Theologie, 111–31.

56. Cf. Matt. 25.18.

whose death stands at his pillows, and he watches, worried, for
    years.

69   It is Satan who teaches, my brothers, wakefulness for the sake of
    wakefulness,
so that we might be asleep to virtues, vigilant and wakeful to vices.

70   Even Judas Iscariot kept vigil an entire night,[57]
and he sold the blood of the Just One Who purchased the entire
    creation.

71   The sons of darkness, who stripped off and shed the Shining One,
    put on darkness,[58]
and with silver the thief sold the Creator of silver.

72   Even the Pharisees, sons of darkness, were awake an entire night;
the dark ones kept vigil to conceal the incomprehensible Light.[59]

73   Keep vigil as bright ones on this bright night;
for even if its color is black, still it is splendid in its power.

74   One who splendidly watches and prays in the darkness
is wrapped in hidden brilliance in the midst of this visible darkness.

75   The way of life of the hateful one who stands in the daylight is the
    way of a son of darkness,
so that even if clothed by light without, he would be girt by
    darkness within.

76   Indeed, my friends, let us not forget in our wakefulness:
illicit is the vigil of one who does not watch as he should.

77   Deep sleep is the vigil of one who watches unworthily;
its opposite, too, is the vigil of one who watches unchastely.

78   The vigil of a jealous man is an abundance full of emptiness,
and his watch is a matter full of scorn and disgrace.

79   If an angry man keeps watch, his vigil is disturbed by anger,
and his watch itself becomes full of wrath and curses.

80   If a garrulous man keeps vigil, his mouth becomes a thoroughfare
useful for the destroying [spirits] but wearisome for prayers.

81   If a discerning man keeps vigil, he chooses one of two:
either he sleeps sweetly, or he keeps vigil righteously.

---

57. The night of his betrayal of Jesus? Cf. Mark 14.32–52 et par.
58. Garment imagery is frequent in Syriac, cf. Brock, Clothing.
59. The trial before the Sanhedrin is apparently meant, cf. Mark 14.53–65 et par.

82 Serene[60] is the night on which shines forth the Serene One Who
came to give us serenity.

Do not allow anything that might disturb it to enter upon our
watch.

83 Let the path of the ear be cleared; let the sight of the eye be
chastened;

let the contemplation of the heart be sanctified; let the speech of the
mouth be purified.

84 Mary today has hidden in us the leaven from the house of
Abraham;[61]

let us, therefore, love the poor as Abraham [loved] the needy.

85 Today she has cast rennet into us from the house of David, the
compassionate one;

let man have mercy on his persecutor as the son of Jesse on Saul.[62]

86 The sweet salt of the prophets today is scattered among the peoples;

let us acquire by it a new taste by which the former people would
lose its flavor.[63]

87 On this day of redemption let us speak a speech of interpretation;

let us not speak superfluous words, lest we be superfluous to [the
day].

88 This is the night of reconciliation; let us be neither wrathful nor
gloomy on it.

On this all-peaceful night let us be neither menacing nor boisterous.

89 This is the night of the Sweet One; let us be on it neither bitter nor
harsh.

On this night of the Humble One, let us be neither proud nor
haughty.

90 On this day of forgiveness let us not avenge offenses.

On this day of rejoicings let us not share sorrows.

91 On this sweet day let us not be vehement.

On this calm day let us not be quick-tempered.

92 On this day on which God came into the presence of sinners,

---

60 *špy*, here rendered "serene," may mean either calm or clear. Ephrem plays on the
various senses of this root in this and the following strophes.

61. Cf. Matt. 13.33 (Pes.)

62. For David's mercy on Saul, cf. 1 Sam 26. In cheesemaking rennet separates the curds
from the whey; here it separates the merciful from those who lack mercy.

63. The apostles are the salt of the earth sent out over all the earth; cf. Mark 9.50 et par.,
and HdP 6.21 and the comments of Beck and Graffin in CSCO and SC editions.

let not the just man exalt himself in his mind over the sinner.

93 On this day on which the Lord of all came among servants,
let the lords also bow down to their servants lovingly.

94 On this day when the Rich One was made poor for our sake,
let the rich man also make the poor man a sharer at his table.

95 On this day a gift came out to us without our asking for it;
let us then give alms to those who cry out and beg from us.

96 This is the day when the high gate opened to us for our prayers;
let us also open the gates to the seekers who have stayed but sought
[forgiveness].

97 This Lord of natures today was transformed contrary to His
nature;[64]
it is not too difficult for us also to overthrow our evil will.

98 Bound is the body by its nature for it cannot grow larger or smaller;
but powerful is the will for it may grow to all sizes.[65]

99 Today the Deity imprinted itself on humanity,
so that humanity might also be cut into the seal of Deity.[66]

---

64. Here Ephrem states one of his central theological themes, the miraculous transformation (šwḥlp') in the incarnation of the Creator, who is by nature unchangeable. The One becomes
many for the sake of self-revelation to the creatures God loves. Cf. de Halleux, Mar Ephrem, 45–
47. Also Virg 4.5–6, 25.12, 28.11.

65. Freedom of the will is important to Ephrem and enters often into his polemics against
other beliefs; cf. T. B. Mansour, "La défense éphrémienne de la liberté contre les doctrines
marcionite, bardesanite et manichéenne," OCP 50 (1984), 331–46.

66. The verb here rendered "imprinted" (ṭbʿ) belongs to the context of coinage, seals and
signets. Hence ṣbt, usually rendered "decorate" or "embellish," is here translated "cut into" since
ṣbt is a denominative verb from ṣebtā, "ornament or embellishment," but also "carved work, gem
of a ring," i.e., intaglio; cf. Margoliouth 473a; gemma annuli, Payne Smith 3360. The language of
seals and sealing (σφραγίς, σφραγίζω) is frequently used in Greek Christian literature, especially in relation to the sacrament of baptism; Ephrem has that use as well, cf. Virg 4–7. But here
his meaning is that the incarnation has divinized human nature in a way similar to Athanasius'
statement, "[The Word of God] became human that we might become divine." Ath. de inc. 54.
Further on Ephrem's use of ṭbʿ and its derivatives, cf. Beck, Bildtheologie, esp. 254–58.

2

In this hymn Ephrem delineates an Old Testament basis for the Christian claim that Jesus is the Messiah, apparently in response to Jewish objections. He begins with a tripartite claim for Jesus as inheritor of the threefold leadership of the Old Testament people of God: He has inherited the lyre of the prophets, the hyssop of the priests and the diadem of the kings (str. 2). Most important here, however, is the kingship (str. 3–23). Like all kings, Jesus is recognized by cities, and like Solomon, he is offered a crown by his mother (str. 3–5), but his royal dignity is as the Son of the Ruler of all Creation (str. 6). The great exaltation of his mother is the result of his choice of her (str. 7–9). Ephrem is on the defensive with respect to the virgin birth (str. 11), sustaining his view in part by claiming that in the guise of an old man the angel Gabriel appeared to Mary while she was at prayer (str. 17–20). Yet the theological justification of Mary's virginity rests on typology: Christ is the second Adam; she is the second Eve (str. 7, 12). Finally, the claim to Davidic kingship is an historical assertion. It rests on Micah's messianic prophecy related to Bethlehem (Ephrata) and the divergent claims of Matthew and Luke that Mary and Joseph, respectively, were from Davidic stock. Ephrem defends a double Davidic heritage for Jesus; the one in the flesh, through Mary; the other, for the sake of the name, through Joseph (str. 13–16). He portrays the incarnation as a divine pedagogical device (str. 21). In the last strophes he takes the offensive, claiming that the Davidic kingship is extinct in Israel as a divine punishment, presumably for disbelief in Jesus the Messiah (str. 22–23).

2

To the melody "Heavenly hosts"

1   In the heavenly host sent for praise,

in the glorious age appointed[67] for salvation,
and in the blessed day preserved for rejoicings,
I have been made a partaker in love by Him—even I, and I have
       burst into song.
With pure hymns I shall sing hallelujahs to Him,
and with a holy melody I shall sing to Him;
this child who saved us I shall praise.

    Refrain: Make me worthy, even me, to offer praise to You on
        Your lyre on the day of Your birth.

2   The lyre of the prophets who proclaimed Him, singing before Him,
and the hyssop of the priests who loved Him, eagerly desiring his
       presence,
and the diadem of kings who handed it down in succession
belong to this Lord of virgins, for even His mother is a virgin.
He Who is King gives the kingdom to all.
He Who is Priest gives pardon to all.
He Who is the Lamb gives nourishment to all.

3   The cities of a king are all accustomed
to offer crowns of gold in their hands.
The cities of Judah are crowns endowed with speech, my Lord.
To You, Jesus, they offer crowns in their mouths—
Bethlehem, Cana and Nazareth,
Bethany, Shechem and Samaria
and the worthy cities[68]—and they crown You.

4   The first crown Your city will offer You [is]
two crowns at once: of Mary and Ephrata,[69]
And then, in ranks, all the cities at once.
Behold! They offer You their crowns from what is Your own.
A king, my Lord, takes without giving.
Your glorious cities are plaiting a crown
and offering it for Your glory.

---

67. The Syriac verb *ršm* again evokes the image of seals, engraving or drawing, cf. Nat. 1.99 above, and Beck, Bildtheologie, esp. 244f. and 256–59. It is usually rendered "engrave" or "draw" in the present translation.

68. Fortified cities (*krk'* as opposed to *mdynt'* in Nat. 2.3.1 and 3 above). The cities named here are possible pilgrimage cities in Ephrem's time; further, cf. Virg 16–23, 32–36.

69. Cf. Mic. 5.1–2.

5 Let His mother worship Him; let her offer Him a crown.
For Solomon's mother made him king and crowned him.[70]
He apostatized and lost his crown in battle.[71]
Behold the Son of David who glorified and crowned the House of
    David!
For You have greatly magnified his throne,
and You have greatly exalted his tribe,
and his lyre You have extended everywhere.

6 Worthy of remembrance is the mother who gave birth to Him;
worthy of blessings is the bosom that bore Him.
[Worthy] too is Joseph, who by grace is called father
to the true Son, Him Whose Father is glorious,
Ruler of all Creation, Who was sent
for the sake of the sheep that was lost and had gone astray,[72]
to bring it to the sheepcote and have it enter in.

7 "Most of all those healed, I rejoice, for I conceived Him;
most of all those magnified by Him, He has magnified me, for I
    gave birth to Him.
I am about to enter into His living Paradise,
and in the place in which Eve succumbed, I shall glorify Him.
For of all created women, He was most pleased with me,[73]
[and] He willed that I should be mother to Him,
and it pleased Him that He should be a child to me."

8 Bethlehem thanks You that she was found worthy to give birth to
    You:
the saying of Micah she plaits into your crown.[74]
The prophecy that became a garden of blossoms
will call the prophets and kings to help her with her crown.
For Moses himself bears the types,
and Isaiah [bears] the symbols that flourish,
and [like] lilies [are] parables in all of scripture.

9 "By the mouth of my glorious ones[75] I give thanks that I received

---

70. Cf. 1 Kgs. 1.11–40.
71. Cf. 1 Kgs. 11 et par.
72. Cf. Matt. 18.12–14, et par.
73. Luke 1.28. The speaker in this strophe is Mary.
74. Cf. Mic. 5.2.
75. The "glorious" or "victorious" (*nṣyḥ'*) are saints, perhaps martyrs or ascetics. They are
to be at the highest level of paradise, above the penitents and the just, and closest to the

the child, the Son of the Hidden One, as He emerged into
    revelation.
To a great height He lifted me with my saints
so that I might glorify Him in the broad and vast heaven
full of His glory but unable
to contain within itself the greatness[76]
of the One who bent down and became small in the manger."

10   Heavenly voices announced to those below;[77]
the ears of earthly beings drank You in with the tidings—
[You,] a new Spring that heavenly ones opened
for the earthly who thirsted for life but did not taste it,
[You,] O Fount untasted by Adam,
Who opened twelve rational springs,[78]
and life filled the earth.

11   Joseph worshipped You; a crown he offered to You—
this troubled just [man] whom the angels reassured.[79]
So that you might increase his reward, he rescued You in his arms.[80]
For who could convince a just man
to carry the hateful son of adultery
and to be pursued from one place to another?

12   Teach me, my Lord, how and why
from a virgin womb it was fitting for You to shine forth for us.
Was He a type of splendid Adam [taken]
from the virgin earth that had not been worked until he was
    formed?[81]
Why then was it necessary that she, a daughter of David,
be betrothed to Joseph[82] and that then Your birth
from her would be without man?

Shekinah, the presence of God, cf. HdF 2.11. Since the speaker is Bethlehem, its "glorious ones" may be the innocents killed by Herod, hence taken to be martyrs, as Beck has suggested, cf. Beck, Paradies, 19–21.

76. Behind Ephrem's image is the concept of God as ἀχώρητος, "uncontainable," frequently found in the Greek apologists, cf. e.g. Just. dial. 127.2 (MG 6.772B), Thphl. Ant. Autol. I.5 (MG 6.1032A).

77. Cf. Luke 2.13 f.

78. The twelve apostles; Ephrem rests here on Jewish traditions that the rock struck by Moses produced twelve streams for the twelve tribes, cf. Murray, Symbols, 208–10.

79. Cf. Matt. 1.18–21.

80. Cf. Matt. 2.14.

81. Cf. Gen. 2.5.

82. Cf. Matt. 1.18 et par.

13   The succession of kings is written in the name of men instead of
        women.
    Joseph, a son of David,[83] betrothed to a daughter of David,[84]
    for the child could not be registered in the name of His mother.
    He became, therefore, Joseph's offspring without seed,
    and His mother's offspring without man,
    and by the two of them He bound Himself to their people,
    so that among the kings He is written, Son of David.

14   It was not fitting that from the seed of Joseph He be born,
    nor without Joseph that from Mary He be conceived.
    He was not registered by the name of Mary, who gave birth to
        Him,
    but Joseph, who registered, did not register his [own] seed.
    Without the body of Joseph, He was united with his name;
    without the betrothed of Mary, He sprang forth, her Son.
    He was Lord to David and son.[85]

15   Moses calls the wife of a man the bride;
    the bridegroom who has not taken her, he calls husband, even him,[86]
    lest the succession of the Son of David be broken.
    Without a man, indeed, how can He be counted the Son of David?
    She considers her bridegroom a husband;
    also our Lord acknowledged Himself in their lineage,
    for they call Him Son of David, and He did not deny [it].

16   Even an adopted son is called a man's son
    although he is alien to his lineage and his people,
    but because he is pleased with him, he is an acceptable heir.
    Who then will doubt concerning the birth of the body of our Savior
    that by this daughter of David He was conceived,
    and in the arms of the son of David He was clasped,
    and in the town of David He was worshipped?[87]

17   What indeed was the pure woman doing at the moment

---

83. Cf. Matt. 1.20.
84. Cf. Luke 1.27. Ephrem's emphasis on the double Davidic descent of Jesus occurs also in his commentary on the Diatesseron; contrary to views held formerly by von Harnack and Vööbus, then, Ephrem provides evidence of Tatian's concern for the Davidic descent of Jesus, cf. L. Leloir, "Éphrem et l'ascendance davidique du Christ," SP (TU 63), 389–94.
85. Cf. Matt. 22.41–46.
86. Cf. Gen. 29.21; Deut. 22.23f.
87. Luke 2.4, 11.

when Gabriel was sent down to her?[88]
She saw him perhaps at the moment of prayer,
for Daniel was also at prayer when he saw Gabriel,[89]
for prayer is next of kin to good tidings.
It is right that they should delight one another
as Mary did Elizabeth, her next of kin.[90]

18 The dove bore good tidings for prayer.[91]
By Abraham's prayer good tidings proliferated.[92]
Hezekiah's prayer hastened and proclaimed good tidings to him.[93]
The centurion's good tidings caused his prayers to be joyful.[94]
and on the roof terrace Simon was made joyful,[95]
And Zechariah [at] the reward[96] of his incense;
his good tidings came because of his incense.[97]

19 All good tidings came to the harbor of petition;
this greatest of all good tidings, the cause of all rejoicing,
found Mary at prayer and eagerly desired her.
For Gabriel, inhabiting an honorable old man,[98]
entered and greeted her so that she would not tremble,
so that the modest girl would not see
a youthful face and be sad.

20 To two pure old men and to a virgin girl,[99]
to them alone Gabriel was sent with good tidings.
In the will their natures are similar and resemble one another.
The virgin and the barren woman and Daniel the faithful:
One brought forth the revelation of the word,
and the other a voice for the wilderness,

---

88. Lit. "was sent, flew and came down." Cf. Luke 1.26.
89. Cf. Dan. 9.20f.
90. Cf. Luke 1.40.
91. Of Noah, cf. Gen. 8.11.
92. Cf. Gen. 15.
93. Cf. Isa. 38.5.
94. Cf. Acts 10.3.
95. Cf. Acts 10.9f., not Matt. 16.17, pace Beck.
96. Unpointed, "roof terrace" and "reward" are the same Syriac word.
97. Cf. Luke 1.9–11; cf. Exod. 37.
98. Gabriel takes on various guises, human and otherwise, to appear to humans, according to non-canonical sources, cf. Ginzberg, Legends, VII, 172. If Ephrem is drawing on an established tradition of Gabriel's appearance as an old man, it is otherwise unattested. This probably reflects his own particular concern to defend Mary's virginity.
99. Zechariah, Daniel and Mary.

and the virgin the Word of the Most High.

21 Lest He bewilder the onlookers by His greatness,
He drew Himself up from all the land of the Hebrews
and from all Judah and all Bethlehem
until He filled a small womb,
and as if He were a seed in our garden
or a small flash of light for our pupil,
He shone forth and diffused and filled the earth.

22 And so that His lineage would be well-explained—whose son He
        was—
Luke and Matthew traced his lineage:[100]
Son of Abraham they reckoned Him—and of David and of Joseph,
so that by the learned mouths of two witnesses—
and of the blind man who called Him Son of David—[101]
let the reproach increase for those who hate Him,
and let the crown become greater for those who love Him.

23. The line of Judah, then, never had been cut off,
its sceptre had never been cut short.
Behold, by our Lord, it has been chastised and thus brought to an
        end,
and the great length of time testifies he has confounded it.
There is no more numbering of generations.
The line reached You and stood still,
for You are the Son of David, and there is no other.

100. Matt. 1.16, Luke 3.23–38.
101. Mark 10.46–52 et par.

3

This is a hymn of praise and thanksgiving for the incarnation. By addressing both God the Father and Christ under a series of titles, Ephrem stresses the paradoxical nature of the incarnation. His choice of imagery achieves an intricate interplay of philosophical ideas with metaphors drawn from everyday life, many of them found also in scripture. Although Ephrem occasionally refers directly to New Testament events (e.g., str. 2, 18), most of the theological imagery of this hymn is not explicitly scriptural. Early in the hymn (str. 3–7) Ephrem shows his acquaintance with philosophical notions of God. God, who by nature is unable to be grasped even by the mind, freely chose to become limited, small and accessible to us by the incarnation; God went so far as even to be bound, fettered and crucified. The unchangeable God's willingness to submit to change has revived the full dignity of our humanity.

After setting forth this theology of the incarnation, Ephrem proceeds to a series of metaphors for redemption: light breaking into darkness (str. 8–9), relief from indebtedness (str. 10), awakening from sleep (str. 19), rescue from drowning (str. 19). God is like a tree or vine giving fruit (str. 15, 17); he is a farmer, ploughman, shepherd, physician, master builder and musician (the last with strong Orphic overtones; str. 14–16, 19–20). In the incarnation God makes a tabernacle (str. 7), palace, temple, garment, armor (str. 20) in which to dwell.

3

To the melody "He consoled with promises"

1   Blessed be the Child Who today delights Bethlehem.
Blessed be the Newborn Who today made humanity young again.
Blessed be the Fruit Who bowed Himself down for our hunger.
Blessed be the Gracious One Who suddenly enriched

all of our poverty and filled our need.

Blessed be He Whose mercy inclined Him to heal our sickness.

Refrain: My Lord, blessed be Your Child,[102]
Who raised to honor our hardness of heart.

2   Thanks to the Fountainhead sent for our salvation.

Thanks to the One Who violated the sabbath in its fulfillment.[103]

Thanks to the One Who rebuked leprosy and it remained not.[104]

Fever also saw Him and departed.[105]

Thanks to the Compassionate One Who bore our pain.[106]

Glory to Your coming that restored humankind to life.

3   Glory to that One Who came to us by His First-born.[107]

Glory to that Silent One Who spoke by means of His Voice.

Glory to that Sublime One Who was seen by means of His Dawn.

Glory to the Spiritual One Who was well-pleased

that His Child should become a body so that through Him His
     power might be felt

and the bodies of His kindred might live again.[108]

4   Glory to that Hidden One Whose Child was revealed.

Glory to that Living One Whose Son became a mortal.

Glory to that Great One Whose Son descended and became small.

Glory to that One Power Who fashioned Him,

the Image of His greatness and Form for His hiddenness.

With the eye and the mind—with both of them we saw Him.[109]

5   Glory to that Hidden One Who even to the mind

---

102. Jesus is addressed as child of God, παῖς θεοῦ in the *Didache*, 9–10, probably also of Syrian origin, and in Hippolytus' Apos. Trad. 7. The title may also mean servant of God, with reference to the Suffering Servant of Isaiah 53.

103. Cf. Mark 2.23–28 et par.

104. Cf. Mark 1.41f. et par.

105. Cf. Mark 1.29–31 et par.

106. Cf. Isa. 52.4f.

107. Here and throughout the verse, the utter ineffability of the Father is stressed. Although Ephrem does not use the term, this is a Logos theology; cf. Beck, Reden, 85f.

108. Through the incarnation of the Child of God, human beings become kindred of the Child of God, thus becoming receptive to the power of God and receiving life. The notion is, again, fundamentally of a Logos theology.

109. God the Father fashioned (ṣwr) the Son as his image. For the use of this term in Ephrem, cf. Beck, Bildtheologie, esp. 244–51. Likewise, for Athanasius, Ath. adv. Ar. 3.23.5, the Son is the "perfect," express image of the Father, but the Father did not "fashion" his image, cf. Ath. adv. Ar. 1.13.58.

is utterly imperceptible to those who investigate Him.[110]
But by His grace through [His] humanity
a nature never before fathomed is [now] perceived.[111]
His hands bound and fettered, His feet nailed and fastened,
by His [own] will He clothed Himself with a body for those who
    seized Him.[112]

6   Blessed is He Whom freedom crucified, when He permitted it.
Blessed is He Whom also the wood bore, when He allowed it.
Blessed is He Whom even the grave enclosed, when He set limits to
    Himself.
Blessed is He Whose will brought Him
to the womb and to birth and to the bosom and to growth.
Blessed is He Whose changes revived our humanity.

7   Blessed is He Who engraved our soul and adorned[113] and betrothed
    her to Him[self].
Blessed is He Who made our body a Tabernacle for His
    hiddenness.[114]
Blessed is He Who with our tongue interpreted His secrets.
Let us give thanks to that Voice Whose praise on our lyre[115]
and Whose power on our kithara[116] are sung.

---

110. Those who are arrogant enough to investigate God will be utterly incapable of perceiving him. Ephrem's sustained polemic against the "investigators" and the "inquirers" is directed against the Arians, who seek to understand the mysterious essence of God. The proper role of humans is to ponder the symbols God has placed in scripture and nature and the sacraments rather than trying to analyze the nature of God. Cf. de Halleux, Mar Ephrem, 42–45; Beck, Theologie, 62–80; Murray, Symbols, 14–20; Brock, Luminous, 10–36.

111. By the incarnation even the divine nature becomes accessible to human beings, but not for investigation!

112. Paradoxically, the incarnate Christ is physically helpless, but he became incarnate by his own will for those who lay hold of him—'ḥd is to be taken in both the physical sense (the seizing of Jesus by his persecutors) and in the mental sense (those who grasp the meaning of Christ, in a positive sense).

113. As in Nat. 1.99, ršm, "engraved," suggests the image of a gemstone or seal, but ṣbt is here rendered "adorned" because of the bridal imagery.

114. The incarnation is like God's presence in the tabernacle.

115. The kinora (knwr) or lyre was associated by Greek pagans with Orpheus, by Jews with David, and by Christians with both David and Jesus; cf. P. C. Finney, "Orpheus-David: A Connection in Iconography between Greco-Roman Judaism and Early Christianity?" JJA 5 (1978), 6–15. Strophe 16 of this hymn clearly invokes Orphic ideas of the taming of wild animals as a metaphor for salvation.

116. Or zither (Syriac, qytr'). Ephrem is fond of musical imagery, as are some of the Greek Patristic writers, particularly Clement of Alexandria; cf. Clem. prot. 1; cf. T. Halton, "Clement's lyre: a broken string, a new song," *The Second Century* 3 (1983), 177–99. Instrumental music in a liturgical context is, however, rejected by all Greek and Latin Christian writers who mention

The peoples came together to listen to His melodies.

8   Glory to the Son of the Gracious One, rejected by the sons of the
Evil One.

Glory to the Son of the Just One, crucified by the sons of the
Wicked One.

Glory to the One who released us and was bound in place of us all.

Glory to that One who pledged Himself to pay the debt.

Glory to the Beautiful One Who portrayed us in His similitudes.

Glory to that Serene One Who looked not at our blemishes.

9   Glory to that One Who begot His Light in the darkness,

and [the darkness] was hidden by its vices that concealed its secrets,

but [the Light] stripped off and took away from us the garment of
blemishes.[117]

Glory to the Heavenly One who mingled

His salt with our mind, His milk with our souls.

His body became bread to revive our mortality.

10   Thanks be to the Rich One who paid the debt in place of us all,

something He did not borrow, but He signed and became indebted
for us again.

By His yoke He brought away from us the shackles that held us
captive.

Glory to the Judge Who was judged,

but He had His Twelve sit down for the judgment of the tribes.

Yet He was found guilty by the ignorant, the scribes of that people.

11   Glory to that One Who never before could be measured by us;

our heart is too small for Him and our intellect too weak.

He dazzles our smallness by the wealth of His forms.[118]

Glory to the All-knowing Who cast Himself down,

and asks to hear and to learn what He already knew

to reveal by His questions the treasure of His benefits.

---

it; cf. Quasten, Musik; E. Ferguson, "The Active and Contemplative Lives: the Patristic Interpretation of Some Musical Terms," SP XVI, 15–23; James W. McKinnon, *Music in Early Christian Literature*, Cambridge Readings in the Literature of Music (Cambridge, 1987). Ephrem apparently differed from his Greek and Roman counterparts since a sixth-century source depicts him playing the lyre while a woman's choir sings; cf. McVey, Singing.

117. The use of imagery of clothing is common in Syriac Christian literature, but the more usual notion is that the garment of light or of glory is lost by Adam and Eve and regained through Christ; cf. Nat. 23.13, Brock, Clothing, and Saber, Theologie, 152–57.

118. God has many forms (*pwršn'*), not by nature but by choice. He is the One, who enters into multiplicity for our sake, cf. Nat. 1.97.

12 Let us worship the One who enlightened our intellect by His
        teaching
    and prepared in our hearing a path for His words.
    Let us thank the One Who gave to taste His Fruit on our tree.
    Thanks be to the One Who sent His Heir
    to draw us toward Himself by Him and to make us heirs with Him.
    Thanks be to that Gracious One, the cause of all our virtues.

13 Blessed is He Who did not reproach, for He was the Gracious One.
    Blessed is He Who did not avert His gaze, for He is also the Just
        One.
    Blessed is He Who was silent and reproached: He restored life by
        both.
    Powerful is his silence, and reproachful.
    Gentle is His strength even though He accuses,
    for He reproached the False One, but He kissed the thief.

14 Glory to the Farmer, the Hidden One of our thought.
    His seed fell on our earth and enriched our intellect.
    Its harvest was a hundredfold[119] for the storehouse of our souls.
    Let us worship the One Who sat down and rested,
    Who walked within the way, and He was the Way on the way[120]
    and the Gate[121] of entry for those who enter the kingdom.

15 Blessed is the Shepherd Who became the sheep for our absolution.
    Blessed is the Vineshoot that became the cup of our salvation.
    Blessed also is the Cluster, the source of the medicine of life.
    Blessed also is the Ploughman Who Himself became
    the grain of wheat that was sown[122] and the sheaf that was reaped.
    He is the Master Builder Who became a tower for our refuge.[123]

16 He is He Who Himself constructed the senses of our minds
    so that we might sing on our lyre something that the mouth of the
        bird
    is unable to sing in its melodies.
    Glory to the One Who saw that we had been pleased

---

119. Cf. Mark 4.20 et par.
120. Cf. John 4.6
121. Cf. John 10.7.
122. Cf. John 12.24.
123. On building images, cf. Vielhauer, Oikodome, esp. 49, 52–54, on the Odes of Solomon and Acts of Thomas.

to resemble the animals in our rage and greed,
and [so] He descended and became one of us that we might become
heavenly.

17   Glory to Him Who never needs us to thank Him.
Yet He [became] needy for He loves us, and He thirsted for He
cherishes us.
And He asks us to give to Him so that He may give us even more.
His Fruit was mingled with our human nature
to draw us out toward Him Who bent down to us.
By the Fruit of the Root He will graft us onto His Tree.[124]

18   Let us thank Him Who was beaten and Who saved us by His
wound.
Let us thank Him Who took away the curse by His thorns.
Let us thank Him Who killed death by His dying.
Let us thank Him Who was silent and vindicated us.[125]
Let us thank Him Who cried out in death that had devoured us.[126]
Blessed is He Whose benefits have laid waste the enemies of God.

19   Let us glorify Him Who watched and put to sleep our captor.
Let us glorify the One Who went to sleep and awoke our slumber.
Glory to God the Healer of human nature.
Glory to the One Who plunged in and sank
our evil into the depth and drowned our drowner.
Let us glorify with all our mouths the Lord of all means [of
salvation].

20   Blessed is the Physician[127] who descended and cut painlessly
and healed the sores with a mild Medicine.
His Child was the Medicine that takes pity on sinners.
Blessed is the One Who dwelt in the womb, and in it He built

---

124. In the second half of the verse, "He" is God the Father rather than the Son. The image of root and fruit is part of Ephrem's usual Trinitarian language for Father and Son; cf. Beck, Reden, 75–77.
125. Matt. 27.14 et par.
126. Matt. 27.50 et par.
127. Ephrem frequently characterizes Christ both as physician and as the medicine of life. The image is especially developed in CNis 26.3–7, 27.1 and CNis 34, where it is applied to Old Testament types and Christian bishops as well. Ephrem's use is firmly rooted in Syriac tradition, cf. Murray, Symbols, 89–91, 199–204. Here, as in str. 17, Ephrem shifts the referent for "Him" without warning from Son to Father, so that Christ is the Physician in the first line, but the Child and the Medicine of the third line.

a palace[128] in which to live, a temple[129] in which to be,
a garment in which to be radiant, and armor by which to conquer.

21   Blessed is the One Whom our mouth is not sufficient to thank,
Whose gift is too great for those gifted with speech.
Nor are the senses sufficient to give thanks for His grace.
for however much we thank Him, it is too little,
and because it is of no use for us to be silent and unnerved,
let our weaknesses return [to God] a song of thanksgiving.

22   Gracious One Who does not demand more than our strength,
how much was your servant judged by principal and interest—
he who did not give what was sufficient and withheld what he
      owed?
Sea of glory without needs,[130]
receive in Your graciousness a drop of thanksgiving,
for by Your gift You have moistened my tongue to praise You.

---

128. *bykl'* may be a palace or temple.
129. *nws'* from Greek ναός, temple.
130. *dl' snyq* is the equivalent of ἀνεπιδεής of the Greek apologists, cf. Clem. str. 7.13,
Meth. symp. proem., Ath. gent. 28, where God is said to be sufficient to Himself.

4

Although this hymn is primarily a nativity hymn celebrating the paradox of the incarnation, it also concerns the feasts of Easter and the Ascension (str. 31–32, 58–59). The primary theological and liturgical theme for the nativity is that the birthday of Christ resembles him in many ways, primarily in its compassion (str. 1–31). Ephrem develops this theme by an extended exegetical section contrasting the life-giving birthday of Christ with the death-dealing birthday of Herod as recounted by the synoptic gospels (Mark 6.21–19 et par.; str. 60–83). The primary theme for Easter is a paradox: the bait catches the fishermen (str. 35–47), and again, as by the wood, wine and rib we were conquered, so Christ conquers by those same means (str. 109–118), and the Lamb destroys Satan as the divine presence in the Ark destroyed the image of the Philistine god Dagon (112–118; cf. 1 Sam 5). The theme of the Ascension is both incarnational and eucharistic: Just as the infinite God was paradoxically present in the infant at the nativity, so also the unlimited God is present in the eucharistic elements (str. 84–96); just as the body of Christ was lifted up to heaven, so those who worthily receive the body and blood of Christ in the Eucharist will be lifted up, spiritualized (str. 58, 97–108).

After alternating these three themes at greater length, Ephrem recapitulates them: 1) in winter when there is little light, the Light came (str. 119–20); like the barren earth, a virgin brought forth (str. 121–22); 2) the lamb born out of season tore apart the wolf (str. 123–29); 3) as the holy One dwelt bodily in Mary's womb, so he dwells spiritually in those who can perceive him (str. 130–42). Ephrem ends the hymn with a long and stirring litany of examples of the apparent powerlessness of the incarnate One with the reality of his hidden power (str. 146–213). The reality can be seen by those able to see it (str. 132–42; actually the metaphor of hearing is much more developed than seeing here); God is revealed to each according to the capacity of the creature (str. 199–202).

4

To the melody "Gather together, let us celebrate in the month of Nisan"

1 Blessed is Your day, my Lord, that first one
by which Your feastday is appointed.[131]

*Refrain: Blessed is He Who gave You to us without our asking,
so that by You we might thank Your Father for His gift.*

2. Your day resembles You, for it is a lover of human beings.
It is handed down and comes with all generations.

3 It is a day that goes to the end of life with old people
and returns with infants.

4 It is a day that renews itself by its love,
so that its strength will renew our old age.

5 When it has visited us and passed by and gone,
in its compassion Your day returns and visits us again.

6 It knows that humanity is needy.
The entire [day] resembles You in its concern for humanity.

7 The creation needs [the day's] spring;
for it, as for You, my Lord, all [creation] thirsts.

8 It is the day whose yoke rules over [all] times,
but length of time conquers all and will not pass it by.

9 For even kings and their images have passed away,[132]
and the festivals to commemorate them have disappeared.

10 The power of Your day is like Your own;
it extends over the generations that have come and will come.

11 Your day resembles You for although it is one,
it branches out and becomes many[133] in order to be like You.

12 My Lord, on this, Your day, that is near to us,
we have seen Your birth, that distant one.

---

131. As in Nat. 2.1, the verb *ršm* carries the sense of engraving.

132. For the king's image, the Syriac *ywqn'*, the Greek εἰχών is used here. It is a word frequently used by Ephrem in a symbolic sense; cf. Beck, Bildtheologie, esp. 240–44. The emperor's image represents the emperor himself and hence is paid respect. When the emperor's power passes away, that respect can no longer be demanded, as the exercise of the *damnatio memoriae* of a dead emperor demonstrated. In the following verse Ephrem contrasts this with God's power and its visible image, the feastday of Christmas/Epiphany.

133. The one birthday of Christ becomes many in its liturgical celebration. Hence it is like God, the One, Who became manifold for our sake; cf. de Halleux, Mar Ephrem, 45–47.

13   Lord, let Your day be like You for us.
     Let it be a means and a pledge of peace.

14   It is Your day that reconciled heaven and earth,
     for on it the Heavenly One descends to the earthly ones.

15   Your day is able to reconcile
     that Just One Who became angry at our sins.

16   Behold our sins are myriad! Forgive us on Your day
     on which mercy shown forth upon the guilty.

17   My Lord, Your day is great; let it not be diminished by us.
     Let it have mercy on our follies, as is its custom.

18   And, my Lord, if every day pours forth Your forgiveness,
     how much more will it increase on this day!

19   All of the days acquire good things
     from the treasury of Your glorious day.

20   All of the feastdays derive their beauty and are adorned
     from the treasures of this feastday.

21   Your mercy pours forth to us, my Lord, on this day.
     Make better known to us Your day than all the [other] days.

22   For great is the treasure house of Your birthday.
     Let it be the one that makes recompense for debtors.

23   Greater is this day than every day,
     for on it the Compassionate One came out to sinners.

24   A treasure of medicines is Your great day
     on which the medicine of life shone forth for the severely wounded.

25   A storehouse of benefits is this day
     on which the light broke forth upon our blindness.

26   Indeed He came bearing us to the bowl[134]
     from which plenitude will pour upon our hunger.

27   The early-maturing cluster is this day
     in which the cup of salvation was hidden.

28   The first-born feastday is this day
     that is first to conquer all the feastdays.

29   In the winter that robs the branches of fruit,
     the Fruit sprang forth for us from the barren vine.

30   In the frost that stripped all the trees
     a Shoot budded for us from the house of Jesse.

---

134. Word play on "bowl" (*kpt'*) and hunger (*kpnwt'*).

31 In January[135] when seed hides in the earth,
the Staff of life sprang up from the womb.

32 In April[136] when the seed springs up into the air,
the Sheaf propagated itself in the earth.

33 In Sheol Death mowed it down and consumed it,
but the Medicine of Life hidden in it burst through.

34 For in April when lambs bleat in the field,
into the womb He, the Passover Lamb, entered.

35 Into the stream from which fishermen come up,
the Fisher of all plunged, and He came up from it.[137]

36 [At] the stream where Simon was catching his fish,
the Fisher of men[138] came up and caught him.

37 With the cross that catches all thieves,
He caught that thief for life.[139]

38 By death the Living One emptied Sheol.[140]
He tore it open and let entire throngs flee from it.

39 Tax collectors and prostitutes [are] unclean snares;
the Holy One caught the snares of the Deceitful One.

40 The sinner who had been a snare for men—
He made her an example for penitents.[141]

---

135. Conun = December–January.

136. Nisan, when Easter was celebrated, is sometimes used more loosely by Ephrem to mean the season of spring. Here Christ's death and resurrection are seen as conception and (re)birth. By an interesting play of paradox, Ephrem makes the nativity and Easter interchangeable: the birth is a resurrection, the resurrection a birth.

137. The image of Christ as a fisherman and fisher of men is rooted in his own words as reported by the synoptics, cf. Mark 1.16f. et par., to which Ephrem specifically alludes in the next verse here. Since the same word in Syriac, *ṣwd*, means both to fish and to hunt or trap, Ephrem's imagery in verses 35–50 is more continuous than a translation is able to show. Further on use of the image in Ephrem and the Syriac context, cf. Murray, Symbols, 176–78; in early Christian literature more generally, cf. Dölger, Ichthus. For the special importance of the fish in pre-Christian Edessa, cf. Segal, Edessa, 53–55, and Drijvers, Cults, 79f.

138. Cf. Mark 1.16f. et par.

139. Cf. Luke 23.39–43. The "good thief" was especially interesting to Syriac Christians; their liturgy portrayed his predicament when arriving at the gates of paradise in advance of Christ, cf. Graffin, Cherubin.

140. Christ's victorious descent into Sheol to release the just, especially the prominent figures of the Old Testament, is a significant theme of Jewish Christianity that made its way quickly into the Syrian Christian environment; cf. Teixidor, Descente.

141. Cf. Luke 7.36–50.

41 The shriveled fig tree that withheld its fruit[142]
    offered Zacchaeus as [its] fruit.[143]

42 Fruit of its own nature it had not given,
    but it gave one rational fruit.

43 His thirst made our Lord lean over the well,
    but He caught the thirsty woman by the water that He requested.[144]

44 He caught one soul out of the spring,
    with her He caught the entire city.

45 The Holy One caught twelve fishermen,
    with them He caught the whole creation.

46 The Iscariot slipped away from among His nets;
    upon his neck fell the noose.

47 The snare of the All-reviving catches for life,
    and one who slips away from it, slips away from life.

48 And who is able to enumerate for me
    the various benefits hidden in You, my Lord?

49 How much is my thirsty mouth able to lap up
    from within the spring of the Deity?

50 Grant us today the voice of our petition.
    May our prayer in words be in deeds.

51 My Master, make us forget whatever we have seen.
    Let Your feastday make pass away the news we have heard.

52 Our mind has been distracted among the voices.
    O Voice of His Father, quiet the [other] voices.

53 Let the inhabited earth be made very peaceful by You,
    by Whom the sea was calmed from its tempests.[145]

54 The demons rejoiced to hear the voice of blasphemy;
    the Watchers will rejoice in us as they are accustomed.

55 From within Your flock [comes] the voice of distress;
    in You, the One Who makes all joyful, let Your herd rejoice.

56 My Master, requite us not, for our murmuring;
    our mouth is apt to complain since it is sinful.

---

142. Cf. Mark 11.12–14 et par.
143. Cf. Luke 19.1–10. Cf. HdF 25.13–15, for another example of Ephrem's linking Zacchaeus with the barren fig tree.
144. Cf. John 4.7–42.
145. Mark 4.36–41 et par.

57　My Lord, on Your day, give all [kinds of] joys;
　　with blossoms of peace may we celebrate Your Pasch.

58　On the day of Your ascension may we be lifted up;
　　with the new bread may we be His remembrance.

59　Our Lord, increase peace for us that we may celebrate
　　the three feasts of the Deity.[146]

60　My Lord, great is Your day; let it not be mocked.
　　Every one honors his birthday.

61　O, Just One, keep, honor Your birthday.
　　for Herod honored his birthday.[147]

62　The unchaste dance pleased the tyrant.
　　May the chant[148] of chaste women please You, my Lord.

63　May the chant of the chaste women dispose You, my Lord,
　　to keep their bodies in chastity.[149]

64　Herod's day resembles him.
　　Your day also resembles You.

65　The day of a turbid man is turbid with sin,
　　but serene like You is Your serene day.

66　The day of the tyrant killed the harbinger;[150]
　　on Your feastday everyone proclaims glory.

67　On the day of the murderer the voice became silent,
　　but on Your day [there are] festive voices.

68　The unclean one on his feastday extinguished the light,[151]
　　so that darkness might hide the adulterers.

69　The time of the Holy One sets lights in array[152]

---

146. Epiphany, Easter and Ascension, cf. str. 31, 32, 58.

147. Mark 6.21–29, et par.

148. *ql'* is "chant", "voice" or "sound."

149. *qdyšwt'* is used in its encratite sense here, but the chaste women of the previous lines are *nkpt'*.

150. John the Baptist.

151. Early Christian apologists defended their communities against the charge of "extinguishing the light," e.g., Min. Fel. Oct. 9.6–7. For other instances, cf. *The Octavius of Marcus Minucius Felix*, trans. and annotated by G. W. Clarke, ACW 39 (New York, 1974), 224f., nn. 124f.

152. If Ephrem indicates a liturgical use of lights here, it is one of the earliest explicit literary attestations of this practice and of its symbolic significance, cf. F. Cabrol, "Cierges," DACL 3.2, 1613–22; H. Leclerq, "Lampes," DACL 8.1, 1086–1221; H. Thurston, "Lights," CE 9.244b–247a; D. R. Dendy, *The Use of Lights in Christian Worship*, Alcuin Club Collection 41 (London, 1959). Since the practice of lighting candles or lamps was primarily associated with death in pre-Christian contexts, it is not surprising that it is first attested at the Easter Vigil and in devotions at martyrs' tombs. Jerome (*c. Vigilantium* vii) and the *Testamentum Domini* I.19, attest to a liturgical

to make the darkness flee with its hidden things.

70 The day of this fox[153] stank as he did;
but holy is the feastday of the True Lamb.

71 The day of the transitory one passed away as he did,
but Your day, like You, will remain forever.

72 The day of the tyrant raged as he did,
for by force he silenced a just voice.

73 The feast of the Humble One is gentle as He is,
Whose sun shone forth on His false accusers.[154]

74 The tyrant knew that he was not the king of kings
so he yielded to the King of kings.

75 My Lord, the entire day is insufficient for me
to set off praise of You against censure of him.

76 May Your day full of compassion excuse my offense
that against the unclean day I have set off Your day.

77 For Your day is beyond comparison,
and it cannot be compared with our days.

78 The day of a human is like an earthly [being].
But the day of God is like God.

79 My Lord, Your day is greater than the prophets' [days].
Yet I undertook to compare it with that of a murderer.

80 You understand, my Lord, as the All-knowing,
You Who hear the comparisons that my tongue makes.

81 On Your day grant to me a request for life,
as on his day he granted a request for death.

82 The needy king swore on his feastday
that half of his kingdom would be the price of the dance.

83 But on Your feastday, our All-enriching One,

---

lighting with symbolic intent in the East, the latter almost certainly in a Syriac environment, cf. F. X. Funk, *Das Testament unseres Herrn und die verwandten Schriften* (Mainz, 1901), esp. 82–87. Further, cf. I. Dalmais, "Le thème de la lumiére dans l'office du matin des églises syriennes orientales, in *Noël, Épiphane, rétour du Christ* (=Lex orandi 40; Paris, 1967), 257–76.

153. Herod Antipas, youngest son of Herod the Great, was tetrarch of Galilee and Peraea during the ministries of John the Baptist and Jesus. In his encounter with Herod, Jesus referred to the ruler as a "fox," cf. Luke 13.31–33. The fox figures in the Bible and in classical literature, especially Aesop's fables, as the crafty but base opponent of the lion; cf. Harold W. Hoehner, *Herod Antipas* (Cambridge, England, 1972), 214–24, and Appendix XI, "The Meaning of 'Fox,' " 343–47.

154. Cf. Mark 14.55–65 et par. To accuse falsely, *ʿṣq*, is the same word used frequently in Nat. 5–18, where I have more often translated it as "slander."

let us cast away, as is right, the crumb of bread.[155]

84   From the thirsty earth gushes forth a Spring
sufficiently to satisfy the thirst of the peoples.

85   From a virgin womb as if from a rock,
sprouted the Seed from which harvests have come.

86   Joseph filled innumerable storehouses,
but they were emptied out and consumed in the years of the
famine.[156]

87   The one True Ear [of wheat] gave bread,
heavenly bread without limit.

88   The bread that the first-born broke in the desert[157]
was consumed and passed away, although He multiplied it greatly.

89   Once again He has broken new bread
that ages and generations will not consume.

90   They consumed the seven loaves of bread that He broke,[158]
and they finished also the five loaves of bread that He multiplied.[159]

91   The one loaf of bread that He broke conquered the creation;
for however much it is divided it multiplies all the more.[160]

92   Again, a great deal of wine filled the water jugs;[161]
it was poured out and consumed although there had been a great
deal.

---

155. Does Ephrem mean to give bread to the poor? If so, the verb *šdʾ* is an odd choice, but cf. Nat. 1.84, 93–95, for similar notions. A second possibility is a reference to Mark 7.24–30 et par. The third, and greatest, possibility is that the "crumb of bread" represents the Old Testament types for the Eucharist, now superseded by the sacrament itself. Strophes 84–108 are clearly eucharistic, stressing the unlimited nourishment available in Christ over against the limitations of its types. Beck attributes Ephrem's understanding of the limitless character of the sacraments to the emphasis on the presence of the Holy Spirit, cf. Beck, Eucharistie, esp. 51–58. It is certain that the presence of the Spirit plays an outstanding role in Ephrem's sacramental theology; further, cf. Graffin, Eucharistie. It is probably unwarranted to assume, however, that every reference to the spirit or to a spiritual presence should be taken as a reference to the Holy Spirit rather than to the divinity in a more general sense, cf. the remarks of J. P. de Jong, in "La connexion entre le rite de la Consignation et l'Epiclèse dans saint Éphrem," SP 2 (1957), (=TU 64), 29–34, esp. 31f. In the present passage the emphasis on the power of Christ, esp. str. 155–213, refers not to the Holy Spirit but is instead best interpreted in the light of Logos theology; pace Beck, Eucharistie, 58.

156. Cf. Gen. 41.49.

157. The manna of the Israelites, Exod. 16.

158. Cf. Mark 8.1–10 et par.

159. Cf. Mark 6.32–44 et par.

160. Cf. Mark 14.22–25 et par. The Eucharist, unlike its types, is inexhaustible.

161. Cf. John 2.6ff.

93   Although small was the drink of the cup that He gave,[162]
      very great was its power—infinite.

94   In the cup that accepts all wines,
      the mystery[163] remains the same.

95   The one loaf of bread He broke cannot be confined,
      and the one cup that He mingled cannot be limited.

96   The grain of wheat that was sown, after three days
      came up and filled the storehouse of life.

97   The bread is spiritual like its Giver;
      it revives spiritual ones in a spiritual manner.

98   But the one who takes it in a bodily manner
      takes it indiscreetly and uselessly.[164]

99   Let the mind take the bread of the Compassionate One
      in a discerning manner as the medicine of life.

100   If sacrifices of the dead in the name of demons
      in a mystery are sacrificed and eaten,

101   how much more fitting it is for us to perform nobly
      the mystery of the consecration of the gift.

102   Whoever eats from the sacrifice in the name of demons[165]
      will become demonic without dispute.

103   Whoever eats of the bread of the Heavenly One
      will become heavenly without doubt.

104   Wine teaches us, since it makes one who
      is allied with it [become] one like itself.

105   For it hates especially the one who loves it;
      it intoxicates and maddens him and mocks him.[166]

106   Light teaches us since it makes the eye
      a source of brightness like itself.[167]

107   The eye by light saw nakedness,
      and modesty hastened to the modest man.

---

162. Cf. Mark 14.22–25 et par.

163. r'z', usually rendered "symbol" is translated here and in str. 100f. as "mystery." For the sacramental use of the term, cf. Beck, Symbolum-Mysterium, 39f.

164. 1 Cor. 11.29.

165. 1 Cor. 8 and 10.

166. Cf. Lewy, Sobria ebrietas.

167. The light comes from the eye to meet the light outside. As Beck has noted, this idea occurs several times in Ephrem's corpus and is of Platonic origin, cf. Beck HdF 73.16, n. 2; further, Dillon, Platonists, 275.

108   Wine made that nakedness
that does not know [how] to spare the modest ones.

109   The First-born put on the weapons of the Deceitful One
so that with the weapons that killed He might, conversely, give life.

110   By the wood[168] with which he killed us, we were delivered;
by the wine[169] that maddened us, we became modest.

111   By the rib[170] plucked out from Adam,
the Evil One plucked out the heart of Adam.

112   There shone forth from the rib[171] the hidden Power
Who cut down Satan as [He did] Dagon,[172]

113   for in that Ark was hidden scripture
that cried out and proclaimed the Conqueror.

114   But there was also in this a revealed symbol,
for Dagon was overcome in his place of refuge.

115   It came to fulfillment following the symbol
that the Evil One was vanquished in his own retreat.[173]

116   Blessed is He Who came and in Whom were fulfilled
the symbols of the left hand and of the right hand.[174]

117   He completed the symbol that was in the lamb
and He completed that type that was in Dagon.

118   Blessed is He Who redeemed us by the True Lamb
and destroyed our Destroyer as [He destroyed] Dagon.

119   In January when the nights are long,
daytime without limit shone forth to us.

120   In winter when the whole creation is gloomy
the beauty that gladdened all of creation emerged.

121   In winter that made the earth barren,
virginity learned to give birth.

122   In January that stilled the birthpangs of the earth,

---

168. Ephrem frequently uses *qys'* to refer to the forbidden tree of paradise and to the cross of Christ.

169. The eucharistic wine is brought into the theme of sober inebriation.

170. Eve.

171. Mary, the second Eve.

172. 1 Sam. 5. The incident is portrayed in Panel WB4 of the synagogue at Dura Europos, cf. C. H. Kraeling, with C. C. Torrey, C. B. Welles and B. Geiger, *The Synagogue, Excavations at Dura-Europos, Final Report*, 8.1 (New Haven, 1956), 101–103 and Pl. LVI.

173. As Dagon was destroyed in his own sanctuary, so Satan is destroyed in his place of refuge, woman!

174. I.e., both evil and good types in the Old Testament are fulfilled in the New.

the birthpangs of virginity came.

123 No one sees the young lamb
at first except the shepherds.

124 At the moment of his birth the good tidings
of the True Lamb also rushed to the shepherds.[175]

125 Perhaps even there the marvel doubled,
for the Lamb [born] out of season spoke and emerged.

126 For the lamb not [born] in season becomes the harbinger
for the Lamb Whose conception was not [merely] natural.[176]

127 The Old Wolf saw the nursling Lamb,
and he was alarmed by Him Who had been transformed.

128 For since the Wolf had put on sheep's clothing,[177]
the Shepherd of all became a lamb in the flock,

129 so that when the Greedy One dared attack the Lowly One,
the Powerful One would tear apart that Devourer.

130 The Holy One dwelt in the womb in a bodily manner,
and behold, He dwells in the mind in a spiritual manner.

131 Mary who conceived Him hated sexual union;
the soul in which He dwells will not commit adultery.

132 When Mary perceived Him, she forsook her bridegroom;
behold, He dwells in chaste women if they have perceived Him.

133 A deaf person cannot perceive a great thunderclap,
nor an insolent person the voice of a commandment.

134 Therefore a deaf person is tranquil at the moment of thunder,
and an insolent one is tranquil at the voice of warning.

135 If the powerful thunderclap terrified the mute one,
if the powerful reproach weighed upon the corrupt,

136 the deaf one who cannot hear is not to blame,
but the one who stops up his ears—this is impudence.

137 From time to time, then, there was a thunderclap;
the voice of the Law thundered daily.

138 Let us not shut up our ears—openings that are open
and cannot be closed—so that they may not accuse us.

---

175. Luke 2.8ff.
176. While Jesus is the True Lamb, whose conception is not natural, John the Baptist is the lamb born out of season, since his parents were old. As the lamb bleats and emerges at birth, John the Baptist, went out to preach.
177. Matt. 7.15. The Wolf is Satan.

139   The gate of hearing is open by nature,
so that by its force it might rebuke our insolence.

140   The will is able to open and close
the gates of the pupils of the eyes and the gate of the mouth.

141   He granted to us to see . . .
To hear news . . . to be closed.

142   . . .
. . . its minutiae by our will.

143   Glory to that Voice that became a body,
and to the lofty Word that became flesh.

144   Ears even heard Him, eyes saw Him,
hands even touched Him, the mouth ate Him.

145   Limbs and senses gave thanks to
the One Who came and revived all that is corporeal.

146   Mary bore a mute Babe
though in Him were hidden all our tongues.[178]

147   Joseph carried Him, yet hidden in Him was
a silent nature older than everything.

148   The Lofty One became like a little child, yet hidden in Him was
a treasure of Wisdom that suffices for all.

149   He was lofty but he sucked Mary's milk,
and from His blessings all creation sucks.

150   He is the Living Breast of living breath;
by His life the dead were suckled, and they revived.

151   Without the breath of air no one can live;
without the power of the Son no one can rise.

152   Upon the living breath of the One Who vivifies all
depend the living beings above and below.[179]

153   As indeed He sucked Mary's milk,
He has given suck—life to the universe.

154   As again He dwelt in His mother's womb,
in His womb dwells all creation.

155   Mute He was as a babe, yet He gave
to all creation all His commands.

---

178. The theme of apparent powerlessness but real power continues through str. 213; for a similar idea, cf. Ath. de inc. 17.

179. Str. 151f. continue the eucharistic theme, cf. Graffin, Eucharistie, 107; Beck, Eucharistie, 58.

156   For without the First-born no one is able
     to approach Being, for He alone is capable of it.

157   Indeed the thirty years that He was on earth,
     who was guiding all creation?

158   Who was receiving all offerings?
     the praise of those on high and of those below?

159   He was entirely in the depths and entirely in the heights;
     He was entirely in all and entirely in each one.

160   While His body in the womb was being formed,
     His power was constructing all the members.

161   While the fetus of the Son was being formed in the womb,
     He Himself was forming babes in the womb.

162   Ineffectual as was His body in the womb,
     His power in the womb was not correspondingly ineffectual.

163   Nor again is it [true] that as weak as this body was on the cross,
     so weak would be His power on the cross.

164   For when upon the cross He revived the dead,
     did His body revive them or His will?

165   Thus although all of Him was dwelling in the womb,
     His hidden will was supervising all.

166   For He saw that all of Him was hanging on the cross
     but His power made all creation tremble.

167   For [His power] darkened the sun and shook the earth;
     graves were torn open, and the dead emerged.[180]

168   See, indeed, that He was entirely on the cross,
     while yet He remained entirely everywhere.

169   In the same way He had been entirely in the womb,
     while yet He remained entirely everywhere.

170   While indeed He was on the cross, He revived the dead;
     just so, while He was a babe, He was forming babes.

171   While He was dead, He was opening graves;
     while He was in the womb, He was opening wombs.

172   Come and hear, my friends, about the hidden Son
     Who was revealed in His body, yet hidden was His power.

173   For the power of the Son is a fluid power;
     the womb did not confine it as [it did] the body.

---

180. Matt. 27.51–53.

174 For while the power dwelt in the womb,
     it was forming babes in the womb.

175 His power embraced the one who embraced Him,
     for if His power were curtailed all would collapse.

176 Indeed the power that contained all creation,
     while He was in the womb, did not desert all.

177 He formed His individuality,[181] the Image, in the womb,
     and He formed in all wombs all persons.

178 Although He grew up among the poor,
     from the storehouse of plenty He provided for all.

179 While again she who anointed Him, was anointing Him,[182]
     with His dew and His rain He anointed the universe.

180 The Magi offered myrrh and gold,
     although hidden in Him was a treasure of wealth.

181 The Magi offered to Him from what was His:
     myrrh and frankincense that He had brought into existence and
          created.[183]

182 By power from Him Mary's womb became able
     to bear the One who bears all.

183 From the great treasury of all creation
     Mary gave to Him everything that she gave.

184 She gave Him milk from what He made exist.
     She gave Him food from what He had created.

185 He gave milk to Mary as God.
     In turn, He was given suck by her as human.

186 Her arms carried Him, for He lightened His weight,
     and her bosom embraced Him, for He made Himself small.

187 Who would be able to measure his grandeur?
     He diminished his measurements corresponding to the garment.[184]

188 She wove it and clothed in it Him Who had taken off His glory;
     she measured and wove for Him Who had made Himself small.

189 The sea bore Him; it became calm and abated;[185]
     and how indeed did the arms of Joseph bear Him?

---

181. Syriac *qnwm'* is the equivalent of Greek ὑπόστασις.
182. Mark 14.3–9 et par.
183. Matt. 2.11.
184. On Christ's body as a garment, cf. Brock, Clothing, esp. 15ff.
185. Mark 6.45–52 et par.

190 The Womb of Sheol conceived Him and burst open;[186]
and how did the womb of Mary sustain Him?

191 With His voice He split stones upon graves;[187]
and how did Mary's bosom sustain Him?

192 You came to humiliation to save all:
glory to You from all who were saved by You.

193 Who is able to speak about the hidden Son
Who came down and put on a body in the womb?

194 He came out and like a babe He sucked milk,
and the Son of the Ruler of All crawled among infants.

195 Openly the youths in the marketplace surrounded Him;
secretly the Watchers surrounded Him in awe.

197 He was cheerful among the infants as a baby;
awesome was He among the Watchers as a commander.

198 Too awesome was He for John to loosen His sandals;[188]
accessible was He for sinners who kissed His feet.[189]

199 The Watchers as Watchers saw Him;
according to the degree of his knowledge each person saw Him.[190]

200 Everyone according to the measure of his discernment
thus perceived Him, that One greater than all.

201 In His Father alone is the measure
the fulness of knowledge of Him, for He knows how much He is.[191]

202 But each according to measure acquires knowledge of Him:
heavenly natures and earthly.

203 He Who is Lord of all, gives us all,
and He Who is Enricher of all, borrows from all.

204 He is Giver of all as one without needs.
Yet He borrows back again as one deprived.

205 He gave cattle and sheep as Creator,
but, on the other hand, He sought sacrifices as one deprived.[192]

---

186. Cf. Teixidor, Descente, and idem, Muerte.

187. Matt. 27.52.

188. Mark 1.7–8 et par.

189. Luke 7.38.

190. The notion of ἐπινοίαι of Middle and Neo-Platonism underlies Ephrem's understanding here. For a very similar use in Origen, cf. F. Bertrand, *La mystique de Jésus chez Origène*, Théologie 23 (Paris, 1951).

191. John 10.15.

192. E.g., Lev. 1.

206   He made water into wine as Maker,
but, on the other hand, He drank some of it as a poor man.

207   From His own He mixed it at the wedding feast—
His [own] wine He mixed and gave [it] to drink where He was
invited.[193]

208   By his love the old man Simeon became great,
so that a mortal offered the One who saved all.

209   It was by the power from Him that Simeon carried Him;
he who offered Him was offered by Him.[194]

210   He gave the laying-on of hands to Moses on the mountain,[195]
and He received it in the midst of the river from John.[196]

211   By the power of His gift, John was competent,
and the earthly one baptized the Heavenly One.

212   By the power that came from Him, the earth bore Him;
it was beginning to collapse, but His power bound it together.

213   From what is His, Martha gave Him food to eat;[197]
she placed before Him the foods created by Him.

214   All who gave have vowed from what is His;
from His treasury they have placed [gifts] on His table.

---

193. John 2.
194. Luke 2.22–32.
195. Cf. Lev. 8.
196. Cf. Mark 1. 9–11 et par.
197. Luke 10. 38–42.

5

This hymn is the first from Ephrem's original collection of Nativity Hymns, which forms the core of the full collection of the manuscript tradition. All thirteen hymns in this original group have the same strophic pattern and are to be sung to the same melody. Further, most contain strophes attributed to the *dramatis personae* of the nativity story, especially Mary. They also share the same subject matter: the paradox of the incarnation and the defense of the virgin birth.

This hymn begins with a celebration of the joys and triumphs of the month of Conun (December–January), in which the incarnation of the Lord of the universe made possible the exaltation and divinization of humankind. After twice enumerating three classes of people—slave, free and royal—in ascending order of dignity, Ephrem strikingly contrasts the exaltation of humans with the *kenosis* of Christ (str. 1–4). The humble righteousness of Christ conquers the rebellious disobedience of Adam (str. 5). After a brief exhortation to chase away boredom (str. 6), Ephrem sets out a series of images for the feast of the Nativity: it is a treasure-house full of spiritual riches (str. 7–9); the garlanding of doorways (str. 1) represents the garlanding of the believer's heart to welcome the Holy Spirit (str. 10); in contrast to earthly kings who collect taxes, God has paid our debt and promised even more (str. 12); the conquering sun of the winter equinox is an appropriate symbol for the victory of Christ the Light (str. 12–15).

The final third of the hymn is a meditation on the paradox of the incarnation put into the mouths of Joseph (str. 16–18) and Mary (str. 19–24). Joseph first ponders his initial misunderstanding of the virgin birth. Then he turns to the implications of his humble trade, on the one hand, and his Davidic descent, on the other. Mary meditates on the incarnation in more theological and philosophical terms: How can she be the mother of an infant who is the Director of all creation and Commander of the universe?

HYMNS ON THE NATIVITY

5

To the melody "Who is able to speak?"

1 This is the month that bears utterly
all joys: for slaves—liberation,
for the free—pride, for doors—garlanding,
for bodies—dainties. And purple [garments]
it showers in its love as if for a king.

Refrain: Praise to You, fair Child of the Virgin!

2 This is the month that bears entirely
all victories: it frees the spirit;
it subdues the body; it brings forth life
among mortals. Divinity
it showers in its love upon humanity.

3 In this month slaves recline
upon rugs, and the free recline
upon carpets, and kings recline
upon tapestries. In a manger
the Lord of the universe reclined for the sake of the universe.

4 Behold, O Bethlehem, David the king
clothes himself in fine white linen. The Lord of David
and Son of David hid His glory
in swaddling clothes. His swaddling clothes gave
a robe of glory to human beings.[198]

5 On this day our Lord exchanged
radiance for shame, as the Humble One.
For Adam exchanged truth for evil
as a rebel. The Gracious One took pity;
His upright [deeds] conquered those of the perverse.

6 Let everyone chase away his boredom
because it was not boring for that Majesty
to be in the womb nine months
for our sake and to be thirty
years in Sodom among madmen.

---

198. The garment of glory, originally bestowed on Adam and Eve but lost through sin, is restored by Christ; cf. Nat. 17.4 and Kronholm, Motifs, 216, 223.

7 Because the Gracious One saw that the human race
   was poor and humble, He made feastdays
   as treasure-houses, and He opened them
   for the lazy, so that the feast would stir up
   the lazy one to rise up and become rich.

8 Behold, the First-born has opened His feastday for us
   like a treasure-house. This one day,
   the [most] perfect in the year, alone opens
   this treasure-house. Come, let us prosper
   and become rich from it before it is closed.

9 Blessed are the vigilant who plunder from it
   the spoils of life. It is a great disgrace
   if one sees his neighbor
   carrying away treasures, yet he in the treasure-house
   reposes and sleeps to come out empty-handed.

10 On this feast let everyone garland
   the door of his heart. May the Holy Spirit
   desire to enter in its door to dwell
   and sanctify. For behold, She moves about
   to all the doors [to see] where She may dwell.

11 On this feast the openings in the curtains
   are joyous, and the Holy One rejoices[199]
   in the holy Temple, and a voice thunders
   in the mouth of babes, and the Messiah rejoices
   in His feast as Commander of the host.

12 On the birth of the Son, the king[200] was enrolling
   the people in the census,
   so that they would be indebted to him. To us the King came out
   to cancel our debts, and He wrote in His name
   another debt, so that He would be indebted to us.

13 The sun conquered and engraved a symbol
   on the degrees that it ascended. Since it ascended
   it is twelve days, and today this is
   the thirteenth:[201] a perfect symbol

---

199. Or, as Beck suggests, "the holy [altar] rejoices."
200. Caesar Augustus, cf. Luke 2.1.
201. January 6, the thirteenth day since December 25, the day of the Conquering Sun. Further on this theme, cf. Nat. 27.16–22, esp. 27.21.

of the birth of the Son and of His Twelve.

14   Moses shut in the lamb in April
on the tenth day[202]—a symbol of the Son
Who came into the womb and closed Himself up
on the tenth day. He came out from the womb
in this month when the light conquers.

15   Darkness is defeated to signify
that Satan is defeated, and light conquers
to shout out that the First-born is victorious.
The Dark One is defeated with the darkness,
and our Light conquers with the sun.

16   Joseph caressed the Son
as a babe. He served Him
as God. He rejoiced in Him
as in a blessing, and he was attentive to Him
as to the Just One—a great paradox!

17   "Who has given me the Son of the Most High
to be a son to me? I was jealous of Your mother
and wanted to divorce her.[203] I did not know
that in her womb was a great treasure
that would suddenly enrich my poverty.

18   "David the king arose from my race
and put on a crown.[204] Great ignominy
have I attained, for instead of a king
I am a carpenter.[205] A crown has found me
for in my bosom is the Lord of crowns."

19   With rival tones Mary was aglow.
She, too, sang: "Who has granted
to the barren one to conceive and give birth
to the One [Who is also] many, to the small [Who is also] great,
Who is fully present in me yet fully present in the universe.[206]

20   "The day when Gabriel entered

---

202. On the tenth of Nisan (April–May), in preparation for its slaughter four days later for Passover, cf. Ex. 12.3–6.
203. Matt. 1.19.
204. Matt. 1.1–16, 20.
205. Matt. 13.55; cf. Mark 6.3, Luke 6.23.
206. Cf. Nat. 4.11.

my poor presence,[207] he made me immediately
a free woman and a servant; for I am servant
of Your divinity, but I am also mother
of Your humanity, [my] Lord and [my] son.[208]

21 "Suddenly a handmaiden has become daughter of the King
by You, Son of the King. Behold, the lowly one [is]
in the House of David because of You!
O Son of David, behold, the daughter of the earth
has reached heaven by the Heavenly One.

22 "Indeed, how much I am amazed that an aged Babe
is set before me—One Who lifts His gaze
entirely to heaven without ceasing.
The murmuring of His mouth—how it seems to me
as if His silence were speaking with God!

23 "Indeed, who has seen a Babe who gazes
entirely everywhere? He gazes
as the Director of all creation
above and below. He looks as
the Commander of the universe.

24 "How shall I open the fount of milk
for You, the Fount? How shall I give
sustenance to You, the All-sustaining,
from Your [own] table? How shall I approach
with swaddling clothes the One arrayed in streams [of light]?"

---

207. Luke 1.26.

208. Although Ephrem's specification that Mary is servant of the divinity and mother of the humanity of Christ has a strongly Nestorian ring, it would be anachronistic to judge his orthodoxy by the standards of the fifth century. In fact, his statement is not even Nestorian, since Nestorius used the term χριστότοκος, "Christ-bearer," not simply ἀνθρωπότοκος, "human-bearer," for Mary. Further, in the next strophe, she refers to herself as "the daughter of the earth [who] has reached heaven by the Heavenly One." Ephrem's concern is with the paradox of the incarnation, not with the precise delineation of the two "natures" of Christ. (But cf. Nat. 6.7–11).

6

This second hymn of the core collection develops the theme of the manifestation of Christ to the world. Most of the New Testament materials on which Ephrem's meditation is based are drawn from the infancy narratives of the gospels of Matthew and Luke. The hymn begins with several strophes (str. 1–6) sung by Mary, who ponders the proper way to address her son. Affirming the virgin birth, still Mary says it is appropriate to call him son of Joseph. Yet he is also Son of God, Son of man, Son of David. Mary complains that she is slandered and persecuted, but she can seek refuge in Christ and his life-giving power.

Turning now to the infancy narratives, Ephrem finds a series of persons who recognize Jesus' true identity. First, thanks to the star of Bethlehem, the Magi found the Divine Infant and worshipped him (str. 7–8). The two harbingers of Christ, the star of Bethlehem and John the Baptist, announce the divinity and humanity of Christ, respectively, correcting adoptionist and docetic tendencies (str. 9–11). Now, turning from the Matthean account to the Lucan, Ephrem recounts the recognition of the prophets, Simeon and Anna (str. 12–14), followed by the recognition of "the barren" Elizabeth, Zachariah and their son, John (str. 15–18). Even Herod, Ephrem claims, returning to Matthew's account, recognized the Lion of Judah enough to try to kill him (str. 19–20). All of creation announced his coming (str. 21). Finally, at the baptism of Jesus, the Father himself proclaimed his Son; the Watchers (angels) and children joined in with their hosannas (str. 22). At last all this jubilation awakens even Sion (str. 23)—Ephrem has shifted to the entry into Jerusalem. Sion, startled but not truly awakened, kills the Awakener. When Christ rises from the dead, he awakens the Gentiles instead of the Jewish people (Sion).

6

The same melody

1   "My mouth knows not how to address You,
    O Son of the Living One. I tremble
    to dare to address You as son of Joseph,
    for You are not his seed. Yet I shrink
    from denying the name of him to whom I have been betrothed.

Refrain: Praise to You, Son of the Most High, Who put on our body.

2   "Although You are the Son of the One, I shall call You henceforth
    Son of many, for myriads of names
    do not suffice for You, for You are Son of God
    and Son of Man and Son of Joseph
    and Son of David and Lord of Mary.

3   "Who made the speechless one
    Lord of speech? With your pure conception
    evil men have slandered me.[209] O Holy One,
    be Your mother's defender. Show miracles
    to convince them whence is Your conception.

4   "For Your sake, behold, I am hated,
    Lover of all. Behold, I am persecuted
    because I conceived and bore the One Place of Refuge
    for human beings. Let Adam rejoice
    for You are his Key to paradise.

5   "Behold, the sea is stirred up against Your mother
    as against Jonah. Behold, Herod,
    the raging surf, seeks to drown
    the Lord of the seas. Where shall I flee?
    Teach me, Lord of His mother.

6   "With You I shall flee to acquire by You
    life in every place. With You, the pit
    would not be the pit, for with You one would

---

209. Jewish criticism of the virgin birth is an issue that constantly recurs in these hymns, cf. McVey, Tol'dot.

ascend to heaven. With You, the grave
would not be the grave, for You are also the resurrection."[210]

7 The star of light[211] that shone forth suddenly
beyond its nature is smaller than the sun
yet greater than the sun; it was smaller
in visible light; it was greater
in hidden power because of its symbol.

8 The morning star shed its rays
among the dark ones and led them
like blind men. They came and received
a great light. They gave offerings
and received life and worshipped and returned.[212]

9 Above and below there were two harbingers
for the Son: the star of light
shouted out joyfully from above, and John
proclaimed from below. Two harbingers:
both an earthly one and a heavenly one.[213]

10 That heavenly one showed his nature
that is from [God's] Majesty. And the earthly one also
showed His nature that is from humanity.
O great wonder!—that His divinity
and His humanity were announced by them.[214]

11 Whoever considered Him earthly—
the star of light would convince him
that He was heavenly. And whoever considered Him
spiritual—John
would convince him that He was also bodily.

12 Into the holy Temple Simeon carried Him
and sang a lullabye to Him, "You have come, Compassionate One,
having pity on my old age, making my bones enter
into Sheol in peace. By You I will be raised
out of the grave into paradise."

---

210. John 11.25.
211. Matt. 2.2–12, the star of Bethlehem. Ephrem begins an enumeration of witnesses to
the dignity of Christ. Cf. Virg 15.
212. Matt. 2.11f.
213. Cf. Nat. 24.23.
214. The star announces the divine nature of Christ; John the Baptist announces his human
nature.

13   Anna[215] embraced Him; she placed her mouth
      upon His lips, and [then] the Spirit rested
      upon her lips, like Isaiah
      whose mouth was silent [until] a coal drew near
      to his lips and opened his mouth.[216]

14   Anna was aglow with the spirit of His mouth.
      She sang him a lullabye, "Royal Son,
      despised son, being silent, You hear;
      hidden, You see; concealed, You know;
      God-man, glory to Your name."

15   Even the barren heard and came running
      with their provisions. The Magi are coming
      with their treasures. The barren are coming
      with their provisions. Provisions and treasures
      were heaped up suddenly among the poor.

16   The barren woman[217] cried out as she was accustomed,
      "Who has granted to me, blessed woman,
      to see your Babe by whom heaven and earth
      are filled? Blessed is Your Fruit
      that brought forth the cluster on a barren vine."[218]

17   Zachariah came and his mouth was opened.[219]
      A noble one, he cries out, "Where is the King
      on Whose account I have begotten the voice
      to proclaim before Him? Hail, Son of the King!
      Even our priesthood will be handed over to You."

18   John approached with his parents
      and bowed down to the Son, and brightness rested
      on his face.[220] He did not leap
      as in the womb. A great wonder
      that here he bows down and there he leaps [for joy].

19   Even Herod, the despicable fox,[221]

---

215. Cf. Luke 2.36–38, where Anna prophesies as Isaiah, but she neither embraces nor kisses the infant.

216. Isa. 6.6f.

217. Elizabeth.

218. Christ, Mary's fruit, made it possible for the barren Elizabeth to bear John.

219. Luke 1.64.

220. Cf. HdF 7.3 on the baptism of Jesus.

221. Luke 13.31–33. On Herod as a fox, cf. Nat. 4.70.

who swaggered as if [he were] a lion—
the fox lay down and howled when he heard
the roar of the Lion Who came to lie down
upon his kingdom, as it is written.[222]

20 But the fox heard that the Lion was a cub
and was like a suckling, and he sharpened his teeth
so that while He was still a newborn, the fox might lie in wait
to strangle the Lion before He had grown strong
and the breadth of his mouth should destroy him.[223]

21 All of creation became mouths
and cried out above Him: the Magi cried out
with their offerings; the barren cried out
with their offspring; the star of light
cried out in the air, "Behold the King's Son!"

22 The sky was opened; the water sparkled;
the Dove hovered over; the voice of the Father,
more weighty than thunder, said,
"This is My Beloved"[224]; the Watchers proclaimed Him,
the children shouted joyfully with their hosannas.

23 By these voices that proclaimed and cried out
above and below, the sleep of Sion
was not frightened away. By His colt she was startled;[225]
he trampled and grieved her; she started and rose up.
She killed the Watcher because He awakened her.[226]

24 The Watcher rose up from within the grave,
for He was sleeping while awake, and He came and found
the peoples asleep. He shouted for joy and cried out
and awakened them. The sleeping [people] thanked
the Watcher who made [them] watchers on earth.

---

222. Gen. 49.8–12.
223. Herod Antipas, the fox of Luke 13, son of Herod the Great, is here confused with his father, cf. Matt. 2.16–18. Jesus, the Davidic Messiah, is the Lion of Judah.
224. Mark 1.11.
225. Ephrem has shifted to the entry into Jerusalem, Mark 11.1f.
226. Sion, the female personification of the Jews, is seen by Ephrem as the killer of Christ, here understood in the language of angel-Christology as the "Watcher." On the watchers, cf. Nat. 1.61, 4.195, CJ 1.8.

7

This hymn begins with the infancy narrative of Luke in which the angelic praise at the nativity is followed by the homage of the shepherds to Jesus. Ephrem uses the theme of shepherds and sheep to draw out several Old Testament types for Christ: the Paschal Lamb, Moses as shepherd of the people in the wilderness, and David. Noah is also included, apparently because his name brings to Ephrem's mind Orphic themes. At the ninth strophe Ephrem universalizes the praise by adding women of various ages and states in life as well as old men. The unity of the hymn is somewhat artificially maintained by alluding again to the infancy narrative, this time from the Matthean version, the slaughter of the innocents.

7

The same melody

1   At the birth of the Son a great clamor
took place in Bethlehem, for Watchers descended
to give praise there;[227] a great thunder
were their voices. With this voice of praise
the silent ones[228] came to give praise to the Son.

Refrain: Blessed is the Babe by whom Adam and Eve grew young again.

2   Shepherds, too, came carrying
the good things of the flock: sweet milk,
fresh meat, fitting praise.
They divided [the gifts] and gave to Joseph the meat,
to Mary the milk, to the Son the praise.

---

227. Luke 2.13.

228. Beck suggests dumb animals, cf. Ps. Matt. 14, HdF 13.10.3. More usually *štyq'* refers to inanimate objects or to people, while *l' mlyl* refers to animals. Yet the content of the following strophes lends support to Beck's view.

3 They carried and offered to Him: suckling lamb
to the Paschal Lamb, the first-born to the First-born,
a sacrifice to the Sacrifice, a temporal lamb
to the True Lamb. A fitting sight
that a lamb to the Lamb should be offered.

4 The lamb bleated while being offered
to the First-born. He thanked the Lamb
that came to free sheep and oxen
from sacrifices, even the traditional
paschal lamb that served as a symbol of the Son.[229]

5 The shepherds approached to worship Him.
With their staffs they greeted Him,
prophesying, "Peace, O Greatest
of shepherds! The staff of Moses
acknowledges Your staff, Shepherd of the universe."

6 For You [are the One] Moses acknowledged—he whose
lambs became wolves and whose sheep became
like dragons and his ewes [like]
savage beasts. In the fearful wasteland
his flock became rabid and attacked him.[230]

7 You, then, the shepherds will acknowledge,
for You reconciled wolves and lambs
in the flock. You are the newborn
Who is older than Noah and younger than Noah,
Who pacified all in the ark.[231]

8 For the sake of a lamb, David, Your father
killed a lion.[232] O Son of David,
You have killed the hidden wolf

---

229. Literally, ". . . the paschal Lamb that was handed down and served as a symbol of the Son." The traditional sacrificial animals are grateful that there is to be no more animal sacrifice after Christ, not even a Passover celebration. Cf. Nat. 18.18–19.

230. Tensions between Moses and the people of Israel in the desert become a basis for Ephrem's portrayal of the Jews as perenially faithless in relation to God and to the leaders chosen by God. On the portrayal of Moses in Syriac Christian literature, cf. R. M. Tonneau, "Moïse dans la tradition syrienne," in *Moïse l'homme de l'Alliance* (Paris, 1955), 245–65.

231. Ephrem plays on *kwl'* in two different vocalizations: *kûlâ* meaning "all, the universe" and *kewelâ* meaning "ark." Elsewhere he plays on *nwḥ* meaning "to rest" as well as "Noah." This pun, the Orphic theme of rest, and the more usual Jewish and Christian association of David with Orpheus perhaps explain Ephrem's mention of Noah here just before David and in the context of shepherd imagery.

232. 1 Sam. 17.34–37.

that killed Adam, the innocent lamb
who grazed and bleated in paradise.

9   By that song of praise brides awoke suddenly
and chose chastity, and virgins
preserved their chastity, and even young girls
were purified. They rose early and came
in throngs to worship the Son.

10 The old women of the town of David came
to the daughter of David, speaking blessings:
"Blessed is our native land whose streets are made light
by the ray of Jesse! Today the throne of David
is established by You, the Son of David."

11 Old men cried out, "Blessed is the Babe
Who restored Adam's youth; he was displeased to see
that he grew old and wasted away, yet the serpent who killed him
shed [his skin] and recovered his youth. Blessed is the Babe
by whom Eve and Adam were restored to youth."[233]

12 The chaste women said, "Blessed Fruit,
bless our fruits, given to You
as first fruits." Aglow, they prophesied
about their children, who, when they were killed,
would be plucked by Him as first fruits.[234]

13 The barren women hovered over and held Him.
They caressed [Him] and said, "O Blessed Fruit [conceived]
without intercourse, bless our wombs
during intercourse.[235] Have pity on our barrenness,
Miraculous Child of virginity."

---

233. The portrayal of Adam and Eve as children is common to several early Christian writers in the Greek and Syriac traditions, cf. Thphl. Ant. Autol. 2.25, Iren. A.H. 3.22.4, 4.38.1, and Demonstr. 12 and 14; Clem. prot. 11.111.1, Virg 12.12, and Murray, Symbols, 304–306. Ephrem uses this idea and adds the notion that in the Eucharist Christ restores their youth, cf. Graffin, Eucharistie. For a negative stress on their youth, cf. Nat. 26.8. As is often the case, Ephrem plays on the words ḥw' and ḥwy', "Eve" and "serpent."

234. Cf. Matt. 2.16–18. The mothers of the slain innocents address Jesus. Their children are types of the resurrected faithful. They are the first fruits of the resurrection, to be plucked by Jesus immediately after his resurrection.

235. Here the temporal sense of the preposition mn is more appropriate than the comparative sense suggested by Beck.

8

This hymn begins with the theme of *kenosis*, God's accommodation to human limitations and sinfulness, in the incarnation. Stressing imagery particularly characteristic of Syriac Christianity, Ephrem elaborates on the theme of incarnation and then moves to soteriology: In the incarnation the divine and human natures are mixed like the pigments of an artist; Christ, salt of the earth, is the new Adam to be swallowed up by the serpent; the lance that barred entrance to paradise has pierced the side of Christ and thereby regained entry to paradise for humankind.

In the fifth strophe Ephrem advocates an understanding of Christ's behavior as a model of nonviolent behavior for human beings. In the subsequent strophes (str. 6–12), Ephrem chooses a variety of images to represent the saving work of Christ as well as his role as divine Logos and judge. Farmers, vineyard laborers and carpenters give thanks to Christ—these professions may have been chosen because they adapt easily to the theological imagery, or they may be indicative of the social and economic positions of the Christian community to whom Ephrem was addressing himself.

Next follows a series of strophes (str. 13–15) recalling women from scripture: Sarah, Rachel, Anna and Elizabeth. Although the first example stresses Isaac as a type of Christ, the emphasis is on the women themselves and their prayers for fertility. These strophes serve several functions in the hymn: 1) they serve as a female counterpart to the strophes immediately preceding, addressing the concerns of the ordinary woman in the Christian community; 2) they elaborate Old Testament types for Jesus and especially for Mary; and 3) they provide a foil of the *qal w homer* type for Mary's prominence; if these women were blessed by God in answering their prayers, how much more was Mary blessed in the birth of a Son greater than all his predecessors and conceived without Mary's even asking (str. 16–17).

The final strophes of the hymn portray the praises of other representative social groupings: bridegrooms and brides, children, women and unmarried girls. Again, it is unclear whether aptness of theological imagery has prompted Ephrem's choice or whether it is an attempt to be as inclusive as possible. Bridal imagery is prominent both with and without ascetic emphasis (str. 21 and 19, respectively). It is tempting to construe the emphasis on poor women (str. 20) as an indication of the social and economic status of Ephrem's audience.

8

The same melody

1 Blessed is the Messenger who came bearing
a great peace.[236] By the mercy of His Father,
He lowered Himself to us.[237] Our own debts
He did not take up to Him. He reconciled
[His] Lordship with His chattels.

Refrain: Glory to Your Dawn, divine and human.

2 Glorious is the Wise One Who allied and joined
Divinity with humanity,
one from the height and the other from the depth.
He mingled the natures like pigments
and an image came into being: the God-man.[238]

3 O Zealous One who saw Adam
who became dust and the accursed serpent
eating him.[239] Reality dwelt
in what had lost its flavor. He made him salt
by which the cursed serpent would be blinded.[240]

4 Blessed is the Compassionate One Who saw, next to paradise,
the lance that barred the way

---

236. Or simply, "a great greeting."
237. Cf. Phil 2.6–11.
238. Cf. SdF 92.
239. Similarly, of Eve, Nat. 17.6. Although Ephrem uses *ḥwy'*, "serpent" or "snake," we are perhaps to be reminded of the "reptile" or "dragon," *tnyn'* that swallowed Adam and Eve, cf. Nat. 1.27 and Virg 37.1. Further, cf. Yousif, Croix, 42–45; also cf. Stephen E. Robinson, *The Testament of Adam: An Examination of the Syriac and Greek Traditions* (SBLDS 52, Chico, Cal, 1982), esp. 142, nn. 29f., and my review in CBQ 47 (1985), 540f.
240. The idea seems to be that the serpent is fooled by the incarnation, a notion common in Gnostic texts but not usually portrayed with the imagery used here.

119

to the Tree of Life. He came to take up
the body that would be struck so that by the opening in His side
He might break through the way into paradise.[241]

5 Glorious is the Compassionate One Who did not use
violence, and without force,
by wisdom He was victorious. He gave a type
to human beings that by power
and wisdom they might conquer discerningly.

6 Blessed is Your flock for You are her gate,[242]
and You are her staff, and You are her shepherd,[243]
and You are her drink; You [are] her pilot[244]
and her overseer.[245] O to the Only-begotten
Who was fruitful and multiplied in all [His] benefits.[246]

7 The farmers who cultivated life
came and worshipped before Him. They prophesied to Him,
bursting into song, "Blessed is the Farmer
by Whom is worked the earth of the heart;
He gathers His grains of wheat into the storehouse of life."[247]

8 The laborers came to give glory
to the offshoot that sprang forth from the root
and the stem of Jesse, the virgin cluster
of a parched vine. "Let us be the vessels
for Your new wine that renews all.[248]

9 "In You may my friend's vineyard that gives sour grapes
find peace. Graft its vines

---

241. For Ephrem, the flaming "sword" of the angel in Gen. 1.24 is a type of the lance that pierced the side of Jesus according to John 19.34. The idea occurs also in HdP 2.1, CJ 3.14.1, Comm. Diat. 21.10, Eccl. 45.3.1, Cruc. 9.2, and in CNis 39.7; cf. Murray, Lance; also Murray, Symbols, 125–27.
242. John 10.7.
243. On Christ the Shepherd, cf. Murray, Symbols, 187–91.
244. Or "salt." Although the punctuation of the ms. and the meter favor "pilot of a ship," (cf. Beck), the references to salt in strophe 3 make that reading also plausible. Perhaps Ephrem is deliberately evoking the double meaning.
245. Or "visitor" of the sick, whence "healer;" cf. Beck.
246. Christ as *yḥydy'*, the Only-Begotten or the solitary one, is represented by the solitary ascetics, who are his imitators par excellence. Ephrem plays on this notion by alluding to Gen. 1.28. On *yḥydy'* cf. Murray, Symbols, 12–16.
247. Cf. Matt. 13.30; on Christ as Farmer and vineyard Laborer, cf. Murray, Symbols, 195–99.
248. Cf. Mark 2.22 et par. On Christ as the "cluster of grapes," cf. Murray, Symbols, 113–29.

with Your slips. Let it be laden entirely
with Your blessings. Let its fruit appease
the Lord of the vineyard who threatened him."[249]

10 Carpenters came because of Joseph
to the son of Joseph. "Blessed is your offspring,
the Chief of carpenters, by Whom was drawn
even the Ark.[250] By Him was constructed
the temporal Tabernacle that was [only] for a time.[251]

11 "Confess in the name of our craft.[252]
that You are our pride. May You make the yoke
that is light and easy upon those who bear it.[253]
May You make the measure in which deceit
cannot be, for it is full of truth.

12 "Also may You construct and make a balance[254]
from justice, so that whoever steps
onto it will be judged, and whoever is perfect
will be celebrated on it. O Just One, may You weigh
mercy and sins in it, as a judge."

13 When Sarah sang lullabyes to Isaac
as to a servant who bore the image
of the King, his Lord: upon his shoulders
the sign[255] of the cross, also upon his hands

---

249. Isa. 5.1–7.

250. Both for Noah's Ark and for the Ark of the Covenant the Peshitta often uses *qbwt'* (cf. Pes. Gen. 6.14–8.19 and Pes. Exod. 25.10–22, 37.1–9). Here Ephrem uses *kwyl'* as in Pes. Luke 17.27 and Matt. 24.38; further, cf. Payne-Smith I, 1693, II, 3451f. On Christ as Architect, cf. Murray, Symbols, 218–28, esp. 223–28.

251. Cf. Exod. 26.1ff., Exod. 36.8ff., Exod. 40. Both the Ark of the Covenant and the Tabernacle were taken as cosmological symbols in Judaism and subsequently in Syriac Christianity; cf. McVey, Microcosm. Thus, Christ the Architect is the Architect of the Cosmos, the δημιουργός or λόγος of Greek philosophy and theology.

252. The Syriac *'wmnwt'* is equivalent to Greek τέχνη. Ephrem's attitude to craftsmen is radically different from the traditional Greek attitude; cf. Virg 11 and 12.2 and Beck, TEXNH; for a consideration of the issue in the Greek and Latin Patristic literature in its classical context, cf. Arthur T. Geoghegan, *The Attitude towards Labor in Early Christianity and Ancient Culture*, Studies in Christian Antiquity 6 (Washington, D.C., 1945).

253. Matt. 11.28–30.

254. On the balance as a symbol of judgment, cf. Patrick Brunn, "Signes, symbôles et monogrammes," Acta Instituti Romani Finlandiae, I (1965), libra s.v.

255. "Sign" stands for Syriac *nyš'* which is usually the equivalent of *r'z'*; cf. Beck, Bildtheologie, esp. 260.

bonds and pains, a symbol of the nails.[256]

14 Rachel cried out to her husband; she said,
"Give me sons!"[257] Blessed is Mary
for, without her asking, You dwelt in her womb
chastely, O Gift
Who pours Himself out upon His recipients.

15 Anna with bitter sobs
asked for a child;[258] Sarah[259] and Rebekah[260]
with vows and words, and even Elizabeth,[261]
again, with her prayer [asked] for a long time.
Although they suffered, afterward they were consoled.

16 Blessed is Mary, who without vows
and without prayer, in her virginity
conceived and brought forth the Lord of all
the sons of her companions who were and will be
pure and just men, priests and kings.

17 Who will sing a lullabye to the child of her womb
as Mary [did]? Who will dare
to call her son, Son of the Maker,
Son of the Creator? Who has ever existed
who called her son, Son of the Most High?

18 Bridegrooms shouted joyfully with [their] brides,
"Blessed is the Babe whose mother was
bride of the Holy One. Blessed [was] the marriage feast
at which You were present: even though its wine
suddenly was depleted, by You it became plentiful again."[262]

19 The children cried out, "Blessed [is] He Who was for us

---

256. Gen. 22.6–9. Isaac carrying the wood and then bound for sacrifice was seen by early Christians as a type of Christ carrying his cross and then crucified. It is a frequent theme of early Christian art; cf. F. Cabrol, "Abraham" DACL 1.9 (Paris, 1907) col. 111–127 and H. Leclercq, "Isaac" DACL 7.2 (Paris, 1927) col. 1553–1577. For the theme in Syriac Christianity and its Jewish antecedents, cf. S. Brock, "Sarah and the Aqedah," *Le Muséon* 87 (1974) 67–77; idem, "Genesis 22 in Syriac Tradition," in P. Casetti et al., eds, *Mélanges Dominique Barthelemy: études bibliques* (Göttingen, 1981); idem, "Two Syriac verse homilies on the binding of Isaac," *Le Muséon* 99 (1986) 61–129.

257. Gen. 30.1.
258. 1 Sam. 1.9–20.
259. Cf. Gen. 16.1ff., 17.15ff., 18.9ff.
260. Cf. Gen. 25. 21f.
261. Cf. Luke 1.5–25.
262. Cf. John 2.1–12.

a brother and companion in the streets.
Blessed is the day that with branches
glorified the Tree of Life
Who inclined His height toward our childishness."[263]

20 Women heard that behold a virgin indeed
would conceive and bring forth.[264] Well-born women hoped
that He would shine forth from them, and elegant women
that He would appear from them. Blessed is Your height
that bent down and shone forth from the poor.

21 Even little girls taken by Him [as brides]
spoke prophetically, "Yours, Lord, let me be,
for I am ugly, to You I am fair,
and if I am lowly, to You I am noble.
The bridal chamber that passes away have I exchanged for You."[265]

22 Since youth is both bold
and talkative, the young girls gathered,
daughters of the Hebrews, wise women,
and the mourners, and with their soft words
changed dirges into prophecy.[266]

---

263. Cf. Mark 11.1–11 et par., esp. Matt. 21. 15f., the source of the notion that children played an important role here. Ephrem plays on the similarity of "streets" *šwq'* and "branches" *swk'*.

264. Isa. 7.14.

265. Bridal imagery is associated especially with asceticism in early Syriac literature, e.g., the Odes of Solomon, Acts of Thomas, Aphrahat and Ephrem, cf. Murray, Symbols, 131–42, 255f.

266. Cf. Jer. 9.16–21, Joel 3.1 and Acts 2.17.

9

This hymn begins by accentuating the uniqueness of Mary's motherhood through the majesty of her Son. In the first strophe Ephrem stresses that Mary addresses her Son as both divine and human. Then he considers these two aspects in turn: as Son of the Creator, he creates his own body in the womb and descends from the presence of his Father (str. 2); in his human aspect he inherits the promises given to the Jewish people (str. 3). He is heir to the priesthood of Melchizedek, the kingship of David and the nation of Abraham. Ephrem's choice of Melchizedek rather than Aaron and Abraham rather than Moses is probably meant to stress the applicability of God's promises to the Gentiles.

Mary is the harbor into which the Old Testament types come to rest as ships. The promises given to David and the prophets are fulfilled in Jesus born of Mary. In this context Ephrem refers to Psalm 110, a basis for both royal and priestly messianic claims traced through David and Melchizedek. Along with Psalms 24 and 68 this psalm provided the scriptural basis for the earliest Christian claims concerning the ascension of Christ.[267] Less typically, Ephrem interprets a number of the psalms as a mystical indication of the divine and human natures of Christ.

But Ephrem's emphasis here is on the female mediators of the messianic promise as much as on the males. Returning to a theme he began in the previous hymn, the presentation of the women of the Old Testament as foils for Mary, Ephrem chooses three women from the Matthean genealogy of Jesus who maintained the continuity of the line from Abraham to David to Jesus through extramarital sexual relations: Tamar, Ruth and Rahab (str. 7 ff.). Stressing Tamar (str. 8–13) and Ruth (str. 12, 14–16), Ephrem construes their behavior as motivated by the anticipation and love of the Messiah, that is, Jesus.

---

267. J. Danielou, *The Bible and the Liturgy* (Notre Dame, Indiana, 1956), 303–18.

9

The same melody

1 Who will dare speak to her son
as in prayer, to the hope of his mother
as God, to her beloved [child] and her son
as man. In fear and love
it is right for Your mother to stand before You.

Refrain: Praise be to You on the day of Your manifestation[268] for Your flock.

2 You are the Son of the Creator, Who resembles His Father.
As Maker, He made Himself in the womb;
He put on a pure body and emerged;
He made our weakness put on glory
by the mercy that He brought from His Father's presence.

3 From Melchizedek, the high priest,[269]
the hyssop came to You; a throne and a crown
from the House of David; a family and a people
from Abraham. Who will speak
so to her son as Your mother to You?

4 "I became a haven for Your sake,
great Sea. Behold, the psalms
of Your father David and also the words
of the prophets, like ships
discharged in me Your great wealth.

5 David, Your father, wove and brought for You
Psalm one hundred and ten,
two numbers, as a crown.
O Victorious One, with them You were crowned,
and You ascended and sat down upon the right hand.

6 The great crown is the number
that is woven with the hundred; with it Your divinity

---

268. Or "sunrise," or Epiphany, cf. Nat. 1.6.
269. Gen. 14.17–20; cf. Ps. 110.4 and Hb. 5.6. In each of these, as in Ephrem's hymn here, the word used is *kwmr'*, a more general designation for priest than *khn'*, a specifically Aaronic or Levitical priest. In other works Ephrem specifies when the transmission of the Old Testament priesthood passed to Jesus: either when Jesus was presented to Simeon in the Temple (de Dom. nos. 50.6) or at the moment of his baptism by John (CH 22.18, and Comm. Diat. p.94f.); cf. Graffin, Eucharistie; Saber, Typologie, 84–86.

is crowned. The small crown,
the number ten, crowns the head
of Your Humanity, O Glorious One.

7 Because of You,[270] women pursued
men: Tamar[271] desired
a man who was widowed, and Ruth[272] loved
a man who was old. Even Rahab,[273]
who captivated men, by You was taken captive.

8 Tamar went out and in darkness
she stole the light, and by filth
she stole chastity, and by nakedness
she entered furtively to You, the Honorable One,
Who produces chaste [people] from the licentious.

9 Satan saw Him and was afraid and ran
as if to hinder [her]; He reminded [her] of judgment,
but she feared not, of stoning and the sword
but she was not afraid.[274] The teacher of adultery
was hindering adultery to hinder You.

10 For the adultery of Tamar was chaste
because of You. For You she thirsted,
O Pure Fountain. Judah cheated her
of drinking You. A thirsty fount
stole Your drink from its source.

11 She was a widow for Your sake.
She desired You, pursued You, and even
became a harlot for Your sake.
For You she longed, You she kept [in memory], and she became
a chaste woman.[275] She loved You.

12 May Ruth receive good tidings, for she sought Your wealth;
Moab entered into it. Let Tamar rejoice

---

270. Cf. Matt. 1.1–17 and Nat. 1.13 and note ad loc.
271. Gen. 38.6–30.
272. Ruth 3.10.
273. Jos. 2.1–22, 3.22–25.
274. Gen. 38.24; as Beck has noted, Judah speaks of burning Tamar, not of stoning or execution by the sword. Lev. 20.10 and Deut. 22.22 prescribe death as the penalty for adultery but do not specify the means.
275. I have not accepted Beck's suggestion that Ephrem has translated the Hebrew qedeša with mqdšt' meaning "sacred [prostitute]" since, as he notes, it does not appear in the Peshitta or in the dictionaries.

that her Lord has come, for her name announced
the son of her Lord, and her appellation
called You to come to her.[276]

13   By You honorable women made themselves contemptible,
[You] the One Who makes all chaste. She stole You
at the crossroads, [You] Who prepared the road
to the house of the kingdom. Since she stole life,
the sword was insufficient to kill her.

14   Ruth lay down with a man on the threshing floor
for Your sake. Her love was bold
for Your sake. She teaches boldness
to all penitents. Her ears held in contempt
all [other] voices for the sake of Your voice.

15   The fiery coal that crept into the bed of Boaz
went up and lay down. She saw the Chief Priest
hidden in his loins, the fire for his censer.
She ran and became the heifer of Boaz.
For You she brought forth the fatted ox.

16   She went gleaning for love of You;
she gathered straw. You repaid her quickly
the wage of her humiliation: instead of ears [of wheat],
the Root of kings, and instead of straw,
the Sheaf of Life that descends from her.

---

276. Ephrem plays on the similarity between the pronunciation of Tamar's name (*tmr*) and the phrase, "Come, my Lord!" (*t' mry*). For the use of similar phrases in the earliest liturgical contexts, cf. 1 Cor. 16.22, Rev. 22.20, and *Didache* 10.

10

This hymn is a strongly-worded defense of the claims of Christianity against criticisms apparently emanating from Ephrem's Jewish contemporaries. He begins with a bare statement that Jesus is superior to the twelve sons of Jacob, the fathers of the tribes of Israel (str. 1). He immediately shifts the focus of the hymn, however, to a defense of the resurrection of Christ evidently against accusations that the disciples stole the body of Jesus (str. 2,3). He proceeds with his defense first by drawing typological links between the tomb of Christ, the den in which Daniel was enclosed and Lazarus' tomb (str. 4). Doubling back to make a more straightforward historical argument, he invokes the Matthean account of the burial of Jesus, which claims that the tomb was sealed and guarded to prevent the disciples' stealing the body; this fact should be sufficient to stop the mouths of the slanderers (str. 5). In a manner that should delight devotees of semiotics or of Freud or Jung, he next argues that the resurrection of Jesus constitutes a proof by analogy of the virgin birth (str. 6–10); further, the typological precedents of the resurrection also apply to the virgin birth (str. 6). Finally, he adds another parallel to show the lack of foundation for the doubts of Jesus' resurrection: Despite belief in the ascension of Elijah, some searched in vain for his body; just as they were proved wrong, so are those who doubt the resurrection of Jesus (str. 11–12).

10

The same melody

1   When Leah and Rachel, Zilpah and Bilhah,
    sang lullabyes to those fair
    twelve that they bore,[277] their soft words

---

277. The four are the mothers of Jacob's children; Zilpah and Bilhah are the maids of Leah and Rachel; cf. Gen. 28.24, 29.

were human; lordly are
all Your lullabyes, Lord of His brothers.

2 So that even Your resurrection might be believed
among the doubters, inside the sealed
grave they placed You, for they sealed [it] with a stone
and guards stood [there].[278] It was for Your sake
that they sealed Your grave, O Son of the Living One.

3 When they buried You, if they had given up,
left You and gone, there would be occasion
to assert falsely that they really stole You,[279]
O All-saving One. Contriving
to seal Your grave, they increased Your glory.

4 Types for You were both Daniel
and Lazarus: the one in the den
that the peoples sealed,[280] and the other in the grave
that the people opened.[281] Behold their signs
and their seals confuted them.

5 Open would be their mouth if they had left open
Your grave and gone away. Since they shut up Your grave
and sealed and secured [it], they have shut up their mouth.
And although they desired it not, all the slanderers
covered their heads[282] since they covered Your grave.

6 But by Your resurrection You convinced them
about Your birth, for the den was sealed
and the grave was secured—the pure one on the den
and the living one in the grave. Your witnesses were
the sealed den and grave.[283]

7 The womb and Sheol shouted with joy and cried out
about Your resurrection. The womb that was sealed,
conceived You; Sheol that was secured,

---

278. Matt. 27.62–66.
279. Matt. 28.11–15.
280. Dan. 14.10, 30; the "peoples" are the Gentiles. Aphrahat makes similar comparisons of Daniel with Jesus, cf. Aph. Dem. 21.18.
281. John 11.39, 41; the "people" is the Jewish people.
282. Beck suggests, plausibly, that they have covered their heads in shame; cf. Tonneau, Gen/Exod CSCO 152 (scr. syr. 71), 81.30f.
283. I.e., the virgin birth and the resurrection.

brought You forth. Against nature
the womb conceived and Sheol yielded.

8   Sealed was the grave which they entrusted
with keeping the dead man. Virginal was the womb
that no man knew. The virginal womb
and the sealed grave like trumpets
for a deaf people, shouted in its ear.

9   The sealed womb, the secured stone:
among the slanderers the conception is slandered,
that it was human seed, and the resurrection,
that it was human robbery. Seal and signet
refute and convince that He was a heavenly one.

10   The people stood between Your birth
and Your resurrection. If they slandered Your birth,
Your death reproved them. [If] they dismissed your resurrection,
Your birth confuted them. The two athletes
have struck the mouth that slandered.

11   Elijah, too—they went seeking him
among the mountains.[284] While those on earth
were seeking him, it became all the more clear
that he had been taken up. Their seeking without finding Him
bore witness that he had been lifted up.

12   But if the prophets who were aware of
the ascension of Elijah, doubted, as it were,
his ascent, how much indeed would impure men
have slandered the Son? By their [own] guards
I shall convince them that He has been resurrected.

---

284. 2 Kgs 2.1–18.

11

In this hymn Ephrem explores the paradoxical relationship of Mary to Jesus as the basis for the paradox of *kenosis*. Inverting the reasoning of the previous hymn, the unnatural conception of Jesus provides a kind of proof of his divinity. If one cannot understand how Mary is both virgin and mother, how much less is it possible to comprehend her Son! (str. 1). Moreover, Mary is mother, sister and betrothed of Jesus (str. 2–4). Finally, the kenotic theme is developed in two respects: First with respect to Mary: She cared for her Son because He willed to become in need of care (str. 5). Second with respect to all creation: By entering Mary's womb he is transformed from Lord, Establisher, Ruler, Nourisher of all into a needy and helpless infant (str. 6–8). Alluding to the Magnificat of the Lucan infancy narrative, Ephrem gives the latter theme a prophetic note of social transformation (str. 7).

11

The same melody

1 Our Lord, no one knows
   how to address Your mother. [If] one calls her "virgin,"
   her child stands up, and "married"—
   no one knew her [sexually]. But if Your mother is
   incomprehensible, who is capable of [comprehending] You?

   Refrain: Praise to You for Whom, as Lord of all, everything is easy.

2 For she is Your mother—she alone—
   and Your sister with all. She was to You mother;
   she was to You sister.[285] Moreover, she is Your betrothed
   with the chaste women.[286] In everything,
   behold, You adorned her, Beauty of Your mother.

---

285. Cf. Nat. 16.1.
286. Cf. Nat 4.132, Virg. 25.16, CH 17.5.

3   For she was betrothed according to nature
before You came; yet she conceived
outside of nature after You came,
O Holy One, and she was a virgin
although she gave birth to You chastely.[287]

4   Mary acquired by You all the attributes[288]
of married women: conception within her
without sexual union, milk in her breasts
not in the usual way. You have suddenly made
the parched earth into a source of milk.

5   If she carried You, Your great mountain
lightened its burden. If she fed You
[it was] because You hungered. If she gave you a drink
[it was] because you willed to thirst. If she embraced You,
the coal of mercy[289] preserved her bosom.

6   A wonder is Your mother: The Lord entered her
and became a servant; He entered able to speak
and He became silent in her; He entered her thundering
and His voice grew silent; He entered Shepherd of all;
a lamb he became in her; He emerged bleating.

7   The womb of Your mother overthrew the orders:[290]
The Establisher of all entered a Rich One;
He emerged poor. He entered her a Lofty One;
He emerged humble. He entered her a Radiant One,
and He put on a despised hue and emerged.

8   He entered, a mighty warrior, and put on fear
inside her womb. He entered, Nourisher of all,
and He acquired hunger. He entered, the One who gives drink to
      all,
and He acquired thirst. Stripped and laid bare,
He emerged from [her womb], the One who clothes all.

---

287. This line seems to imply *virginitas in partu;* for a discussion, cf. Beck, Reden, 104. It is more clearly implied at Nat. 12.3.

288. The word is more usually translated "generation," "story," "matter," "subject," or ὑπόστασις. Beck translates "Eigenschaften."

289. Isa. 6.6–7; the implication is that Mary's role is a prophetic one; cf. str. 7, below, and HdF 10.10.

290. Luke 1.46–55.

12

Ephrem continues the kenotic theme and the theme of the transformation of might to lowliness in Mary's womb. Here he adds several new dimensions to these themes. After briefly meditating on the Infant who is older than his mother (str. 1), he turns to the idea of a sealed royal treasure. Here he evokes imagery associated with Jewish Hekhalot mysticism, on the one hand, and with Middle and Neo-Platonism, on the other. Mary's womb is a palace in which the King dwelt (str. 2). Miraculously, while the treasury remained sealed, Christ, the Signet of the King of Kings, the Logos of God, emerged (str. 3). Next, he turns to the natural symbol by which these religious mysteries are revealed to all: the physical evidence of virginity in all women (str. 4). This leads him to the issue of the remaining strophes: the role of the Christian women among his contemporaries who are dedicated to the celibate life (str. 5–11). He argues that the virginity of Mary is continued in these women dedicated to chastity, since Christ is also present in them in a unique way (str. 6). His remarks about "slanderers" seem to indicate the opposition of his rabbinic Jewish contemporaries to the Syrian Christian emphasis on celibacy as well as criticism of the belief in Mary's virginity (str. 7, 9).

12

The same melody.
1 Who indeed has seen the Babe Who is more ancient
   than His bearer? The Ancient One entered
   and became young in her. He emerged an infant
   and grew by her milk. He entered and became small in her;
   He emerged and grew through her—a great wonder!

HYMNS ON THE NATIVITY

Refrain: Glory on Your day to Your hidden sunrise[291] and to the Father Who sent You!

2   Babe in the womb, since the seal[292] of virginity
    abides, the womb was for You
    the royal palace, and the curtain.
    Evidence of virginity upon it, evidence of virginity outside,
    a fetus inside—a great paradox!

3   O to the chest that was empty
    and sealed and, while [it was] secured,
    from within emerged the Great Signet[293]
    of the King of Kings! The witness cries out
    that this gift is not of nature.

4   Womankind possessed the evidence of virginity
    because of You, to affirm that Yours
    was a holy conception. Within the seals
    dwelt Your purity. The seal refutes
    one who falsely claims that Your mother made false pretenses.

5   Within the seal You dwell even now
    within chaste women, and if anyone slanders
    Your brides,[294] the silent seal,
    the curtain, rages out to meet him.
    The seal cries out that our King is there.

6   The seal witnesses to Your brides
    and to the one who bore You. Within the seal
    You were dwelling in Your mother, and in Your chaste women
    [You dwell] within the sign.[295] Your seal will justify

---

291. Or "manifestation," "Epiphany."

292. The Syriac *ḥtm'*, "seal," indicates the wax or molten metal that was stamped with a signet to identify letters and possessions in antiquity. It is the equivalent of the Greek σφράγισμα.

293. The Syriac *ṭb'*, "signet," is the instrument with which the wax or metal is stamped to identify the owner or sender of the material that it seals. It is the equivalent of the Greek σφραγίς. On the use of this imagery by Ephrem, cf. B. Vandenhoff, "Eine unveröffentlichte Abhandlung Ephräms des Syrers Über die Bedrückten und Bedrängten," in *Theologie und Glaube* 4 (1912), 239–41, and Beck, Bildtheologie, esp. 254–58. On its use in early Christian literature in general and its Greco-Roman background, cf. Dölger, Sphragis.

294. Here and especially in strophes 7 and 9 Ephrem seems to indicate contemporary strife on this issue.

295. Although he uses *ṭb'*, Ephrem seems to intend the meaning of "seal" rather than "signet."

134

Your brides as it did Your mother.

7 Since chastity is [so] great that it is unbelievable
among the unclean, the seal and signet
of the King of kings persuades [them] that the pearl[296]
is preserved. Your maidservants acquire
good advocates among the slanderers.

8 If with a seal this treasure-house[297]
was not believed, without a signet
who would be able to believe
that it had not been pillaged? God convinced
[all] people for the sake of His saints.

9 You dwelt in Mary, but the unclean said falsely
that the fetus was not Yours.[298] Since You dwell now
within chaste women, behold they are slandered
as [if they were] pregnant. They slander the pregnant one
and those who are not pregnant—a great atrocity!

10 Your bulwark keeps Your brides
as [it did] Your mother. If there were a thief
who came to steal, by You he would be thwarted
and consumed, and if there were a slanderer
who came to slander, by You he would be silenced.

11 Praise to You [Who] purify your flock
as Your mother, and Your chaste women
as the one who bore You, and Your handmaids
as the one who nursed You. From them and from her
and from all of us glory be to Your name!

---

296. On virginity as the "pearl of great price," cf. Virg 2.4.
297. I.e., Mary.
298. I.e., not divine.

13

Ephrem continues to focus on women, beginning this hymn by invoking the image of the women of Israel singing joyful songs rather than laments (str. 1). Their joyful songs are the expression of their joy at the accomplishments of their offspring—in Ephrem's eyes, not as an end in themselves but as types of the accomplishments of Christ. Beginning with Eve who rejoices in anticipation of her rescue from Sheol by "the Son of her daughter" (str. 2), Ephrem proceeds to a rather vague indication of Sarah's appreciation of Isaac as a type of Christ (str. 3). Isaac's importance as a type of the crucified Christ has already been mentioned in an earlier hymn (Nat. 8.13), but this notion will be extended in this hymn to make Isaac a type of the rule of non-retaliation against wrong inflicted (str. 17).

First Ephrem finds types for Christ's victory over Satan in Samson and Samuel (str. 4–5). But they are not just representatives of victory, they also anticipate the "sweetness" of Christ: Samson in the honeycomb found in the carcase of the lion and Samuel who wept over Saul. Thus they represent Jesus, both divine and human, whose "judgment is powerful" while his "love is sweet" (str. 6–9).

The circumstances and behavior of Christ meet with the expectations neither of a Davidic messiah (str. 10–11) nor of an infant (str. 12–13) nor of a just God (str. 14–15). But, especially in the final strophes (str. 15–17), Ephrem suggests that Christ is "greater than the Law which requires recompense," and that he is the norm by which the leaders of the Old Testament and their religion are to be judged, rather than the reverse.

13

The same melody
1   The Hebrew daughters, who sang
     the laments of Jeremiah instead of the laments
     of their scripture, intoned lullabyes

from their Bible.[299] Hidden power
was prophesied in their words.

Refrain: Praise be to You from all that You have created on this Your feastday!

2 Therefore they answered, "Today let Eve
rejoice in Sheol, for behold the Son of her daughter
as the Medicine of Life[300] came down to save
the mother of His mother—the blessed Babe
Who will crush the head of the serpent that wounded her.[301]

3 Your type looks out from the youth
of the fair Isaac. At You looked
Sarah who saw that Your mysteries dwelt
upon his childishness: "O son of my vows
in whom is hidden the Lord of my vows!"

4 The Nazirite, Samson, gazed at the type
of Your courage. He tore the lion apart,
the likeness of death.[302] You ripped [death] asunder
and made the sweet life[303] emerge
from its bitterness for human beings.

5 Anna, moreover, in You embraced
Samuel also, for Your justice
was hidden in him who tore Hagag apart[304]
as [You did] the Evil One. He wept over Saul,[305]
for Your goodness was also portrayed in him.

6 How humble You are! How powerful You are!
O Infant, Your judgment is powerful!
Your love is sweet! Who is able
to stand against You? Your Father [is] in heaven
and Your mother on earth. Who is able to speak about You?

---

299. "Scripture" and "Bible" here translate Ephrem's *spr'* and *ktb'*, both in the plural. They
do not appear to be distinguished for any technical reason but simply for the sake of variety; cf.
Beck, Bildtheologie, 252.

300. Cf. Ign. Eph. 20.2.

301. Gen. 3.15. On the punishment of the serpent, cf. Kronholm, Motifs, 112–18, also
Nat. 17.6, 21.15, 22.31, 26.8 and 28.5.

302. Judg. 14.6. Perhaps the spirit of Samson's riddles, Judg. 14.14 and 18, Ephrem
engages in word play here with *dwmy' dmwt'*, "the likeness of death."

303. Another play on words: *ḥy' ḥly'*, "sweet life."

304. 1 Sam. 15.32f.

305. 1 Sam. 15.35.

7   If anyone seeks Your hidden nature
    behold it is in heaven in the great womb
    of Divinity.[306] And if anyone seeks
    Your revealed body, behold it rests and looks out
    from the small womb of Mary!

8   The mind wanders among your attributes,[307]
    O Rich One! Copious inner chambers
    are in Your godhead, contemptible appearances
    in Your humanity. Who will measure You,
    Great Sea Who made Himself small?

9   We came to see You as God.
    Behold! You are a human being. We came to see You
    as a human being—the banner of Your godhead
    shines forth! Who can bear
    Your transformations, O True One?

10 We came to see the way of life that was Your lot
    from the House of David. From [among] his beds
    You inherited a manger.[308] From [among] his palaces
    a cave was Your lot.[309] Instead of his chariot
    the despised ass now is Your lot.[310]

11 Who would believe that You have inherited
    the throne of David? We go away to scorn,
    to disregard You. Heaven cries out
    and the earth below. After we have scorned
    we bow before You, the Hidden Power!

12 How bold You are, Babe, Who bestows Himself
    upon all. At everyone who meets You

---

306. For an important precedent for Ephrem's graphic use of feminine language for God, cf. Odes of Solomon 19.

307. Here and in the following strophe Ephrem considers the "transformations" undertaken by the immutable Deity for the sake of self-revelation to finite creatures. Cf. Virg 28.11. For a discussion of the theological importance of this idea, cf. de Halleux, Mar Ephrem, 45–47.

308. Luke 2.7.

309. The cave does not appear in the canonical infancy narratives, but it is mentioned in non-canonical and Patristic literature, cf. Prot. 18–21, Just. dial. 78, Or. c. Cels. 1.51. By the fourth century it was a pilgrimage site, and a Constantinian basilica was constructed there. For further discussion of the site, cf. Wilkinson, Pilgrims, 151f. and H. Chadwick, *Origen's Contra Celsum*, (Cambridge, England, 1965), 47, n.5. The tradition of the cave was well-established in the Byzantine iconographic tradition of the Nativity; cf. Ouspensky, Icons, 157–59.

310. Matt. 21.5 et par. Ephrem may also have Zech. 9.9f. in mind since there the Messiah brings peace and banishes chariots along with other instruments of warfare.

You smile. To meet everyone who sees You
You eagerly wait. It is as if Your love
hungers for human beings.[311]

13 You distinguish not Your parents
from strangers, nor the one who bore You
from maidservants, nor the one who nursed You
from harlots. Is this Your boldness[312]
or Your love, all-merciful One?

14 What moves You to bestow Yourself
upon each who has seen You—upon the rich
and upon the poor? With them You take shelter[313]
without their invoking You. From where did it come to You
so to hunger for human beings?

15 What is Your love that if anyone rebuke [You],
You are not angry, and if one cry out,
You are not terrified, and if one scolds You
You are not gloomy? Are You indeed greater
than the Law that requires recompense?

16 Meek was Moses, yet harsh was his zeal,
for he struck and killed.[314] Elijah also,
who revived the youth, let the mob of boys
be torn apart by the bears.[315] Who are You, youth,
that Your love is greater than [the love] of the prophets?

17 That son of Hagar who was a wild ass,
kicked Isaac. He endured and was silent,
but his mother was jealous.[316] Are You his symbol
or is he Your type? Do you resemble Isaac,
or, indeed, does he resemble You?

---

311. Literally, "Your love resembles [a love] that hungers."
312. "Boldness" or perhaps better "impulsiveness," *ḥwsp'* is here opposed to "love," *ḥwb'*. Further on this theme, cf. Nat. 14.1, where Ephrem assumes that "boldness" is inappropriate to royalty as well as to divinity.
313. The same word means "to represent as a type," a denominative verb from *twps'*.
314. Num. 12.3 and Exod. 2.11f.
315. 2 Kgs 4.18–37 and 2 Kgs 2.23–25.
316. Gen. 16.12 (Pes.); cf. HdF 79.3; and Gen. 31.9.

14

In this hymn Ephrem picks up the question he posed in the previous hymn and answers it from a different perspective. The question is, "Ho *v* can this infant be son of David or Son of God?" (Nat. 13.10–15) Ephrem begins his answer with the idyllic image of the royal child at rest in his mother's lap (str. 1). This child is son of Mary and son of David (str. 1), yet he is also son of the "chaste one" and Son of the Hidden One (str. 2). He brings to humankind rest, peace and joy, for he is Philanthropos—a virtue appropriate to kings as well as to God (str. 1–6).

To elaborate the point that Jesus is truly son of David, Ephrem comments on David's dance and Michal's criticism of it (2 Sam. 6; str. 7–9. David anticipates Jesus' triumphal entry into Jerusalem, while Michal anticipates both the Jewish rejection of Jesus as son of David, i.e., as royal messiah, and the contemporary critics of Christianity (str. 8, 10).

In the remaining strophes Ephrem argues first that the Jewish skepticism of Mary's virginity and of the virginity of the "daughters of the covenant" is not unexpected. The Mosaic laws concerning the testing of accusations of female unchastity show this to be true (str. 11–15). Second, he argues that chastity was the source of superhuman power exercised by Elijah, Elisha and Moses (str. 16–19). Unlike Zipporah, who was chaste despite her pagan parentage, "the daughter of Abraham," i.e., the Israelites, went whoring with the golden calf (str. 19).

Ephrem's argument in the second half of this hymn is an interesting variant on the usual Patristic approach to the Old Testament. It is fairly predictable that a fourth-century Christian writer would divide the *dramatis personae* of the Old Testament into positive and negative characters and interpret the positive figures as antecedents of the Christians while negative figures are seen as the forerunners of the Jews.[317] What is different here is the principle of choosing the positive models; the figures chosen from the Old Testament narrative are not unexpected—Elijah, Elisha and Moses. But the understanding of their importance is unex-

---

317. For discussion of this approach, cf. Ruether, Fratricide, esp. 117–82.

pected; they are presented as the equivalent of neo-Platonic holy men, the *theioi andres* of the Old Testament.[318]

14

The same melody

1 Come rest and be quiet in the lap[319] of Your mother,
  Son of the Honorable One.[320] Boldness is not fitting
  for the sons of kings. You are son of David,
  that honorable one, and son of Mary,
  who keeps her beauty in the inner chamber.

  Refrain: Praise be to You Who on this day delight all.[321]

2 Who resembles the cheerful Babe,
  the fair Child, Whose mother is chaste,
  and His Father [is] the Hidden One Whom not even the Seraphim
  are able to see?[322] Whom do You resemble?
  Tell us, Son of the Compassionate One.

3 You delighted in the angry who came
  to gaze at You. They mingled their laughter
  with one another's. The wrathful were made sweet

---

318. For the definition of the term θεῖος ἀνήρ and for a treatment of its growing significance for Christians in Late Antiquity, cf. L. Bieler, *θεῖος ἀνήρ: Das Bild des "Göttlichen Menschen" in Spätantike und Frühchristentum* (Wien, 1935; rep. Darmstadt, 1967); P. Brown, "The Rise and Function of the Holy Man in Late Antiquity," JRS 61 (1971), 80–101; D. L. Tiede, *The Charismatic Figure as Miracle Worker*, SBL Diss. ser. 1, (Missoula, Montana, 1972). P. Cox, *Biographies in Late Antiquity* (Berkeley, 1985); G. P. Corrington, *The "Divine Man": His Origin and Function in Hellenistic Popular Religion*, American University Studies, ser. 7, Theology and Religion 17 (New York, 1986), with an overview of the literature, 1–58, reviewed by Tiede in CBQ 49 (1987), 497–99. For a similar phenomenon in rabbinic Judaism, cf. Neusner, HJB II, 236–40 et passim.

319. Or "bosom" or "womb." The Syriac is *'wb'*.

320. I.e., Son of God, cf. str. 2; or within the context of this strophe, simply son of David. One suspects that Ephrem enjoys the ambiguity.

321. Or "offer the Passover for all." Despite the unseasonableness of such a reference in a nativity hymn, the ambiguity here may be deliberate on Ephrem's part since this hymn emphasizes the sweetness and alleviation of anger brought by Christ.

322. SdF 1.43.; Beck, Reden, 52. Simply put, since Mary is chaste, the Father of Jesus is God.

by You, Pleasant One. Who are You, O Youth,
that even the bitter are sweetened by You?

4 Who has seen a babe who eagerly awaits
those who approach? From the bosom
He reaches out toward those far away.
A fitting sight: The Babe Who muses
entirely on everyone that they may gaze at Him.

5 One who came to see you with a worry—
his worry fled, and one who was brooding
in You forgot his brooding. In You the hungry one forgot
even his food. And the one who had been sent out
by You was enticed to forget his way.

6 You Yourself are at rest, but have released humankind[323]
to their affairs. You are a son of the poor;
know what is the spirit[324] of each of the poor
who ceased to work and came. Lover of humankind,[325]
You have enveloped humankind in Your joy.

7 David the king, that honorable one,
took branches, and on a feastday,
dancing among the children,
he gave glory.[326] Is it not the love
of David Your father glowing in You?

8 In that daughter of Saul the demon of her father
spoke.[327] She called dissolute
that honorable one who gave an example
to the elders of the people to take branches
with the children on the day of Your praise.[328]

9 Who will not fear to reproach You
with rashness? For behold, because Saul's daughter
vomited forth evil, her womb was deprived[329]

---

323. Ephrem uses alliteration here: *šly npš' wšry 'nš'*.
324. "Spirit" here translates *npš'*, which usually means life principle or soul rather than an attitude. Although it is unattested in this sense, it seems appropriate here. (Beck declines to translate it.)
325. The Syriac *rḥm 'nš'* seems to be the equivalent of Greek φιλάνθρωπος.
326. 2 Sam. 6.5, 14.
327. 2 Sam 6.16–22, 1 Sam 18.10f.
328. Mark 11.1–11 et par.
329. The Syriac involves a pun: *gst* "she vomited" and *gzt* "it was deprived."

of childbearing. Since her mouth mocked,
the wage of her mouth was her barrenness.[330]

10   Let mouths shrink in fear from blaspheming You,
lest they be stopped up. Daughter of Sion,
hold your tongue about that Son of David
Who surpasses you in glory. Be not
like the daughter of Saul whose family history is complete.[331]

11   God saw how much the unclean people,[332]
whoring and envious,
were slanderous, but He had pity
upon women. For our sake
He increased His strategems[333] among the slanderers.

12   If her spouse should hate her,
he was to write to dismiss her,[334] and if he were jealous,
they tested her [with] water,[335] and if he slandered her
[her father] presented the cloth.[336] All slander
was frustrated in the presence of Mary, who was sealed.

13   Moses had already exposed
how slanderous they were, for although cloths
of virgins are possessed by their families,
they have accused them and killed them.
How much more they slandered the mother of the Son!

14   By water ordeals and by cloths
He taught them, so that when the Lord of conceptions
came to them, and they slandered that womb
in which He dwelt, pure evidence of virginity
concerning her conception would convince us about it.

15   If, therefore, the evidence of virginity made public
would save the wife of a man
from the sword, O wise women,

---

330. Cf. 2 Sam. 6.23.

331. Or, more innocuously, "whose story is completed;" cf. Beck, "deren Erzählung in Erfüllung ging."

332. The Jewish people in the Old Testament.

333. *pwrs'* from Greek πόρος; i.e., the tests for adultery were God's way of protecting innocent women against false witness.

334. Deut. 24.1–4.

335. Num. 5.11–30.

336. Deut. 22.13–19, which mentions both parents, but here the verb is masculine singular.

preserve it and be preserved by it. It is weapon that,
turns around and does battle with its master, if he is guilty.[337]

16 Since Elijah repressed
    the desire of his body, he could withhold the rain
    from the adulterers.[338] Since he restrained his body,
    he could restrain the dew from the whoremongers
    who released and sent forth their streams.

17 Since the hidden fire, bodily desire,
    did not prevail in him, the fire of the high place
    obeyed him,[339] and since on earth he conquered
    fleshly desire, he went up to [the place] where
    holiness dwells and is at peace.[340]

18 Elisha, too, who killed his body,
    revived the dead.[341] That which is by nature
    mortal, gains life by chastity,
    which is beyond nature. He revived the boy
    since he refined himself like a [newly] weaned [infant].

19 Moses, who divided and separated himself
    from his wife,[342] divided the sea
    before the harlot.[343] Zipporah maintained
    chastity, although she was the daughter of [pagan] priests;[344]
    with a calf the daughter of Abraham went whoring.[345]

---

337. Deut. 22.19.
338. 1 Kgs. 17–18, esp. 17.1
339. 2 Kgs 2.1–11. For holy high place *rwm'*; cf. 1 Kgs 18.38 and 2 Kgs 1.10.
340. The ambiguity of the Syriac *qdyšwt'* ("holiness" or "chastity") better suits the context.
341. 2 Kgs. 4.32–38.
342. Ephrem thinks that the dismissal of Zipporah (Exod. 18.2) was for the sake of chastity and that it was provoked by the angel's visitation in Exod. 4.24–26; cf. Pr. Ref. II.75, 35–45.
343. Israel.
344. Pagan priests, *kwmr'*.
345. Exod. 32.

15

Ephrem places this hymn in the mouth of Mary and at the moment of the offerings of the Magi (str. 4). In it he stresses four themes, all of which contribute to a portrayal of Mary and her role in prophetic terms. At the same time he toys with the language and imagery of fertility religion (str. 1), arguing, in effect, that the new message of Christianity is the reinterpretation of fertility in allegorical and spiritual terms (str. 5–6). First, Mary is the instrument of Christ's will in his role as Logos or Son of God (str. 1, 4–5). Second, God chose poor people rather than the rich for his revelation (str. 2–3). Third, Mary is the lyre, the mouthpiece of Christ. Despite slander and oppression she sings a new song (str. 5–7). She will be vindicated as Tamar was (str. 8). Finally, David prophesied the visit of the Magi in his psalms, which must all be interpreted Christologically (str. 9–10).

15

The same melody
1   "With You I shall begin, and I trust
that with You I shall end. I shall open my mouth,
and You fill my mouth.[346] I am for You the earth
and You are the farmer. Sow in me Your voice,[347]
You who are the sower of Himself in His mother's womb.

---

346. Ps. 81.10, where the filling of the mouth is with food; here, it is with the prophetic word. Cf. HdF 10.1.

347. Up to this point, Ephrem has combined the language of fertility religion with prophetic language. Despite the fact that "voice" (Syriac *ql'*) is not the equivalent of Word (λόγος, Syriac *mlt'*), this phrase seems to suggest divine impregnation of Mary as yet another level of meaning for the entire strophe. The final line shows that this is Ephrem's intent. On the use of fertility language in an ascetic context, cf. Beck, Mariologie, 31; also Nat. 17.6, 21.16–18, 26.8, Virg 24.11, 52.1f., and Kronholm, Motifs, 218, 223.

HYMNS ON THE NATIVITY

Refrain: Glory be to You, my Lord, and through You to the Father, on the day of Your nativity.

2   "All the chaste daughters of the Hebrews
and virgin daughters of rulers
are amazed at me. Because of You, a daughter of the poor
is envied. Because of You, a daughter of the weak
is an object of jealousy. Who gave You to me?

3   "Son of the Rich One, Who despised the womb
of rich women, what drew You
toward the poor? For Joseph is needy,
and I am impoverished. Your merchants
brought[348] gold to a house of the poor."

4   She saw the Magi;[349] her songs increased
at their offerings: "Behold Your worshippers
surround me, and their[350] offerings
encircle me. Blessed be the Babe
Who made His mother the lyre of His melodies.

5   "And since the lyre looks toward its master,
my mouth looks toward You. Let Your will arouse
Your mother's tongue.[351] Since I have learned by You
a new way of conceiving, let my mouth learn by You
a new [way of] giving birth to new glory.

6   "If difficult things for You are not difficult
but easy, so that the womb conceived You
without intercourse, and without seed
the womb gave birth to you, it is easy for the mouth
to be fruitful and to multiply[352] Your great glory.

7   "Behold, I am slandered and oppressed,
but I rejoice. My ears are full
of scorn and disdain, but it is a small matter to me
how much I shall endure, for a single [word of] consolation from
      You

---

348. Literally, "carried and brought."
349. Matt. 2.1–12.
350. Although Beck's text reads "Your," it is apparently in error since he translates "their" offerings, which makes more sense.
351. Cf. HdF 25.1–3.
352. Cf. Gen. 1.22, 28.

is able to chase away myriads of griefs.

8 "Since I am not despised by You, my Son,
I am confident. I who am slandered
have conceived and given birth to the True Judge
Who will vindicate me. For if Tamar
was acquitted by Judah,[353] how much more will I be acquitted by
        You!

9 "David, Your father, sang a psalm to You
before You came, that to You would be offered
gold of Sheba.[354] The psalm
that he merely sang [now] in reality
heaps before You myrrh and gold.

10 "The hundred and fifty psalms he sang
were flavored by You since all the words
of prophecy are in need
of Your seasoning. For without Your salt
all wisdom would lose its savor."

---

353. Gen. 38.26.
354. Ps. 72.15.

147

16

In this hymn, presented as Mary's song to her infant, Ephrem has crafted a theological treatise on the nature of God's presence in Mary and the manner in which that instance of God's presence in the world is related to other manifestations of God in the world. The first strophes concern the ways in which Christ is present in the world other than His presence in Mary's womb: in the lives of Christians (str. 1), ruling the world as Logos and Son of God (str. 2–3), in the eucharistic bread and wine as well as in the human mind (str. 4–7).

Recapitulating Mary's multiple roles with respect to Jesus (str. 9; cf. Nat. 11.2–4 and 16.1), Ephrem adds one more: Along with all other Christians, Mary is Jesus' daughter, brought forth by him in blood and water at baptism (str. 8–11). Again, like all Christians, in baptism Mary put on the "glory" of Christ, the glorious body that had been lost at the Fall. Conversely, in the incarnation, Christ put on the garment of the body made for him by his mother (str. 11). Through the paradox that the mother of Jesus is also his daughter, Ephrem has led us back once more to the mysteries of the incarnation and the virginity of Mary.

In the final strophes Ephrem uses imagery drawn from the Jewish priestly cult to describe Mary's role. The virginity of Mary and of all the "daughters of the covenant" is the vestment of the High Priest, who is Christ (str. 13). Like the Ark of the Covenant, Mary is honored not for herself but for the divine presence within her (str. 16). She is also the Tablets containing the teachings of the Mosaic Law (str. 17). To grasp the significance for Ephrem of these metaphors one must remember that in Syriac "virginity" (*btwlwt'*) is synonymous with "chastity" (*qdyšwt'*), which also means "holiness." Behind the coincidence in meanings between "chastity" and "holiness" is ultimately a notion of mysterious power, untouchable sacral presence. Mary as the virgin *par excellence* is uniquely suited to be the holy one in whom—or almost the holy place in which—God deigns to be present.

16

The same melody

1 "I shall not be jealous, my Son, that You are both with me
and with everyone. Be God
to the one who confesses You, and be Lord
to the one who serves You, and be brother
to the one who loves You so that You might save all.

2 "While You dwelt in me, [both] in me and outside of me
Your majesty dwelt. While I gave birth to You
openly, Your hidden power
was not removed from me. You are within me,
and You are outside of me, O Mystifier of His mother.

3 "When I see Your outward image
before my eyes, Your hidden image
is portrayed in my mind.[355] In Your revealed image
I saw Adam, but in the hidden one
I saw Your Father who is united[356] with You.

4 Have You shown your beauty in two images
to me alone? Let bread and the mind
portray You.[357] Dwell in bread
and in those who eat it. In hidden and revealed [form]
let your church see You as [does] the one who bore You.

5 "Whoever hates Your bread is like that one
who hates Your body. A distant one
who loves Your bread [is like] a near one
who cherishes Your image. In bread and body
the former and the latter have seen You.

6 Indeed, Child, Your bread is far more honorable
than Your body. For even the unbelievers[358]

---

355. The hidden image is of the divine nature; it is the *imago dei*. The outward, revealed, image is the human nature, as the following lines show. Ephrem's distinction between inner (or hidden) and outward (or revealed) knowledge is reminiscent of the ἐπιστημονικὸς λόγος and δοξαστικὸς λόγος of Middle Platonic epistemology; cf. Dillon, Platonism, 273f.

356. Literally, "mixed" (Syriac *mzg*); Ephrem's language would be problematic for post-Chalcedonian Christology.

357. A second dimension is added to the ways of knowing God; for believers after the time of the incarnation the Eucharist and the mind become the outward and inner ways.

358. Or "doubters," a term Ephrem often applies to the Jews, but here it would seem to include any of Jesus' contemporaries who did not join his following. Rather than referring to the

saw Your body, but they do not see
Your living bread. The distant ones rejoiced;
their portion surpassed that of the near ones.

7   "Behold Your image is portrayed with the blood of the grapes
upon the bread[359] and portrayed upon the heart
by the finger of love with the pigments
of faith. Blessed is He Who made
graven images pass away by His true image.

8   "You are not [merely] a human being that in an ordinary way
I should sing You a lullabye. For Your conception is a new thing,
and Your birth is a miracle. Without the Spirit
who could sing to You? A new utterance
of prophecy seethes in me.

9   What can I call You, a stranger to us,
Who was from us? Shall I call You Son?
Shall I call You Brother? Shall I call You Bridegroom?
Shall I call you Lord, O [You] Who brought forth His mother
[in] another birth out of the water?[360]

10   "For I am [Your] sister from the House of David,
who is a second father.[361] Again, I am mother
because of Your conception, and bride am I
because of your chastity. Handmaiden and daughter
of blood and water [am I] whom You redeemed and baptized.[362]

11   "Son of the Most High Who came and dwelt in me,
[in] another birth, He bore me also
[in] a second birth. I put on the glory of Him
Who put on the body, the garment of His mother.

12   Amnon disgraced[363] Tamar who was
from the House of David, and virginity

---

disciplina arcana as Beck suggests, Ephrem alludes to those who saw Jesus in the flesh but did not believe.

359. Dölger, AC 5 (1936), 275ff.; and cf. CH 35.1.

360. Although *mwld*, here translated "Who brought forth," is used of men as well as women, the immediate context is more appropriate to birth than to begetting. On Jesus as mother in Greek and Latin Patristic literature, cf. Bradley, Background.

361. David is second after God the Father (or Joseph?) rather than after Jesus; cf. Nat. 6.1–2.

362. Despite Ephrem's emphasis on Mary's role as second Eve, here he makes it clear that she is redeemed along with all humankind by Christ; cf. Beck, Mariologie, 28.

363. The *pael* perfect rather that *p'al* participle (as it is pointed in Beck's text) is necessary for the sense of the passage. 2 Sam. 13.1–22.

fell and perished from the house of both of them.[364]

My pearl, placed in Your treasury,

has not perished, for You have put it on.[365]

13 "May all evidences of virginity of Your brides

be preserved by You. They are the purple [robes]

and no one may touch them

except our King. For virginity

is like a vestment[366] for You, the High Priest.[367]

14 "Tamar reeked of the smell of her father-in-law,

for she had stolen perfumes.[368] Not even the slightest scent

of Joseph wafted from the garments of his bride.

For the Balsam that I conceived, Your conception, became for me

a wall of fire, O Son of the Holy One."

15 The blossom lost its scent, for the fragrance of the Glorious Lily

was strong. The Treasure of Perfumes

had no need of the flower

or of its fragrances.[369] The flesh stayed away,

for it saw in the womb the conception of the Spirit.

16 Woman serves in the presence of man,

who is her head.[370] Joseph rose

to serve in the presence of his Lord

Who was within Mary. The priest serves

in the presence of Your Ark[371] because of Your holiness.

---

364. Or, with Beck, this could be translated "from between both of them." Since both Amnon and Tamar were from the house of David, the present translation seems preferable.

365. The pearl is Mary's virginity (cf. Virg 2.4–5, 2.10, 3.12), but virginity is also the vestment of the High Priest (cf. str. 13 below and note ad loc.) and the body is a garment (Nat. 4.187–88 and note ad loc.). Thus Jesus "puts on" the pearl (virginity) of Mary—and it is his body. Ephrem's metaphor's are mixed, but deliberately!

366. The same word *šwšp'* is used for the cloth that constituted proof of a bride's virginity; cf. Nat. 14.12.

367. Ephrem uses *kwmr'* rather than *khn'*, following the usage of the epistle to the Hebrews rather than Leviticus. Like the author of the epistle, Ephrem stresses a priestly heritage extrinsic to the Mosaic covenent; cf. Hb. 5.1, 7.1ff.

368. Cf. Gen. 38.1–30. The imagery in this and the following strophes is loosely related to the Song of Songs, esp. 1.3, 1.12–2.3.

369. The Syriac is alliterative: *pqḥ' pkh hw'* . . . *šwšn šwbḥ'* . . . *symt bsm'*. The presence of Christ (the Glorious Lily and the Treasure of Perfumes) in Mary's womb made sexual intercourse with Joseph (the flower) superfluous, as Ephrem states more directly in the following line.

370. 1 Cor. 11.3.

371. Jesus is not only the presence of God (Emmanuel—God with us) and thus prefigured as the presence within the Ark, but he is also the Word of God (λόγος), hence prefigured by the scripture contained within the Ark; Mary is the Ark; cf. Nat. 4.113 and 12.3.

17 Moses bore the tablet of stone
that His Lord had written. And Joseph escorted
the pure tablet in whom was dwelling
the Son of the Creator. The tablets were left behind
since the world was filled with Your teaching.[372]

---

372. Cf. Exod. 32.15; here, too, the understanding of Jesus as λογος, Word of God,
provides the connection with "God's writing" on the tablets. During her pregnancy Mary is,
then, the tablet. The tablets of the Mosaic Law are rendered superfluous by the teaching of
Christ.

17

This hymn begins with an ascension motif. Like many of the supposed authors of Jewish and Christian apocalyptic literature, Mary is transported into the air to receive a revelation. The divine person of Christ in the form of a great bird is not only bearer and revealer but also the subject of the revelation. The content of the revelation to Mary is the cosmic role of Christ: "He promised me, 'the height and the depth will be your Son's.' " (str. 1). Mary names a series of others who recognized the dignity of Christ: Gabriel, Simeon, Herod and Satan (str. 2–3). These are drawn from the canonical infancy narratives.

By providing the body of Christ, Mary, the new Eve, has provided for all the garment of glory, the resurrection body (str. 4). The life of consecrated virginity is the means by which the new creation continues to transform the world. In contrast to Eve, especially, the woman consecrated to virginity is the dwelling place of God. (str. 5–6). Yet all, male and female, slave and free, clean and unclean, are encouraged to take up the yoke of virginity (str. 8–11).

Christ is "the Son of the Creator Who came to renew the whole creation" (str. 11.4–5). This renewal has both cosmic and human dimensions (str. 12–14). In an anti-Marcionite vein, Ephrem argues that Jesus' healings and his bringing the dead back to life prove that he is the Son of the Creator and himself the Creator as well. Jesus' love for the human body is shown by his healings. They demonstrate that Jesus is not, as Marcion would have it, son of a Strange God, but he is Son of the just Lord of the Universe (str. 15–18).

17

The same melody
1   "The Babe that I carry has carried me,"
     said Mary. "He bent down His pinions

153

and took and put me between His wings
and soared into the air. He promised me,
'the height and the depth will be your Son's.' "[373]

Refrain: Praise to You, Son of the Creator, Who loves all!

2   "I saw Gabriel who called him Lord
and the High Priest, the aged servant[374]
who solemnly carried him. I saw the Magi
bowing down and Herod
dismayed that the King had come.

3   "Satan, too, who drowned boys
so that Moses would perish, kills boys [now]
so that the Living One will die. I shall flee to Egypt[375]
since [Satan] has come to Judah, so that he will become weary and
confused—
he who seeks to hunt his Hunter.

4   "In her virginity Eve put on
leaves of shame.[376] Your mother put on,
in her virginity, the garment of glory
that suffices for all. I gave
the small mantle[377] of the body to the One who covers all.

5   "Blessed is the woman in whose heart
and mind You are. She is the King's castle[378]

---

373. A similar motif occurs in *The Apocalypse of Abraham* 15. After Abraham and an angel have been carried up to the presence of God on the wings of a pigeon and a turtledove, respectively, Abraham joins in an angelic song of praise to God; cf. *The Apocalypse of Abraham*, ed. and trans. by G. H. Box, SPCK (London, 1918). I am grateful to Martha Himmelfarb for pointing out this parallel. The representation of Christ as a bird also has some parallels in early Christian literature. In Matt. 23.37 Jesus compares himself to a mother hen. Various Greek and Latin Patristic writers saw the mother hen as a particularly appropriate image for Christ as the Divine Wisdom; cf. Bradley, Background, esp. 103–108. Beck comments briefly on this passage in Beck, Mariologie, 25.

374. Simeon; cf. Luke 2.25–35.

375. Matt. 2.13–18; in Ephrem's version, Mary rather than Joseph seems to be the initiator of the flight. Ephrem explicitly draws the parallel implied by Matthew's account; cf. Exodus 1.22.

376. Cf. HdP 2.7 and 6.9, Virg 35.2.

377. The word *prys'* is rich in meanings. In addition to any small covering, mantle or rug, it may mean the breastplate of the high priest, the veil of the Temple, or (as a feminine) the flat wafer of the Eucharist (Margoliouth 460b). Further, cf. Beck, Mariologie, 30.

378. The Syriac is *byrt'*, not *hykl'*.

for[379] You, the King's Son, and the Holy of Holies
for You, the High Priest. She has neither the anxiety
nor the toil of a household and husband.[380]

6   "On the other hand, Eve became a cave and grave
for the accursed serpent, for his evil counsel
entered and dwelt in her; she who became dust
became bread for him.[381] [But] You are our bread,
and You are our bridal chamber and the robe of our glory.

7   "If she who is chaste[382] is afraid,
behold the guard [of her chastity]. If she [commits] a wrong,
behold its pardoner. If she has a demon,
behold its pursuer. And [for] those who have pains,
behold the binder of their wounds.

8   "Whoever[383] has a body, let him come to be
a brother to my Beloved. Whoever has a daughter
or kinswoman, let her come to be
the bride of my Honorable One. And whoever has a slave,
let him release him to come to serve his Lord.

9   "My Son, one is the wage of the free-born man
who has taken up Your yoke. But the slave who has borne
the double yoke of two lords,
of the One above and one below, receives two blessings
and the two wages of the two burdens.

10 "My Son, the free-born woman is also Your handmaiden
if she serves You, and the enslaved woman
in You is a freewoman. By You she is consoled
that she is a freed woman. Invisible emancipation
is placed in her bosom if she loves You.

11 "O chaste woman, eagerly await my Beloved
so that He may dwell in you, and unclean women, too,

---

379. Or "by You."
380. The freedom of the virgin—male or female—from the anxieties of the householder is a common theme is early Christian ascetic literature. Although the authority of 1 Cor. 7.32–35 is often invoked, the catalogue of woes owes much to pagan literature, e.g., Tert. exh. ad. cast. 12; Greg. Nyss. de virg. 3; John Chrys., de virg. 14.6, 56.1.
381. The serpent is condemned to crawl on his belly and eat dust, cf. Gen. 3.14.
382. Literally, "who has chastity."
383. In this strophe the hypothetical person having a son or daughter is addressed as female, whereas the hypothetical slaveowner is addressed as male.

so that He may purify you; churches, too,
so that He may adorn you. He is the Son of the Creator
Who came to restore the whole creation.

12   "He renewed the sky since fools worshipped
all the luminaries. He renewed the earth
that had grown old because of Adam. A new creation[384]
came to be by His spittle,[385] and the All-sufficient
set straight bodies and minds.

13   "Come, you blind, and without money[386]
receive sight. Come, you lame,
receive your feet. You mute and deaf,
receive your voices. And let those with maimed hands[387]
receive [whole] hands.

14   "The Son of the Creator is He Whose treasures are full
of all benefits. Let the one
who needs eyes come to Him.
He will make clay and transform it.
He will make flesh. He will enlighten eyes.

15   "With a little clay He showed that by His hand
our dust was formed.[388] The soul of the dead man
also witnessed that the human soul
was breathed in by Him.[389] By the latter witnesses
it is verified that He is the Son of the First One.

16   "Gather, you lepers, and without effort
receive your purification. For He does not need
as Elisha [did] to have [you] plunge in
seven times.[390] Nor again will He weary [you]

---

384. The Syriac word, *ghylt'* from the root *gbl* "to form, to shape" suggests the image of a potter. The image and the word itself (*gbl*) appear in str. 14 and 15.

385. I.e., by his miracles of healing, cf. John 9.6.

386. I.e., without paying a doctor or healer.

387. The Syriac has a singular here, plural in the following line.

388. Ephrem interprets John 9.6 in relation to Gen. 2.7; the healing shows that Christ is the same One Who created the first human being; cf. also Job 4.19, 10.9. Although Ephrem's interpretation of this detail in the Johannine pericope is not supported by modern scholars, the same idea was elaborated with the same anti-Marcionite polemical intent by Irenaeus in Adv. Haer. V.15.2; cf. Brown, Gospel According to John, I, 369–82, esp. 372.

389. John 11 is here interpreted in the light of Gen. 2.7. On the Creator breathing life into Adam, cf. Kronholm, Motifs, 216.

390. 2 Kgs. 5.10.

as the priests did with their sprinklings.[391]

17   "The seven of Elisha in a symbol cleansed
the seven spirits,[392] and hyssop and blood
are a great type:[393] There is no place
for strangeness; the Son of the Lord of the universe
is not estranged from the Lord of the universe.[394]

18   "For if the Just One makes the body leprous,
and You purify [it], [then] the One Who formed the body
hates the body and You love it!
But You formed it! The pledges[395] that you have cast
upon it cry out that You are the Son of the Creator.

---

391. Lev. 1.1–32. Here the Syriac word for priest is *khn'*.

392. The seven washings prescribed by Elisha typologically represent the seven evil spirits cast out from Mary Magdalene; cf. Luke 8.2 and Mark 16.9. Or the reference may be to the seven evil spirits who replace one in the parable, cf. Matt. 12.45, Luke 11.26.

393. The priestly remedies, cf. Lev. 14.4–7, are also antetypes of Christ the High Priest.

394. Here and in the final strophe Ephrem makes an explicitly anti-Marcionite polemic: the Father of Jesus is not a Stranger God but is the Creator of the universe.

395. I.e., the healings, as Beck suggests.

18

Ephrem begins this hymn by invoking the association of the birth of Jesus with the reign of Caesar Augustus. This association has its basis in Luke 2.1–3, but for Luke it probably had an apologetic significance that was also appreciated by Ephrem.[396] The reign of Augustus was seen as a peaceful Golden Age, and Christians were quick to appropriate the imagery as the cornerstone of their apologetic historiography: Good emperors, beginning with Augustus, favor Christianity, while the bad rulers persecute it.[397] Ephrem gives Luke's theme his characteristic typological twist: Augustus is a type of the real King who is Christ (str. 1–3).

The bulk of the hymn is a recounting in thirty-one strophes the thirty years of Jesus' life. Each strophe calls upon an element in the creation to give thanks for the incarnation. Ephrem's principle in choosing the participants in the hymn of praise is somewhat obscure. Only two years have associations from the presumed chronology of Jesus' life: the twelfth year associated with the Temple, and the thirtieth year associated with the dead. For the rest, Ephrem begins with three groups of angels: Cherubim, Seraphim and "the house of Michael." He proceeds to major elements in the cosmos: the sky, sun, air, dew, all creation, the earth, Mt. Sinai[!] and the sea. Then there are major New Testament images for Christ: the Lamb and the Vine; images common in parables: leaven and salt; and Old Testament antetypes of Jesus: Isaac, Moses and Job[!]. Other imagery is drawn from the court of law: lawyers and judges; or is representative of various forms of power: diadems, wealth, armor and swords, and mighty men. In every case Ephrem plays on a paradoxical correspondence between the person or thing in question and the actions of Jesus in the incarnation. The power or vastness of the creature is contrasted with a carefully chosen instance of the *kenosis* of the Son of the Creator.

---

396. For a discussion and further bibliography, cf. Brown, Messiah, 412–18, esp. 415f., 547–56.

397. T. D. Barnes, "Legislation against the Christians," JRS 58 (1968), 32–50, esp. 32–35.

18

The same melody

1 In the years of that king, who is called
"Radiance,"[398] our Lord shone forth
among the Hebrews, and "Radiance" and "Dawn"[399]
came to rule: a king on earth
and the Son on high. Blessed be His power!

Refrain: To You be praise Whose on this feast bestowed gladness upon all [people].[400]

2 In the days of the king who enrolled people
for the poll tax,[401] our Savior descended
and enrolled people in the Book of Life.[402]
He enrolled [them], and they enrolled Him. On high He enrolled
     us;
on earth they enrolled Him. Glory to His name!

3 His birth [was] in the days of the king
whose name is "Radiance." The symbol and the truth[403]
encounter one another: king and King,
"Radiance" and "Dawn." That kingdom bore[404]
His cross. Blessed be the One Who exalted [the kingdom]!

4 For thirty years[405] He remained on earth
in poverty. My brothers, let us plait
hymns of praise in all varieties
for the years of our Lord: for thirty years
thirty crowns. Blessed be His nativity!

5 In the first year, mistress of treasures
and full of graces, let the Cherubim who bore

---

398. Caesar Augustus is clearly meant, but it is not clear how he is called "Radiance." Beck suggests a pun on Greek ἀπαύγασμα.

399. For *dnḥ'* as a messianic title, cf. Zech. 3.8, 6.12. (Pes.); also in LXX ἀνατολή, and in Vulg. *oriens*.

400. Or, "this feast celebrated the Passover for all." Cf. str. 18 below.

401. Luke 2.1–3; cf. also Acts 5.37.

402. Phil. 4.3 and Rev. 13.8, but in the Pes. both with *ktb'* rather than *spr* as Beck has noted.

403. *qwšt'* instead of the more usual *šrr'* as antithesis to *r'z'*.

404. The word may be taken either in the sense of "supported" or "tolerated."

405. Cf. Luke 3.23, which gives, about thirty years to the beginning of the ministry. If this is his source, Ephrem apparently takes *'yk* in the sense of "almost" thirty years, then apparently counts the ministry as less than a year.

the Son in glory give thanks with us.[406]
He left His glory and labored and found
the sheep that was lost.[407] To Him be thanksgiving!

6 In the second year let the Seraphim multiply
thanksgiving with us. Those who called "holy" to the Son,[408]
on the other hand saw Him reviled
by the unbelievers. He endured scorn
yet He taught praise. To Him be glory!

7 In the third year let the house of Michael[409]
give thanks with us. Those who serve
the Son on high saw that He served
on earth—washed feet,[410]
cleansed souls. Blessed be His submission!

8 In the fourth year let the sky[411] give thanks with us;
its entirety is too small for the Son.
It was amazed to see Him recline on the couch
of the despised Zacchaeus.[412] He filled the couch,
and He filled the sky. To Him be majesty!

9 In the fifth year let the sun that scorches
the earth with its breath give thanks to our Sun,
Who inclined His height and softened His might
so that the feeble eye of the hidden soul
could see Him.[413] Blessed be His dazzling light!

10 In the sixth year let all the air
give thanks with us. In [the air's] majesty

---

406. The Lord is enthroned upon the Cherubim, 1 Sam. 4.4; cf. Ezek, 1.5–21; hence they are particularly representative of the glory of God. Ephrem freely places the Son on the throne or chariot borne by the Cherubim; cf. CJ 3.17. Cramer argues that Ephrem's references are to the ascension rather than to the theophany described by Ezekiel; cf. Cramer, Engelvorstellungen, 132–34. However, Ephrem, like virtually every Christian writer from the second century onward, freely treats any Old Testament theophany as referring to the Son of God rather than (or as well as) God the Father.

407. Matt. 18.10–14, Luke 15.3–7; on the basis of CH 26.6 Beck understands the lost sheep explicitly as Adam.

408. Isa. 6.2–5.

409. I.e., the angels. Ephrem does not systematically set apart the archangels as a group; cf. Cramer, Engelvorstellungen, 72f.

410. John 13.3–17.

411. Or "heaven."

412. Luke 19.1–10.

413. Cf. Nat. 16.3.

the universe exults.[414] It saw its Lord,
the Great One who became a small babe
in a small womb. Blessed be His dignity!

11   In the seventh year, O clouds and winds,
rejoice with us, and, dew, sprinkle
upon the blossoms. For they have seen the Son
Who subjected His brightness and accepted mockery
and filthy spittle.[415] Blessed be His redemption!

12   Also in the eighth year,[416]
let creation give glory. She, whose fruits drink
from her springs, worshipped when she saw
the Son in the womb, and the Pure One drank
pure milk. Blessed be His will!

13   In the ninth year let the earth give praise.
Her barren womb, when moistened,
soon gives birth. She saw
that the Fruit of the parched earth, Mary,[417]
was a great sea. To Him be exaltation!

14   In the tenth year let Mount Sinai give glory,
for it melted[418] in the presence of its Lord.
It saw that they took up stones against its Lord.[419]
It took stones to build His church.
upon stones.[420] Blessed be His building!

15   In the eleventh year let the great sea
give thanks to the hand of the Son
that measured it,[421] and let it be amazed to see
Him descend to be baptized; in the little waters
He cleansed the creation. Blessed be His victory!

16   In the twelfth year let the holy Temple
give thanks that it saw the boy

---

414. Cf. HdP 9.14.
415. Mark 14.65 et par.
416. Literally, "Again in the year, the eighth one."
417. Literally, "that the parched earth, Mary, gave" cf. Nat 8.8, 11.4.
418. The reference is unclear.
419. John 10.31.
420. Matt. 16.18? More probably, as Beck suggests, the reference is to Juliana Saba, who built a church on Mt. Sinai; cf. Jul. Sab. 19.13–18.
421. Isa. 40.12.

sitting among the elders.[422]
Silent were the black [sheep], for the Festal Lamb
bleated on His feastday. Blessed be His atonement!

17 In the thirteenth year let diadems
give thanks with us to the King who was victorious
and was crowned with a crown of thorns.[423]
He plaited for Adam a great diadem
upon the right hand.[424] Blessed be His glory!

18 In the fourteenth year let the paschal lamb of Egypt
give thanks to the Paschal Lamb who came
and offered the Passover for all.[425] But instead of Pharaoh
Legion sinks; instead of horsemen
He drowns demons.[426] Blessed be His vengeance!

19 In the fifteenth year let the lamb of the flock
give thanks that our Lord did not kill him
as Moses [did],[427] but with His blood He redeemed
humankind. This Shepherd of all
died for all. Blessed be his Begetter!

20 In the sixteenth year let the grain of wheat[428]
give thanks in a symbol to that Farmer
Who sowed His body in the barren earth
that had failed to produce anything. It sprouted and gave
new bread. Blessed be the Conqueror!

21 In the seventeenth year let the vine
give thanks to our Lord, the True Vineyard.
Souls were like young plants;[429]
He cultivated [His] vineyard, but He destroyed the vineyard
that gave sour grapes.[430] Blessed be the One Who uproots!

22 In the seventeenth year let the vine

---

422. Luke 2.41–51.
423. Mark 15.16–20 et par.
424. Cf. HdF 50.5.
425. Or "and delighted all." The same expression is used in the refrain of the present hymn and of Nat. 14.
426. Mark 5.1–20, esp. 5.13 et par.
427. Ephrem's polemic against Judaism extends to a rejection of animal sacrifice on principle; cf. Nat. 7.4 and 18.30.
428. John 12.24.
429. Ephrem's wordplay produces a Syriac tongue twister here! *ḥwy npšt' 'yk nṣbt'*
430. Isa. 5. 1–6.

eaten by the boar of the forest give thanks
to the True Vinedresser, who Himself worked
and guarded His fruit and offers fruit
to the Lord of the vineyard. Blessed be its Vinedresser!

23　In the eighteenth year, too,
let out leaven give thanks to the true leaven,[431]
that moves through and expands all minds
and made them one mind
by one teaching. Blessed be your teaching!

24　In the nineteenth year let salt
give thanks to Your body, O Blessed Babe.
The soul is the salt of the body,
and faith is the salt of the soul,
by which it is preserved. Blessed be Your preservation!

25　In the twentieth year let temporal riches
give thanks with us. For the perfect
have forfeited them because of the curse,
and they have come to love poverty
because of its blessing.[432] Blessed be one who prefers it!

26　In the twenty-first year let the water that became sweet[433]
as a symbol of the Son give thanks.
By the honeycomb of Samson the peoples whom he destroyed
became bitter.[434] They have come to life again by the cross
that redeemed them. Blessed be Your sweetness!

27　In the twenty-second year let armor and sword
give thanks. They were not sufficient to kill
the Enemy of our age. You have killed him,
but You attached the ear that Simon's sword
had cut off.[435] Blessed be your healing!

28　In the twenty-third year let even the ass
give thanks. For she gave a foal

---

431. The leaven in the parables of the New Testament is not Christ but his kingdom; cf. Matt. 13.33 et par. cf. HdF 12.12, 25.9, CH 2.12.
432. Luke 6.20–24.
433. Exod. 15.25.
434. Judg. 14.5–20.
435. Cf. John 18. 10f. and Luke 22.51f. Although the other synoptics include the incident, cf. Mark 14.47 et par., only John identifies Peter as the assailant and only Luke includes the detail of Jesus' repair of the wounded ear.

upon which He might ride Who opens the mouths
even of wild asses.[436] The progeny of Hagar[437]
gave a shout. Blessed be Your shout!

29 In the twenty-fourth year let wealth
give thanks to the Son. Treasures marveled
at the Lord of treasures, as He grew
among the poor. He made Himself poor
that all might become rich. Blessed be Your mingling!

30 In the twenty-fifth year let Isaac
give thanks to the Son who spared him on the mountain
from the knife and became in his place
the sacrificial lamb.[438] The mortal escaped
and the universal Life-giver died. Blessed be His offering!

31 In the twenty-sixth year let Moses
give thanks with us. For he was afraid and fled
from killers.[439] Let him give thanks to the Son
Who entered Sheol on foot,[440]
plundered it, and emerged. Blessed be Your resurrection!

32 In the year that is twenty-seventh,
let eloquent lawyers give thanks to the Son.
They did not find a stratagem for our case.
When He conquered He was silent in the court;[441]
yet he acquitted us. Glory to Him!

33 In the twenty-seventh year let all judges
give thanks. They, as just men,
have killed evil men. Let them give thanks to the Son
Who, in place of bad men, died as a good man
although He was Son of the Just One. Blessed be His mercy!

34 In the twenty-eighth year
let all mighty men give thanks to the Son.
For they did not save us from the Captor.

---

436. Literally, "the opener of mouths even for wild asses." Matt. 26.5, quoting Zech. 9.9.
437. Either the Arab tribes, as Beck suggests, or possibly it is the sedentary non-Jewish Semites who are meant.
438. Gen. 22.
439. Exod. 2.11–15.
440. Perhaps better as Beck translates, "after him"—essentially reading *lrglwhy* in place of *brglwhy*. Beck cites CH 55.3 and HdP 8.10 as grammatical and contextual basis.
441. Mark 14.61 and 15.5 et par.

One alone is worshipped—He Who, being slain,
attained our salvation. Blessed be Your deliverance!

35 In the twenty-ninth year let Job
give thanks with us. He endured sufferings
for his own sake, but our Lord endured
spitting and scourging, thorns and nails
for our sake. Blessed be His compassion!

36 In the year that is thirtieth,
let the dead who were revived by His dying,
[and] the life that returned by His crucifixion,[442]
and the height and the depth that were pacified by Him
[all] give thanks with us! Blessed be He and His Father![443]

---

442. Matt. 27.52.

443. The principal ms. tradition adds the following colophon to this, the last hymn in its collection: "Completed are the hymns of the nativity of our Lord that holy Mar Ephrem composed. Glory to the Father and to the Son and to the Holy Spirit now and in all times and for ever and ever. Amen."

19

Mary sings this hymn as a representative of the Jewish people (str. 3, 8, 18). Ephrem portrays the offering of the Magi to the infant Jesus as a reversal of the Assyrian Domination and the Babylonian Captivity. Their offerings of gold, frankincense and myrrh rectify the injustices and suffering of the eighth to sixth centuries B.C. by bringing atonement for the Assyrians and Babylonians and consolation for the Jews (str. 1–4). The defeats of the past are contrasted with the homage rendered to the infant, Emmanuel (str. 5–11). Isaiah's prophecy of the birth of Emmanuel provides a scriptural link between past humiliation and present honor (str. 7–8). In a sense Ephrem is arguing that Isaiah's prophecy proves the accuracy of his own interpretation of the visit of the Magi.

In the second half of the hymn Ephrem argues that the majesty of Christ is much greater than what was lost (str. 12–17). Contact with Christ makes "even worthless [things] become beautiful" (str. 14). The references to the New Testament and to exaggerated awe for things touched by Christ (str. 15–16) suggest a context of pilgrimage. Finally, Mary closes with a rhetorical request that her Son teach her now to be silent and to rest (str. 18–19).

19

1   "Uzziah and Jotham and Ahaz were defeated
    in their wars.[444] Instead of captives
    who went down to Assyria, the Magi came to us
    with caravans. In our streets wafted
    the good odor of their spices.

---

444. 2 Kgs. 15.1–7, 15.32–38, 16.1–20 (and 2 Chr. 26–28) indicate that only Ahaz suffered military defeats, although the others were chastised in other ways. The oracles of Isaiah mention all three, cf. Isa. 1.1.

HYMN 19

Refrain: To You be praise, Son of the Lord of the universe, Who saved all.

2   "Being the Son of the Compassionate One, You took pity on them
in Your kindness. Being the Son of the Zealous One,
You avenged them with your might.
Being the Son of the Rich One, according to [Your] love of them,[445]
they have paid their debts with their offerings.

3   "You juxtaposed [events] so that You might not grieve us
and You might save them: Those who had seized our[446] silver,
brought gold. Those who had wounded our bodies,
brought myrrh. Those who had burned our sanctuary
offered frankincense to Your divinity.

4   "Their myrrh intercedes for their swords
with which they killed us. Their gold intercedes
for our treasures, for they plundered the treasuries
of the House of Hezekiah.[447] Their frankincense appeased
Your divinity, for they had angered Your Father.

5   "Whereas Ahaz sent [word] to Assyria,
'Come and save me!'[448]—those who had been humbled,
by You were exalted. They came
with their pledges to You instead of Jechoniah,[449]
the hostage captured from the House of David.

6   "Where by his envoys Ahaz subjected
himself to Assyria,[450] by You they are subjected
in their envoys. Whereas the sceptre of the lion's cub[451]
rendered homage, the mighty who had received homage
rendered homage to you, O Worshipful One.

---

445. Although the meaning could be "their love," the objective genitive, viz., "love of them," is more appropriate to the context.

446. Mary speaks as a member of the Jewish people, referring to the Assyrian invasions of Israel under Tiglath-Pileser III, Shalmaneser, Sargon II and Sennacherib in the late eighth century B.C.; cf. 2 Kgs. 16–18 and Isa. 5.26–30.

447. 2 Kgs. 18.14f.

448. Ephrem quotes precisely the words of Ahaz to the Assyrian king, according to the Pes., 2 Kgs. 16.7.

449. Ephrem confuses matters by interjecting into his discussion this reference to considerably later events. Jechoniah, son of Jehoikim, was deported to Babylon under Nebuchadnezzar at the beginning of the sixth century B.C.; cf. 2 Kgs. 24.10–16 and Jer. 24.1, 27.20, 28.4.

450. 2 Kgs. 16.7.

451. Gen. 49.9. Since Judah is the lion's cub, Ahaz, king of Judah, is the sceptre of the lion's cub.

7 "When Aram and Ephrem dared to attack,
Zion was afraid lest she be left bereft
of the House of David.[452] When Ahaz took flight
and abandoned [her],[453] Isaiah
gave her Your good news of Emmanuel.

8 "Behold a virgin shall conceive and give birth"[454]
without intercourse. Am I having a dream
or a vision that, behold, upon my lap
is Emmanuel? I shall cease all [else]
and give thanks to the Lord of the universe each day.

9 "Whereas they despised virginity in Zion,
they honored Your mother, O virginal Child
Who put on the evidence of virginity of His mother
and emerged with it. To me You are Child,
Bridegroom and Son, even God.

10 "The Babylonians, too, came up [and] afflicted
the children in Judah.[455] By You the children
have found peace, for by You the vicious
have become worshippers. Those who despised old men
honor a Child who is older than all.

11 "Babylon, too, sent offerings
to Hezekiah; the envoys who saw
his treasures were amazed.[456] What did you show to
the Magi? You showed a wonder
for they rendered You homage although You were poor.

12 "However great was the ivory palace
of the kings of our people,[457] greater
and more beautiful is the little cave
in which I bore You. In swaddling clothes
the shepherds saw Your glory.

13 "A small nature, if it wears a diadem,
by the diadem becomes great. Your nature is great,

452. This occurred during the reign of Ahaz, cf. Isa. 7.1–9, esp. 7.2.
453. Literally, "abandoned [her] and took flight and left."
454. Isa. 7.14–16. Emmanuel = "God with us."
455. Cf. note on Nat. 19.5.4 above.
456. Isa. 39.1–2 et par.
457. 1 Kgs. 22.39.

O son of poor people, and through You something small
becomes great; if someone places
thorns on Your head, they are like a diadem.

14 "A worthless body may be adorned
with jewels. Through You, Honorable One,
even worthless [things] become beautiful.
So great is contact with You that even if someone
cast a stone at You, it would be a pearl.

15 "Even your sweat, for one who is worthy,
is a baptism,[458] and the dust of Your garments,
for one who is infirm, is a great fount
of all aids,[459] and even Your spittle,
if it reach the face, would enlighten the eyes.[460]

16 "If upon a stone You should rest Your head,
they would divide and tear it apart, and if You slept
upon a dunghill, it would become a church
for prayers, and if, again, You broke
ordinary bread, for us it would be the medicine of life.[461]

17 "Who will revile You? For even Your abuse
is a blessing of the peoples. Who will kill You?
For even Your death is the Word of life
for humans, And even if You mount
a cross, You are the Paschal Lamb!

18 "Since You, O mountain, are greater than the one who bore You,
I shall sit down and be quiet. Be a harbor for me,
and I shall take refuge in You. Great nature

---

458. If the verb is taken as Pael, this would read "for one who wipes [it] away." Perhaps it is a reference to an early version of the Veronica legend or to the ἀχειροποίητος of Edessa. Cf. Acta Thaddaei 3; E. von Dobschütz, *Christusbilder: Untersuchungen zur Christlichen Legende*, TU, ser. 2, III (Leipzig, 1899); more recently, Averil Cameron, "The Sceptic and the Shroud," Inaugural Lecture, Departments of Classics and History, King's College (London, 29 April 1980); Wilkinson, Pilgrims, 84, 88, 98, 167b.

459. Mark 5.25–34 et par.; cf. Eusebius EH 7.18–672, for reference to a fourth century pilgrimage site at Panais in Palestine with a statue thought to represent the woman. This woman is later called Veronica, and her story becomes confused with the Veronica of the later Latin legend; further, cf. Wilkinson, Pilgrims, 167b.

460. John 9.6.

461. In this strophe Ephrem puts into Mary's mouth an attestation of the excesses of pilgrims. The parallel reference to the Eucharist probably indicates his observations should not be taken as criticisms of pious gullibility.

that cannot be interpreted, permit Your mother
to be silent about You, for her mouth is weary.

19 "Withhold Your gift from Your lyre
that it may rest a little. Since You have taught me
everything I have said, teach me
how to be silent. Since you have wearied me,
let me rest. Glory be to Your Father!"

20

Unfortunately this hymn is only partially preserved. The hymn is a Christian midrash on the story of Abraham and Sarah, with the emphasis on Sarah. As in the case of other women of the Old Testament in the ninth nativity hymn, Ephrem explains the behavior of Sarah as if she were motivated by the expectation of the Messiah. She was jealous of Hagar and she pretended to be Abraham's sister not for any personal reasons but because she knew the Messiah would come through the line of Abraham and herself (str. 1,4). Ephrem argues further that Abraham has only one blessed seed (str. 2–3). The implication seems to be that the one seed is Christ rather than "a multitude of blessed seeds," namely, the people of Israel.

20

1 Because of You Sarah was jealous,[462]
which [was] not her custom. She was not jealous
of the boy's mother, where even chaste women
are jealous; she was jealous of the slave
because of You, O Free-born Son!

Refrain: From the House of Sarah[463] and from the peoples to You be glory!

2 For the sake of Your manifestation Isaac prayed
on behalf of his wife;[464] at once she conceived
the wolf and the lamb. It showed that Abraham

---

462. Gen. 16.1–16, esp. 16.5.

463. Note the use of the "House of Sarah" rather than "House of Abraham." Ephrem's purpose is less to emphasize Sarah's importance vis-à-vis Abraham than to emphasize the uniqueness of the blessed progeny of Abraham; the line through Hagar is not included. Yet the effect is to raise Sarah to greater prominence.

464. Rebekah. Gen. 25.19–27.45; esp. Gen. 25.21.

did not have blessed seeds:
Only one is his seed that blesses all.[465]

3   If Abraham has a multitude
of blessed seeds—behold Esau
and Ishmael are first-born sons
of the House of Abraham. By two cursed [men]
[scripture] showed that the blessed seed is one.

4   Son of the King, Sarah loved You,
but she hated the king,[466] nor was the palace
pleasing to her when she walked about
with the exile.[467] She was inclined to him
for she saw Your manifestation hidden in him.

5   Ninety years[468] were not too wearisome for her
to wait for You. You came in the nineti[eth year]
to Sarah. And you came in the hundred[th year]
to Abraham. You gave . . .

   . . .

---

465. Gal. 3.16.
466. Gen. 12.10–20.
467. Abraham. In his Commentary on Genesis and Exodus, Ephrem explains that even if he spoke from a human perspective in asking Sarah to pretend to be his sister, two purposes were filled: 1) to teach Sarah that she, rather than he, was sterile (!), 2) to show "her love for her husband that she did not exchange the exile for the king." In this she is a type for her descendents since "just as she did not love the kingdom of Egypt, they would not love the idols and garlic and onions of Egypt. And as all the house of Pharaoh was smitten to free her, so all Egypt was smitten to free her children." Tonneau, Gen/Exod, CSCO 152 (scr. syr. 71) 67.17–31.
468. Gen. 17.17.

21

This hymn begins with a comparison of the reward of the singer at Herod's birthday feast with the singer at the birthday of Christ (str. 1). One who sings and keeps vigil on the eve of the Nativity becomes like the angels (str. 2–4). The song to be sung is one of praise and thankgiving for the paradox of the incarnation: the Incomprehensible and Unlimited One was confined to the womb of Mary (str. 6–8); the All-powerful One became the abused servant of his servants (str. 13–15). This recurrent theme is given several new expressions in this hymn: First, Divinity is portrayed weaving a garment for herself—the body of Christ (str. 5). Second, God responded to the human penchant for idolatry, the worship of creatures, by the incarnation—the best example of the gentleness of God (str. 9). Third, God is able to reverse the usual order both in nature and in history: The barrenness of a married woman (Elizabeth) and the conception of a virgin (Mary) are symbolic of the rejection of the Jewish people and acceptance of the Gentiles (str. 16–18).

21

Change of melody

1 About the birth of the First-born on His feastday let us speak.
On His day He gave hidden helps.
If the unclean one on his feast and in commemoration of his day
gave a gift of anger, a head upon a platter,[469]
how much [more] will the Blessed One give blessings to one
who sings on His feast.

---

469. Mark 6.14–29 et par. For a longer comparison with Herod's birthday, cf. Nat. 4.60–83.

HYMNS ON THE NATIVITY

Refrain: Blessed is He Who became small without limit to make us great without limit.

2 Let us not count our vigil as everyday vigils;
it is a feastday whose wage increases a hundredfold.
For it is a feast that attacks sleep with its vigil,
a speaker who attacks sleep with his voice.
He snatches all good things; he is head of the hosts of the feasts.
and of all joys.

3 Today the angels and even the archangels
came down to sing a new song of praise on earth.
by this mystery they come down and rejoice with vigils.
At that time when they sang praise, blasphemy filled [the earth].
Blessed is the birth on which a generation thundered
with hallelujahs of praise.

4 For [this] is the night that mingles heavenly Watchers with vigilants.
The Watcher came to make watchers in creation.
Behold vigilants have been made partakers with the Watchers.[470]
Praisegivers have been made companions with the Seraphim.
Blessed is he who became a lyre for Your praise,
and whose wage was Your mercy.

5 But let us sing the birth of the First-born—how
Divinity in the womb wove herself a garment.[471]
She put it on and emerged in birth; in death she stripped it off
again.
Once she stripped it off; twice she put it on.
When the left hand snatched it, she wrested it from her,
and she placed it on the right hand.[472]

6 The Power that governs all dwelt in a small womb.
While dwelling there, He was holding the reins of the universe.
His Parent was ready for His will to be fulfilled.

---

470. Christ is the Watcher who by his incarnation makes it possible for humans to participate in the angelic service of praise, that is, to make them "watchers in creation." On watchfulness, cf. Nat. 1.61, 4.195, 6.22–23, 7.9, 21.4.

471. The feminine pronouns refer to "Divinity," which is grammatically feminine in Syriac; since weaving is a feminine task in antiquity, it is appropriate to preserve the feminine rather
than shifting to a neuter or masculine. On the imagery of the body as a garment, cf. Nat. 4.187–
88, 5.4.4–5, 16.11–13, 17.4.

472. The death, resurrection and ascension of Christ are meant.

The heavens and all the creation were filled by Him.
The Sun entered the womb, and in the height and depth
His rays were dwelling.

7   He dwelt in the vast wombs of all creation.
They were too small to contain the greatness of the First-born.
How indeed did that small womb of Mary suffice for Him?
It is a wonder if . . . sufficed for Him.
Of all the wombs that contained Him, one womb sufficed:
[the womb] of the Great One Who begot Him.

8   The womb that contain Him, if it contained all of Him,
is equal to the wonderful womb that is greater than [the womb] of
       His birth.
But who will dare to say that a small womb,
weak and despised, is equal to [the womb] of the Great Being?
He dwelt [there] because of His compassion and since His nature is
       great,
He was not limited in anything.

9   Reconciling Peace, sent to the peoples,
Gladdening Flash, Who came to the gloomy,
Powerful Leaven, conquering all in silence
Patient One, Who has captured the creation little by little.
Blessed is he who makes Your joys dwell in His heart
and forgets his griefs in You.

10   The mouth[s] of the Watchers and vigilants shouted a joyful "peace."
The good news brought by the Watchers[473] met the vigilants.
Who will go to sleep on that night that awakened creation?
For they brought a "peace" where enmity had been
Blessed is the Babe who rules with His silence the Majesty
That the speech-endowed had angered.

11   The Watchers mingled with watchers; they rejoiced that the world
      revived.
Put to shame was the Evil One who became king and plaited a
      diadem of deceit.
Like God, he set his throne on the inhabited earth.
The Babe in a manger[474] cast him from his power.

---

473. Literally, "The good news of the Watchers, she brought it."
474. Literally, "The Babe Who was put in a manger."

The sun returned worship; by his Magi he honored Him.
In his worshippers he worshipped Him.

12 God had seen that we worshipped creatures.
He put on a created body to catch us by our habit.[475]
Behold by this fashioned one our Fashioner healed us,
and by this creature our Creator revived us.
His force did not govern us. Blessed is He Who came in what is
 ours
and mingled us into what is His.[476]

13 O [You] Greater than measure Who became immeasurably small,
from glorious splendor[477] You humbled Yourself to ignominy.
Your indwelling mercy inclined You to all this.
Let Your compassion incline me to become praiseworthy in my
 evil.[478]
Blessed be the one who became a source of melodies
and entirely gave thanks to all of you.

14 He became a servant on earth; He was Lord on high.
Inheritor of the height and depth, Who became a stranger.
But the One Who was judged wrongly will judge in truth,
and He in Whose face they spat, breathed the spirit into the face.[479]
He Who held a weak reed was the sceptre for the world
that grows old and leans on Him.

15 He Who stood [and] served His servants, sitting, will be
 worshipped.
He Whom the Scribes scorned—the Seraphim sang "holy" before
 Him.
This glory Adam wanted to steal secretly.
The serpent who cast him down saw to what height [Adam] was
 raised.

---

475. Ephrem plays on the similarity of sounds in *dl'byd'* and *db'dn* in this and the previous
line.
476. In the incarnation God came in the flesh or in human nature and thereby mingled us
into his divine nature; this is a favorite idea of Ephrem's; cf. Nat. 8.2, Virg 37.2.
477. The Syriac is more redundant or alliterative—"glorious glory" or "splendid splendor."
478. The sense seems to be "despite my evil," but the Syriac does not express this
unambiguously.
479. That is, Christ in His divine role as Creator breathed life into Adam, cf. Gen. 2.7. For
Ephrem, the breathing of the soul into Adam is the source of the *imago dei* in human beings;
hence, it plays an important role in his theology; cf. Kronholm, Motifs, 57–67. On the role of
Christ in the creation of the world and especially of Adam, cf. ibid. 39–43, 46–51.

He crushed him because he harmed him; Eve's feet trampled him
who had poured gall in her ears.

16 The wife became barren and failed to produce fruits,
but Mary's womb conceived chastely.
To marvel at fields and to wonder at plantings!
This one refused to take, and without a loan, she paid back!
Nature confesses he was conquered, the womb deceived him!
And without his giving to her, she repaid him.

17 By Elizabeth Mary was judged innocent.
Barrenness petitioned so that the Will that was able
would close the open gate [and] open the closed one.
He deprived the married womb; He made fruitful the virgin womb.
since the People was unfaithful, He obstructed the wife
before the pure one.[480]

18 The One Who is able to moisten barren and dead breasts,
deprived them when they were young, made them flow when old.
He forced and changed nature in its time and not in its time.
The Lord of natures changed the nature of the virgin.
Since the people was barren he made the old woman
a mouth on behalf of the young woman.

19 And as He began in birth, He continued and completed in death.
His birth received worship; His death repaid the debt.
As He came to birth, the magi worshipped Him.
Again, He came to suffering and the thief took refuge in Him.
Between His birth and death He placed the world in the middle;
By [His] birth and death He revived it.[481]

20 A thousand thousands stood; ten thousand ten thousands ran.

---

480. Ephrem's intent here is not only to contrast the initial barrenness of Elizabeth despite her married state with the conception of Mary despite her unmarried state. In the following strophe he emphasizes the overturning of nature in both cases and, thence, the sense in which Elizabeth vindicates Mary. Just as God overturned nature to make Elizabeth barren in her youth yet fruitful in her old age, God reversed the natural order by having Mary conceive while a virgin.

481. The last six strophes are culled from Hymns 4 and 7 on Faith. (20–22 = HdF 4.1–3; 23 = HdF 4.7; 24 = HdF 4.11; 25 = HdF 7.5). They have the same melody, and the subject is basically compatible, but the addition seems to be the work of a later hand. The emphasis on avoiding investigation, so typical of Ephrem's anti-Arian writings seems most germane to the Hymns on Faith. A more technical reason for preferring the Hymns on Faith as the original context is the change of addressee from the member of the congregation to the Son of God and back again in the added strophes. For this reason the additional strophes have not been included in the prefatory discussion of the hymn.

Thousands and ten thousands were not able to investigate the One.
All of them in silence, therefore, stood to serve Him.
He has no consort except the Child that is from Him.
Seeking Him is in silence. When Watchers went to investigate,
they reached silence and were restrained.

21   The First-born entered the womb, but the pure one perceived not.
He arose and emerged with birthpangs, and the fair one felt Him.
Glorious and hidden His entry; despised and visible His emergence,
since He is God at His entry, but human at His emergence.
[What] a wonder and confusion to hear: Fire entered the womb,
put on a body and emerged!

22   Gabriel—that head of the angels—called Him Lord.
He called Him Lord to teach that He is his Lord and not his equal.
For Gabriel, Michael is the equal.
The Son is Lord of the servants. His nature is as great as His name.
A servant is not able to investigate Him since, however much the
        servant becomes greater,
the One Whose servant [he is] is greater than him.

23   When the Watchers stand before You in [their] glories,
they do not know on what side they should look for You.
They sought You above on high; they saw You below in the depth.
They sought You in heaven; they saw You in the abyss.
They considered You as divine; they found You in the creation.
They came down to You and sang praise.

24   You are utterly a wonder. In every side that we seek You,
You are near and far, but who is it that reaches You?
Investigation is not able to stretch it[self] to reach You.
Whenever it stretches out to reach [You], it is cut off and falls short.
It is too short for Your mountain. Faith reaches [You]—
and love and prayer.

25   The Magi, too, sought Him, and when they found Him in the crib,
worship instead of investigation they offered Him in silence.
Instead of empty controversies, they gave Him offerings.
You, too, seek the First-born, and if you find Him on high,
instead of confused searchings, open your treasures before Him
and offer Him your deeds.

22

This hymn is an alphabetical acrostic comprised of one to five strophes for each of the twenty-two letters of the Syriac alphabet. The main theme is the need to know the disease in order to appreciate the healer (str. 1–3). In the case of the coming of Christ the disease is idolatry and healing is the freedom from idolatry not only for the worshipper but especially for the creature wrongly worshipped (str. 4–5, 7, 9, 35–36). The sun, moon, fire, material possessions and graven images are prominent among the creatures that have been worshipped through the devices of error and Satan (str. 10–18). But the wisdom and mercy of God led God to turn the human proclivity for idolatry to our own good by the incarnation, "to draw us by a created body toward the Creator" (str. 16, 18).

God released the creation from idolatry in stages: The prophets were sent to the Jewish people; the apostles to the Gentiles (str. 21). The incarnation itself took place in stages: first the conception, then the birth (str. 20, cf. str. 6, 36–37). The gold, frankincense and myrrh brought by the Magi represent the release of these created things from inappropriate human use (str. 26–29). The ancient semitic cults of the high places as well as Chaldean astrology are ended (str. 30–32). Humanity is transformed by the incarnation, resurrection and ascension (str. 35, 38–40). The hymn ends with an invocation of the Paraclete, the Spirit of truth (str. 40–41).

22

Change of melody

'1   O peoples sing praise on the feast, the First-born of all feasts!
Recount the sufferings that took place and the bruises and pains
so we may know what a wound was healed by the Child Who was
      sent.
Blessed is He Who was sufficient for our pains!

HYMNS ON THE NATIVITY

Refrain: Most blessed of all is He by His birth! (Repeat)

'2   Confess, O redeemed peoples, the Savior of all at His birth!
Even my weak tongue has become a lyre by mercy
to sing the triumphs of the Firstborn on His feastday.
Blessed is He who made us worthy of His feast.

'3   How indeed can one marvel at a healer
unless one hears and learns what the pains were?
When our wound has been proclaimed, then our Healer is
     magnified.
Blessed is He who triumphed over our pains!

B4   Creatures were worshipped since the worshipper was foolish.
He worshipped everything so that the One they did not worship
came down [and] compassion broke the yoke that enslaved the
     universe.
Blessed is He Who released our yoke!

G5   The mercy of the High One was revealed, and He came down to
     free His creation
In this blessed month in which manumission takes place,[482]
the Lord came to slavery to call the slaves to freedom.
Blessed is He Who brought manumission!

G6   The Lord of the months chose two months for his actions:
His conception took place in April[483] and His birth in January.[484]
In April he sanctified those conceived, and those born He freed in
     January.
Blessed is He Who gladdens with His months!

G7   The sun bellowed out in silence to the Lord against his
     worshippers.

---

482. Ephrem seems to refer to a particular time when manumission of slaves took place, perhaps on some festival. Beck's suggestion of Yom Kippur, cf. Lev. 25.9f., does not seem correct since Ephrem should be referring to January, the date of the nativity celebration. In the Roman Empire manumission of slaves was the prerogative of the owner at any time by prescribed legal procedures; cf. Westermann, Slave Systems, 154f. et passim. Constantinian edicts of 316 and 323 C.E. associated this prerogative particularly with the church, the *manumissio in ecclesia*, but I have not found any reference to manumission on a particular date in either the pagan or Christian Roman Empire; ibid. E. J. Jonkers, "De l'influence du Christianisme sur la législation relative à l'esclavage dans l'antiquité," *Mnemosyne*, ser.3, 1(1933–34), 241–80, esp. 265.

483. Nisan.
484. Conun.

It was a suffering for him, the servant, that instead of his Lord he
    was worshipped.
Behold the creation is joyful that the Creator is worshipped!
Blessed is the worshipful Child!

G8   Three months plaited [a crown] and with victories they crowned
    Him.
The blessed [month] served His birth, the desirable His
    resurrection,
the joyful His ascension. The months carried His crowns.
Blessed is the One Who triumphed in His months!

G9   Unveil, make joyful your face, O Creation, on our feast!
Sing, O Church, with a voice! Heaven and earth [sing] in silence!
Sing and confess the Child Who brought manumission for all.
Blessed is He Who cut to pieces the letters of bondage![485]

D10 Since fools honored the sun, they diminished him in his honor.
Now that they know he is a servant, by his course he worships his
    Lord.
All the servants are glad to be counted servants.
Blessed is He Who set the natures in order!

H11 We have done perverse things that we should be servants to
    servants!
Behold, our freedom forced our Lord to be a servant to us.
The sun, servant for all, we have made lord for all.
Blessed is He Who has restored us to Him!

W12 Even the moon that had been worshipped was freed by His birth.
For it is a wonder that by the light that enlightens eyes,
eyes were darkened so that they looked upon it as a god.
Blessed is the Flash that enlightened us!

Z13 Fire approved of Your birth to drive worship away by it.
The Magi used to worship [fire]—they worshipped You!
They left it and worshipped its Lord; Fire they exchanged for fire.
Blessed is He Who baptized us in His light!

Ḥ14 Instead of the foolish fire that eats its own body itself,
the Magi worshipped the Fire Who gave His body to those who
    eat.

---

485. Cf. Col. 2.14.

The coal drew near to sanctify unclean lips.[486]
Blessed is He Who has mixed His fire with us!

T15 Error blinded humankind that we should worship creatures.
Fellow-servants were worshipped, and the Lord of the universe was
     denied.
The Worshipful came down to birth and gathered worship to
     Himself.
Blessed is He Who is worshipped by all!

Y16 The All-Knowing saw that we worshipped creatures.
He put on a created body to catch us by our habit,
to draw us by a created body toward the Creator.
Blessed is He Who contrived to draw us [to Him].

Y17 The evil one knew [how] to harm us; with the luminaries he
     blinded us.
With possessions he maimed us, by gold he made us poor.
With graven images he made us a heart of stone.[487]
Blessed is He who came to soften it!

K18 They carved stones and set them up that humankind might stumble
     on them.
They did not put them on the road that the blind should stumble
     on them.
They named them gods that on them the seeing might stumble.
Blessed is He Who unmasks false gods!

K19 Sin spread its wings to cover everything
so that no one could see the truth from above it.
Truth came down to the womb, emerged [and] rolled away error.
Blessed is He Who dispelled [sin] by His birth!

L20 For the Compassionate One did not endure seeing the way closed.
Coming down in the conception, He opened the way a little.
Emerging in birth, He trod it out and set His milestones on it.
Blessed is the peace of Your way!

L21 He chose the prophets; they made smooth the way for the People.
He sent the apostles; they cleared a path for the peoples.
The snares of the evil one were put to shame since the weak
     cleared them away.

---

486. Isa. 6.5–7.
487. Cf. Ezek. 11.19f.

Blessed is He Who made straight our paths!

M22 Graven images were blinding their carvers in secret.

They carved an eye in stone, but they blinded the eyes of the
soul.[488]

Praise be to Your birth that opened [the eyes of] blind seers.

Blessed [is He] Who restored sight!

N23 Let chaste women praise that pure Mary.

Since in their mother Eve their disgrace was great,

behold in Mary their sister their triumph was magnified.

Blessed is He Who shone forth from them!

N24 Let the peoples praise Your birth when they acquired eyes to see.

When He shook off their wine and they saw the humiliation of
their soul,[489]

they were judges for them[selves], and they worship their
Deliverer.

Blessed is He Who taught remorse!

S25 His worship humanity has scattered everywhere.

You did not seek the worshipful one to offer Him worship.

But the worshipped did not tolerate [being worshipped] by errant
worshippers.

Blessed is He Who came down to be worshipped!

S26 The gold of images [of gods] worshipped You Who drew it out for
alms.

What was devoid of use in dead [images] [was] for the use of the
living.

It ran to Your moneybox as it ran to Your manger.

Blessed is He Whom the creation loved!

S27 Frankincense that [had] served demons worshipped Your birth.

It was gloomy in its vapor; it rejoiced to see its Lord.

Instead of the incense of error, [Your birth] was offered to God.

Blessed is Your birth that is worshipped!

S28 Myrrh worshipped You on its own behalf and for similar sweet
spices.

Loathsome graven images had made it loathsome since they had
anointed its ointments.

---

488. Or "of the self," i.e., "their own eyes."
489. Or "their own humiliation."

By You the sweet spices smelled sweet in the oil with which Mary
    anointed You.[490]

Blessed is Your scent that made us smell sweet!

S29   Gold, that had been worshipped, worshipped You as the Magi
    approached.

What was worshipped in molten [images] gave You worship.

With its worshippers it worshipped You; it confessed that You are
    worshipful.

Blessed is the One Who demanded His worship!

'30   The evil one who had exulted in the inhabited earth fled with his
    hosts.

At the high place they sacrificed a calf to him; in the gardens they
    killed bulls for him.

He swallowed the entire creation; the prey filled his belly.

Blessed is He Who came and annihilated him!

'31   About him our Lord said that he would fall from heaven,[491]

that the loathsome one would magnify himself [and] would fall
    from his greatness.

The foot of Mary has trampled him, who was bruised by Eve on
    his heel.[492]

Blessed is He Who by His birth humbled him!

P32   The Chaldeans were wandering everywhere and they went astray.

They were confused in the inhabited earth, the announcers of
    error.

They were silenced and conquered by the announcers of truth.

Blessed is the birth that was announced!

P33   Sin has spread her nets for the catch.[493]

Praise to Your birth that ripped up the nets of error.

The soul that had been captured in the depth flew out to the
    height.

Blessed is He Who acquired wings for us!

S34   His will would also have been able to set us free by force.

---

490. John 12.1–8, esp. v.3.
491. Luke 10.18.
492. Gen. 3.15.
493. Ephrem plays on ṣwd, "capture," and its derivatives, "nets" and "catch" throughout
this strophe.

Since it was not by force we were guilty, He did not grant us
    victory by force.
The evil one by guile enslaved us; Your birth beguiled him to
    revive us.
Blessed is He Who schemed to revive us!

Q35   Creatures complained that they were worshipped; in silence they
    sought manumission.
He Who frees all heard, and since He [could] not tolerate [this], He
    came down.
He put on the servant in the womb, emerged [and] freed the
    creation.
Blessed is He Who made profits for His creation!

R36   Mercy on high was greatly moved by the voice of creatures that
    appealed for help.
Gabriel was sent; he came to announce Your conception.[494]
When You arrived at birth, the Watchers announced Your
    emergence.[495]
Most blessed of all is Your worship!

R37   For greater is the joy of the birth than the conception.
Indeed one angel announced to us Your conception;
the joy of Your birth throngs of Watchers announced.
Blessed is Your announcement on Your day!

S38   I, too, will offer You glory on Your day, Worshipful One.
Take from the fruit I have, and give me the compassion You have.
If I give [from] the evil that is mine, how much more will You give
    Who are good.
Blessed is Your wealth in Your servant!

T39   The two things You[496] asked, we have by Your birth.
You put on our visible body; let us put on your hidden power.
Our body became Your garment; Your spirit became our robe.
Blessed is He Who was adorned and adorned us!

T40   The depth and height wondered that Your birth subdued the
    rebels.

---

494. Luke 1.26–38.
495. Luke 2.13f.
496. Cf. John 17. Beck reads "we" with one ms., but this seems to be an allusion to Jesus'
requests on behalf of the believing community in the farewell discourse.

Since we gave You hostages, You gave us the Paraclete.[497]
When the hostages ascended from us, great power came down to
    us.
Blessed is He Who took and sent!

T41   Come all you mouths, pour out and become a type
of water and wells of voices; let the Spirit of truth come!
Let Her sing praise in all of us to the Father Who redeemed us by
    His Child.
Most blessed of all is His birth!

---

497. Cf. John 15.26, 16.7. The "hostages" are the body and soul[?] or spirit[?] of Christ. Beck has noted the similar notion in Aphrahat, cf. Dem. 21.18 and 23.50 (Parisot II,98.24–26). In the first case, within an extended comparison of Jesus with Daniel, he says, "Daniel was taken with the hostages for the sake of his people, and the body of Jesus was a hostage for the sake of all peoples." In the second instance, in the context of a discussion of the general resurrection in which he alludes to John 14.3 and 20, Aphrahat says, "Therefore let us rejoice in the hostage who was led from us and sits in glory with the Glorious King." Both citations in Aphrahat have "hostage" in the singular, whereas the passage in Ephrem has the plural. Beck translates in the singular without comment. The reason for Ephrem's use of the plural may lie in his application of theological anthropology to the resurrection of Jesus; that is, he envisages the body, soul and spirit of Jesus as hostages. For Ephrem's anthropology, cf. Kronholm, Motifs, 45–66, esp. 58; n. 33. For an interesting parallel, cf. Origen, dial. c. Her. 138.

23

This hymn plays on a familiar theme, the paradox of the incarnation. As always, however, Ephrem gives the theme a new flavor. The miracle of the incarnation is not only that the magnificently transcendent God should become a small child (str. 1, 8), but also that the Logos indwelling the entire creation should confine himself to a tiny part of it (str. 2, 11). Always stressing the power and majesty of Christ (str. 3, 4, 12), Ephrem asks why he should choose the path of *kenosis*. The answer is threefold: the grace of God (str. 3), the gift of hope for humankind (str. 6), the return of life to Adam and to us all (str. 5, 13, 14). The liturgical celebration brings us close to the moment of the birth of Christ, so that we, like the Magi, can come from afar to experience the incarnation through our faith (str. 7, 9, 10).

23

Change of melody

Refrain: Glory to You utterly from all of us. (Repeat).

1 Who, being a mortal, can tell about the Reviver of all,
   Who left the height of His majesty and came down to smallness?
   You, Who magnify all be being born, magnify my weak mind
   that I may tell about Your birth, not to investigate Your majesty,[498]
   but to proclaim Your grace. Blessed is He Who is [both] hidden and
      revealed in His actions!
2 It is a great wonder that the Son, Who dwelt entirely in a body,
   inhabited it entirely, and it sufficed for Him. Although limitless, he
      dwelt in it.

---

498. Throughout his anti-Arian polemics Ephrem insists that they erroneously believe they can investigate God's nature.

His will was entirely in Him; His totality was not in Him.
Who is sufficient to say that although He dwelt entirely in the body,
still He dwelt entirely in the universe? Blessed is the Unlimited
      Who was limited!

3   Your majesty is hidden from us; Your grace is revealed before us.
I will be silent, my Lord, about your majesty, but I will speak about
      Your grace.
Your grace seized hold of You and inclined You toward our evil.
Your grace made You a Babe; Your grace made You a human being.
Your majesty contracted [and] stretched out. Blessed is the power
      that became small and became great!

4   Glory to Him Who became earthly although heavenly by His
      nature!
By His love he became first-born to Mary although He is First-born
      of Divinity.
He became in name the child of Joseph although He is Child of the
      Heavenly One.
He became by His will a human although He is God by His nature.
Glorious is Your will and Your nature! Blessed is Your glory that
      put on our image!

5   My Lord, Your birth became mother of all creatures,
since, again, she labored and gave birth to humanity which gave
      birth to You.
[Humanity] gave birth to You physically; You begot her spiritually.
Your birth became Begetter of all. Blessed is He Who became young
      and restored youth to all!

6   Since human hope was shattered, hope was increased by Your birth.
The heavenly beings announced good hope to human beings.
Satan, who cut off our hope, cut off his hope by his [own] hands
when he saw that hope increased. Your birth became for the
      hopeless
a spring gushing hope. Blessed is the hope that brought the Gospel!

7   Your birthday resembles You, being, like You, desirable and lovable.
Without having seen Your birth, we love it as if in its time.
On Your day we see You just as when You were a babe,
beloved of everyone. Behold the churches rejoice in it.
Your day adorns and is adorned. Blessed is the day that came to be
      for our sake.

8   Your day gave us a gift like which the Father has no other.
     It was not the Seraphim He sent us, nor the Cherubim came down
          to us.
     Nor did attending Watchers come, but the First-born Who is
          attended.
     Who is able[499] to give thanks that Majesty without measure
     is lying in a despised manger? Blessed is He Who gave us all that
          He gained!

9   Your birth made that generation glad, and Your day makes our
          generation glad.
     Double is the bliss of that generation who saw the birth and the day.
     Small[er] is the bliss of the later people who see only the day of
          your birth.
     But since the nearer people doubted, greater is the bliss of the
     later people who believed in You without seeing You. Blessed is
          Your bliss that was increased for us!

10   The Magi rejoiced from afar; the scribes proclaimed from nearby.
     The prophet showed his erudition, and also Herod his fury.
     The scribes showed interpretations; the Magi showed offerings.
     It is a wonder that to one babe the kinspeople rushed with their
          swords,[500]
     but strangers with their offerings.[501] Blessed is Your birth that
          stirred up the universe!

11   Mary's lap astonishes me that it sufficed for You, my Lord, and
          embraced You.
     The entire creation was [too] small to hide Your majesty.
     Earth and heaven were [too] narrow to be like laps
     to hide Your divinity. [Too] small for You is the earth's lap,
     but large [enough] for You is Mary's lap. He dwelt in a lap, and He
          healed by the hem [of His garment].[502]

12   He [was] wrapped [in] swaddling clothes in baseness, but they
          offered Him gifts.[503]

---

499. The Syriac adds "to be sufficient."
500. Matt. 2.16–18.
501. Matt. 2.9–11.
502. The same word *knp'* means "lap, bosom, arms" and "border, flap, hem of a garment;"
Margoliouth 218b. Cf. Matt. 9.20–22, Luke 8.43–48.
503. Luke 2.7.

He put on the garments of youth, and helps emerged from them.

He put on the water of baptism, and rays flashed out from it.[504]

He put on linen garments in death,[505] and triumphs were shown by them.

With His humiliations [came] His exaltations. Blessed is He Who joins His glory to His suffering!

13 All these are changes that the Compassionate One shed and put on when He contrived to put on Adam the glory that he had shed.

He wrapped swaddling clothes with his leaves and put on garments instead of his skins.[506]

He was baptized for [Adam's] wrongdoing and embalmed for his death.

He rose and raised him up in glory. Blessed is He Who came down, put on [a body] and ascended!

14 Since Your birth sufficed for the sons of Adam as [for] Adam,

O Great One Who became a babe, by Your birth again You begot me.

O Pure One Who was baptized, let Your washing wash us of impurity.

O Living One Who was embalmed, let us obtain life by Your death.

I will thank You entirely in Him Who fills all. Glory to You entirely from all of us!

---

504. Cf. Mark 1.9–11 et par. None of the evangelists speaks of rays flashing from the water, but Ephrem refers presumably to the presence of the Holy Spirit.

505. Mark 15.46 et par.

506. Gen. 3.7.

24

This hymn is an extended comment on the second chapter of Matthew's gospel, the visit of the Magi, the flight into Egypt and the slaughter of the innocents. In his handling of these materials Ephrem's midrashic style shows a remarkable consonance with Matthew's.[507] For example, he clearly understands Matthew's intent to evoke the Exodus (str. 3). More remarkable, however, is his perception that Balaam is the principal model for the Magi.[508] Ephrem cites the prophecy of Balaam early in the hymn (str. 4.1), and he refers to it again explicitly near the end in a strophe that recapitulates the major themes of the hymn (str. 20). Throughout the hymn his emphasis is on the star as a sort of prophet that discriminates between good and evil listeners (str. 5-8, 13). Closely linked is the theme of the futility of the opposition of the tyrannical king to the plan of God (str. 8, 9). He also stresses the irony of a Babylonian seer who prophesies for Israel (str. 4, 13, 15). He uses an unusually rich and varied range of imagery to describe the persecution and slaughter of the innocents, notably, the chase of animals of prey (str. 3, 6), and destruction of a garden (str. 7, 17–18). In the latter passages he skillfully blends in eucharistic images as well.

As is often the case, he chooses to emphasize the anti-Judaic direction of the Matthean story (esp. str. 11). He uses the Magi as representatives of the Gentiles and contrasts their belief with the unbelief and hostility of Herod and his soldiers, whom he takes as typifying the Jewish people (str. 4; cf. Nat. 23.10). With the advent of Jesus, Israel's line of priests, prophets and kings has come to an end (str. 2). In a sense the line of prophecy has crossed over from the prophets of Israel to the Magi and the star as a consequence of the deafness and blindness of Israel (str. 12–16, 19–20).

After the insertion of a personal prayer (str. 21), several manuscripts

---

507. On the infancy narratives as *midrashim*, cf. Brown, Messiah, 557–63.
508. For the story of Balaam, cf. Num. 22–24. For this as the background of the story of the Magi, cf. Brown, Messiah, 190–96.

continue with four additional strophes (str. 22–25), which fit very well with the rest of the hymn, continuing the anti-Judaic theme and relating the theme of the star to John the Baptist. Like the star John proclaimed Christ, but unlike the star he proclaimed the same message to all despite the fact that it led to his own death (str. 23–24). The star, on the other hand, hid its message from evil men to delay the death of Christ until the proper time (str. 25, cf. str. 17).

24

Change of melody and [to] the same melody [as . . .][509]

1 The babes were slain because of Your all-reviving birth.[510]
But since the King, our Lord the Lord of the kingdom, was a slain [king],
slain hostages were given by that cunning tyrant.[511]
The heavenly ranks received, clothed in the mysteries of His slaying,
the hostages whom earthly beings offered. Blessed is the King Who magnified them!

Refrain: To You be glory from all mouths on this day of Your birth!

2 As keepers of deposits all the kings of the house of David
handed down and passed on the throne and diadem of the Son of David.
The priests, prophets and kings came to an end; they were confined and limited to One
Who came, the Lord of everything, and took everything from them.
He ended all successions.[512] Blessed is He Who was clothed in what belonged to Him.

---

509. The manuscript tradition is confused as to which is the appropriate melody for this hymn.

510. Matt. 2.16–18. The murdered innocents are types, anticipating the death of Christ.

511. Beck suggests an alteration of the text to make the tyrant the subject, but the same sense may be obtained by taking "that cunning tyrant" as *casus pendens*, the plural verb as a passive, and the pronoun "*lh*" as referring to Herod rather than to Christ and as the agent of the passive verb.

512. Literally, "the successions of everything."

3   The doves in Bethlehem murmured since the serpent destroyed their
       offspring.[513]

The eagle fled to Egypt to go down and receive the promises.[514]

Egypt rejoiced to be the capital for repaying her debts.

She who had slain the sons of Joseph[515] labored to repay by the Son
       of Joseph

the debts of the sons of Joseph. Blessed is He Who called Him from
       Egypt!

4   The scribes read every day that a star would shine forth from
       Jacob.[516]

The People have the voice and the reading; the peoples have the
       shining forth and the explanation.

They have the books and we have the deeds; they have the branches
       and we their fruits.

The scribes read in books; the Magi saw in actions

the flash of that reading. Blessed is He Who added for us their
       books!

5   Who is able to speak about the secrets and the revelations

of the star of light that went before the bearers of offerings?

The diadem was revealed and announced; the body was veiled and
       hidden.

It became the Son's in two ways: announcer and guardian:

It guarded His body and announced His diadem. Blessed is He
       Who makes His announcers wise!

6   The tyrant gazed at the Magi who asked, "Where is the king's
       son?"[517]

Although his heart was gloomy, he sought an appearance of joy.[518]

With the sheep he sent wolves to slay the Lamb of God.[519]

The Lamb went to Egypt to judge from there those

---

513. Cf. Matt. 2.17f.
514. Cf. Matt. 2.13f.
515. Cf. Exod. 1.8.
516. Num. 24.17.
517. Matt. 2.2.
518. Literally, "Although his heart was a gloomy one, he sought an appearance of a joyful one." Cf. Matt. 2.3.
519. Here and in the following strophe Ephrem implies that the soldiers accompanied the Magi, but they were sent later according to Matthew, cf. Matt. 2.7–18; however, cf. Num. 22–24, e.g. Num 22.20, where Balaam is accompanied by the elders of Moab and Midian.

whom he had delivered from there. Blessed is He Who enslaved
   them again![520]

7 The Magi declared to the tyrant, "When your servants mingled with
      us,
   the star of light was hidden and the paths were veiled."[521]
   The good men did not know that the bitter king [had] sent
   villains as worshippers to destroy the sweet Fruit
   Whom bitter men eat and become sweet. To You be glory, Medicine
      of life!

8 But since the Magi received the command to go and seek Him,[522]
   it is written of them that they saw the star of light and rejoiced.[523]
   It is known that it was well-hidden since they rejoiced in its sight.
   It was veiled to hinder the villains; it rose up to summon the
      worshippers.
   It defeated one side and summoned the other. Blessed is the one
      who triumphed on both sides!

9 How did the unclean one who slew the infants overlook the Infant?
   Justice hindered him who supposed the Magi would return to
      him.[524]
   While he delayed, he postponed catching the Worshipped and His
      worshippers,
   his hands let everything escape; the offerings and the worshippers
      fled
   from the tyrant to the King's Son. Glory to Him Who knows every
      contrivance!

10 The guileless Magi, asleep on their couches, were thinking
   so that sleep became a mirror and a dream rose up like light;[525]
   they saw the slayer, his deceit and his sword flashing, and they were
      terrified.
   His deceit reached out to the men; he sharpened the sword for the
      infants.

---

520. Probably the measures taken against the Jews by Titus and Hadrian are meant, as
Beck suggests.
   521. This is not in the canonical account, which has no indication that Herod's men
accompanied the Magi.
   522. Matt. 2.8.
   523. Matt. 2.10.
   524. Matt. 2.16.
   525. Matt. 2.12; cf. Num. 22.8,13,19f.

The Watcher taught the sleeping men. Blessed is He Who makes
    wise the guileless!

11   The simple believers[526] recognized two advents of Christ,
but the foolish scribes were not aware of even one advent.
Yet the peoples received life from one and there at the other they
    will be revived.
The one advent scattered the People whose understanding was
    blind;
The second will blot out its memory.[527] Blessed is the King Who has
    come and will come!

12   The Redeemer shone forth to the blind, but they looked to others.
The Sun showed His rays, but they were clothed in darkness.
The Resplendent One sent His light, and it summoned the sons of
    light
to reveal to the sons of darkness, "Behold in your midst is the light,
but over your eyes a veil."[528] To You be glory, New Sun!

13   The prophets announced His birth but did not specify His time.
He sent the Magi, and they came and declared His time.
But the Magi who made known the time did not specify where the
    Infant was.
The glorious star of light ran and showed where the Infant was.[529]
This glorious succession! Blessed is He who by all of them was
    interpreted!

14   They[530] rejected the trumpet of Isaiah that sounded the pure
    conception;[531]
they stilled the lyre of the psalms that sang about his priesthood;[532]
they silenced the kithara of the spirit that sang of His kingship.[533]
Under a great silence they closed in the great birth that made

---

526. Literally, "who believed."
527. Like many Patristic writers, Ephrem attributes the Roman dispersal of the Jews to their rejection of Jesus. He extends this to the eschaton, contrary to Paul's view in Rom. 11.25–36.
528. 2 Cor. 3.14. Ephrem's meaning is that the star sent by God summoned the Magi, the sons of light, to reveal Christ to the Jews, the sons of darkness, the blind. The alterations of the text here suggested by Beck are not necessary.
529. Matt. 2.9.
530. I.e., the Jewish people.
531. Isa. 7.14.
532. Ps. 110.4.
533. Ps. 145.10–13.

heavenly and earthly beings shout out. Blessed is He Who shines
    forth from within the stillness!

15   His voice became a hidden key, and it opened the mouth of the
    Magi.
Since in Judea the announcers were silent, [the Magi] sounded the
    voice in creation.
The distant ones came bearing the news they [had] rejected.
The ungrateful[534] began to heed the voices of the strangers,
crying out about the Son of David.[535] Blessed is He Who silenced
    them with our voice!

16   Since the People withheld offerings and did not approach the King's
    Son,
His ambassador[536] went out to the peoples and brought them with
    their offering.
But it did not bring all of them since the small womb of Bethlehem
could not suffice for them, so that the womb of the holy church
opened wide and enclosed her children. Blessed is He Who made
    fruitful the barren one!

17   In Bethlehem the slayers mowed down the fair flowers so that with
    them
would perish the fair Seed in which was hidden the Living Bread.[537]
The Staff of life had fled so that is might come to the sheaf in the
    harvest.
The Cluster that fled while young, gave Himself in the trampling
to revive souls with His wine. Glory to You, the Medicine of life!

18   The villains entered the garden full of young fruits.
They shook down the blossoms from the branches. Buds and shoots
    they destroyed.
Unknowing, the agitator offered pure gifts[538]—
to him woe, to them grace. Bethlehem brought forth early and gave
virgin fruits to the Holy One. Blessed is He Who received the first
    fruits!

---

534. This is the *nomen agentis* for the word *ṭlm* translated as "rejected" in the line above.
535. Cf. Num. 22.1–14, 24.17; cf. Nat. 23.10 and Nat. 24.20, below.
536. I.e., the star.
537. Cf. Matt. 2.16ff. and John 6.22–71, esp. 35.
538. I.e., the innocents were gifts offered to God to their benefit and to the deficit of Herod, who offered them.

19 Since the scribes were silent with envy and the Pharisees with
jealousy,
people of stone who acquired a heart of stone cried out and
praised;[539]
They sang praises before the rejected Stone that became the head.[540]
The stones were softened by the Stone and they acquired speaking
mouths.
Stones cried out by means of the Stone.[541] Blessed is Your birth that
made the stones cry out!

20 As is written in the scripture, distant peoples saw the star
that the near People might be put to shame. O the learned and
proud People who by the peoples have been retaught how and
where they saw
that rising of which Balaam spoke![542] A stranger declared it;
strangers were those who saw it. Blessed is He Who made His
kinspeople jealous!

21 Let my request approach Your gate and my need Your treasury.
Grant me, my Lord, without reckoning, as God [grants] to man
that even should You increase as the Son of the Gracious and add as
a King's Son
[and] should I be ungrateful as one of dust—like Adam is the child
of Adam,
and like the Gracious is the Son of the Gracious. Glory to You, One
like His Father![543]

22 The People who possessed the scriptures did not perceive that they
proclaimed its faults,
they cried out about its exile, and they told about our entry.[544]

---

539. Cf. the entry into Jerusalem, Mark 11.1–10 et par.; for hearts of stone, cf. Ezek.
11.19f. and Nat. 22.17.
540. Mark 12.10 et par. On Christ the Stone or Rock, cf. Virg 14.6–7.
541. Luke 19.40.
542. Num. 22–24, esp. Num. 24.17. Just as Balaam was brought from a distance to put to
shame the king of Moab and his people, the Magi were brought from afar to put to shame King
Herod and his people, cf. str. 15 above.
543. Although the ms. tradition and the meter of this strophe present no problems, the
content bears no resemblance to the previous strophes. It appears to be a final invocation
intended to end the hymn. This is perhaps the reason for the loss of the following strophes from
some of the mss. It is my judgment that str. 22–25 belong to the original hymn.
544. On this anti-Jewish use of the Hebrew scriptures, especially of the prophets, cf.
Ruether, Fratricide, 124–49.

Behold the fool reads in his scriptures the promises that were
    distributed to us!
As he boasts in his scriptures, he reads to us his [own] accusation,
and he witnesses our inheritance to us! Blessed is He Who wearied
    them to give us rest.

23   The pair of announcers expressed the properties of the Only-
    Begotten:
the star of light and John—one a shining forth, the other a voice.[545]
For the One Announced was also a Word and a Light.
Voice and ray serve Him. The shining forth announced His light
and the voice His wisdom.[546] More blessed is the First-born than
    His announcers!

24   John gazed at Him and cried, "This is the Lamb of God!"[547]
The Lamb grew fat and matured, and He came to be an offering.
John was not afraid to cry, "Behold, it is He!"[548]—
not even if the slayers attack, even if it was the time of sprinkling[549]
so that forgiveness would be by His blood. Blessed is the
    Compensator of our sins.

25   The glorious star of light was not like John,
for there was a [place] where it rose and made straight the way for
    the simple,
but there was [a place] where it sank and made the path of the
    wolves go astray.
It kept the Lamb from the slaughter so that the day for the slaughter
    would come,[550]
that in Him the flock would be pardoned. Blessed is He in Whom
    His possessions were redeemed!

---

545. Cf. Nat. 6.9.
546. Although Beck's text erroneously (?) gives the plural here, he translates the singular.
547. John 1.29.
548. John 1.30.
549. The Day of Atonement, cf. Lev. 16.1–34. Jesus' death is so interpreted, e.g., in Heb. 9.11–10.18. Here, Ephrem refers to the death of Christ, but he also seems to have John's death in mind as an antetype of Christ's, like the deaths of the innocents in str. 1–3.
550. Cf. str. 17 above.

This hymn links the liturgical festivals of the church to the mystery of the incarnation. The first ten strophes, addressed to the church, celebrate the blessings bestowed on it. The festivals and scripture of Judaism have been transferred to Christianity (str. 1 and 9). The festivals of the church have been honored by angels, Magi and good kings (str. 2–4). The prophets Isaiah, Micah and Daniel and King David have honored the church by their predictions about the Messiah (str. 5–8). In the Sermon on the Mount Jesus bestowed ten blessings on the church—ten because it is the perfect number (str. 10).

By introducing a notion of cosmic and mysterious significance, the tenth strophe broaches the theme of the latter half of the hymn: the infinitude, incomprehensibility and eternity of the Incarnate One. First Ephrem addresses Bethlehem-Ephrata, the insignificant town where the Infinite One made himself finite, where the Timeless One had a beginning (str. 11–13). Then, similarly, he turns to Mary, the one best able to know the Unknowable One; she was wise enough to know not to inquire but to praise (str. 14–15). Finally, Simeon—perhaps as a figure for all Christian priests—is portrayed offering the Father's Child to the Father (str. 16). Through the incarnation "the earth became . . . a new heaven" in which the angels sing praises—reemphasizing the first theme of Christian festivals of praise and perhaps alluding to the understanding of Christian liturgy as heavenly praise (str. 17).

25

On the melody, "Blessed are you, Ephrata!"

1 Blessed are you, O church in whom resounds
  the great feast, the festival of the King!

Abandoned Sion thirsts[551] for them very much,
but her gates are bereft of festivals.
Blessed are your gates that are opened but not filled
and your courtyards, extensive but not empty.
Within you graze the peoples—behold they cried out
and silenced the People.

Refrain: Glory to the One Who sent Him! (Repeat)

2 Blessed are you, O church, upon whose festivals
Watchers rejoice among your feasts.[552]
For the Watchers praised one night
on the earth that restrains and refuses praise.
Blessed are your voices that have been sown and reaped,
and in heaven they have been gathered into storehouses.
Your mouth is a censer, and your voices like sweet spices
rise up on your festivals!

3 Blessed are you, O church, to whom come
all offerings on this feast.
The Magi, once, among deceivers
offered their gifts to Truth.
Blessed is your habitation in which the King's Son,
worshipped with gifts, condescended to dwell.
Gold of the West and spices of the East
are offered on your festivals.

4 Blessed are you, O church, who have
no king, no tyrant and harmer of babes.
For in Bethlehem he slew infants indiscriminately
so that the Child who is Reviver of all might die.
Blessed are your children who were emulated and honored
by kings who were seasoned by your worship.[553]
The crown of the East trampled your loved ones
that he might be trampled by those you love.[554]

---

551. *zbyn*, a pun on *zbywn*, Sion; Ephrem continues with *ṣdyn*, "are bereft."
552. There are several similar sounding words here: church ('*dt*'), your festivals ('*d'dyky*), Watchers ('*yr*'), and your feasts ("*dyky*).
553. Constantine and his successors.
554. Shapur II, Sassanid ruler of Persia, persecuted Christians in his realm and also carried on extensive military campaigns against the Roman rulers, but the Roman victories were not so decisive as Ephrem here pretends.

5 Blessed are you, O church, in whom rejoices
even Isaiah in his prophecy:
"Behold a virgin will conceive and bring forth
a child" whose name is a great mystery.[555]
O for the explanation that was revealed in the church!
Two names were joined together and became one:
Emmanuel.[556] El is with you always,[557]
Who joins you with His members.

6 Blessed are you, O church, by Micah who cried out
"A shepherd will come out from Ephrata."[558]
For He came to Bethlehem to take
from it the rod of Jesse and to rule the peoples.[559]
Blessed are your lambs sealed with his Seal[560]
and your sheep kept by His word.
You, O church, are the eternal Bethlehem,
since in you is the bread of life.[561]

7 Blessed are you, O church, in whom behold
even Daniel, the man beloved, rejoices.[562]
He declared that the glorious Messiah would be slain
and the holy town would be destroyed by His slaying.[563]
Woe to the People that was rejected and did not repent!
Blessed are the peoples who were called and did not turn away.
Those invited declined and others instead of them
enjoyed their marriage feasts.[564]

8 Blessed are you, O church, by whom
David the King sings with his lyre.
By the Spirit he sang about Him, "You are my Son.

---

555. Isa. 7.14.

556. Strictly speaking Emman and El are not two names for God, but the following lines indicate that this is the division Ephrem means. The two parts are joined by what appears to be the conjunction *w* but is actually the enclitic *hw*. Ephrem's remark is a kind of theological grammarian's pun.

557. In Syriac, as in Hebrew, Emmanuel means "God [El] is with us."

558. Mic. 5.2.

559. Cf. Isa. 11.1–16 and Mic. 5.3–7.

560. Cf. Rev. 7.1–8.

561. Ephrem's meaning is based on a pun in the Syriac, since "Bethlehem" means "house of bread."

562. Dan. 9.23.

563. Dan. 9.26.

564. Luke 14.15–24; cf. Matt. 22.2–10.

I"—by the glories of holiness—"have begotten You today."[565]
Blessed are your ears, cleansed to hear
His day as His body.[566] Keep vigil and honor Him.
Be chastened by Sion who made the festival mournful.
Make joyful Him Who made you joyful.

9   Blessed are you, O church, since all festivals
fled from Sion and alighted with you.
In you the weary prophets have found rest
from that labor and shame in Judah.
Blessed are her scriptures unrolled in your temples
and her festivals celebrated in your temples.[567]
Sion is bereft, and behold today the generations shout at your
    festivals.

10   Blessed are you, O church, with ten blessings[568]
that our Lord gave; a perfect mystery.
For every number depends on ten.[569]
Therefore ten blessings perfected you.
Blessed are your crowns into all of which were plaited
holy blessings mingled in every crown.
Blessed One, crowned with every blessing,
bestow a blessing on me too!

11   Blessed are you, Ephrata, mother of kings,
from whom shone forth the Lord[570] of diadems.
It was Micah who announced to you, "He is from eternity
and the length of His times is incomprehensible."[571]
Blessed are your eyes that met Him before all!
You He found worthy to see Him when He shone forth:
the Origin of blessing and Beginning of joys.
You received Him before the universe.

12   Blessed are you, Bethlehem, whom fortified towns

---

565. Ps. 2.7.
566. The meaning is unclear.
567. Two different words *hykl'* and *nws'*—the first of Semitic origin, the second Greek ναός—are used here for temple. In this context both refer to the Christian churches.
568. I.e., the first ten strophes of this hymn, but also, as Beck has noted, the beatitudes are counted as ten: Matt. 5.3, 5.4, 5.5, 5.6, 5.7, 5.8, 5.9, 5.10, 5.11b [with Luke 6.27a], Luke 6.21; cf. Aph. Dem. 2.19.
569. Cf. Nat. 26.12 and 27.2–4.
570. The indication of plural in Beck's text is apparently an error.
571. Cf. Mic. 5.2.

and fortified cities envied.
Mary, like you, women envied—
and virgin daughters of powerful men.
Blessed is the girl He found worthy to indwell,
and also the town He found worthy to inhabit.
A needy girl and a small town
He chose to humble Himself.

13 Blessed are you, Bethlehem, in whom was the beginning
for the Son, Who is in the Father from eternity.
It is difficult to comprehend that He is before Time[572]
Who in you subjected Himself to Time.
Blessed are your ears that were first [to hear when] in you bleated
the Lamb of God Who rejoiced in you.
In your manger He became small, but He extended in all directions
and was worshipped by all creatures.

14 Blessed are you also, Mary, whose name
is great and exalted[573] because of your Child.
Indeed you were able to say how much and how
and where the Great One, Who became small, dwelt in you.
Blessed is your mouth that gave thanks but did not inquire
and your tongue that praised but did not investigate.
Since His mother was awed by Him, although she bore Him,
who is sufficient [to know] Him?

15 O you, woman that no man knows,
how shall we see the Son you have brought forth?
For the eye is not able to understand
his glorious transformations.
For tongues of fire dwell in Him
Who sent tongues at His ascension.[574]
Let every tongue be warned that our investigation is stubble
and our scrutiny [is] fire.

16 Blessed is the priest[575] who in the sanctuary
offers to the Father the Father's Child,
the Fruit plucked from our tree,

---

572. The Syriac uses a plural here and in the following line.
573. This word, differently vocalized, is Mary's name!
574. Cf. Acts 2.3.
575. Simeon, cf. Luke 2.22–35.

although He is entirely from majesty.
Blessed are the consecrated hands that offer Him
and his lips wearied with kissing Him.[576]
The Spirit in the Temple longed to exalt Him,
and when he was crucified it tore [the veil] and went out.[577]

17   That chief of the angels greeted you[578]
as the pledge of holiness.
The earth became for him a new heaven
in which the Watchers came down and praised.
The sons of the height gathered around your dwelling
because of the King's Son Who dwelt in you.
Your earthly habitation became like heaven above
by their vigil.

---

576. Here I have departed from Beck's text, reading *wlspwth* rather than *wlsybth*, and leaving *d't'mly* unchanged.

577. Cf. Mark 15.28 et par. and Luke 2.27.

578. Mary. On Gabriel as "chief of the angels" rather than Archangel, cf. Cramer, Engelvorstellungen, 95f.

26

This hymn is a meditation on the biblical account of the seven days of creation in relation to the Christian understanding of the incarnation (esp. str. 3–10).[579] Evidently because of the liturgical context, other materials related to the birth and infancy of Jesus provide a framework for the hymn (str. 1–2, 11–13). Thus, Ephrem begins by relating the first year of Jesus' life to the first day of creation (str. 1). Next he considers events attributed to the second year of Jesus' life: the visit of the Magi and the slaying of the innocents (str. 2). But this direction is temporarily abandoned in favor of a theological consideration of the days of creation.

In the central portion of the hymn he discovers a typological aspect in the description of each of the days of creation in Genesis. The creation of light on the first day provides a meditation on the role of Christ as Light of the world (str. 3). The first day, like Christ the First-born, the Logos, represents the pillar of creation and root of the universe (str. 1 and 4). Just as on the second day the waters of the firmament were separated, Christ separated from heavenly beings to come down and give us water to drink (str. 5). The third day, on which plants were created, recalls Christ the Holy Blossom as well as the source of all growth (str. 6). The fourth day brings a meditation on the sun and moon, light and sight (str. 7). The creation of reptiles on the fifth day provokes a consideration of Satan and the Fall (str. 8). Adam's creation on the sixth day provides an opportunity to contrast the poison of the forbidden fruit with the Medicine of life (str. 9). The day of God's rest is symbolic not only of the sabbath rest and the divine care for creatures but also of subjection and freedom (str. 10).

Leaving the Genesis account of creation, Ephrem returns in the last few strophes to themes related to the infancy of Christ. The eighth day recalls the circumcision of Jesus and Christian rejection of the practice (str. 11). The tenth day is remembered due to the perfection of the

---

579. The hymn and its theology are discussed in el-Khoury, Interpretation, 49–62, as well as in Kronholm, Motifs, 41f.

number ten (str. 12). Finally, without mentioning the fortieth day,[580] Ephrem recalls the day of purification as a symbol of Christ, the Purifier of all (str. 13).

26

Change of melody

Refrain: Blessed is Your birth that makes all Creation glad!

1 The first year of our Redeemer's birth
is the source of blessings and foundation of life.
For by it are borne a multitude of victories
and the sum of helps.
As the first day "in the beginning"
the great pillar of the creation
bears the building of the creation,
so the first-born day [bears] the helps for humanity.

2 In the second year of our Redeemer's birth
the Magi are glad, the Pharisees are gloomy,
treasures are opened, kings are hastening,
and infants are slain.
For in it are offered in Bethlehem
desirable and fearful gifts.
For love offered gold,
but envy [offered] infants by the sword.

3 The day of the All-Illuminating is glad at His birth.
It is a pillar of rays that pursues with its beams
the works of darkness in a type of that day
on which light was created
and tore away the darkness
spread over the beauty of creation.
The ray of our Redeemer's birth
entered and tore away the darkness upon the heart.

---

580. Although Luke was confused about the relation between purification and circumcision, Ephrem seems to realize the purification would be later; cf. Brown, Messiah, 447f. and Lev. 12.1ff.

4 The first day, the source and beginning,
is a type of the root that germinated everything.
Much greater than it is our Redeemer's day[581] planted in the
     universe.
For His death is like a root[582] inside the earth,
His resurrection like the summit in heaven,
His words [extend] in every direction like branches,
and like His fruit [is] His body for those who eat it.

5 Let the second day sing praise on the birth
of the Son, the Second,[583] and the Voice of the First.[584]
He commanded the firmament and it came into existence; He
     divided the waters above,
and He gathered the seas below.
He Who separated the waters from the waters
separated from the Watchers and came down to humankind.
Instead of the waters He commanded and they were gathered,
He let flow a source of water and gave [it] to drink.

6 Let the third day weave with hymns
a crown of psalms[585] and offer [it] with one voice
for the birth of Him Who made flowers and blossoms grow
on the third day.
But now He Who makes all things grow,
came down and became a Holy Blossom.
From the thirsty earth He sprouted, and He went up
to adorn and crown the victorious.

7 Let the fourth day confess fourfold
the birth of Him Who created on the fourth day
the pair of luminaries that fools worship
and they are blind and unseeing.

---

581. The two phrases are inverted in the Syriac.

582. The Syriac word is not the same as a few lines previous.

583. I.e., second after the Father. Although this seems susceptible to an Arian interpretation, the following phrase makes it the most likely reading. Another, less likely, possibility is that "second" should be attributed to "birth" rather than "Son," meaning the birth from Mary in the incarnation as opposed to the birth from the Father before all time.

584. I.e., the Voice of the Father. Ephrem's Logos theology is evident here. For some discussion cf. Kronholm, Motifs, 39–43.

585. The phrases are inverted in the Syriac.

He, the Lord of the luminaries, came down,
and like the sun He shone on us from the womb.
His radiances have opened [the eyes of] the blind;
His rays have enlightened the straying.

8   Let the fifth day praise Him Who created
on the fifth day creeping things and dragons
of whose kind is the serpent. He deceived [and] led astray our
          mother,
a young girl without understanding.[586]
Since the deceiver mocked the young girl,
the fraudulent one was exposed by the Dove
Who shone forth and emerged from an innocent womb,
the Wise One, Who crushed the crafty one.

9   Let the sixth day praise Him Who created
on Friday Adam whom the evil one envied.
As a false friend he pleased him [by] offering him poison in [his]
          food.
The Medicine of Life diffused Himself to them both.
He put on a body and was offered to them both.
The mortal tasted Him and lived by Him;
the devourer who ate Him was destroyed.[587]

10   Let the seventh day cry "holy" to the Holy One
Who sanctified the Sabbath to give rest to living beings.
The untiring Gracious One took care of humanity and He took care
          of animals.
Since freedom fell under the yoke,
He came to the birth and was subjected to free [it].
He was struck a servant's slap in the court.
As Lord, He broke the yoke upon the free.

11   Let the eighth day that circumcised the Hebrews
confess Him Who commanded His namesake Joshua[588]
to circumcise with flint the People whose body [was] circumcised
but whose heart was unbelieving from within.

---

586. Eve's childishness makes her vulnerable to the serpent. On this theme, cf. Kronholm, *Motifs*, 98–107, but his stress on her "infantilism" is too negative since naïve innocence is an equally important nuance, cf. Nat. 7.7, 7.11 and note ad loc.
587. On the punishment of the serpent, cf. Nat. 13.2 and note ad loc.
588. In Syriac, as in Hebrew, Jesus and Joshua are the same name.

Behold on the eighth day as a babe
The Circumciser of all came to circumcision.[589]
Although the sign of Abraham was on His flesh,
the blind daughter of Sion has disfigured it.

12 Let the tenth day praise its number
for yodh, the letter of the fair name of Jesus,
in counting is ten. This [number] that is like a lord
reverses the numbers.
For whenever counting goes up to ten,[590]
it goes back to begin from one again.
O great mystery that [is] in [the name] Jesus
Whose power turns Creation back again!

13 The First-born, Purifier of all, on the day of His purifying
purified the purification of the first-born and was offered.[591]
The Lord of offering was in need of offerings
to make an offering of a bird.[592]
By His birth were completed the archetypes:
He came and paid the debts by His descent;
by His resurrection He ascended and sent treasures.[593]

---

589. Luke 2.21.
590. Cf. Nat. 25.10, 27.2–4.
591. Cf. Luke 2.22–24.
592. Ibid.
593. According to Ephrem the true meaning of the offering of birds in Judaism was fulfilled in the incarnation and resurrection of Christ—His coming down and going up like a bird.

This hymn is a calendrical speculation on the relation of solar phenomena, numbers and letters of the alphabet to the conception and birth of Jesus and to the name of Jesus. Ephrem reads these details as divine hints pointing to Jesus' status as "Son of the Lord of the universe." Especially prominent here is the association of Jesus with Sol Invictus, the Unconquered Sun.

Six and ten, perfect numbers, are the dates of Jesus' birth and conception. Further the letter yodh, which represents the number ten in Syriac, is also the first letter of Jesus' name—thus indicating his mysterious status. The names of Joseph and John the Baptist begin with the same letter as Jesus, and Mary's name begins with the same letter as Messiah—all to indicate the power of Jesus, the Messiah (str. 2–13).

Christ is represented by the sun in three ways. The descent and ascent of Christ are prefigured by the sun's setting and rising (str. 14–16). The conceptions of John the Baptist in a dark month and of Jesus in a light month are types of the two births of Christ: the first birth from the Father, hidden from all; the second from Mary, revealed to all (str. 17–20). Finally, and most important, the conception and the birth of Christ take place at the moments of the sun's victories in spring and in winter (str. 1 and 21–22).

27

Change of melody
1   Light was like a harbinger
    to that Bright One to Whom Mary gave birth,
    for His conception was in the victory of light,
    and His birth was at the victory of the sun. Blessed be the
        Conqueror!

HYMN 27

Refrain: To You be glory, Son of the Lord of the universe! (Repeat).

2   "Yodh" stands at the beginning of Your name.[594]
    It stands at the tenth in the month of April.
    On the tenth You entered the womb.
    Your conception was in a symbol of the perfect number.
3   The number ten is complete;
    on the tenth of April You entered the womb.
    The number six is also perfect;
    on the sixth of January Your birth gave joy to the six directions.
4   The number ten is the sum,
    and the sixfold is the sum of sums.[595]
    On the tenth [was] His conception, on the sixth His birth.
    His birth gave joy to the four directions [and the height and depth].
5   Joseph's name was not sufficient
    for him to be Your father since it was [too] weak.
    Your name gave [his name] the letter "yodh";
    Your name strengthened Joseph's name to be father to You.
6   "Messiah," too, in its compassion,
    gave the first of its letters to Mary's name.
    Behold! Their names depend on His names
    even as their bodies, with all creation, depended on His power.
7   For Mary, that [woman] who bore Him
    in the womb and on her lap—Him, the Messiah—

---

594. The mystical interpretation of numbers in relation to the letters that represent them is a standard device of rabbinic exegesis, gematria; cf. C. Levias, "Gematria," JE 5, 589–92, and G. Scholem, "Gematria," EJ 7, 369–74.

595. Ten is the sum of the numbers one through four. Six times six is the sum of the numbers one through eight. In contrast to the mixing of numbers and letters characteristic of rabbinic gematria, the mystical interpretation of the properties of the numbers themselves originated with the Pythagoreans, made its way into popular Hellenistic culture and eventually, through Philo and the Alexandrian Christian exegetes, to Augustine and the medieval West; cf. V.F. Hopper, *Medieval Number Symbolism: Its Sources, Meaning and Influence on Thought and Expression* (New York, 1938); M. Comeau, *Saint Augustin, exégète du quatrième Evangile*, 2d ed. (Paris, 1930), 127–42; M. Pontet, *L'exégèse de S. Augustin prédicateur* (Paris, 1945), 278–303. Similar notions are to be found in Syriac and Greek Patristic sources; cf. R. W. Thomson, "Number Symbolism and Patristic Exegesis in Some Early Armenian Writers," *Handes Amsorya* 90(1976), 117–38; A. Guillaumont, *Les 'Kephalaia Gnostica' d'Evagre le Pontique et l'Histoire de l'Origénisme chez les grecs et chez les syriens*, Patristica Sorboniensa 5 (Paris, 1962) 34f.; McVey, Microcosm, 100; but no study to date has investigated Ephrem's sources for these ideas or their relation to the rabbinic gematria.

211

the first of the letters of [her] name was messiah.
She bore His name as His power bore her body.

8   For without His power
Mary could not bear His body.
He showed the hidden by way of the revealed,
since not even their names could exist without Him.

9   He gave the heads of His letters
to His parents who were His heads,
and as their bodies were adorned by Him,
so, too, He adorned their names with His names.

10   Nor again did that John
baptize His body without His power.
"Yodh" bore the name of John
as Jesus' power bore John.

11   But if He bestowed the beauty
of His letters on their names,
if he mixed some of His glorious beauty in their names,
how much, indeed, did He mix His hidden power in their names!

12   Just as enumeration
has only ten levels,
there are six sides to the creation:
the height and depth and four directions filled by You.

13   The letter "yodh" of Jesus, our King,
is the Queen of all numbers.
On her perfection depend all reckoning
as in Jesus all meanings are mixed.

14   The Greatest of all descended utterly
to unspeakable humiliation.
He returned from that humiliation
to seize the unlimited height on the right hand.

15   [It is] a great wonder that from that height
He did not proceed little by little
to descend [and] come to smallness.
He flew from the womb of Divinity to humanity.

16   For the sun—that sun of Yours—
announces Your mystery as if by mouth.
In the winter, as Your type, it descends to a low level;
in summer, like You, it ascends to the height and rules over all.

17   Also the type of Your conception, my Master,
    and [the conception] of John, Your harbinger,
    the mystery of Your conceptions and Your births,
    by light and darkness are portrayed and revealed to one who
         perceives.

18   The conception of John took place
    in October in which darkness dwells.[596]
    Your conception took place in
    April when the light rules over darkness and subdues it.[597]

19   I give thanks for Your first birth
    hidden and concealed from all creatures.
    I also give thanks for Your second birth,
    revealed and younger than all creatures who yet [are] in Your
         hands![598]

20   The births of the Only-Begotten,
    one above and one below,
    one the stranger, strange to all,
    and one the kinsman, allied utterly to humanity.[599]

21   Again, as if by a symbol
    the day of Your birth falls in January
    when light snatches from darkness
    the hours it swallowed, just as You snatched us from our
         swallower.[600]

22   April portrays Your conception when it cried out
    "Behold the Light confined in the womb!"
    In January the pair of lights emerged:
    You from the womb and the sun with You from within the dark.

---

596. Tishri (October–November) is after the autumnal equinox, hence nights are lengthening. Ephrem has apparently deduced the time of John's conception by extrapolation from the Lucan infancy narrative, cf. Luke 1.24–26.

597. The vernal equinox in Nisan (April) marks the point when the days begin to be longer than the nights.

598. The first birth is of the divine Son from the "womb of the Divinity" before the creation of all things; the second is the birth from Mary of the incarnate Christ.

599. Here Ephrem, like other anti-Arian polemicists, contrasts the utter uniqueness of the generation of the Son by the Father (or, to use the female imagery Ephrem often prefers, the birth of the Son from the womb of the Father) with the familiar human birth of the incarnate Son.

600. Conun (December–January) contains the winter solstice. On the theme of Christ as the Unconquered Sun, cf. Nat. 5.13–15.

28

The hymn is a meditation on Mary's virginity as appropriate to the indwelling of the Son of God in her. She is a holy thing, set aside for God's presence on earth. Just as the animals in Noah's ark were chaste, he begins, how much more should Mary be chaste (str. 1). This is not because marriage is unacceptable, but because chastity is better, a heavenly and angelic state (str. 2–4). Paradoxically Mary is both virgin and mother (str. 5). Her virginal conception implies the freedom from sexual desire since such a desire would have no purpose (str. 6). The Divine Presence suffused Mary entirely during her pregnancy (str. 7). Even from Holy Scripture, Error may gather poison for those who love her (str. 8), but the church is like a bee gathering the nectar from the Egyptian and Hebrew fields (str. 9). Since the Jewish people have not accepted it, it has been gathered by the Gentiles. (str. 10)

28

The same melody[601]

1   If the animals in the precious tent
     in the ark were chaste,
     how much [more] would Mary in whom dwelt Emmanuel
     turn against marriage.
     Your will increased you and sanctified you.[602]
     Your Lord increases and adorns you, as well.
     The animals of Noah were compelled by force,
     but you [chose] by your will.
     Refrain: Glories to His birth!

---

601. I.e., the melody is the same as in Nat. 25, which precedes this hymn in the manuscript chosen by Beck.
602. Mary is addressed here.

2   That chief of the angels greeted you[603]
      as the pledge of holiness.
      The earth became for him a new heaven
      in which the Watchers came down and praised.
      The sons of the height gathered around to serve you
      because of the King's Son Who dwelt in you.
      Your earthly habitation became like heaven above
      by their vigil.

3   But intercourse is not defiled,
      nor is marriage accursed.
      Chastity's wings are greater and lighter
      than [the wings of] marriage.[604]
      Intercourse, while pure, is lower.
      Its house of refuge is modest darkness.
      Confidence[605] belongs entirely to chastity,[606]
      which light enfolds.

4   Light shone forth upon your[607] residences
      and gave no space to marriage,
      for there were no doers of the secret [deed].
      Inside your[608] dwelling full of glory
      the shadows of dissoluteness and desire
      were dispersed by the Savior's rays.
      Spiritual woman, all of you has become spiritual
      since you have given birth to the spiritual man.[609]

5   The conception hinders our saying, "she is a virgin,"
      and [if we say] "a man's wife," the signs of virginity cry out.[610]
      The body is one and does not allow us
      to say she is [both] a virgin and a man's wife.
      It was a wonder and a marvel for the vigorous,[611]

---

603. Mary is addressed. This strophe is identical with Nat. 25.17.
604. For the wings of chastity, cf. Virg. 1.7.
605. Literally, "baring of the face," perhaps equivalent to the Greek παρρησία. For a similar idea, cf. Virg. 3.3.
606. Literally, "Is entirely chastity's."
607. The addressees are the angels.
608. The addressee is Mary again.
609. This is addressed to Mary.
610. Cf. Nat. 11.1.
611. i.e., the ascetics.

It was a vexation and a torment for the learned.[612]
The signs of virginity were hidden, but the breasts were full.[613]
To Him be praises because of all.

6 Earthly conception is the cause of its impulse,
the bodily desire that is in the members.
Your refined conception wipes clean [and] dissolves
the impulsive desire of your members.
Holiness and purity he poured forth [and] filled you
with holy floods. He purified you,
so that one who saw you would say, "How good is she[614]—
that glorious woman!"

7 Since the Conception[615] is the Glorious One, He stamped Himself,
as if by a signet upon your mind.[616]
Although He was begotten,[617] indeed He was in you
so that entirely gazing out from your members
was His brightness, and upon your beauty was spread
His love, and upon all of you He was stretched out.
You wove a garment for Him,[618] but His glory extended
over all your senses.

8 How Error has erred in culling
bitterness from sweet flowers,
in the same manner as she eats sweet fruits,
and by her they are transformed to deadly gall!
Even from fragrant scripture Error culls
poison for her lovers.[619]

---

612. Or "for scribes," i.e., the rabbis.

613. Cf. Nat. 11.4.

614. Literally, "how her goodness."

615. The Syriac word, *btn'*, used here and in the previous strophe, may have the sense of either the act or moment of conception or the thing conceived, the fetus.

616. For the signet or seal as a representation of the Logos, cf. Nat. 1.99.

617. Or, "although He was born"—the translation preferred by Beck. Beck understands Ephrem to say that even after the nativity, Christ was present in Mary. I think, instead, that Ephrem is making his frequently-stated point that the presence of Christ in Mary as a fetus did not prevent His simultaneous presence in the universe as Logos; cf. Nat. 4.126–213.

618. During her pregnancy, Mary wove the garment of Jesus' body for Him; pace Beck ad loc. and at Epiph. 13.3, where he rejects his earlier understanding as stated in Beck, Mariologie, 30. Ephrem likes the image of Jesus' body as a garment woven variously by the Deity, cf. Nat. 21.5, or by Mary, as here. The weaving of new baptismal garments by the Holy Spirit in Epiph. 13.3 does not demand a consistency, which is not present in Ephrem's use of the image.

619. On the dangers of faulty exegesis, cf. HdF 53.7.

They receive the cup, in which the sons of the serpent[620]
have mixed the dragon's gall.[621]

9   Now for you, good Church, a bee
who has many sweet blossoms,
one is Egyptian,
the second is Hebrew.[622]
From holy flowers you cull.
From all of them you gather all help.
Good Church, from the blossoms of your temple,
you gather sweetness.

10   Your type is portrayed by the bee[623]
who left the blossoms in her region,
flew, not a little [distance], to diffuse the smell
of the sweet Blossom that sprouted in Judea,
and came and gathered in her ears
the sweetness of her proverbs and brought [them] forth.
But Jerusalem made her pour out the sweetness
so that the Gentiles ran [and] collected it.

---

620. Heretics, cf. CH 1.13.

621. On the Fall as a poisoning for which Christ, the Medicine of life, is the antidote, cf. Nat. 26.9, but for the venom of the heretics, cf. CH 1.11.5.

622. The Syriac calendar divided Nisan, the season of Spring, into two parts, which correspond to the two months, March and April. Beck suggests that the allusion here is to the Exodus and the Christ-event.

623. Literally, "the bee portrays your type." Clement of Alexandria uses a similar image to describe his teacher, Pantaenus; cf. Clem. str. I.1.

Hymns against Julian

On the Church

This first hymn concerning Julian was composed in anticipation of his arrival in Nisibis soon after the apostate emperor's accession. From the beginning Ephrem sets forth his central theological theme: There is no reason to fear that God has abandoned his church; the true Christian must not lose hope but persevere under conditions of duress (str. 1). As the examples of Elijah and Daniel show, the courage to rebuke idolatrous tyrants is required of us by our Creator, and we will be vindicated for it (str. 4–7). The hymn is particularly rich in vineyard imagery.[1] The incarnation itself is symbolic of the fact that God does not ever forget us, for Christ the True Vine bent down to rescue us (str. 8–9). The present time is a transitory period of trial in which the true fruits will cling to the True Vine while the wild grapes are cast away (str. 5, str. 10–11). Now that the plenitude of summer has been replaced by winter, true Christians will continue to love the Vinedresser (str. 12–14). Or alternatively, now that the refreshing shade of the Christian emperors has been withdrawn "to make us mindful of our drought," we have an opportunity to show fidelity and perseverance (str. 14–15).

On the Church

Again, on the melody of paradise.

1   Rely on the truth and fear not, my brothers,
    for our Lord is not weak that He should desert us in trials.
    He is the power on Whom depend[2] the creation and its inhabitants.
    On Him depends the hope of His church.
    Who is able to cut off its[3] heavenly roots?

---

1. Cf. Murray, Symbols, 106–13.
2. Throughout the hymn Ephrem plays on the literal and figurative meanings of *tl'*, "to hang, to depend."
3. I.e., hope's.

Blessed is He Whose power came down and was mingled with his
>> churches!

2 Bestow on yourselves, my brothers, the treasure of consolation
from the word our Lord spoke about His church,
"The bars of Sheol cannot conquer her."[4]
If, indeed, she is mightier than Sheol,
who among mortals can frighten her?
Blessed is He Who made her great yet has tested[5] her that she might
>> be greater!

3 Reach out,[6] indeed, your hands toward the Branch[7] of Truth
that has torn asunder[8] the arms of warriors without being bent.
She bent down from her height and came down to the contest.
She tested the true, who hung on her,
but those hanging with an [ulterior] motive withered and fell.
Blessed is He Who brought her down to go up in triumphs!

4 Elijah, then, was drunk with the love of the True One,
and without fear he seethed and confronted the house of Ahab,[9]
who demeaned the Creator and worshipped creatures:
Jezebel led her retinue to Sheol.
The crowns of seven thousand men were glorious.[10]
Blessed is He Who revealed to his servant concerning hidden
>> treasure!

5 The sons of truth, then, grow large on this Branch of Truth;
they have been perfected and have become fruits fit for the
>> kingdom.
But, although the Branch is living, on it are also
dead fruits that blossom [only] apparently.

---

4. Matt. 16.13–20, esp. 18.

5. Literally, "but has turned and tested."

6. Ephrem puns on "reach out," *pšwṭw*, here and "has torn asunder," *pšḥt*, below.

7. The word *swkt'*, "branch," is grammatically feminine. Since it is customary to refer to the church with feminine pronouns, this convention is easily followed here insofar as the Branch of Truth represents the church. However, it also represents Christ or the Second Person of the Trinity, to whom it is not customary for us to refer with a feminine pronoun. In the context of *kenosis* other early Christian traditions refer to the motherhood of Jesus or use the feminine Sophia rather than Logos to refer to the Second Person of the Trinity; cf. Bradley, Background. With this in mind I have followed the Syriac more literally, translating with feminine pronouns all references to the Branch of Truth.

8. Here Murray suggests "has wearied," cf. Symbols, 107, n. 5.

9. For similar expressions regarding prophetic utterances, cf. Nat. 5.19.1, 6.14.1, 7.12.3.

10. I.e., the 7,000 who did not worship Baal; cf. 1 Kgs. 19.18.

The wind[11] tested them and shook down the wild grapes.
Blessed is He Who crowned by it[12] those who held fast in Him!

6   The love of the All-reviving tested Daniel
by the contract contrived by the cunning[13] to hinder
his acceptable prayer that exposed their idols.[14]
They demeaned their graven images, unwittingly.
He brings to nought their acts of worship that One may be
     worshipped by all.
Blessed is He Whose true ones confounded the erring!

7   She bent down [and] shed her friends into the fire.
Her leaves bore dew [and] cooled the furnace.
Conquered were the arms of the conqueror who had decreed
that the Most High would bow down before his images.
His friends who did not abandon Him were not abandoned by
     Him.
Blessed is He Who, instead of an image, is praised by His
     worshippers!

8   Jesus, bend down to us Your love that we may grasp
this Branch that bent down her fruits for the ungrateful;
they ate and were satisfied, yet they demeaned[15] her who had bent
     down
as far as Adam in Sheol.
She ascended and lifted him up and with him returned to Eden.
Blessed is He Who bent her down toward us that we might seize
     her and ascend on her.

9   Who indeed will not weep that although the Branch is great,
the weakness of one unwilling to seize her greatness
maintains that she is a feeble branch—
she who has conquered all kings and cast a shadow
upon the entire world! By suffering her power has increased.
Blessed is He Who made her greater than that vine from Egypt![16]

10   Who will not hold fast to this Branch of Truth?

---

11. Or "spirit."
12. I.e., by the wind or spirit.
13. The Syriac is active.
14. It is more a decree than a contract, cf. Dan. 3.3–7.
15. Literally, "but they turned and demeaned."
16. Ps. 80.8.

She bore the true ones; she shed the false.
Not because they were too heavy for her[17] did she shed them.
For our sake she tested them in the breeze;
it shook down the shriveled; it ripened the firm.
Blessed is He Who rejected the vineyard that was a source of wild
      grapes![18]

11   Because they were unfaithful to that Branch of life—
in the time of her exaltation they sit in her shade.
In the time of her humiliation they are ungrateful—
they resemble the momentary passers-by
who turn aside and pluck the fruit but abandon[19] the vines.
Blessed is He Whose workers remain in His vineyard!

12   But because the summer by its fruits has forced
the greedy to become friends to the laborer,
winter can argue persuasively that the unfaithful
loved not him but their bellies.
In summer they ran after him; in winter they fled from him.
Blessed is He Who made a crucible that tries the two sides!

13   Because, indeed, the summer adorns the things of summer
so that like itself they, too, are workers in the vineyard,
it is winter that exposes those who plucked and carried away,
while the true worker remained.[20]
He was crucified with the wood Whose fruits he ate.
Come, let us be hung on the wood that gave us the Bread of life!

14   Since Our Lord granted me, too, to enjoy myself in summer
with fruits and the shadows of this Branch of the universe,
let me be among the workers, the demeaned, the winter ones,
lest, indeed, I have two seasons:
in summer within her, in winter far from her.
Grant, my Lord, by Your grace that we all may hold fast to You!

15   The kings who used to provide shade, cooled us in the droughts.[21]
We ate their fruits; we were ungrateful for their branches.
Our soul luxuriated in the bounties and shadows.

---

17. Literally, "for her strength."
18. Isa. 5.2–6.
19. Literally, "let go and abandon."
20. Literally, "who plucked, carried and took away, but he who was a worker remained."
21. Constantine and Constantius, cf. CJ 1.12.1.

ON THE CHURCH

Our mouth raved and attacked[22] our Creator.
Battles in the shadows we waged with our investigations.
He has stripped away our shade to make us mindful of our drought!
Blessed is He Whose grace provides shade for us!
Blessed is He Who worked in us grace without measure!

---

22. Or "mused upon, studied"—the double meaning is appropriate since Ephrem characteristically reproaches the Arians for arrogantly examining the nature of God.

1

This is the first of four hymns explicitly against Julian, composed after the apostate emperor's defeat and death. Having assured his church in the previous hymn that despite appearances, God has not abandoned his flock, Ephrem now extends his argument to encompass the new events and to offer a positive interpretation of the whole. There has been a cosmic alignment of forces, of all the good against all the evil. On the one side with God are the church and the angels; on the other are Satan and his demons, Julian, all the wild, repugnant and monstrous forces, the pagans with their idols, the heretics and the Jews. For Julian was not a true king, whose sceptre drives away the wild animals like a shepherd's crook (str. 1). Instead of protecting his flock, he had left them open to the ravages of the wild animals, that is, the Persians, his true allies (str. 2). The rejoicing of the wild beasts, the resuscitated idols, and Satan and his demons were short-lived, since they all fell with the emperor (str. 3–7). But first there had been a period of persecution, apostasy of those less firmly rooted, and suffering for the faithful (str. 8–11). The peaceful harmony of the reigns of Constantine and Constantius had allowed untried Christians to mingle unnoticed with the true (str. 12–13). Unwittingly, the forces of Error had glorified the true by exposing the hidden apostasy of faithless Christians (str. 14–15). The Jews, too, Ephrem claims, were exposed as idolaters, seeing in Julian's coinage the golden calf of Sinai, and following him as they had followed Jereboam (str. 16–19). Like Nebuchadnezzar, the apostate has been rebuked by God (str. 20).

HYMN 1

Against Julian,
The King Who Apostatized
&
Against The Heretics and The Jews

1

On the melody: Rely on the truth

1 The sceptre of kingship shepherds humankind,
cares for cities, drives away wild animals.[23]
The opposite was the sceptre of the king who apostatized.
the wild animals saw it and exulted:[24]
the wolves were his partisans; the leopard and the lion raged;
even the foxes raised their voices.

2 The wolves saw the clouds, rain and whirlwind.
Calling to one another, they attacked. Ravenous, they rampaged.
Utterly hemmed in, they were all furious.
They surrounded the blessed flock.
But the sceptre that had gladdened them was broken and moved
       them to regret.
a crushed reed[25] was the support of the left hand.[26]

3 They fled back into their caverns, dark and primeval.
The fear they had stripped off, they put on again in their dens.
The creation that had been gloomy, brightened and exulted,
but the rebels were trampled.
The heads of leviathan were smashed in the midst of the sea,[27]
and his crawling tail was shattered in the midst of the dry land.

4 The living dead[28] awoke and were resuscitated.
Thinking themselves revived, they were rebuked—how they were
       disgraced!

---

23. The *casus pendens* construction of the Syriac is difficult to translate into graceful English.
24. The Sassanid Persians are meant.
25. 2 Kgs. 18.21 (Isa. 36.6).
26. I.e., the forces of evil.
27. Ps. 74.13–14.
28. I.e., the pagans.

Being resuscitated, they revived graven images.[29]
The idols confuted the apostates.
One is the death of pagans and tares,[30]
all of whom took refuge at once in the same one.

5 At that time, then, the mud seethed and spewed out
vermin of all sizes and worms of every sort.
They bred, and the earth was full of them in the middle of winter.[31]
The breath of the dragon made the earth seethe,
but the One equipped with the sandal of truth
despised the poison of the stings of the sons of error.[32]

6 Those who stood with the overthrown[33] fell with the fallen.[34]
They persevered, thinking even they could stand firm.
The fools clung to one another, but as it transpired they all fell.
Their fall attested their impediment:
although divided, they agreed on the stumbling block.
In the love of one king they were joined.[35]

7 When demons rejoiced, they suddenly revived with them.
When the Evil One was jubilant, they exulted with him.
As if by a mystery, time arranged
for all of them at once to be dependent on one.
They made themselves brothers and members of one another,
for they all depended on the head of the left hand.

8 For while the right hand was grieved over sinners,
the children of the left hand rejoiced greatly.

---

29. On the importance Julian ascribed to the revival of pagan cult, and for a discussion of the date of its restoration, cf. Bowersock, Julian, 55–110 et passim, esp. 61, 70, 86f.

30. The tares are heretics. This agricultural imagery, rooted in the New Testament, esp. Matt. 13.24–30 et par., is common to early Christian literature, but recieved relatively little emphasis in Syriac Christian literature before Ephrem, who uses it frequently; cf. Nat. 3.15, CNis 20, 29, 31, 33, and Murray, Symbols, 195–99. For the more common Early Syriac theme of the vineyard, cf. ibid. 95–130.

31. Ephrem alludes to Julian's seizure of power in December 361. A traditional portrait of Julian as the hesitant and fortuitous heir to Roman power is presented by Browning, Emperor, 95–122. Bowersock portrays Julian's rise to power as more calculated, Bowersock, Julian, 46–65.

32. Although the identity of the champion of truth here is unclear, Christ probably is meant, and the contest portrayed is between Christ and Satan. It is also possible, however, that Ephrem alludes to the rumors that Julian had arranged for Constantius to be poisoned; cf. King, Julian, 27, n.1.

33. I.e., the idols.

34. Julian. The word may also mean "deserter," thus alluding to his apostasy as well as his death in battle.

35. The king is not only Julian but also Satan, as the following strophe shows.

HYMN 1

In the season of the penitents, angels alone rejoice.
Without realizing it, fools behave in the opposite way.
Only the church agrees with the Watchers in both:
she suffers over the sinners but rejoices over penitents.[36]

9   The Evil One saw that he had intoxicated and confused people.
He rejoiced and mocked freedom all the more
that people have so thoroughly enslaved themselves to him.
The Evil One was astounded how much he tore us to pieces,
but the fools, torn to pieces, did not feel their pains.
Although the Physician was near, they despised the cure.[37]

10   The ugly, dark, all-gloomy winter[38]
robbed the beauty of the all-rejoicing spring.[39]
Thornbushes and tares were disgorged and sprang up.
The dry frost moistened

---

36. Cf. Luke 15.10. In this strophe Ephrem uses the two words most commonly chosen by him to denote angels: *ml'k'* and *'yr'*, here translated "angels" and "watchers." The first has the root meaning of "messenger," is the most common designation of angels in the Bible, and carries the specific meaning characteristic of angels in the canonical scripture. "Watchers" is, on the other hand, the most common general designation of angels in Ephrem, especially in his earlier writings, and is characteristic of his angelology. Rooted in Iranian conceptions of Amesa Spenta and Mithra as heavenly beings who are constantly alert, never sleeping, this sort of angel appears in the extra-canonical I Enoch as well as in Syriac literature before Ephrem in the *Acts of Thomas* and in the writings of Aphrahat. The word *'yr'* occurs in the Book of Daniel, thus giving a kind of biblical pedigree to a notion fundamentally unlike the usual biblical angel. Ephrem is aware of the root meaning of the word and sometimes indulges in elaborate word play on it. Watchfulness is symbolic of holiness; its opposite, sleep, represents sin and death. So Christ is the "Watcher" par excellence, who makes it possible for faithful Christians to be "watchers" and ultimately to live the angelic life, i.e., eternal life. For him the human life most like the angelic life is the ascetic life, a proleptic participation in the paradisal state. His angelology probably derives from the general cultural context father than from a particular literary work. Cf. W. Cramer *Die Engelvorstellungen bei Ephräm der Syrer*, OCA 173 (Rome, 1965), esp. 68f., 165–81.

    The watching angels are here portrayed in one of their characteristic roles as a chorus viewing the drama of human salvation, rejoicing with those who repent or who resist temptation; cf. ibid. 64, 148–52, and for the same in Aphrahat, ibid. 49.

37. The common metaphor of Christ as physician is particularly prominent in Syriac Christian literature from the *Acts of Thomas* onward, and it also figures significantly in the Manichaean literature; cf. Murray, Symbols, 199–203. Ephrem uses the image frequently in his Diatesseron commentary and develops it especially in CNis 34; ibid. 200f.

38. Literally, "the month of *šbṭ*" (February–March). Ephrem may have in mind Julian's edict of 13 March 362, by which Christian clergy were no longer permitted to seek exemption from the decurionate; cf. Cod. Theod. XII.I.50; Bowersock, Julian, 73f. More probably, however, this is a broader allusion to the winter and spring of 361–62, which were marked by purges, reforms, new appointments and the gradual emergence of Julian's lack of tolerance for religious and philosophical views other than his own. For the sequence of events, cf. ibid. 66–85. For the suggestion that here *šbṭ* may mean "winter" as *nysn* often means "spring," cf. Beck, CSCO 175, 66, n.9.

39. *nysn.*

229

brambles in the inner rooms and thistles in the courts.
In this time the naked[40] and the barefoot[41] shivered.

11 How the late seeding was afraid and terrified![42]
For without effort it was sown and took root.
Uprooted were the aftergrowth, the self-sown growth sprouting
      throughout the world,[43]
and that which had quickly risen to the surface,
but the seed of effort that struck root profusely—
its fruit came a hundredfold, sixty and thirtyfold.

12 The truth-loving kings[44] in the symbol of two bulls
yoked together equally the two Testaments.[45]
With the yoke of harmony they worked and adorned the earth.
But the thorns clothed themselves in the beauty of the wheat,
and the seed spread its appearance even upon the tares.
Those who stripped away beauty did so in freedom.

13 Some of them were brambles, and some were wheat.
Some were gold, and some were dust.
The tyrant became a crucible for the beauty of the true ones.
Who has ever seen such a glorious sight?
For Truth entered and was tested in the crucible of the False One.
Unwittingly, Error has glorified the true ones.

---

40. *šlyḥ'* may mean "naked" or "apostle," hence, as Beck suggests, "bishop." Ephrem's pun is probably intentional since he uses the same double entendre in HdF 74.7–9; cf. Murray, Symbols, 80f.

41. Again, a pun is possible since "barefoot" is a designation for ascetics in the Pseudo-Ephremic writings on monasticism; cf. Beck, CSCO 175, 67, n.12; idem, Asketentum, 341–62.

42. Cf. Matt. 13.4–9, 18–23, et par.; weak Christians, possibly recent converts who have apostatized under persecution.

43. The Syriac is approximately equivalent to Greek οἰκουμένη, the inhabited world.

44. Constantine and Constantius. On Constantine as champion of orthodoxy against heresies due to his summoning of councils, cf. CH 22.20.10. Although he portrays Constantius as pious, pure and favored by God, cf. CJ 2.19, 2.25, 3.8, 3.10, 4.15, Ephrem passes over the question of orthodoxy with regard to this emperor. Given Constantius' well-known Arianism and Ephrem's polemics against that heresy, it is clear that the hymnodist consistently overlooks Constantius' heretical views of the sake of his contrast with Julian. Elsewhere, comparing him with Pilate, he exculpates him of responsibility for the Arian persecutions of the orthodox; cf. HdF 87.21, noted by Murray, Symbols, 66, n.2; discussed at greater length by Griffith, Ephraem, esp. 31–37. Similarly Gregory of Nazianzus in his invective against Julian makes only slight reference to these persecutions; cf. Greg. Naz. Orat. 4.37, and Murray, Symbols, 61f.

45. The precise meaning is unclear. Ephrem evidently intends to constrast orthodox Christianity with both Marcionite rejection of the Old Testament and Jewish rejection of the New Testament. It is remotely possible that he also intends a pun of Syriac *twr'*, "bull," and Hebrew *Torah*, the "Law."

14 All who were apostates rejoiced in the apostate—
the sons of the left hand in the head of the left hand.
In him they could see who they themselves were,
since he became a mirror for all of them.
Those who rejoiced over his victory shared his lot,
inasmuch as disgrace befell them from his death.

15 For it was the church alone that opposed him utterly,
and they and he together opposed her utterly.
Without dispute this is sufficient to teach
that they were on one side and she on the other.
The furtive ones, who were believed not to belong to them,
hastily associated themselves with them.[46]

16 The People raged and raved and blared the trumpet.
They rejoiced that he [was] a soothsayer and were jubilant that he
        was a Chaldean.
The circumcised saw the image that suddenly was a bull.[47]
On his coins they saw the shameful bull,
and they began to keep its feast with cymbals and trumpets,
for they recognized in that bull their ancient calf.

17 The bull of paganism engraved on his heart
[Julian] imprinted on that image for the People who love it.[48]
Perhaps the Jews cried out to that bull,
"Behold the gods who will lead
your captives up from Babylon into the land they devastated,

---

46. The Syriac is more vivid: "they strung themselves with them [like beads] on a chain."
The partisans of Julian here seem to be lukewarm Christians or even secret pagans, who like the
emperor himself, disguised their beliefs until the death of Constantius. Possibly, however, he
alludes to Jewish supporters of Julian, as in the following strophe.

47. As the following line indicates, Ephrem refers to the image on Julian's bronze bull
coinage. Its iconography has been variously explained as: 1) the Egyptian god Apis (Eckhel,
Babelon, Stein, Mattingly, Elmer), 2) a rhetorical symbol of the good emperor (Kent), 3) a
Mithraic bull (Thieler), 4) the zodiacal symbol Taurus, allegedly Julian's birth sign, thus a
representation of Julian himself (Gilliard); for discussion and bibliography, cf. F.D. Gilliard,
"Notes on the Coinage of Julian the Apostate," JRS 54 (1964), 135–41, esp. 138–41. Bowersock
argues that Ephrem's construal of the bull as the golden calf shows either that virtually no one
understood the iconography (cf. Julian, 104), or that Julian issued the coins on an occasion having
to do with his relations with the Jews (cf. *Numen* 28 [1981], 88–93, esp. 91). But Ephrem's
association of the bull with the golden calf may be simply an idiosyncratic juxtaposition for the
sake of his invective, meant especially to discredit the Jews by association with this *locus classicus*
of idolatry.

48. Or "who love [Julian]" or "whom [Julian] loves."

as the molten calf led you out of Egypt!"[49]

18   A king, the Babylonian king, suddenly became a wild ass,[50]
but he learned to be subjugated; he who used to kick, kicked no
    more.
A king, the Hellenic king,[51] suddenly became a bull
and gored the churches, but he was dragged away.
The circumcised saw the bull imprinted on the staters,
and they rejoiced that the calves of Jereboam were revived.[52]

19   Perhaps because of that silver coin on which the bull was portrayed,
the Jews were overjoyed that [Julian] carried it in his heart
and also in his purse and in his hand
as a type of that calf of the wilderness
that was before his eye and heart and mind;
and probably in his dreams he used to see the calf.

20   A king, the Babylonian king, went mad and went out into the
    countryside.
He was made to wander in order to be gathered in; he was
    maddened in order to come to his senses.[53]
He made God rejoice and made Daniel exult.
A king, the Hellenic king, has been rebuked,
for he angered God and denied Daniel,[54]
and there near Babylon he was judged and condemned.[55]

---

49. Exod. 32.8.

50. Although the reference is clearly to Nebuchadnezzar, as Beck suggests, cf. Dan. 4.28–33, it is odd that Ephrem refers to him as a "wild ass," (*'rd*) where the Peshitta uses "bull" or "wild ox," *twr*, the same word he used for the image on the coinage and in the next lines for Julian, "the Hellenic king."

51. In referring to Julian as "the Hellenic king" (*mlk ywn*) Ephrem emphasizes his "Hellenism," i.e., his pagan beliefs. If he meant to refer simply to Julian as Roman Emperor, the metrically equivalent *mlk rwm'*, would be more normal parlance since Syriac writers continued to refer thus to the emperors well into the Byzantine period.

52. Jereboam instituted a rival to the Jerusalem cult by setting up golden calves at Bethel and Dan and telling the people this was the god who brought them up out of Egypt, as in str. 17 above; cf. 1 Kings 11.26–15.34, esp. 12.26–32.

53. Cf. Dan. 4.31–37.

54. By attempting to rebuild the Temple in Jerusalem, Julian denied the testimony of Daniel 9.24–27, which Ephrem and many other Patristic writers understood to prophesy the permanent destruction of the Temple, cf. CJ 4.20.

55. Julian's death on the Persian campaign is the divine punishment for his apostasy; further, cf. CJ 3.1–9, 13–17.

2

Here Ephrem alludes to the tenth chapter of John's gospel which portrays the good shepherd whose sheep know him and who lays down his life to protect them from the wolf. Like Jesus, Constantius was a true shepherd, but Julian is a wolf in sheep's clothing. Characterizing the Jews as goat kids, he enlarges on the theme introduced at the end of the previous hymn, Jewish acceptance of Julian's leadership (str. 1). He implies that the emperor was a false messiah for them since he played the roles of prophet, king and priest (str. 2). Alluding to the attempt to rebuild the Temple in Jerusalem, he claims that the emperor's "pledge" swayed them to continue to accept him after he shed his "sheep's clothing" by declaring his polytheistic beliefs (str. 1, 3.4). This shows, he argues, that the Jewish rejection of Jesus had been motivated by a hidden yearning for polytheism (str. 3).

Ephrem then returns to the larger theme of the divine purpose in these events. God has made Julian a mirror in which to see the falsity of pagan religion and the destruction that awaits those who put their trust in its oracles (str. 4–15). He claims that, despite the personal asceticism of the emperor, his religion is characterized by lascivious revelry, resembling the Israelite worship of the golden calf (str. 4–7). Just as the golden calf was destined for destruction, Julian, like an unwitting goat kid, was prepared for sacrifice by the falsity of his pagan oracles (str. 8–15). Nisibis is also a mirror displaying a contrapuntal lesson: As long as the people placed their trust in God and were faithful to him, they were preserved from Persian capture; only when they succumbed to idolatry was the city lost to the Persian forces (str. 16–27). Ephrem describes the dramatic and successful earlier defenses of Nisibis, associating their success with the piety of Constantius as well as of the city's inhabitants (str. 19–20, 25). The city was taken only when the inhabitants restored an idolatrous cult, and when they were led by an emperor who entrusted his plans to soothsayers, who nevertheless proved vulnerable even to the mundane deceit of traitors (str. 12, 15, 17, 18, 25). Even Shapur grasped the lesson God intended all to see in the fate of Nisibis, for he showed respect for the Christian religion but not for Julian's paganism (str. 22–24, 27). Although the apostasy of some of the city's Christian inhabitants and the restitution of the pagan cult have resulted in God's anger and the loss of the city, the freedom of its inhabitants to emigrate to Roman territory rather than being exiled eastward into the Persian realm is a sign of divine mercy (str. 26–27).

2

1   The wolf borrowed the clothing of the True Lamb;
the innocent sheep sniffed at him, without recognizing him,
for he had greatly deceived that shepherd who died.[56]
But when the wolf emerged from within the lamb,
stripped off [and] shed his beauty, the kids took his scent.
They hated the ewes, but loved him as a shepherd.

> *Refrain: Blessed is He Who blotted him out*
> *and has afflicted all the sons of error!*

2   They rejoiced that he was a Chaldean; they were jubilant that he
was a soothsayer.
They became arrogant that he was king; they were joyful that he
was a priest.
They rejoiced that he filled the place of many,
of kings and queens of the sort
of Ahab[57] and Jeroboam,[58] of Jotham[59] and Manasseh,[60]

---

56. The Emperor Constantius, unaware of Julian's pagan beliefs, had appointed him Caesar.

57. Ahab is best remembered for marrying Jezebel and introducing Baal worship in Israel, cf. 1 Kgs. 16.29–34.

58. Cf. CJ 1.18.6 and note ad loc.

59. Jotham, son of Uzziah, ruled Judah for sixteen years. Although he is presented in 2 Kings and 2 Chronicles as a good king, Ephrem apparently wishes to recall the criticism that he did not put an end to the worhsip in the high places that Jeroboam had reestablished, cf. 2 Kgs. 15.32–38, 2 Chron. 27.1–9.

60. Manasseh not only reinstated the Baal worship his father had ended, he also practiced child-sacrifice, augury, divination and magic, and he introduced an idol into the Temple at Jerusalem. When he was captured by the Assyrians and taken in chains to Babylon, however, he repented. Restored to power, he later purified the worship of Judah and regained the favor of Yahweh, cf. 2 Chron. 33.1–20.

234

of Jezebel[61] and Athaliah,[62] sources of paganism.[63]

3 They rejected the Savior, the witness of the True One,
Who, when they asked Him, taught, "One alone is God."[64]
Being pagans, they crucified Him and went astray with many
    [gods].
They rejoiced in the abominable pledge.[65]
Through his sacrifices he hired and brought ten gods[66]
to heap up sheaves of thorns for Gehenna.

4 He led his gods and the goddesses he forged.
He clothed himself in auguries and set out—he and the soothsayers
    and conjurers.
All the sons of error equipped him with their prayers,
and he set out with the promises of powerful men.
He took his conveyance[67] and smote it and brought
a crown of disgrace for all his partisans.

5 The goddesses rampaged with his gods,
and the one who denied chastity[68] was not ashamed to proclaim

---

61. Jezebel, wife of King Ahab, came to her Baal worship naturally, being the daughter of Ethbaal, King of Tyre. Her corrupting influence on Israel is well-known, as is her persecution of the prophet Elijah and his successors, and her ignominious death, cf. 1 Kgs. 16.31, 1 Kgs. 18, 19, 21, and 2 Kgs. 9.30–37.

62. Athaliah, who was a daughter of Omri, a consort of Ahab and the mother of Ahaziah, ruled for six years. A devotee of Baal, she was killed when Jehoiada, a priest of Yahweh, led a revolt against her, cf. 2 Kgs. 8.26 and 11.1–20.

63. In his second invective against Julian, Gregory Nazianzen also invokes the images of Ahab and Jeroboam in connection with the rebuilding of the Temple, but rather than the other kings and queens of Israel whom Ephrem mentions here, he adds Nebuchadnezzar and Pharaoh to his list; cf. Greg. Naz. Orat. 5.3.

64. Mark 12.29.

65. The pledge is Julian's promise to rebuild the Temple, cf. CJ 1.16–20 and 4.18–25.

66. The Syriac word here indicates a group of ten, for which there is no English equivalent. "A dozen gods" would give the sense loosely.

67. The Syriac here can mean chariot or throne. Since the context is a description of Julian's setting out on the Persian campaign, possibly this is an allusion to his fleet and its destruction as Beck suggests ad loc.

68. The Syriac word *nkpwt'* may mean modesty or chastity in a general sense, or it may be a *terminus technicus* for monasticism. Julian was critical of Christian monasticism, which he saw as akin to the "pseudo-Cynicism" of his time; cf. Bowersock, Julian, 81f. and Malley, Hellenism, 148–55. The emperor was, however, himself very dedicated to an ascetic lifestyle, justified in neo-Platonic terms; cf. Amm. Mar. 25.4.2–6, Libanius Orat. 18.179, Bowersock, Julian, 79–93, and Malley, Hellenism, 226–35. Even his devotion to the Great Mother (Cybele-Atargatis) was compatible with his asceticism since she had acquired astrological and philosophical underpinnings by this time, as Julian's hymn to her demonstrates; cf. the introduction II, D. Ephrem's point, however, is that this juxtaposition is not possible. John Chrysostom voices a similar complaint about Julian's devotions to Aphrodite, probably another reference to the same syncretistic cult; cf. *Liber in Sanctum Babylam Contra Julianum et Gentiles* 14, noted by Beck ad loc.

male idols who raved after female idols.[69]

A he-goat and also a priest he was for them.

For a shameful [goddess] he abstained [from cutting] his beard and
      let it grow,

and he bent down to let the smoke of the fumes rise into it.[70]

6 Agreeable to him was the feast of the detestable idol

on whose feastday women and men rave,

virgins fornicate, and wives become lascivious,

vomit out [and] speak words of shame.[71]

He loved filthy feasts and despised the blessed

feastdays of chastity and the Pasch of honor.[72]

7 The pagans carried their idols and raved,

and the circumcised blew trumpets and raged,

and all of them chanted with their voices and behaved wantonly.[73]

It was a festival like the one in the wilderness.

The Gracious One Who chastened those who rampaged with a calf,

[and] Who chastened the many who rampaged with a king—

8 He broke that calf to pieces to cut short the rampage,

and He undid that diadem to cut off the frenzy.

Like a physician He cut off the cause of the rampage.

---

69. Or "and lusted after" or "raved in pursuit of female idols." The Syriac is alliterative.

70. Clearly aware that Julian's beard is intended to symbolize his philosophical and theological commitments, Ephrem mocks this idea by the use of the root *nzr*, "to abstain, to become a Nazirite." In the context of Israelite prophecy the Nazirite vow to abstain from wine and the razor was a sign of a charismatic call; cf. Num. 6.1–21, 1 Sam. 1.22, Judg. 13.2–7. The notion carried over into early Christianity and especially in the Jewish-Christian encratite environment; cf. Brown, Birth of the Messiah, 210f. Given his insistence that Julian was promoting obscene worship, his use here is strongly ironic, and the characterization of the emperor as a he-goat both alludes to his beard and carries the suggestion of lewdness. Popular mockery of his beard in Antioch had led Julian to write his satirical *Misopogon*, where he himself refers ironically to goats; cf. Jul. Imp. Misop. 338C–339B, and Bowersock, Julian, 13. The criticisms continued and included mockery of his "billy goat's beard" as well as his excessive sacrificial offerings and his inappropriate assumption of priestly prerogatives, so that they called him "a slaughterer rather than a high priest," cf. Amm. Mar. 22.14.2–3.

71. For a similar description of the feast of the "raving goddess," cf. CH 9.8.3.

72. Alternatively "and honorable merriment," but since the pagan celebration of which he complains here is probably the festivities of the Great Mother in late March, cf. CJ 2.5.2 and note ad loc., a specific comparison with Easter is more likely.

73. Although it sounds as if pagans and Jews celebrated a festival together, for his polemical purpose Ephrem has merged the celebrations of the two communities. Possibly he has in mind the celebration of Passover which would be at about the same time as the Great Mother's feast. In addition, Julian's announced intention to rebuild the Temple in Jerusalem may have been the cause of additional rejoicing for the Jewish community. Further cf. CJ 4.18–23 and notes ad loc.

HYMN 2

In the south[74] both were overthrown.

By means of hard iron He destroyed that calf,

and with a terrible spear he destroyed that king.[75]

9   He-goats from the people[76] of that goat-kid,

who grew their curls and stank in their beards,[77]

surrounded the black one who did not look at marriage,

who was continent and purified for his shameful [goddess].[78]

The flocks of the left hand stirred up by their oracles

the goat-kid who set out to become a victim in the midst of Persia.[79]

10   By their oracles they broke the reed of the tares,[80]

the pillar and column upon which had been supported

thorns, sons of his people, and brambles, sons of his race.[81]

As he set out he threatened the grains of wheat

that he would return and bury them in the thicket of his
paganism.[82]

The Cultivator of justice destroyed the tares.

11   That haughty and arrogant thornbush, as it is written,[83]

---

74. In Sinai and Babylon, respectively.

75. In the case of the calf, the precise allusion is unclear, cf. Exod. 32.20, but for Julian's case, cf. CJ 3.14.

76. Here and in CJ 2.10.3 "his people" is *gnsh*, from Greek γένος, not '*mm*' as in references to the Jewish people.

77. Ephrem puns on *spry* "goat-kid" and *zprw* "they stank." The emperor's philosphers and religious advisors are the subject here.

78. Here and in CJ 2.5.5 one might read "for his shame" or "to his disgrace" rather than "for his shameful goddess," but Beck's suggestion that this is an allusion to a goddess is most probable since the word may refer to an idol (*bhtt*'; cf. Margoliouth 37a). On Julian's preference for continence, cf. CJ 2.5 and note ad loc. He specified the relationship between the Great Mother's cult, allegorically interpreted, and abstinence of various sorts, cf. Jul. Imp. Orat. 5 174B–178D.

79. The pagan oracles and interpreters of omens encouraged Julian to undertake his Persian campaign. Yet, at least according to the hindsight of Ammianus, it seems that many omens were negative or at least ambiguous as the campaign proceeded; cf. Amm. Mar. 22.12.6–8, where Ammianus expresses doubt over the qualifications of some of those consulted; Amm. Mar. 23.1.4–7, 23.2.6–8, 23.5.6, and 24.6.17 for unfavorable omens; Amm. Mar. 23.3.3, for unfavorable dreams; Amm. Mar. 23.3.6 and 23.5.8–14 for omens Julian mistakenly interpreted as favorable. As a convinced pagan, Ammianus had an interest in showing that Julian's disastrous campaign was not encouraged by the gods, just as Ephrem wished to show that the emperor had the best advice available from pagan sources.

80. Ephrem alludes both to Pharaoh as a broken reed (2 Kgs. 18.21) and to the parable of the wheat and tares (Matt. 13.24–30).

81. The Syriac is *twhmh*.

82. Julian's anti-Christian measures reached a peak in spring 363 as he set out on his Mesopotamian campaign, cf. Bowersock, Julian, 79–93, esp. 92.

83. 2 Kgs. 14.9. The thornbush of Lebanon writes to the cedar of Lebanon asking for his

determined to bend down cedars and cypresses
and willed to grow thorns and tares.
[God] made it a broom,[84] but it did not disperse.
The Just One swept together in him the abomination of paganism
and took [and] hurled his paganism into a distant place.

12 For Truth to conquer one at a time would have been a small thing.
He swept together [and] bound up the diviners and soothsayers in
      one king
and gave them the opportunity to put on a helmet and arm
      themselves,
and in the one he conquered all of them,
and upon all of them he stretched out the measuring line of disgrace,
for the sons of error lied, all of them in everything.

13 If all of them together lied in their oracles,
taken individually how much each one lied in his oracle!
Hogs got down [and] wallowed in their detestable filth.
This is the herd [of swine] that defiled the world,
who came down and rolled in dust and got up and shook themselves
      off.
It has happened and does happen that they lead many astray.

14 The king, the king of Babylon, confuted the Chaldeans,
nor did he summon others, for he tested one in another.[85]
He cast them out [and] expelled them; to slaughter he gave them.
That one, indeed, whose own they were, renounced them.
But if they misled him, how much indeed will they mislead you!
For if all of them lie, who indeed will trust one?

15 For [Julian] foretold and promised and wrote and sent to us
that he would come down and trample it; Persia he would
      disperse.[86]
Singara he would rebuild.[87] [This was] the threat of his letter.

---

daughter to be given in marriage to his son; he is trampled by the animals of Lebanon as they
pass by.

84. For *mknšt'* as "broom," cf. Payne-Smith I, 1774f., *scopa, verriculum*. This meaning suits
the context here and in the remainder of the strophe where God is portrayed as the Great
Housekeeper in the Sky.

85. Dan. 2.1–13. When Nebuchadnezzar tested the soothsayers in his kingdom, on the
basis of the answers of some, he convicted all and condemned them to death.

86. The Syriac also contains a pun: Persia . . . disperse = *lprs mprs'*.

87. Singara had been taken by the Persians in 360, Amm. Mar. 20.6.

Nisibis was taken away by his campaign,
but by his conjurers he cast down the power in which they
    believed.[88]
As a [sacrificial] lamb, the city saved his encampment.[89]

16 Nisibis that was captured—as a type of mirror[90]
[God] set it up, that we might see in it the pagan who set out
to take what was not his; he lost what was his.
For it was the city that proclaimed to the world
the shame of his conjurers and became his constant reproach.
He surrendered the constant unwearying herald.

17 This is the herald that with four mouths[91]
cried out into the whole world the disgrace of his conjurers.
The gates that were opened by the sieges also opened
our mouth for the praise of our Savior.
Behold! Shut up today are the gates of that city
that the mouth of pagans and heretics might be shut up with them.

18 Let us seek the cause how and why
the shield[92] of all the cities, that city, was given up.
The madman raged and set fire to his ships near the Tigris.
Without his being aware the bearded ones deceived
the he-goat who promised that he knew secret things.[93]

---

88. *Pace* Beck, who citing Ephrem's claim of widespread paganism in the Roman army, cf. CJ 3.10, here translates, "das Heer, das an ihn glaube."

89. I.e., Nisibis was ceded to Persia in exchange for safe passage for the Roman army.

90. The image of the mirror is used variously by Ephrem. Here the image in the mirror serves as a warning example, cf. Beck, Spiegel, esp. 10–16.

91. The four mouths are the city gates; thus the news went out in all directions.

92. The word has the same root as "shut up" in the previous strophe, *skr*.

93. According to Libanius, Julian simply decided to burn his fleet rather than risk the Persians' acquisition of it or the continued commitment of manpower needed to bring it in the upstream retreat (Libanius, Orat. 18.262–3; repeated by Zosimus, *Historia Nova* 3.26, 28, 29). The same explanations are offered by Ammianus Marcellinus, but he mentions traitors who admit to deceit when they are tortured, and he describes a belated reversal of the decision to burn the boats (Amm. Mar. 24.7.4–6). The fullest explanation would seem to be in Gregory Nazianzen's second invective against Julian (Greg. Naz. Orat. 5.11–12). According to Gregory, Julian was deceived by a Persian nobleman who represented himself as alienated from Shapur, but who was in reality still in the service of the Persian ruler. Using essentially the same arguments that Libanius and Ammianus attribute to Julian himself, this supposed renegade persuaded him to burn his fleet and promised that he himself would conduct him by a secret overland route to his troops in the north. Once the ships had been torched, however, the Persian had disappeared. The discussion in Bowersock, Julian, 114f., is most helpful. Browning's account of two Persian noblmen who confess when put to torture, is apparently a conflation of Ammianus Marcellinus' and Gregory's accounts, cf. Browning, Emperor, 208f. The only discrepancy between Gregory's version and Ephrem's is that Ephrem, like Ammianus Marcellinus,

He was deceived in visible things to be disgraced in hidden things.

19 This is the city that had heralded the truth of its Savior:
seas broke through suddenly, battered it, but were overcome.
The earthworks were brought down, but the elephants were
    drowned.
The king by his sackcloth preserved it.[94]
The tyrant by his paganism cast down the victory
of the city that prayer had crowned with triumphs.

20 Truth was its bulwark and fasting its rampart.
The Magi came, threatening, but Persia was disgraced in them,
[as] Babylon in the Chaldeans and India in the sorcerors.
For thirty years the truth encompassed it.[95]
In the summer in which an idol was set up in the city,[96]
compassion fled from it, and anger overran it.

21 For empty sacrifices emptied its fullness.
Demons, sons of the wasteland, laid waste to it by libations.
The [pagan] altar[97] that was built, rooted out and expelled
that altar whose sackcloth[98] had delivered us.
The feasts of frenzy silenced His feastday.
While the sons of error served, they put to an end His service.

22 The Magus who entered our place regarded it as holy, to our
    disgrace.
He neglected his fire temple but honored the sanctuary.[99]
He cast down the [pagan] altars built by our laxity;
he destroyed the enclosures[100] to our shame.

---

refers to two or more men, rather than a single man. On the other hand, if Gregory were somehow aware of Ephrem's remarks as well as Ammianus' account, his version could be an elaboration on them.

94. In the third siege of Nisibis in 350, the Persian strategy, which entailed damming the Mygdonius River to flood the city walls, met with some success, but the Nisibenes managed to rebuild the walls and save the city; cf. CNis 1–3. Ephrem here credits the success to the piety of Emperor Constantius.

95. As Beck notes, the precise period between the first attacks and the fall of Nisibis was twenty-six years, 337–63 C.E.

96. For further evidence of the idolatry in Nisibis, cf. Beck ad loc. and Soz. HE 5.3.

97. Literally "high place," *'lt'*, in contrast to *mdbh'* in the following line.

98. Cf. CNis 4.27, and Beck's remarks ad loc.

99. Syriac *mqdš'*, apparently the Christian church.

100. Syriac *ḥbwšt'*. Beck suggests that heretical cult rooms are meant, citing CH 1.18.1, where the reference is to the Bardaisanites. That is, the cult places are destroyed by Shapur to the shame of Christians, who should themselves have destroyed them.

For he knew that from one temple[101] alone emerged
the mercy that had saved us from him three times.[102]

23 How much indeed truth revealed its face in our city!
Everywhere it showed itself through our breaches
to the point that even the blind saw it in our preservation.
The king in our deliverance recognized it.
Since he had seen it outside of our city in triumphs,
when he entered into the city, he honored it with offerings.

24 The war was a crucible, in which the king saw
how beautiful the truth and how ugly falsehood is.
He learned through experience that the Lord of that house
is gracious and just in all things.
For He wearied him and did not give him the city that believed in
Him,
but when the sacrifices angered Him, He surrendered it without
effort.

25 The sackcloth of the blessed one preserved the city that was head
of the region of Mesopotamia, and it was magnified.
The tyrant by his blasphemy humbled and abased it.
Who can weigh how great is its dishonor?
For the city that had been head of the entire West
was made the hind feet[103] of the East.

26 [This] city was not considered like all the [other] cities.
For how many times did the Gracious One deliver it from within
Sheol
[in] the battle under the earth and the battle above it,
but when it refused its Savior, He abandoned it.
The Just One, Whose anger is mighty, mingled His love with anger,
so that He did not lead us away as captives and exile us, [but] let us
dwell in our land.[104]

---

101. Syriac *hykl'*.
102. That is, he recognized that the Christian God had saved the city in the three unsuccess-
ful sieges.
103. Literally, the "other heels."
104. That is, God did not punish the people of Nisibis by allowing Shapur to exile them to
the distant East, as in the case of Singara, cf. Amm. Mar. 20.6.7, and Fiey, Nisibe, 36. Although
it is unclear whether "our land" refers to the Syriac-speaking region or the Roman Empire, in
either case Edessa would be included. Alternatively, but less plausibly, one might surmise that
Ephrem composed this hymn before learning of the need to vacate the city.

27 Whereas the [Roman] king became a [pagan] priest and dishonored
     our churches,
   the Magian king honored the sanctuary.
   His honoring our sanctuary has doubled our consolation.
   [God] saddened and gladdened us but did not exile us.[105]
   He reproved that errant one by means of his erring counterpart;
   since the priest oppressed, He rewarded the Magus.[106]

---

105. Alternatively, the subject could be Shapur rather than God.

106. Again, the subject could be Shapur, translating as Beck, "while the priest oppressed,
the magus rewarded." The more obvious sense, however, is that God reproved Julian by reward-
ing Shapur.

3

Ephrem continues the argument he began in the previous hymns, that the loss of his city to Persia was a great divine lesson on the errors of idolatry. The keynote here is the coincidence in time of the raising of the Persian standard over the city and the bringing of Julian's corpse into the city, to which he has himself been witness (str. 1–3). The poet portrays himself mocking the corpse of the emperor and his presumptuous claims, meditating on the transience of temporal power as compared with God's, and mourning the folly of those who succumbed to the pretenses of Julian (str. 4–6). Next he addresses the principal difficulty in his view: the lengthy and inconclusive struggle for survival under Constantius (str. 7–12). The war remained without a decisive victory in the first half of the fourth-century not because the Christian God was unable to bring victory but because he was waiting for Julian's paganism to come into evidence so that he could serve as an example for all the world of the inefficacy of the Hellenic deities and their oracles (str. 7–9). Even Roman defeats under Constantius and the standard of the cross can be explained away as the fault of hidden pagans among the soldiers, just as Joshua's defeat at Ai was not a sign of the weakness of the Ark of the covenant but of the disbelief of some of the army (str. 10–11). Finally, Ephrem, to whom human freedom is supremely important, argues that Julian's death was the just and freely chosen consequence of his pride coupled with his stubborn refusal to admit the error of his religious beliefs and the injustice of his anti-Christian measures (str. 12–16). Divine justice and respect for human freedom does not, however, prevent God's providing an intricate interlacing of symbolism for the edification of all. In this case Ephrem discovers a fourfold mystery of lances (str. 14), and a pun linking Julian's mocking epithet of the "Galileans" with the angelic "wheels" of God's mighty chariot (str. 17). To his way of thinking these relationships serve as substantiation of his argument no less than the example of Joshua at Ai.

3

1   A wonder! By chance the corpse of that accursed one,
crossing over toward the rampart met me near the city!
And the Magus took and fastened on a tower
the standard sent from the east,[107]
so that this standard-bearer would declare to the onlookers
that the city was slave to the lords of that standard.

Refrain: Glory to the One Who wrapped the corpse in shame!

2   I wondered, "Who indeed set a time for meeting
when corpse and standard-bearer both at one moment were
        present?"
I knew it was a prearrangement, a miracle of justice
that when the corpse of the fallen one crossed over,
the fearful standard went up and was put in place to proclaim
that the evil of his conjurers had surrendered that city.

3   For thirty years Persia had made battle in every way
but was unable to cross over the boundary of that city;
even when it had been broken and collapsed, the cross came down
        and saved it.[108]
There I saw a disgraceful sight:
the standard of the captor set up on the tower,
the corpse of the persecutor laid in a coffin.

4   Believe in "yes" and "no," the word of a trustworthy man,[109]
that I went right up, my brothers, to the coffin of the filthy one,
and I stood over him and derided his paganism
and said, "Is this indeed he who exalted himself
against the Living Name and forgot that he is dust?"

---

107. Ammianus informs us that the standard was erected by the Satrap Bineses, as noted by Beck, cf. Amm. Mar. 25.9.1. But Ammianus takes this as the sign that all must leave the city, and he stresses Jovian's incompetence and his responsibility (rather than Julian's) for the situation; cf. Amm. Mar. 25.9.2–12. Like Ephrem, he praises the constancy of Nisibis, Amm. Mar. 25.9.8–11.

108. Cf. CJ 2.20.4 and CJ 2.19.

109. Cf. Matt. 5.37.

[God] turned him back into his dust to let him know he was of
    dust.[110]

5   I stood and wondered at him whose downfall I had so fully seen.
"This is his majesty and this is his pomp!
This is his kingship and this is his chariot![111]
This is a clump of earth that has disintegrated!"
I argued with myself, "Why in [the time of] his power
did I not foresee this would be his end?"

6   I wondered about the many who, in seeking to please
the diadem of mortality, denied the universal Life-giver.
I looked above and below and was amazed, my brothers,
that our Lord [is] His height, the Glorious One,
and the accursed one in [his] downfall, and I said, "Who will fear
this corpse and deny the True One?"

7   He prevented the cross that came down from gaining victory,
not because the victorious [cross] was unable to gain victory,
but so that a pit might be dug for the evildoer
who came down with his conjurers to the east.
But since he came down and was struck, the discerning saw
that the battle in which he would be put to shame had been lying in
    wait for him.

8   Know that because of this the time was long and delayed
so that the pure one might complete the years of his kingship
and the accursed one might also complete the measure of his
    paganism.[112]
But when he had completed his story, he came to ruin.
So both sides rejoiced, and so there was peace
through the believing king, companion of the glorious [kings].[113]

---

110. Cf. Gen. 3.19. The Syriac word '*pr*' here translated "dust" and its derivative '*prn*', "of dust," are different from the word "dust" in the previous line *dḥyḥ*'.

111. The Syriac *mrkbt*', rendered "conveyance" at CJ 2.4, may allude again to Julian's fleet, but it also has the sense of "throne" or "chariot," cf. CJ 3.17.

112. That is, Constantius was to finish his reign and Julian to complete his anti-Christian measures before God would permit a decisive end to the conflict betwen Rome and Persia.

113. That is, both Romans and Persians rejoiced at the conclusion of a peace treaty by Jovian, an orthodox Christian elevated by the *imperium* by the troops after Julian's death. Although Jovian, then, actually ceded Nisibis to Persia, Ephrem credits him with the peace but blames Julian for the loss of the city. Ammianus takes the opposite tack, cf. CJ 3.1 and note ad loc.

9   The Just One by all [manner] of deaths was capable of destroying
        him,
    but he kept [for him] a downfall fearful and bitter,
    so that on the day of his death all things should be drawn up before
        his eyes:
    Where is that oracle that reassured him?[114]
    and the goddess of weapons that she did not come to his aid?
    and the companies of his gods that they did not come to save him?

10   The cross of the All-knowing marched before the army.
    It endured being mocked: "It cannot save them!"[115]
    It kept the king in safety; it gave the army to destruction,
    for it knew that paganism [was] among them.[116]
    Let the cross of Him Who searches all, therefore, be praised—
    [the cross] that fools without discernment reviled at that time.

11   For they did not persevere with the standard of the Savior of all.
    Indeed that paganism that they showed in the end
    was manifest to our Lord from the beginning.
    Yet although He knew well that they were pagans,
    His cross saved them, but when they apostatized from Him,
    they ate corpses there; they became a parable there.[117]

12   When the People was defeated at Ai of the weak,
    Joshua tore his garments before the Ark [of the covenant]
    and spoke fearful [words] before the Most High.
    A curse [was] among the People, without his knowing.[118]
    Just so paganism was hidden in the army,
    but instead of the Ark they were carrying the cross.

13   But Justice summoned him with wisdom,
    for not by force did she govern his freedom.
    By an enticement he marched out to the lance that struck:
    he saw that he subdued citadels, and he became proud.
    For adversity did not cry out to him to turn back
    until he marched out and fell into the midst of the vortex.

---

114. Cf. CJ 2.9.6 and note ad loc.
115. Cf. Mark 15.29–32 et par. The cross was among the standards at the head of the Christian Roman army.
116. As Beck suggests, the events of 347 and 359–60 are meant here, and the "King" is Constantius.
117. The idea seems to be that the desperation of Julian's army in 363 became proverbial.
118. Cf. Josh. 7.1–26.

14   The lance of Justice passed through the belly of him[119]
who despised Him Who made the lance of paradise pass away.[120]
The divination of the conjurers tore open a pregnant [animal].
[Julian] groaned at length[121] to recall
what he had written and published that he would do to the
     churches.[122]
The finger of Justice blotted out his memory.

15   The king saw that Easterners came and deceived him.
Simple men [deceived] the wise man; common men[123] [deceived] the
     diviner.
Those whom he, wrapped up in his vestment,[124] summoned,
confined his wisdom by ignorant men,
and he gave orders to set fire to his victorious ships,

---

119. Julian was struck in the liver, cf. Amm. Mar. 25.3.6, and Bowersock, *Julian*, 116ff. Gregory Nazianzen similarly dwells on the notion that the "soothsayer" was wounded in the entrails; cf. Greg. Naz. Orat. 5.13. Unlike Ephrem, who does not mention who hurled the fatal lance, Gregory knew four different versions of this part of the story: that Julian's killer was 1) a Persian, 2) a disillusioned Roman officer, 3) a barbarian camp follower, 4) a Saracen desirous of fame; cf. Bowersock, *Julian*, 116 and J. Fontaine, *Ammien Marcellin, Histoire* v.4.2 (Paris, 1977), 213f.n.528 and 251, n.623. Although he initially assumed that Julian's assailant was "some Persian," Libanius later became convinced that Christians conspired to kill him either directly or through the agency of "some Arab" (for the assumption that a Persian killed him, cf. Lib. Orat. 17.32; for the rejection of that notion and the implication that Christians were responsible, Lib. Orat. 18.274.5; for the Arab acting at his leader's command in expectation of a reward, apparently from the Christians, cf. Lib. Orat. 24.6; for Libanius' insistence that the miscreants are privileged Roman Christians and should be punished, Lib. Orat. 24.8, 11, 17–41). The notion of a Christian plot against the life of the apostate emperor was taken up enthusiastically by the fifth-century ecclesiastical historian, Sozomen (HE 6.2), and more recently by Gore Vidal in *Julian* (New York, 1965), 411–31. Recent biographers of Julian have been more sceptical. Browning leaves the question open, 213–15. After a considerably more detailed discussion, Bowersock concludes that the Arab is the most probable culprit. For this conclusion the corroboration of Philostorgius is crucial (HE VII.15, ed. Bidez, GCS 21, 101, Eng. trans. E. Walford [1855], cf. Bowersock, 117f.)

120. Ephrem refers to the flaming sword barring the way to paradise, cf. HdP 2 and Graffin, Cherubin.

121. This translation, suggested to me by Glen Bowersock, seems preferable to Beck's "[Gott] schlug [ihn] und er stöhnte."

122. Possibly Ephrem alludes to Julian's *Against the Galileans* (cf. CJ 3.17 and note ad loc.), but more likely to his legal measures or the threats mentioned in CJ 2.10.

123. Or "swarthy, dark-complected men."

124. That is, Julian was wrapped in a priestly vestment. I have taken the participle *ṣryr* as masculine singular construct, dropping the final yodh of Beck's text. With that final yodh it could be plural but then should have seyame; in that case, those summoned would be in priestly vestments, but the vestment and its pronoun modifier are singular. Since the *šwšp'* is normally the vestment or robe of a judge, king or prophet (cf. Margoliouth 569b), Ephrem seems to be mocking Julian's notion of himself as a wise man, diviner or priest.

and his idols and diviners were entangled in a trap.[125]

16 But when he saw that his gods were confuted and exposed
and that he could neither gain victory nor flee,
[that] between fear and disgrace he was prostrate and beaten,[126]
he chose death to escape into Sheol.
Cunningly he stripped off his armor in order to be wounded,
in order to die so that the Galileans would not see his shame.[127]

17 For he had mockingly named the brothers Galileans.[128]
Behold in the air the wheels[129] of the Galilean king!
He thunders in His Chariot; the Cherubim bear Him.
The Galilean revealed [the chariot][130] and handed over
the flock of the soothsayer to the wolves in the wilderness,
but the Galilean herd increased and filled the whole earth.

---

125. Cf. CJ 2.18 and note ad loc.

126. Or "laid low and pulled apart."

127. Ammianus Marcellinus confirms that Julian was without his armor at the fateful moment, but he attributes this to Julian's rash courage; cf. Amm. Mar. 25.3.3–6, and Lib. Orat. 18.268. Gregory Nazianzen repeats Ephrem's accusation that Julian chose to die rather than to admit the hopelessness of his situation and the disgrace of his gods adding an apocryphal tale of Julian's attempt to throw himself into the river after being wounded, the better to be deified if his corpse were not found; for discussion, cf. Greg. Naz. Orat. 5.12, 5.14 and 4.59, the remarks of J. Bernardi ed., Grégoire de Nazianze, Discours 4–5: Contre Julien, SC 309 (Paris, 1983), 164–67, 314–21, and Bowersock, Julian 116.

128. No longer independently extant, Julian's anti-Christian polemic, Against the Galileans, has been reconstructed through Cyril of Alexandria's refutation. For the Greek text with English translation, cf. Jul. Imp. Galil. It has been carefully studied in Malley, Hellenism, and by P. Evieux, Cyrille d'Alexandrie, Contre Julien, T. 1, Livres I et II, Introduction, texte critique, traduction et notes, par P. Burguiere et P. Evieux, SC 322 (Paris, 1985), esp. 21–58; cf. also Bowersock, Julian, 102.

129. Ephrem puns on gll the root of "Galilean" and ggl the root of "wheel" as well as gl' "to reveal." The "wheels" are one of the groups of angels, who are associated especially with God's chariot; cf. Virg. 36.9.1, also Cramer, Engelvorstellungen, 73–75, and Beck, Reden, 109.

130. Although Beck alters the text since he considers "revealed" to be out of the question, I have translated the received text under the assumption that the chariot is the direct object and that Ephrem alludes either to esoteric speculation on the chariot or, more simply, to the revelation of the power and majesty of God through these events; on the merkabah in Jewish sources, cf. Scholem, Mysticism, 40–79 et passim.

4

Having established both that Julian's death met the criteria of divine justice and that it was provided with clear symbolic indications of its importance for all, in this hymn Ephrem enlarges on its universal didactic purpose. That is, he returns his attention from the ethical lessons to be drawn from the faults of Julian as an individual to the lesson that Christianity is true whereas the emperor's paganism and his attempt to rebuild the Jewish Temple were mistaken religious policies. In tempting and persecuting the church, Julian had merely separated true believers from the false (str. 1-2). Had he only considered the signs, he could have realized the error of his ways. The wretched death of his uncle Julian was a clear warning for the apostate emperor of the death awaiting him (str. 3-4), but like Ahab, he preferred to listen to false prophecies (str. 5). Since he worshiped every other god except that of the Christians, it is abundantly clear which God is responsible for his defeat and ignominious death (str. 6). Likewise, the emperor's consultation of the best sorcerors proves the utter folly of their religion (str. 7).

As on the personal level, so on the religious level, Julian's death shows a kind of ironic suitability (str. 8-14). Foolishly he presumed that the god of the Babylonians would abandon his traditional worshippers to give victory to this upstart devotee (str. 8-11). Even had he found such extraordinary favor in the eyes of the sun-god as to be victorious over the Persians, Julian would have disproved his own religion by showing the injustice of its god and the folly of loyalty to such a tyrant (str. 12-14). The piety and modesty of Constantius, by contrast, were rewarded by his long rule and peaceful death (str. 15-16). Just as God used the sun to teach Jonah a lesson, He used an earthquake to teach a lesson to Julian and the Jews who accepted his plan to rebuild the Temple in Jerusalem (str. 17-20). The words of Daniel and of Jesus clearly state that the Temple will not be rebuilt and that this is the punishment for the crucifixion of Jesus (str. 21-23). The true consolation of Jerusalem and Zion lies not in the rebuilding of the Temple but in the visits of Christian pilgrims (str.

23-25). Ephrem ends by reiterating his major theme: All the claims of paganism have been proven false in the fate of Julian (str. 26).

4

1   Oh, how cunning [is] the crucible that tested the king's daughter![131]
He made merry with her, but she rejoiced not, cast gloom over her,
      but she feared not,
gave to her, but she took not, pillaged her, but she succumbed not.
She uprooted his altars, and he was shaken.
When he tore away her limb, he experienced her courage.[132]
Wisely he ceased,[133] lest he increase her[134] triumph.

Refrain: Glory to the One Whose truth confuted the liars!

2   In one member of her, therefore, he proved that all her members
were ready to take their crowns.[135]
But seeing that force did not prevail over the true,
he put on enticement[136] and approached them.
He poured his rennet into her milk; unwittingly he strained it;
hers he left with her, but his he drew to himself.[137]

---

131. Julian is the crucible, and, as Beck suggests, the king's daughter is the city of Antioch. Ephrem's alternating sentences describe well the emperor's first currying the favor of its citizenry, then angrily attempting to force them to change their ways. His attempts to reform the curia of Antioch to provide a firmer economic base for the city met with no success. Moreover, he objected to the luxurious living, the prominence of the games and theater in the life of the city and the neglect of the traditional pagan religion, especially at Daphne. Julian's difficulties there are documented in his own *Misopogon* as well as by Ammianus Marcellinus and Theodoret, cf. Bowersock, Julian, 79–105.

132. After the body of the martyr Babylas had been removed from Daphne—in Julian's view, in order to purify the shrine—the Temple of Apollo was burned. He blamed the Christians, who denied responsibility; cf. Amm. Mar. 22.13.1–3, Theod. HE 3.6–7. Ephrem portrays the subsequent persecution of the church of Antioch as the torture of a female martyr.

133. Julian abandoned his persecution in favor of other measures, cf. Soz. HE 5.4.

134. Beck's text erroneously reads "his"—a misprint unless Ephrem has changed the referent from the Christian church to the martyr Theodore, to whom he alludes in the following strophe.

135. Theodore's fortitude under torture was proof that the church of Antioch would endure persecution.

136. Ephrem puns here on "enticement," *šdl*, and "poured," *šd*, in the following line.

137. Rennet, or whey, is the agent used to curdle milk, separating it into curds and whey for cheesemaking. The persecution of the church separates it into apostates, represented by the

3   He also saw his kindred in his kinsman
    who, while living, swarmed with worms and was destroyed.[138]
    In the worm of this world he saw that of the world to come.[139]
    The Just One cut off his arm with worms,[140]
    and he went out armless to inform us that in battle
    [Julian] would be hewn down and not gain victory; he would be
        overthrown and not triumph.

4   He was his own flesh and blood; in him he was fully portrayed.
    With one visible name the two of them were imprinted,
    just as with one hidden demon they were possessed.
    His kinsman made a statement about him by his worms.
    In his other half he saw himself and what would befall him.
    In his death he saw his own killing, in his worm his own torment.[141]

5   On her lyre Error played; she captured these:
    Ahab with promises, this one with assurances.
    The prophets of the house of Baal, the possessed of the house of
        falsehood—
    in all of them a single chant resounded:
    to Ahab to go up,[142] to this one to go down.[143]
    Ahab went up and fell, and this one went down and was struck.

6   Who else has so increased altars?
    Who else has so honored all the evil spirits?
    Who else has so pleased all the demons?
    He angered only the One, and he was broken.

---

whey, useless except for curdling other milk, and the faithful Christians, the curds, kept to make the cheese. Unknowingly, then, Julian has performed a useful service for the church.

138. Julian's uncle Julian, Prefect of the Orient, is meant. As punishment for his persecution of Christians in Antioch after the destruction of the Temple of Apollo and especially for his defiling of the altar vessels (according to Sozomen) or of the altar (according to Theodoret), he was tormented by an intestinal disease; cf. Theod. HE 3.7–9 and Soz. HE 5.8.

139. Isa. 66.24, cited by Mark 9.48, associates the worm with fire as instruments of divine punishment. Only Sozomen's version of the events in Antioch includes worms in the punishment.

140. The *comites* or order of Imperial Companions had been created by Constantine. The office of *comes orientis* held by Julian became more permanent and had higher rank than others for reasons that are unknown; cf. Jones, Social and Economic History, I, 104f. Thus Julian, the *comes*, is the arm of the Emperor Julian, although there are more than two *comites!*

141. Julian and his uncle were kinsmen, had the same name and were both persecutors of Christians. This means that they shared in the same reality in a mysterious, symbolic sense. They are even two halves of the same person. Ephrem uses his technical language of typology here: ṣwr, "portray," ṭbʿ, "imprint," glyʾ, "visible" and ksyʾ, "hidden."

142. I.e., to Ramoth-gilead.

143. I.e., to Julian to go down to Seleucia-Ctesiphon.

In him was confuted the entire faction of wrong,
a force unable to support its worshippers.

7   The chief sorcerors, the best of the Chaldeans,
the most-skilled sons of error he chose lest
perhaps some of the ignorant[144] should fail to comprehend.
They labored everyday in everything;
they plunged into and researched the recesses of hidden matters.
Although they thought they understood, they found disgrace.

8   The Just One measured Saul[145] with his [own] measure;
since he consulted a conjured spirit, He cast gloom on him by it.
Listening, he heard from him a note that sickened his heart.[146]
This one, too, who followed in his footsteps,
who loved Chaldeans—[God] surrendered him to the Chaldeans.[147]
He worshipped the sun and fell before the servants of the sun.[148]

9   Since he denied God Who can never be divided,
He surrendered him to Satan who can never be in agreement.[149]
The errant one wandered and went down to destroy the errant ones.
He worshipped the sun, yet again he dishonored it
since he went down to kill its servants and worshippers.
This is the faction of Satan, which is entirely treacherous and
        duplicitous.

10   If by the sun's power, therefore, he went down to conquer
those who for a long time had offered libations to the sun,

---

144. For the translation, "some of the ignorant," cf. Nöldeke, §209A.

145. There is a pun on "Saul," *š'wl*, and "consulted," *š'l*.

146. Saul's conjuring of the spirit of Samuel, cf. 1 Sam. 28.3–25, informed him of his own imminent defeat and death.

147. That is, since Julian loved astrologers, God surrendered him to the Persians. Ephrem plays on the two senses of "Chaldean."

148. Julian wrote a hymn to Helios for December 25, the celebration of Sol Invictus, probably at Antioch in 362; cf. Jul. Imp. Orat. 4, and Bowersock, Julian, 102f. The work shows Julian's contemplative religiosity, a fusion of Neo-Platonism and traditional religion with the sun taking the role of the Logos as metaphysical mediator between the One and the many, cf. ibid., 103, and Malley, Hellenism, 182–87 et passim. Ephrem was himself capable of combining Christian belief with the imagery of Sol Invictus, cf. Nat. 27.

149. Cf. Mark 3.20–30 et par. The division of error as opposed to the unity of truth is a common rhetorical and apologetic device, which recurs below in CJ 4.13. Throughout this strophe Ephrem plays on the various senses of *šw'*, "to be worthy, to agree," and of *ṭ'*, "to wander, err," and of *plg*, "to divide, deceive," Ethp. "to have doubts."

he himself would have prevailed over the sun [to which] he offered a
   libation.[150]
Unwittingly he confuted the signs of the Zodiac,
for if he learned from them that he would go down to victory,
why did he not find out that he would go down to defeat?

11   If, then, while honoring the sun, he determined to march,
it escaped his notice that it was worshipped especially there.
If, moreover, the Chaldeans' home is in Babylon,
should he, a stranger, be exalted?[151]
For if he was confident in the error that befell him,
how much more confident in it would be his indigenous
   predecessors!

12   If, moreover, he found out[152] that he would march to victory
over those who had worthily offered libations to the sun,
he would dissipate his [own] faction: He was both honoring the sun
and unwittingly bringing reproach on it.
For if [the sun] rejected[153] the diligent [worshippers] of old,
it would show itself a tyrant, and in vain would he honor it.

13   The one divided against himself is the root
of the factions of the sons of the Evil One who are utterly in
   disagreement.
For if two kings looked at the signs of the Zodiac,
the erring ones have dissipated their [own] argument.
For if by [these signs] this one learned he would be victorious,
from them also that one learned he would conquer!

14   If he and also they are worshippers of the sun,
if he and also they are gazers at auguries,
if he and also they are consulters of oracles,

---

150. That is, if Julian had defeated the Persians, he would have defeated his own god, the
sun, since they had a longer history of sun worship than he did. But Julian's approach could be
interpreted instead as a normal religious military strategy, the calling out of the gods from a city
under siege, inviting them to join the gods of the attacker; cf. V. Basanoff, *Evocatio: Étude d'un
rituel militaire romain*, Bibliothèque de l'École des hautes Études, Sciences réligieuses 61 (Paris,
1947). Here my translation differs from Beck's, "dann hat er sich selbst besiegt."

151. That is, since Babylonia is the source of astrology, the power behind astrology would
favor the Persians rather than Julian. The emperor himself had addressed this issue in his *Hymn
to King Helios*, arguing that the Greeks had perfected the astrology of Babylonia and hence
presumably were the rightful heirs of its power, cf. Malley, Hellenism, 92f.

152. The Syriac adds "and learned."

153. Ephrem puns on *ṭlm*, "reject" and *ṭlwm'*, "tyrant" in the following line.

it is the Evil One who is divided against himself.

Their accursed instruction lies to its teachers.

Their mad learning speaks falsely to its proclaimers.

15   For behold the son of the king,[154] a sea of calm,

was inexhaustible, but he never proclaimed he would be victorious.

He knew this was the hidden concern of the [Most] High.

His diadem he entrusted to the Omniscient One.

If he were not victorious and triumphant, all the more was he
    victorious and triumphant

whose prayer for forty years preserved his kingdom.[155]

16   He was a cedar that in his time bent quietly

and fell into his couch and, resting, fell asleep in peace.

From their sweet root there emerged in succession

the sapling of paganism,[156] who, it was supposed,

would live long and weary mountains in his shadow.

Overnight he sprouted, and overnight he dried up.

17   Instead of Jonah's [head], the sun beat down on the heads

of [Julian's] accursed partisans—the discriminating sun

that refreshed the true but tormented the infidels.

For if Jonah suffered because he stood

against the penitents, how much more afflicted would be

everyone who fights against the saints.[157]

18   At that time terrors[158] were stirred up as a rebuke;[159]

---

154. Emperor Constantius.

155. Although Constantius had no decisive victory on the Eastern front, at least, Ephrem claims, he neither predicted a great victory nor experienced a resounding defeat. His rule lasted approximately 40 years, as *caesar* from 324–37 and *augustus* from 337–63; cf. Boak and Sinnigen, 438, and R. MacMullen, *Constantine* (London, 1969), 142f., 217–20, Pl. XI, XII.

156. From the "sweet root" of Constantine and his son Constantius emerged the apostate "sapling," Julian, Constantine's nephew.

157. Cf. Jonah 4.8–11. Ephrem uses the plant that sprouted and under which Jonah rested as a symbol of Julian's brief glory. With it he frames a *qal w ḥomer* exegetical argument (cf. Nat. 1.57 and note ad loc.): If God afflicted Jonah for the sake of the penitents of Nineveh, how much more will he afflict Julian, the persecutor of the saints. For further reflections on Jonah, cf. Virg. 42–50.

158. The Syriac word *qwnḥ'* normally means the terror caused by an earthquake. It should be plural to agree with the verb, as per Beck's translation but not his text. According to some ancient sources the attempt to rebuild the Temple was thwarted by one or several earthquakes; cf. Amm. Mar. 23.1.2–3. For discussion of the historicity of these events, cf. Brock, Temple, (which includes a translation of CJ 4.18–23, p. 283f.), Bowersock, Julian, 88–90, 120–22, and Levenson, Attempt.

159. The Syriac here is translated as the Afel infinitive of *kss* "to rebuke, confute." Alternatively it may be the Pael infinitive of *nks* "to put to death"—hence "deadly terrors were stirred up."

He[160] proclaimed in the whole world a truth for souls:
that cities were overthrown by the disgrace of paganism.[161]
Jerusalem found very guilty
the accursed ones and crucifiers who dared to decide to enter[162]
to build the desolate place desolated by their sins.[163]

19 Fools and simpletons, they desolated what had been built,
and now that it has been desolated, they decide to build it.
When they possessed it, they demolished it, but when it was
    desolate, they loved it.
Jerusalem trembled when she saw
her demolishers entering again and disturbing her calm.
She complained to the [Most] High about them, and she was heard.

20 Winds He commanded, and they blew; He beckoned to
    earthquakes, and they came into being,
to the lightning bolts and they blazed forth, to the air and it became
    dark,
to the walls and they were overthrown, to the gates and they were
    opened.
Fire came out and devoured the scribes
who read in Daniel that [Jerusalem] would be destroyed forever,
who read but did not learn; they were severely stricken, and they
    learned.[164]

21 They scattered her with the Humble One[165] Who gathered her
    chicks,[166]
and they thought the soothsayer's error would gather her.
They overthrew her with the steadfast,[167] but supported her with
    the unsteady.
They wanted to build her again.

---

160. If the terrors are plural, God rather than the events must be understood to be the subject here.

161. The preposition may express the agent with the passive verb, as translated here, or it may indicate purpose: "for the disgrace of paganism."

162. Or "to threaten to enter." Especially if the latter is the correct translation, Ephrem does not indicate clearly whether or not the work had begun.

163. Ephrem repeats the Christian anti-Jewish τόπος that the destruction of the Temple was a divine punishment of the Jews for their rejection of Christ.

164. Cf. CJ 1.20.5 and note ad loc.

165. Matt. 21.5, quoting Zech. 9.9, at the entry into Jerusalem.

166. Matt. 23.37.

167. Although the received text is plural, Beck takes this as singular and refers it to Christ.

They scattered His[168] great altar by the slaughter of the Holy One,
and they thought the rebuilder of [pagan] altars[169] would reestablish
    it.

22   They broke her by the wood[170] of the Living Architect,[171]
but they sustained her by the broken reed of paganism.[172]
They disheartened her with Zechariah[173] who had made her rejoice,
    "Behold your king!"
But they encouraged her with the diviner of the madman.
They announced to her, "Behold there comes one possessed who will
    build you.
He will enter to offer sacrifice in you, to pour libations to his
    demons in you."

23   But Daniel passed judgment on Jersualem and determined
that it would not be rebuilt, and Zion believed him.
They themselves wailed[174] and wept: he cut off and cast out their
    hope.
Cana by its wine consoled
the two wailers and gave them advice,
"Do not reject by your wailings the rewards of the Gracious One.

24   "Behold, you are at rest; you are at peace, then, and freed
from demonic things and contact with evil spirits.
They became confused and raved and crucified the Reviver of all,
and they have always torn to pieces the two of you.
In you they killed the prophets; in you they mulitplied idols.
With the image of four faces[175] they put your faces to shame.

---

168. *Sic*—referring to the Holy One, but Beck translates it as feminine, referring to
Jerusalem.

169. As in CJ 2.2, the altar of the Temple, *mdbh'*, is contrasted with pagan altars, *'lt'*, built
by Julian.

170. The Syriac *qys'* here clearly refers to the cross, but Ephrem likes the ambiguity of the
word, which may also mean "tree" or simply "wood."

171. On Christ the Architect, cf. Nat. 3.15 and 8.10 and notes ad loc.

172. 2 Kgs. 18.21.

173. The pun on "Zechariah," *zkry'*, and "his diviner," *zkwrh*, (in the following line) helps
to set out the parallelism—and hence Ephrem's irony—between the announcement of the
prophet and that of Julian's diviner.

174. Although the seyame are missing, the form and context demand the feminine plural;
the understood subject is Jerusalem and Zion.

175. Cf. 2 Chron. 33.7 in the Pes., where Manasseh put a four-faced image of the golden
calf in the Temple, cf. HdF 87.4.3, SdF 3.357 and Beck's remarks ad loc. The 3rd pl. masc.
subject may be either the "demonic things" and "evil spirits" or the "scribes" of strophes 21ff.

25   "Better for you than that inhabited land of paganism
is the wasteland without sins and the desert without oracles,
Bethlehem and Bethany both pledged to [you] two
that instead of that People that was uprooted
from all the peoples they should come with Hallelujahs
to see in your wombs the grave and Golgotha."[176]

26   Who will again believe in Fate and the horoscope?
Who will again trust soothsayers and conjured spirits?
Who will again err with divinations and signs of the Zodiac?
For behold all of them have lied in all things.
So that the Just One [need] not persuade those in error one by one,
He broke that one who erred that they might learn by him.[177]

---

176. Ephrem is an early witness to Christian pilgrimage to the Holy Land; cf. Nat. 19.14–16, Virg. 16–23 and 32–36.

177. B. M. Add. 14571 adds, "Completed are the five hymns about King Julian, the pagan."

The Hymns on Virginity
and on the
Symbols of the Lord[1]

---

1. Although the superscript of the principal manuscript entitles this collection simply "Hymns on Virginity of Saint Ephrem," a postscript gives this fuller title. I have used it here since it is a better description of the contents of this collection of fifty-two hymns.

1

In this, the first of three hymns on the theme of virginity, Ephrem begins with the image of the body as garment and exhorts the virgin to put off the garment of the old, pre-baptismal self (str. 1). The body of the baptized is a temple and palace built by the Carpenter of life (str. 2). Enunciating the central theme of the collection of hymns, Ephrem states that scripture and nature serve as guides for the Christian life (str. 3–5). The next few strophes are an exhortation to avoid both extremes of asceticism and opposition to virginity (str. 6–8). Finally, the dangers threatening the virgin are the subject of the last strophes. The danger of rape is mitigated by the power of the will to resist (str. 9). More perilous are the dangers of wine (str. 10–11) and especially of love (str. 12–14). The description of the power of infatuation, despite Ephrem's intent, is charming.

1

To the melody: "The royal bride"

1   O body, strip off the utterly hateful old man,
     lest he wear out again the new [garment] you put on when you were
         baptized.[2]
     For it would be the inverse of paying his due
     that he, if renewed, should wear you out again.
     O body, obey my advice; strip him off by [your] way of life,
     lest he put you on by [his] habits.

       Refrain: From all the chaste[3] on earth and in heaven,
       glory to the Father and to the Son and to the Holy Spirit.

---

2. Col. 3.9.
3. The Syriac word, *qdyšyn*, can mean "holy" but is most often used as a technical term for celibates or for married couples living chastely; cf. Murray, *Symbols*, 12–16.

2   For by baptism our Lord made new your old age—
He, the Carpenter[4] of life, Who by His blood formed and built a
   temple[5] for His dwelling.
Do not allow that old man
to dwell in the renewed temple.
O body, if you have God live in your Temple,
you will also become His royal palace.[6]

3   Scripture that teaches, nature that proclaims: both admonish man.
Set between the two is his iniquity,
so that nature admonishes him if he lead to sin one without the Law,
and scripture will rebuke him if he lead to sin one of the Law.[7]
Satan wounds, but they heal us:
compunction of soul enters on the heel of iniquity.

4   They scorned the rebellious, mended the penitent and judged the
   judge.
Again, they will reprove rebels but heal the penitent.
For they endure with the Evil One who is
young in every generation and accompanies everyone and does harm
   at every moment.
They also accompany everyone and are young
in each generation and found in every moment.

5   Listen to nature and the Law, relating [man's] evil corruptions, for
   that People committed adultery with the Law;
without the Law the peoples changed their natures
and without nature they have become new.
Nature and Law have complained against [man]
that the seditious have perverted their ordinance.[8]

---

4. Elsewhere Ephrem uses the image of the architect, but here the word is clearly carpenter.

5. The Syriac word is from the Greek ναός. For a similar idea, cf. Clem. str. 7.

6. The Syriac word, *hykl'*, is a cognate of the Hebrew, hence perhaps is related to Jewish "Hekhaloth" mysticism, cf. Scholem, Major Trends, 45–79, 356–68 et passim.

7. Jews have the Law via scripture; Gentiles have "natural law." Although Ephrem does not use this term, the concept is implied here.

8. Beck takes the referent in the first line to be the people, i.e., the Jewish people, rather than humankind. In this context, however, it seems more appropriate to understand the universal human need for redemption: the Law complains against the Jews who were to follow it; nature complains against the Gentiles who were to follow natural law through their consciences.

6 The Evil One stole the weak from marriage in the name of
         conversion,[9]
   and when they were in the midst, he placed behind them the
         disgrace of the offense,
   and before them he again placed beauty
   that is a snare of hateful desire.
   Ashamed to assume the condition of marriage,
   they fell into the snares of sin.

7 O body, why do you persecute virginity that came down to earth[10]
   and lives with us as a sojourner; if one pursues her and uproots her
         nest,
   because she is not able to rebuild it,
   her wing quickly carries her to the height—
   this bird on high who grows old in one nest—
   but if she departs, she leaves [the nest] forever.[11]

8 When the dear friend of Watchers[12] takes flight, the companion of
         demons enters:
   desire, which is the hatred of the virginity pursued by Joseph.
   For virginity loved the Watchers;
   she flees to ascend the height of the Watchers.
   Who will not weep because instead of this quiet one,
   this inflamed one[13] entered and lived there?

9 If a robber seizes you and you are raped[14] in the field,
   the unclean man's force will be persuasive evidence[15] that you are
         chaste
   just as Sarah in the bosom of Pharaoh was chaste,
   for she did not commit adultery by her own will.[16]

---

9. An anti-encratite section—a Christian group recommending celibacy, apparently otherwise orthodox, is criticized for causing some to fall into sin by forbidding marriage. This could be the remnants of the earliest Syriac-speaking Christian community.

10. Literally, "to our place."

11. That is, either one must remain celibate for a lifetime or abandon that vocation. Ephrem argues again here against the earlier tradition of encratism.

12. The "Watchers," as before, are angels. Their "dear friend" is virginity, since the celibate life was seen as the angelic life, cf. Cramer, Engelvorstellung, 49f., 157–61.

13. Ephrem puns on "quiet one," *mšynt'*, and "inflamed one," *mšḥnt'*, virginity and desire, respectively.

14. Literally, "your modesty is exposed."

15. Literally, "will persuade concerning you."

16. Gen. 12. 10–20.

The will has become a priest who by his hyssop
purifies those who have been defiled by force.

10   Fear wine that exposed the honorable Noah, victorious in his
    generation.[17]

A handful of wine prevailed over him who could prevail over the
    flood of water.

This one whom the Deluge had not vanquished outwardly,
wine vanquished inwardly.

The wine that exposed [and] cast down Noah, the head of families—
how much more will it conquer you, solitary woman![18]

11   May you fear[19] the desire of wine that took Lot by force in old
    age.[20]

Wine accomplished difficult things so that by it women stole
    conception.

How much more will it accomplish this easy thing:
that men by it steal the signs of virginity.

The girls pillaged the treasure of the old man;
you keep your treasury from the young [men].

12   One drunk on wine is more tolerable than one drunk on hateful
    love.

Firm bonds enfeeble him; despised is his sceptre and weak [his] staff.

Chastisement and reproof
traverse his ears like fables,

and to him as well reproach is like pleasure,
and spittle in the face he reckons as dew.

13   For the path of the voices that batter his ears does not lead to his
    heart.

The gates of his ears are open one to the other: A word that entered
    by his [one] ear

went out on the opposite [side] by the other ear.

While his teacher supposes that he is listening to him,
he does not perceive that his warning is pouring forth outside,
because there is no place in his heart to receive [it].

---

17. Literally, "Noah, who prevailed" or "conquered." The same word appears twice in the
following line. Gen. 9.20–27. Cf. Kronholm, Motifs, 207–10.

18. Ephrem uses the *gal w homer* type of rabbinic exegesis here.

19. The syntax here is unclear; there is some textual uncertainty.

20. Gen. 19. 30–38.

14   For full and congested and cramped is the spacious gulf[21] of his
        reason
from one drop of the love that surged and became a great sea.
Thoughts plunge in and arise
like a sailor whose ship is wrecked.
Thought is afloat in waves of desires
like a ship whose navigator has abandoned it.

---

21. or "womb."

In this second hymn on the theme of virginity, Ephrem adduces women from Jewish scripture to illustrate his argument. The first nine strophes are a meditation on the treasure of virginity and the inevitability of the punishment of its thief. He begins with the recollection of Amnon's rape of Tamar, vividly describing his desire and deceitful plan (str. 1–3) and Tamar's despair (str. 4–5). The punishment not only of Amnon but also of Shechem illustrate the fate of the destroyers of virginity (str. 6–9). In a more positive vein, though straying farther from the intent of the original story, he finds examples of heroically chaste women in Jephthah's daughter and in Susanna (str. 10–15). Ignoring the fact that his emphasis on permanent virginity as a positive value is utterly foreign to the story of Jephthah's daughter, he takes her as a model for chaste women and even as a type of Christ (str. 10–11, esp. 11.3–6). She and Susanna serve as models for chastity among virgins and married women, respectively (str. 12). The final strophes constitute an explicit exhortation to women to persevere and to be thoroughgoing in their chastity (str. 13–15).

2

The same melody

1 In a lamb's garment the crafty Amnon approached that ewe.[22]
   Scheming to lead her astray by her service,[23] he performed his
        service.
   The sick one, laid low, rose to the conflict
   and laid hold of the crown that was found for his shame.
   Since he saw that virginity was secure in her nest,
   he dissembled to make her enter his den, and so he caught her.

---

22. Cf. 2 Sam. 13.1–22.
23. This word, *dyl'* is apparently from *dwl*, to serve or minister, in Pael.

HYMN 2

Refrain: From all the chaste, glory to the Chaste One Who gave virginity among the Gentiles.

2 Crafty is your hunger, O virgin, but you are innocent, since Amnon
      who sought you
  was seeking food—the astute one, who was not [really] seeking.
  By the meal for which he did not hunger, he served the desire of the
      flesh,
  for which he did hunger.
  O the deceiver who sought something that he does not really seek
  so that by means of it he might find what he seeks!

3 Hearts he was seeking—O the rational one[24] who made hearts for
      the heartless one!
  For he was a snake who in his cunning
  clothed himself in the attire of illness,
  so that she would fail to notice him, and he would wound her.
  Since desire deceived and defiled virginity,
  rage deceived and destroyed desire.

4 Tamar tore her garments when she saw her pearl had perished.
  Instead of her tunic she could acquire another,
  but her virginity did not have a successor,
  because it is not able, if stolen, to be sought out again.
  O you, virginity, your destruction is simple for all,
  but your restoration is easy only for the Lord of all.

5 Tamar feared to be silent, but she was also ashamed to speak.
  Since she was able neither to be silent nor to speak,
  she tore her garments so the visible shreds
  would cry out in silence that her hidden signs of virginity were
      stolen.
  The multitude of pearls on her did not console her
  about that one greatest [pearl].

6 The king's daughter was a maiden whose limbs bore many beryls,
  but her virginity, although [only] one, surpassed them all.
  Therefore the defiled one despised the beryls but ploughed the seals;
  he rejected the stones but stole the signs of virginity.

---

24. I.e., virginity.

The thief knows your value, virginity,
but you are not aware how much you are worth!

7   This athlete, seeing he could not lay her low by standing firm,
hastened to fall and lay her low.[25]
He broke the yoke of marriage and committed adultery;[26]
the iniquity he sowed in the inner chamber, he reaped in the open
    field.
The sword destroyed him who destroyed virginity.
and he who spattered him[self] with her blood, bathed in his
    blood.[27]

8   In the inner chamber and in the wilderness they lie in wait, O
    virginity,
so that if you entered the inner chamber, the crafty Amnon stole
    your riches.
[If] you went out to the field, [if] you resisted in the desert,
Shechem the thief stole your treasure.[28]
Where, indeed, will you go, solitary dove,
whose hunters are numerous everywhere?

9   Venerable one, your hunters[29] are hunted in return,
since the defiled Shechem, who met you in the wilderness and took
    you captive, was killed in his house,
and Amnon, too, who lay in wait in the inner chamber and caught
    you,
was dragged away into the field.
Your destroyers were destroyed and were hunted; in them is a type
that whoever destroys you will be destroyed.

10   Jephthah's daughter bowed her neck to the sword;
her pearl, delivered from all dangers, remained with her and
    consoled her.[30]

---

25. Literally, "He was an athlete who, although he saw that however much he stood firm,
he could not lay [her] low, but he hastened and fell and laid her low."

26. Tamar asked Amnon to marry her after the rape, but he refused.

27. Amnon's death is punishment for his crime, which is in Ephrem's eyes more a crime
against virginity than against Tamar!

28. The allusion here is to the rape of Dinah, cf. Gen. 34.

29. The Syriac adds redundantly, "who hunted you."

30. Judg. 11. 29–40. Ephrem misses the point of the story of Jephthah's promise to Yahweh
to offer the first person he saw as a holocaust when he returned home if he received victory over
the Ammonites. The first he saw was his daughter, his only child. She accepted death willingly
after being allowed two months in the wilderness to "mourn her virginity."

But distress will be the companion in death
of the woman whose pearl perishes here.
Again on the day of resurrection there will be fear
before that Judge, [even] when she has repented.

11 Jephthah's daughter willed to die to fulfill her father's vow.[31]
Do not annul by your eyes the vows of virginity your mouth has
vowed.[32]
Jephthah poured out his daughter's blood,
but your Bridegroom shed His blood for love of you.
Therefore that Only-Begotten blood bought
that blood by which your gate is sealed.[33]

12 A married woman willed to die to put an end to adultery.[34]
A virgin died to fulfill her father's vow.
A married[35] mother of offspring willed to die
lest she receive a stolen seed whose sowing is cursed.
The Virgin will not steal a defiled seed in secret
lest the pure Infant inside her be a lawless one.[36]

13 Chaste woman, do not complete your course in the trackless waste
of desires,
lest your enemy then work in you, take your power and discharge
your wellspring.
lest your old age come to shame,
lest your hateful way of life be reproached.
Your way of life made light of youth in the contest,
so that the crown might adorn your old age.

14 For when one ages and becomes ugly, the chaste ways of youth
come to mind;

---

31. The Syriac is passive here and in the following strophe, Virg. 2.12.2.

32. Beck suggests that discipline of the eyes to preserve chastity is meant here; cf. Eccl.
33.1. If so, it recalls the story of Ephrem's rebuke of a woman who stared at him, Soz. E.H.
3.16. On the probable lack of historical value of the story, cf. Outtier, Saint Éphrem, 21.

33. Only-Begotten, a title used often for Christ, has a special nuance in Syriac. It means a
solitary one and is a technical term for a person who has chosen an ascetic life in imitation of
Christ; cf. Murray, Exhortation. Ephrem's graphic imagery here is startling to modern ears. He
addresses consecrated virgins here; Beck has noted similar imagery in CH 47.1, Nat. 14.12,
Virg. 3.14.

34. Susannah, cf. Dan. 13.43.

35. Since the Syriac reads "of marriage", dšwtpwt', not dšwtpt', it is here translated as
"married." Again, Susannah is meant.

36. Here Ephrem seems to be concerned with polemics against the virgin birth, cf. Nat.
5–20.

they abhor his old age because of its infirmity,
but they cherish the infirmities of the body
who see that the adornments of the spirit are hidden in the soul.
O virginity, portray with your senses your glories
that you might be honored by them when you are old.

15   Let chastity be portrayed in your eyes and in your ears the sound of
      truth.
Imprint your tongue with the word of life and upon your hands
      [imprint] all alms.
Stamp your footsteps with visiting the sick,
and let the image of your Lord be portrayed in your heart.
Tablets are honored because of the image of kings.
How much [more will] one [be honored] who portrayed his Lord in
      all his senses.[37]

---

37. The language of art and coinage is frequently used by Ephrem, cf. Nat. 1.99. Here the image of God is imprinted on all the senses through pious actions.

3

In this third hymn on the theme of virginity, Ephrem urges the consecrated virgin to cultivate modesty. After a warning on the fleeting nature
of youthful beauty, he enlarges on the dangers of sexual temptation (str.
1–7). The kiss of Judas is a warning, as is the devouring nature of fire that
death hides beneath the deceptive allure of sexual desire (str. 5, 7). Exercise of the will and a constant disposition to repentance are necessary for
one betrothed to Christ (str. 8–16).

3

The same melody

1 Youth resembles a branch of fruit, pleasing in summer.
When its fruits are stripped away, it is thrown away,
and everyone turns his face away from it,
and what was found desirable to all [becomes] ugly to everyone.
Girl, do not show your beauty to outsiders,
so that when it has been disfigured, onlookers would scorn it.

Refrain: From each who has struggled and held fast to virginity, to You, Lord, and to
Your Anointed be praise!

2 How swift, O virginity, are your wings that reach your Lord.
Flee from the advice of your enemy whose capital disconcerts the
    merchants.
He impoverished the treasures of great Adam[38]
who did business with the cargo of harms.
Do not borrow from the one who lends and does not demand,
for if you repay his money you would make him poor.

---

38. On the original attributes of Adam, cf. Nat. 5.4 and note ad loc.; also Virg. 16.9, 29.11,
48.15, 51.7.

3 Great fear and shame accompany his desires;
   they are troublesome and sadden for a lifetime those who enact
        them.
   But open and pure are the faces
   of those who are chaste, who are weaned from all desires.
   Be not seized, O body, by hateful love;
   although its doing is dead, the thought of it is living.

4 For his teaching is cunning, so that he may be with everyone and
        like everyone.
   His gift is poured forth for the good; he bribes the belly and is
        bribed by it,
   so that the eye will look away and the mouth will be silent,
   and the ear will pass over its hateful news.
   His silent wine is endowed with speech by its drinkers.
   It sings with their voices instead of its master's.

5 Beforehand in his cunning he placed at the mouth of his trap food
        for the prey.
   For his love precedes his hate, like Judas who kissed and killed.
   For the Pure One kissed the unclean Judas
   to denounce the Evil One in Judas:
   Even if his enticements are sweet like the kiss of Judas,
   death is secretly woven into them.

6 He is the one who, if he arises in you, is able to repay you [with] a
        fall,
   so that when he has stood up, he will cast you down, for his desire
        is dead, my beloved,
   but your flesh is able to revive and vivify it.
   When it lives in [your flesh], it kills [the flesh] in return.
   O body, if you give life to its death,
   there will be death for your life.

7 Let fire be an example for you
   since it is buried in wood and is dead,
   but the friction of [one piece of] wood with another revives[fire] for
        the perishing of both.
   Having revived, it returns to ignite by contact the substance that
        revived it.
   O the type: That wood becomes a grave for fire,
   and when [fire] is awakened from [wood], [the fire] is consumed with it.

8   For our freedom is like a soul for desires, and by it they live,
but if it sheds them, it is as if they were dead.
Therefore [our freedom] is self-governing since by its will debts
        stand,
and by its will sins fall.
It is like the Heavenly One Whose power contains the universe,
and if He retracted it, all would fall.

9   Therefore our Judge is very just, since He does not immediately
        demand our debts;
because of this comes remorse,
so that if one repent, it blots out his evildoing.
But if he rebel, it takes from him his defense.
On that account remorse appears with all sins.
in order to bear witness to the law court.

10   Acquire repentance that persists and not momentary remorse,
for repentance heals our bruises by its constancy,
but remorse has this [character]
that builds up and tears down pains momentarily.
Body, if you are accustomed to repent and to sin again,
the seal of your letter of bondage is remorse.

11   O eye, beware of stealing the beauty in which are hidden the flaws
        of old age.
For a maiden's limbs bear a pleasing sight,
but old age rebukes them.
For a feigned beauty inhabited them;
although it inhabits and dwells in the face of youth, it is beauty
that [soon] departs and flees from it.

12   Your pearl, too is quickly lost from the presence of two thieves;
for it belongs to solitary merchants, and if they are defiled, both lost
the greatest of all treasures.
But the fool hands it to the thief.
O pearl that is lost by it possessor
nor does it remain in the treasury of the thief![39]

13   If a virgin is dishonored in the open field, Moses petitions for her

---

39. The sense seems to be that the virgin who willingly yields the pearl of virginity becomes a thief along with the one who steals it. Yet, having stolen it together, ironically, both have lost it.

that the maiden shouted and cried out and there was no help.[40]
Who will petition on your behalf, O virgin,
who are peacefully taken captive[41] and are silent?
Let you not give yourself to captivity peacefully
lest peace judge you in the law court.

14   It is written that if a husband renounces his wife, her father should
          bring out her proof of virginity,
but since your Betrothed is the High One Who sees in secret,
show the hidden proof of virginity in secret to your hidden Lord—
not on your cloth[42] but on your body.
Rejected women show proof of virginity on a cloth;
let you show your proof of virginity to your Betrothed.

15   Will you lose your Betrothed and acquire instead of Him a false
          betrothed
that you may console yourself, saying, "Even if I lost [one] still I
          found [another]."
Because his love lies and is deceitful and dwells upon all,
he is not able to be your companion.
Then your remorse will increase,
when you are left bereft on both sides.

16   By the true [Betrothed] you have been left because you left him,
but that lying one gave up and left you and made you go astray
          among the ways.
So now where will you turn you gaze?
A dove uprooted her nest and went out in desire of the serpent.
May you not discover Eve's discovery![43]
[Instead] will you discover remorse in her?

---

40. That is, she is given the benefit of the doubt since no one would have heard if she did cry out; cf. Deut. 22.25–27.
41. P'al in the text, but apparently in the sense of the Ethp., as Beck notes.
42. The same word is used in Matt. 14.12.
43. Ephrem puns on ḥwy', "serpent," and ḥw', "Eve," as well as on various words formed on the root škḥ, "to find."

4

Through the theme of baptismal anointing the three hymns on virginity are linked to the following sub-collection of four hymns, "On oil, the olive and the symbols of the Lord." These four hymns provide a good illustration of the way in which Ephrem intertwines the various types of symbols: linguistic, scriptural, natural and sacramental. Here he plays on the notion of Christ, the Anointed One, the Messiah, whose presence and significance is anticipated in nature by the oil of the olive with its many uses—most notably its healing properties and its use in providing fuel for lamps; these symbolize Christ the Physician and the Light. Likewise, the anointed ones of scripture, the priests, prophets and kings, and the healers of both the Old and New Testament find their meaning and their power in Christ. In the baptismal anointing the Christian enters into this rich symbolic system, being sealed with the signet that is Christ.

At the start of this first hymn Ephrem prepares us for the wealth of symbolism he is about to evoke by painting a vivid picture of the wealth of a merchant brought into harbor (str. 1–4). But the focus of this hymn is on oil as a healing and restorative substance: Just as the oil of the olive gives life to the body through its healing properties, it gives life to the mind by its symbolism (str. 3). Not only the healings recounted in the New Testament, but also those of the Old Testament found their source in Christ, the Anointed One, Whose name intimates to us the connection with oil (str. 4–8). The natural restorative properties of oil are indicative of the spiritually restorative character of the sacraments, especially baptism (str. 9–14). He closes the hymn with a characteristic rhetorical apology for his hymnological efforts (str. 15–16).

4

To the melody, "I shall open my mouth with knowledge"

1 Open for us, my Lord, the gate of Your treasure, You Whose wealth eagerly desires the needy

that it might increase the minds of speakers as [if they were]
    merchants.
For Your silver increases and lends on interest; it is the merchant of
    its merchants.
In Your talent are gathered the riches of the treasure of life.
Profitable is the abundance of Your silver that goes out after profit:
    the mina increases tenfold, and the talent by five times.[44]

*Refrain: Glory to the Anointed Who rose and enlightened the symbols that were
veiled.*

2   Let [my] mouth have Your teaching, my Lord, as a merchant [has]
    capital,
    for on [Your teaching] depend all forms of wisdom and from the
      olive a treasury of symbols.[45]
    Let my tongue do business with its riches; let my word be a snare
      for it;
    let me enclose in it his hidden symbols as in the depth.
    Let me gather them for nourishment of the ear that hungers for
      secrets.
    For Your net gathered enough for the mouth that hungers for
      revelations.

3   My gaze succumbed and was conquered by its beauties that gave a
    glimpse [and] gazed into the treasure-house
    of the olive tree in which His symbols rest: as its oil the Light
      entered
    and it bore His types as fruits. And who is able to pluck the fruit,
    hidden and revealed, of this glorious tree that bears
    openly the fruits and leaves and secretly the symbols and types,
    and it gives life to the body with its visible things and to the mind
      with its secrets?

4   For in its oil is a likeness to the sea and by it helps flow
    to the limbs as to a harbor to give healings there.
    Even the disciples, merchants of all helps, succeeded by them—
    they who with the Healing Spirit went away to the sick.[46]

---

44. Cf. Luke 19.16–18 and Matt. 25.16. 6 obols = 1 denarius, 100 denarii = 1 mina, 60 minas = 1 talent.
45. A pun here on *tl'*, "to hang down, to depend."
46. Cf. Matt. 10.1 and Luke 10.8–9.

HYMN 4

Within the oil flowed their words, ships full of helps,
and they entered [and] their healings were sufficient within bodies,
   harbors of the sick.

5 Oil gave itself to the sick[47] that they might gain by it all helps,
as the Anointed Who gave Himself to gain by Him all glories.
The Anointed is One and Only-begotten, but He has many names
that mix with all titles all helps.
Oil also, although one, receives many names
that are compounded with all herbs for the healing of all ills.

6 For oil is rich in strategems and is able to be all with all
so that with powerful herbs it is harsh although it is mild,
and with ablution and cooling it becomes cold, although it is warm,
like the Anointed Who is all with all, so that for doubters
He is powerful, although He is merciful, and with worshippers He
   is sweet.
He resembles each in everything, although He resembles His Father
   alone.[48]

7 The name of oil,[49] therefore, is like a symbol, and in it is portrayed
   the name of the Anointed.
The name of oil was crowned for it is the shadow of the name of
   the Anointed One.
For also that Master of the disciples accompanied them when they
   were sent out,
and when they anointed and healed by oil,[50]
the Anointed was portrayed in secret, and He persecuted all ills,
as on the hem of the garment[51] the flow of blood saw Him and dried
   up.

---

47. Especially in this stanza, Ephrem plays on *mšḥ'* and *mšyḥ'*, "oil" or "ointment" and "Anointed One, Messiah," respectively.

48. In this and in the previous stanza, Ephrem implicitly uses the Middle Platonic notion of *epinoiai* to show the availability of Christ to all at a level appropriate to each. Yet in this final line he counterpoises a Nicene emphasis on His full divinity—characteristically allowing the tension between the two concepts to stand without comment.

49. Throughout these hymns, the Syriac *mšḥ'* has been translated "oil" but it could be rendered "ointment"to replicate the word play of the original.

50. As Beck notes, Luke 10.9 is combined with Jas. 5.14.

51. Syriac *pylwn'* (more commonly *pyn'*) is for Greek φελόνιον (more commonly φαινώλης), "a cloak," cf. Margoliouth 444A. As Beck notes, Ephrem himself and VS have *mrṭwṭ'* instead at Matt. 9.20 (Luke 8.44). Cf. Mark 5.25 et par.

8   The name of oil indeed is His symbol and the shadow of the name,
the Anointed.

The shadow of His name indeed fell upon their sick, and they were
cured,

as the shadow of Simon fell upon the ailing, and they recovered.[52]

The shadow of His name is like His pledge He gave to His apostles

that their shadow was going to heal. Elisha stretched out[53] his body

upon the boy when he brought him to life, but Simon [stretched out
merely] his shadow.

9   Oil filled the place of lineage for strangers whom it accompanied.

On the road it gave rest to their weariness;[54] in vexation it bandaged
their heads,

as our Lord refreshed in every place the afflicted who accompanied
Him.

In sleep oil stole the fatigue of sleeping bodies,

and while it anointed, in baptism it stole sin.

The weariness of sleeping bodies it stole; the sins of waking bodies
it stole.

10   Oil is the sceptre for old age and the armor for youth.

It supports sickness and is the bulwark of health.

It is one, but it is many in its uses: it gives chrism for altars,

and they bear the offering of reconciliation. Who will be sufficient
for this

which is extended to the evil as to the good, and soothes the
oppressed[55] as the just,

which, like its Lord, has opened its treasure-house to carry from it
every help?

11   An abundance is oil with which sinners do business: the forgiveness
of sins.

By oil the Anointed forgave the sins of the sinner who anointed [his]
feet.[56]

---

52. Cf. Acts 5.14–16.
53. 2 Kgs. 4.34. Ephrem discovers yet another pun here, *mšḥ*, "to stretch out," as an
accompaniment to his use of the same root in the sense "to anoint."
54. The Syriac is plural.
55. The sense would suggest "oppressor" rather than "oppressed," but the Syriac is passive.
56. Mark 14.3–9 et par. As usual, Ephrem identifies the sinful woman as Mary, presumably Mary Magdalen.

With [oil] Mary poured out her sin upon the head of the Lord[57] of
    her sins.
It wafted its scent; it tested the reclining as in a furnace:
it exposed the theft clothed in the care of the poor.[58]
It became the bridge to the remembrance of Mary to pass on her
    glory from generation to generation.[59]

12   In its flowings is hidden joy for oil does indeed gladden the face.
It brings its shoulder to all burdens in rejoicing and grieving with
    everyone:
for it serves joy, yet it is obeyed by gloom,
for faces joyful of life by it are resplendent,
and the gloomy face of death with it is prepared for burial and dies.
. . . who mourn as our Lord [mourned] for Lazarus.[60]

13   The force of oil like [that] of the Anointed chases away the iciness in
    the body
that maddens and removes help so that this suffering is even a
    second demon.
Strong is the power against diseases of oil that soothes the limbs,
like its Lord who soothes bodies and punishes demons.
He took pity on the man; He oppressed the legion; He persecuted
    the fierce demons
who had made fierce the man on whom grace took pity.[61]

14   The river of Eden is divided in four directions in a symbol,[62]
and the flowing of oil is divided in the churches in a glorious
    symbol.
That one waters the Garden of Eden; this one enlightens the holy
    church.
That one gladdens trees, and this one bodies.
That one of Eden has four names, the heralds of rivers,
and oil has three names, the trumpets of baptism.[63]

---

57. Beck's text (erroneously?) has a plural here.
58. Ephrem has in mind the Johannine account of the anointing at Bethany. The story occurs in all four gospels, cf. Mark 14.3–9 et par., but Luke omits the complaint about wasting money that should be given to the poor and Jesus' reply. Only John attributes the complaint to Judas and attributes it to his own thievery from the common purse.
59. Mark. 14.9 et par.
60. Cf. John 11.35.
61. Cf. Mark 5.1–20 et par.
62. Gen. 2.10–14.
63. The divine names, Father, Son and Holy Spirit are meant.

15 My feeble tongue has made bold and has defiled the riches of
       majesty.
    It was not that it was able to give; the recipients are worthy to take.
    For the source did not give the desirable treasure that is in it;
    as a steward it distributes streams for thirsty mouths.
    If sweet is the flow of my speech, this belongs to the Truth,
    but if it is insipid, feeble and weak, this is from the earth into which
       the source crossed over.

16 I confess, my Lord, a mouth that became a merchant and upon
       Your table
    cast down the silver that acquired the symbols of the olive tree and
       the types of oil.
    Who has seen the branches of the olive tree that gave symbols
       instead of fruits?
    A type germinated instead of leaves. Who again has seen
    oil that became a simile of the sea and the symbols in it a simile of
       fish,
    and the tongue that sings, a banquet to hungry ears!

The second hymn on oil or ointment stresses the use of oil as a fuel for lamps and thence the role of Christ the Light of the world. The first strophe clearly enunciates this notion: "Without light all would be devoid of usefulness, and without the Anointed everything would be lacking fulfillment" (str, 1.7–10). The prophets are lamps, but Christ is the sun and the apostles His rays (str. 2). The menorah with the Tabernacle represents the lights of the cosmos—the sun, moon and planets; yet all point mysteriously to Christ the Light (str. 3). Just as the oil of a lamp floats on water, Christ walked on water and enabled Simon to do so as well (str. 4). Since the lamp makes even the hours of day and night, it represents God's justice (str. 7). As the light consumes darkness, so the Messiah consumes death; the lost are found by the lamplight and by the Messiah (str. 8). John the Baptist, the virgins who await the bridegroom in the New Testament parable, and the prophet Hezekiah all provide meditations on Christ the Light (str. 9, 10, 12).

The final few strophes depart from the theme of light to develop a few other uses of oil of symbolic import: oil as soothing food—hence like the Eucharist (str. 11); oil as protection against rust—symbolic of Christ's sharpening of the mind (str. 13); for consoling the barren and for women in childbirth (str. 14); and for the persecuted (str. 15). The last two are fortified with scriptural examples. In the final strophe he elaborates with reference to the oil of the olive the broader notion of the symbols of God in the creation and in scripture.

5

The same melody

1   Again, oil fixes for us a lamp, a luminary in the height,
      and the glory of the Anointed, the true Light, shone forth from
            Golgotha.

By the luminary all is arranged, and by the Anointed all is
  explained.
Without light all would be devoid of usefulness,
and without the Anointed everything would be lacking fulfillment.
The light is sufficient for visible things and the Anointed for all
  hidden things.

Refrain: Glory to the Anointed Who came, and the symbols ran to His fulfillment.

2   By the Anointed again and by His power, lamps resist in the
      darkness,
    and by the Holy Spirit the prophets were strong within the People.
    Oil strengthens lamps to struggle with darkness
    until the sun comes with its breath and dispels it.
    The Spirit sustained the prophets so that falsehood was mitigated[64]
      by truth
    before the Sun Who pursues error by the twelve rays that He
      extends.

3   Again, oil served as a beam in the temporal Tabernacle
    since in a seven-branched candlestick its flow served seven flames
    in a symbol of our Lord from Whom seven lights of seven spirits
      shone.[65]
    The seven-[branched] candlestick brought forth the light of its seven
      brightnesses[66]
    by which the temporal Tabernacle enlightens. Mary brought forth
      the Luminary
    of the seven holy brightnesses that illuminate for us all creation.[67]

4   Just like the Anointed, oil is empowered to run upon the waves.[68]
    It also gave power to the flame to walk on water.
    As his Lord gave Simon [power] to walk on the waves.

---

64. The *ettaf'al*, otherwise unattested, is used here, as Beck has noted.
65. Rev. 3.1, 4.5, 5.6. As Beck notes, Justin Martyr interprets the sevenfold spirit of Isa.
11.2 as descending through seven Jewish "prophets" to Christ; Just. dial. 87. In addition there
may be some allusion to Jewish mystical traditions such as the *Sefer Yetsirah;* cf. Scholem, Major
Trends, 75–78.
66. The Syriac word also means "manifestation" or "epiphany." In the course of the hymn,
Ephrem calls upon each of these nuances.
67. That is, the sun, the moon and the five planets known in antiquity: Saturn, Jupiter,
Mars, Venus and Mercury; cf. G.E.R. Lloyd, *Early Greek Science: Thales to Aristotle* (New York,
1970), 82, n. 1.
68. Cf. Matt. 14.22–33.

Like the Anointed, oil rescues the sinking flame
that flickers in the womb of water like Simon in the sea of water.
By a flame oil enlightens the house; by Simon the Anointed
    enlightened the inhabited earth.

5 Again, oil labors; even in a lamp it works
to make the tree of light great, to extend its brightness in the
    darkness.
Since the eye in [darkness] hungers for light, after the sun [sets],
    then there is the lamp;
it consoles the pupils deprived of luminousness.
  . . .

6 Therefore the lamp is like an ombudsman[69] of the eye cheated by
    the dark.
In the nights of November,[70] when the dark overreaches the light,
so that diligence does not suffice for work since the day is short,
the lamp claims for [diligence] the hours that the dark overreached
so that [diligence] may work in the long night until the short day
    rises.
Truth judged the overreaching: what the dark overreached, the light
    claimed.

7 Who has seen the diligence that became like a balance
to weigh night and daytime and make them ascend in the same
    proportion.
For the short day grieved[71] the diligent who did not complete the
    course,
and the long night extended the joy of the cowardly.
But the lamp and diligence balanced the night and daytime,
so that idleness would not distress the best, nor would the cowardly
    rejoice in loss.

8 Darkness is the food of light,[72] since where it finds [darkness], [light]
    swallows it.

---

69. Throughout the stanza, Ephrem contrasts *tb'*, "to claim, vindicate, avenge," with *'lb*, "to oppress, defraud, surpass, take advantage." It is difficult to find an English word for each of these that has all the nuances contained in the Syriac words.

70. Tishri (two months, October and November).

71. A pun on the two meanings of *kr'*, "to be short" and "to be sad, grieved."

72. The words used here for darkness and light are not the same as those used earlier in this hymn.

[This is] a revealed symbol of the Anointed Who by His life
    consumes death.
By the lamp, again, are found the things lost in the dark,
and by the Anointed, too, is found the soul that was lost.
The lamp returned our lost things, and the Anointed also [returned]
    our treasures.
The lamp found the coin, and the Anointed [found] the image of
    Adam.[73]

9   A weak lamp is the symbol of John since they both have a short
    time.
The lamp is not bridegroom of the eye, nor is John bridegroom of
    the church.[74]
They are friends of the two bridegrooms and beloved of the two
    brides.
They were not bridegrooms; they were icons of the Only-begotten
    Bridegroom.
The eye sees in the lamp the likeness of the sun, her rightful
    bridegroom.
The church saw in John the likeness of her true Partner.[75]

10 Oil enriches the light of the lamps symbolically.
The Anointed enriches the lamps of the virgins espoused to Him.
The lamps take types from the visible lamps.
For small is the light of a lamp whose [supply of] oil is small.
Since the time of the Bridegroom is not revealed to us, you virgins
    have become our Watchers[76]
so that your lamps might gladden, and your hosannas might glorify.

11 Oil with meals soothes its eaters like its Lord,
Who also soothes His eaters with the tastes of all helps.
The Anointed captures for the sick restoration from the house of the
    dead.
For a lamp that has sputtered and gone out returns by oil,

---

73. The Syriac word translated here as "image," ṣlm', is used to refer to the image on coins, so here Ephrem alludes not only to Luke 15.8–10, but also to the theological idea of the restoration of the *imago dei* by Christ.
74. Cf. John 3.27–30.
75. The reference seems to be to the vision of the church in the Book of Revelation. Possibly the argument against overestimation of John the Baptist is an anti-Mandaean polemic.
76. Ephrem refers both to the angels called Watchers and to the gospel parable of the wise and foolish virgins, Matt. 25.1–13.

and lamps that had been stifled, by oil returned from death,
for He was God Whose helps are much swifter than His lightning
    bolts.

12 Our body resembles a lamp, since it flourishes and sputters.
Our oil resembles our Anointed since it shows the symbols of our
    God.
Our world resembles our lamp, and they both resemble Hezekiah.
Hear, my brothers, [these] three symbols how they are portrayed:
A lamp awakes by oil; by means of the sun Hezekiah awoke.
But the world awoke and shone by means of the Anointed, the
    Flood of mercy.

13 Oil smears the edge of a sword; the Anointed polishes the mind.
The sword makes the killer tremble, and the tongue of truth [makes]
    doubters [tremble].
Oil preserves the sword from rust that is brought forth on it
since contact with the earth harms it—a hateful symbol.
The Anointed dwells in the mind and restrains from it harms
that are brought forth by laxity like a maggot [brought forth] by
    negligence.

14 Therefore, [oil is] like God, Who loves virginity:
the daughter of the symbol of the house of Michael and kinswoman
    of the house of Gabriel.[77]
[Oil] consoles the barren women like Sarah and Rebekah and
    Rachel.
It also strengthens those who bring forth [children]
like Leah, Zilpah and Bilhah, since to [oil] marriage is pure,
since [marriage] is a vine planted on earth, and like fruits the babes
    hang on it.

15 Again, oil became an image for the persecuted, envied Jacob.[78]
. . .
The sceptre . . . openly, oil and his symbol secretly.
Oil ran like an envoy and etched and made
parables whose explanations became easy because of our Lord:

---

77. Virginity is the angelic state. Cf. Virg. 1.8.
78. Cf. Gen. 27.41–45.

He espoused the soul to God instead of the stone that Jacob
    signed.[79]

16   For oil became the key of the hidden treasure-house of symbols.

It propounds for us the similes[80] of God Who became human.[81]

The whole creation gave Him all the symbols hidden in it.

The scriptures also gave their parables,[82] and they were explained in
    Him.

And the writings [gave] all their types and the Law also its
    shadows.[83]

The olive tree stripped off and gave to the Anointed the comeliness
    of the symbols upon it.

---

79. When Jacob poured oil on the rock, Gen. 28.18, he "signed" it with the symbol of Christ, the Anointed One. Since Jacob designated the rock as the House of God, it represents for Ephrem the type of the church, which is the bride of Christ (cf. Eph. 5.21–33, and CH 17.5). Here, though, it is the bride of the Father, an unusual usage.

80. Syriac *dmwt'*, here in the plural, is most often translated "likeness," as in Gen. 1.26, cited by Ephrem in HdF 6.7. It may also mean a picture either in the sense of a likeness either exact or merely similar; cf. Beck, *Bildtheologie*, esp. 261–63. The best analogy to this passage is Virg. 28.2, where Christ adds the pigments to the symbols presented by the Jewish scripture to create his own likeness; ibid.

81. Literally, son of man, *br 'dm*.

82. Syriac *mtl'* essentially has the meaning of parable, proverb or simile, and Ephrem uses it as the equivalent of *r'z'*, *twps'*, *tll'*, or *dmwt'*, as much as for *pl't'* cf. Virg 8.1–8 and ibid. 261–68.

83. Although his use of *spr'*, *ktb'* and *nmws'* is tantalizingly reminiscent of the rabbis' threefold division of scripture into Law, Prophets and Writings (Torah, Neviim and Ketubim), Ephrem is using them synonymously rather than to indicate discrete portions of scripture; cf. ibid. 263f.

6

In this hymn Ephrem argues that the priesthood and the kingship of the Chosen People have passed through Christ to include the Gentiles along with the Jews. Through Moses and Solomon these offices were bestowed on the Jewish people (str. 1). Zechariah's prophetic vision of two olive trees shows the continuation of these two lines in two covenants, one for Jews, the other for Gentiles (str. 2), but it also presents the typological key for understanding that Jesus is the Messiah, the Anointed One. The olive branch brought back by the dove after the Flood symbolizes not only peace but also Jesus, the Anointed, the First-born of the dead (str. 3–4). The entry into Jerusalem from the Mount of Olives, the anointing of Christ by the sinful woman, the preparation of the way of Christ by John the Baptist all are interwoven with the oil of the olive tree, thus implying that Jesus is heir to the priesthood and kingship (str. 5–9). The properties and uses of olive oil itself also point to Christ and his followers: steadfastness (str. 10), the anointing of athletes (str. 11–13), oil as a means of easing conflicting forces (str. 14).

6

The same melody

1   Oil in the likeness of the Heavenly One became the giver of
        kingship.
  From the horn [of oil] a pure cloud descended upon the head of a
        body,[84]
  as God descended upon the top of the mountain[85] and gave
        brightness to Moses,
  and Solomon received brightness symbolically

---

84. The "body" is the People of Israel.
85. Literally, the "head" of the mountain; cf. Exod. 24.15–18, 34.29–35.

from the horn of messiahship.[86] From the People to the peoples it
went out.

Instead of the few, many will be anointed and cleansed.

*Refrain: Blessed is He Who gave eyes to the peoples to see the symbols of the Son, the
Anointed.[87]*

2   Again, Zechariah saw two olive branches as sources;

[from] the one would flow priesthood, and [from] the other its
companion, kingship.[88]

In the Captivity the treasure of the two poured forth [and] gave two
branches:

atonement and redemption after the Captivity

to the polluted and constrained People. He gave, again, two
covenants:

purification and redemption to the polluted and oppressed peoples.

3   The olive tree, again, became the first-born of the trees that were
buried

in the Flood, in the likeness of its Lord Who became the First-born
from the house of the dead.

Therefore the olive tree passed through the Deluge, and before all
[else] it was revived.[89]

It rose up [and] gave its leaf as a pledge for the revival of all.

The dove found and eagerly desired it—the bird that seeks our
inhabited land.

[The dove] announced that there was a survivor, and [the olive tree]
sent a greeting in her mouth.

4   [The olive tree] passed through the waves [and] rose up as king and
sent its envoy of peace,

and it gave good tidings to the confined and brought forth praise in
the mouth of the silent.

Plucked from it was consolation, a leaf that enlightened the eyes of
all.

It announced to Noah that anger was defeated, and mercy was
victorious.

---

86. Cf. 1 Kgs. 1.39.
87. The Syriac permits but does not demand the causal connection here.
88. Cf. Zech. 4.11–14.
89. Gen. 8.10–11.

The sight of the leaf, although mute, sowed exultation with the
sorrowful.

For them it became a mirror of peace in which they saw the peace
of the earth.

5   In the descent of the Mount of Olives palm trees and olive trees
partook:

two whose leaves were not worthy for our Lord . . . who shed His
garments.

. . . a sweet voice . . .

That a sweet voice . . . was . . . for the Lord . . .

And the olive tree that . . . openings of lamps with its flash of light.

With its branches [the palm tree] enriches the babes praising with
their hosannas.[90]

6   For the olive tree is like John.[91] He foretold a symbol of his Lord.

The king, the Anointed, shone forth and came; the olive tree went
out to meet its Lord;

with children who bore his tree branches, he was stripped [and]
divided his branches.

It was prophesied that his Lord would shed [and] divide his
garments.[92]

The olive tree that bore symbols witnessed to the One Who came to
complete his symbols.

He sent a crown from his branches to the Slain One Who would
conquer death.

7   The dove gave rest to Noah[93] in the Flood, and the dove's
kinswoman, Mary,[94]

with good oil instead of a leaf portrayed the symbol of the Son's
death.

The oil jar she poured on Him emptied out a treasure of types on
Him.[95]

In that moment the symbols of oil took shelter[96] in the Anointed,

---

90. Cf. Mark 11.1–11 et par.
91. The Baptist.
92. Cf. Mark 15.20, 24 et par.
93. A pun on the two vocalizations of the root *nwḥ* meaning "Noah" and "to rest."
94. Mary Magdalen, identified with the sinful woman of Luke 7.37–50.
95. A pun on *šp'*, "to pour," and *spq*, "to empty, pour out."
96. A pun on two meanings of the verb *tps*, "to take refuge" and "to symbolize." The use of
the preposition "b" indicates that the former meaning is the literal sense here.

and the treasurer of the symbols of oil completed the symbols for
    the Lord of symbols:
the creation conceived His symbols; Mary[97] conceived His limbs.

8   Therefore many wombs brought forth the Only-begotten.
The belly brought Him forth by travail, and the creation also
    brought Him forth by symbols.
He put on one body of limbs and another of glories.
Eternal power does not become weary; He worked but gave us rest
    since it wearied the creatures to bear the symbols of His
    majesty.
They were weighed down by His symbols like the belly that carried
    Him.

9   Oil is next of kin of priesthood like John, a son of priesthood.
He opened out a path in the hearing where formerly the voice had
    been stopped up,
and the word flows into the ear so that it portrays the will of the
    speaker in it.
But in this path opened out by John
the Word of the hidden Father flowed. Since the image of Him Who
    sent Him is portrayed by Him,
by Him is beautified the ugliness of the peoples, who acquired His
    comeliness.

10 The confident olive tree does not fear the lion that frightens all.
In the pains of cold winter its leaves resist as the steadfast [do].
They are a type of the steadfast who held fast to the Anointed, the
    Olive Tree.
In persecution the doubters fell like leaves
that do not stay on their trees, but the anointed ones depend on[98]
    the Anointed
like the leaves of the olive tree in winter, entirely rooted in it.

11 Again, a symbol of God is the olive that is upright and good in the
    contest,
for it grasps the beginning [and] also girds the ends.
   . . .

---

97. Here Ephrem shifts from Mary Magdalen to Mary, the Mother of Jesus. This is not
unusual for him, cf. Murray, Symbols, 146–48.
   98. or "hang from."

12   . . .

For the oil in a contest gives the crown to the victor.
The Anointed, Who is Truth, gives us true freedom, my brothers.
Athletes with a temporal crown acquire time;
from the burden . . . the Anointed sets free with a crown of praise.
From the slavery of sin He freed His church by His victory.

13   With oil athletes smear . . .
. . . disciple . . . learns.
He, if he fails, feels ashamed . . .
The athlete . . . his companion is praised,
The disciple who neglects to take from his companion learns.
If . . . is worshipped; if . . . is glorified.

14   Oil teaches acceptableness to disobedient harshness,
that it might appear to comply sweetly with harsh force that grasps
it.
But the Anointed made us oppressed so that instead of one blow we
might be struck two,
that we might mix double harshness with sweetness,
and instead of a mile we might go two, . . . [99]

---

99. Matt. 5.39–41 et par. Strophe 15 is illegible.

7

Although the relationship among the motifs is sometimes elusive, this fourth and final hymn on oil and the olive focuses primarily on baptismal themes, especially on the concept of baptism as rebirth.[100] Repentance and diligence are both necessary, the former for success in the world of the spirit, the latter for success in this world (str. 1). Both fall and spring represent fresh beginnings (str. 2). Whereas Jezebel's evildoing stultified these natural processes, Elijah as agent of the Lord restored them, bringing rain as well as immediate food for the hungry (str. 3–4). Since oil is used for painting, the oil of baptism symbolizes the restoration of the image of God in the baptized (str. 5–6). Oil is not only appropriate to priesthood but also for those about to die, hence its use in baptism symbolizes death and rebirth as well as forgiveness (str. 6–8).

The use of oil to blot out debts on a written document further enhances the symbolic action of the baptismal anointing (str. 9). Oil's characteristic of floating on water brings to mind the immortal divine nature of Christ, whose voluntary death is like the rescue of a drowned man, Adam (str. 10). Elisha's payment of a debt with oil to save the widow's children from enslavement provides a scriptural type for salvation through Christ (str. 11–12). By its oil, its branches and its leaves, the olive represents the mortality, the victory and the resurrection of Jesus (str. 13). As a vessel of oil acts as a mirror, so also Christ has many faces, each appropriate to the beholder (str. 14). Finally, with a touch of humor, Ephrem portrays himself sinking in waves of oil, the plethora of his symbolic interpretations, crying out like Peter for help (str. 15).

---

100. A translation of this hymn appears in Brock, Harp, 59–61.

7

The same melody

1   Repentance and diligence: for both worlds they are required.
For the work of the earth, diligent [people]; for the work of the
    spirit, penitents.
Although he may not become rich, a diligent man's prosperity
    stands on its own,
and though he may utterly fail, the penitent is one of the victorious.
Miserable people and sinners put on the entire evil name,
for the idle have shame, and sinners have reproach.

*Refrain: How much can we marvel at You, our Savior? Your glory is greater than
our tongue.*

2   October[101] revives the weary from the dust and dirt of summer;
its rain bathes and its dew anoints[102] even the trees and their fruits.
April[103] revives fasters, anoints, dips and whitens;
it scours the dirt of sin from our souls.
October tramples the oil for us; April increases mercy for us.
In October fruits are harvested; in April debts are forgiven.

3   Since Jezebel refused the truth, the earth refused her ingathering.
A reproach bereaved the womb of the seed that the farmers lent her.
It choked seeds inside it since her dwellers bereaved truth,
and the bearer became barren, which was not in her custom,
and the pitcher and horn,[104] barren, brought forth and were
    fruitful—which is not in their nature,
since the voice that bereaved the earth made barren wombs fruitful.

4   But hunger overran the earth, and the reserves [of food] fell short,
so that full storehouses were emptied, and cellars, too, were left
    bare.
Elijah joined together flour and oil as a yoke,[105]
and he who was taken up in a chariot and conquered death,[106]

---

101. Tishri (two months, October and November).
102. A pun on *msh*, "to bathe" and *msh*, "to anoint."
103. Nisan (April, or often simply the season of spring).
104. a vessel for oil.
105. Cf. 1 Kgs. 17.8–16.
106. Cf. 2 Kgs. 2.1–12.

conquered hunger in two symbols. Rain was the end of his course
since the Lord of the clouds extended to him a crown of plenty from
    His floods.[107]

5 With visible pigments the image of kingship is portrayed,
and with visible oil is portrayed the hidden image of our hidden
    King.
With the drawings[108] that baptism labors to bring forth in her
    womb,
from the portrayal of the primal man who was corrupted
she portrays a new image, and she gives birth to them with three
    labor pangs
that [are] the three glorious names of Father and Son and Holy
    Spirit.

6 Oil is, therefore, the friend of the Holy Spirit and Her minister.
As a disciple it accompanies Her, since by it She seals priests and
    anointed ones,
for the Holy Spirit by the Anointed brands Her sheep.
In the symbol of the signet ring that in sealing wax marks its
    imprint,
also the hidden mark of the Spirit is imprinted by the oil on bodies
anointed in baptism and sealed in the dipping.

7 For by the oil of departure are anointed for absolution
bodies full of stains, and they are whitened, without being beaten.[109]
They descended in debts as filthy ones and ascended pure as babes
since they have baptism, another womb.
[Baptism's] giving birth rejuvenates the old just as the river
    rejuvenated Na'man.[110]
O to the womb that gives birth to royal sons every day without
    birthpangs!

8 Priesthood is a servant to this womb in her giving birth.
Anointing rushes before her; the Holy Spirit hastens upon her
    floods;

---

107. Cf. 1 Kgs. 18.45–46.
108. Here and in the following strophe the Syriac *ršm* and its derivatives have been translated variously to suit the context; the nuances range from drawing to sealing, imprinting and
stamping, to engraving, etching and branding.
109. The image is of laundry washed in a river.
110. Cf. 2 Kgs. 5.1–14.

the crown of Levites surrounds her; the High Priest was made her
    servant.

The Watchers rejoice in the lost that were found by her.

O to the womb that, having given birth, is nourished and educated
    by the altar![111]

O to the babes who immediately eat perfect bread instead of milk!

9   The Anointed, source of all helps, accompanied the body, source of
    pains.

For oil blots out debts as the Flood blotted out the unclean.

For the Deluge, like the Just One, justly blots out evil people.

Since they did not conquer their lust, those who deluged [the earth]
    with it, floated.

But oil in the likeness of the Gracious One blots out our debts in
    baptism.

Since sin is drowned in the water, let it not be revived by desires.

10   Oil by its love became companion to the diver who in his need
hates his life and descends and in water buries himself.

Oil, a nature that does not sink, becomes a partaker with the body
    that sinks,

and it dove down to bring up from the deep a treasure of wealth.

The Anointed, a nature that does not die, put on a mortal body;

He dove down and brought up from the water the living treasure of
    the house of Adam.

11   Oil gave itself for purchase instead of orphans that they not be
    sold.[112]

For the orphans it was like a guardian that restrained force that
    entered to tear away

from the root of freedom two brothers like shoots[113]

and onto the root of slavery to graft them.

The payment of oil silenced the promissory notes crying out against
    the debtors.

It cut off those coming to cut off a mother from her children.

12   Oil by its love in a symbol of the Anointed repaid the debts that
    were not its own.

---

111. The Syriac is active.
112. Cf. 2 Kgs. 4.1–7.
113. The translation here is based on the text emended as per Beck's suggestion.

A free treasure was found in an earthen vessel for debtors[114]
like the Treasure found for the peoples in an earthly body.
Oil became a slave for purchase for the the freeing of the noble.
The Anointed became a slave for purchase for the freeing of the
    slaves of sin.
Both in name and in deed oil portrayed the Anointed.

13   Oil acknowledges You entirely, for oil revives all.
It serves as the Anointed, Reviver of all; in streams, branches and
    leaves it portrays Him.
With its branches it praised Him through children; with its streams
    it anointed Him through Mary;
with its leaf, too, through the dove it serves as His type.
With its branches it portrays the symbol of His victory; with its
    streams it portrays the symbol of His mortality;
with its leaf it portrays the symbol of resurrection, and like death
    the Flood vomited it up.

14   That face that looks at the vessel that oil fills
sees an image of itself there, and one who looks at it secretly
by its symbols sees the Anointed and His many beauties.
The olive, too, has many symbols . . .
The Anointed is all faces and the oil is just like a mirror;[115]
from wherever I look at the oil the Anointed looks out at me from
    within.

15   Who, indeed, buried me, a weakling, among the pounding waves?
It is as if the waves of oil took me [and] gave me to the concerns of
    the Anointed.
The waves of the Anointed struck me and gave me to the symbols
    of oil.
The waves appease the waves, but I am in the middle.
I, too, am grieved, like Simon; draw me out, my Lord, as You did
    Simon![116]
Myriads of waves have sunk me! Merciful One, draw me out, a
    weakling!

---

114. Cf. 2 Kgs. 4.1–7.
115. Cf. Beck, Bildtheologie, 270f.
116. Cf. Matt. 14.28–33.

8

This is the first of three hymns that share not only the same melody and the alphabetical acrostic form but also the theme of the fulfillment and consequent obsolescence of Jewish scripture and customs through Christ. This first hymn has only the first seven letters of the alphabet—aleph through teth—and it often intersperses strophes that do not fit the acrostic.[117] Although the third strophe enunciates the characteristic theme of the entire collection of hymns, the symbolic presence of Christ in scripture and in nature, it also indicates the focus of his hymn on Christ as the fulfillment of Jewish scripture: He is king, prophet and priest.

Paradox, often a favored tool of Ephrem, plays an important role here as he wields the double-edged sword of typological exegesis: Christ both fulfills and abolishes the Jewish religion. He not only completes and explains all of Jewish scripture (str. 1–8), but he also puts to an end all Jewish customs (str. 9–11). He completes the truth and beauty of Judaism (str. 12), and John the Baptist, last of the prophets, is succeeded by the apostles (str. 13). The Patriarchs and Jewish religious and political leaders symbolize Christ, his apostles and his Church (str. 14–17). The Levitical priesthood has been replaced by the Christian apostolic priesthood (str. 18–21). Despite the envy of the Jewish people, here clearly held responsible for the death of Jesus, the cross of Christ is the proper interpreter of the Torah (str. 22–23).

8

To the melody, "Rich by His symbol"

' 1   He came to us in His love, the blessed Tree.
Wood dissolved wood. Fruit was annihilated by fruit,
the murderer [annihilated] by the Living One.

---

117. On the content of the additional strophes, cf. note on str. 9, below.

HYMNS ON VIRGINITY

Refrain: Blessed is the One Whom the prophets portrayed.

B 2   In Eden and in the inhabited earth are parables of our Lord.[118]
Who is able to gather the likenesses of the symbols of Him,
all of Whom is portrayed in all?

B 3   In scripture He is written; in nature He is engraved.
His diadem is portrayed by kings, and by prophets His truth,
His atonement by priests.

4   He is in the rod of Moses and in the hyssop of Aaron
and in the diadem of David. The prophets have His likeness,
but the apostles have His gospel.

5   In the beginning[119] again upon the wood alighted the weary dove.
On You, the Tree of Life, came, took refuge,[120] and alighted
the weary Testament.[121]

G 6   Revelations gazed at You; similes awaited You;
symbols expected You; likenesses longed for You;
parables took refuge in you.

G 7   [God] revealed Your symbol in the rod that [both] rescued and
drowned.[122]
Its interpretation is in Your cross.[123] oppressors drowned by it,
but the oppressed rose up by it.

G 8   His power perfected the types, and His truth the symbols,
His interpretation the similies, His explanation the sayings,
and His assurances the difficulties.

9   By His sacrifice He abolished sacrifices, and libations by His
incense,
and the [Passover] lambs by His slaughter, the unleavened [bread]
by His bread,
and the bitter [herbs] by His Passion.[124]

---

118. For *pl't*, parable, cf. Beck, Bildtheologie, 264–68.
119. Or "in Genesis." The allusion is to the dove at the end of the Deluge, Gen. 8.6–12.
120. Or "symbolized, typified."
121. Christ, Tree of Life, completes and gives meaning to the "Old Testament," just as the olive tree gave a resting place to the dove sent out by Noah.
122. Cf. Exod. 14.16, 21, 26–27.
123. The same word means wood or tree as well as cross; it is translated variously in this hymn to suit the nuances. Ephrem's poetry, however, hinges upon the multiple meanings of the single word.
124. Like the Epistle to the Hebrews, Ephrem argues that the death of Christ ended the sacrificial cult of the religion of Israel, but he also argues that it ended the Passover celebration. The latter is an important issue in early Christian polemics against rabbinic Judaism. This

HYMN 8

10   By His healthy meal He weaned [and] took away the milk.
By His baptism were[125] abolished the bathing and sprinkling
that the elders of the [Jewish] People taught.

11   By His food refused were[126] food tithes,
for food is not unclean; thought is defiled,
and envy . . . [127]

12   In the genuineness of His truth and the power of His light
He showed His beauty [to] His own. His adornments came [and]
were beautiful on Him;
His sufferings came [and] were completed in Him.

13   In John [the Baptist] He set a limit and restrained the prophets,
and he called and sent apostles. He dismissed and put to rest the
former,
and put to work and wearied the latter.

14   On Abel your flock is imprinted;[128] in Noah is portrayed Your
church.[129]
Your flock[130] [is portrayed] in Jacob, and in the rod of Moses
is portrayed the rod of Your flock.

H 15   On the tribes of Jacob Your twelve are[131] imprinted:
on Judah your robe, and on Levi Your censer,
and Your dispensation on Joseph.[132]

16   In Shem your likeness exults,[133] in Abraham Your joy.[134]

---

strophe and several others (viz., 4–5, 9–14, 16–17, 19, 23) do not fit the form of the alphabetical acrostic and contain markedly stronger anti-Judaic or anti-Judaizing polemics. Possibly they were added later by Ephrem or someone else to reinforce the polemic of strophes 20–22, which are formally congruent with the beginning of the hymn.

125. The Syriac is singular.
126. The Syriac is singular.
127. Mark 7.14–23 et par.
128. Cf. Nat. 1.42 and note ad loc.
129. Cf. Nat. 1.22f., 45, 56–58 and notes ad loc.
130. A different word from that used in the first line of this stanza.
131. The Syriac is singular.
132. The first lines allude to the twelve apostles as the fulfillment of the types of the twelve tribes of Israel. The last three lines give the attributes of Judah's kingship and Levi's priesthood to Christ; perhaps the fact that none of the twelve tribes is associated with prophecy explains the choice of Joseph for the third type.
133. As Beck suggests, citing CH 5.11–12, probably this should be Seth. For Seth as the likeness of Adam, cf. Gen. 5.3. Since Christ is the new Adam, Seth is in the likeness of Christ, cf. Tonneau, Gen/Exod 5.1, CSCO 152 (scr. syr. 71),54; cf. Nat. 1.21 and note ad loc. But on Shem, cf. also Nat. 1.24.
134. Cf. Nat. 1.59.

299

Isaac bore Your cross.[135] The former and the latter
were clothed [in] Your likenesses.

17 In the sings and the dew of Gideon Your teaching was portrayed,
  for it fell in drops and came down and moistened the dryness of
      the peoples.
  Their fruits were pleasing to You.

H 18 By David was written the oath of Your Father
  that Your priesthood is true. Brought to an end are the temporal
      priests;
  "You shall be a priest forever."[136]

19 This oath . . .
  . . . from Your flock went out
  blessings for the universe.

Z 20 More noble is Melchizedek[137] than the priests of the People.
  Among the peoples he is a priest and teaches that the Priest Who is
      coming to the peoples
  will be slain by the People.

H 21 Envious of You is the tribe of Levi for they are aware of Your
      hyssop
  that whitens the peoples. By You the apostles became priests
  so that the Levites were brought to an end by You.

T 22 Jealous of You is the People that is aware that You will teach the
      peoples.
  By means of death they silenced You. Your death itself became
      endowed with speech;
  it instructs and teaches the universe.

23 The scribes knew that by You the writings of Moses
  would be dispersed in the inhabited earth. Although they fastened
      You on a cross,
  Your cross explained the scripture.

---

135. Isaac carried the wood for his own sacrifice, a popular type of Christ among early
Christian writers; cf. Nat. 8.13.
136. Ps. 110.4.
137. Cf. Nat. 1.24 and note ad loc.

9

This second anti-Jewish polemic hymn in acrostic form begins with the second letter of the alphabet—beth—and continues to the middle—mim—with a few letters missing or out of order. The following hymn begins with the next letter—nun—and completes the alphabet; no doubt they constitute two halves of a single hymn. This hymn focuses on the conflicting messianic views of Jews and Christians and argues strongly that the Messiah has come; he is not still to come. The primary metaphor here is a flowing of the "types and symbols of scripture" like streams into the sea, which is Christ.

9

The same melody.

B 1 With the advent of our Sun lamps served[138] and passed away,
and types and symbols ceased. With hidden circumcision
visible circumcision was abolished.

Refrain: Glory to the First-born, the Anointed One!

D 2 The Testament[139] of Moses awaited His gospel.
All the old things took flight and came to perch
on His New Testament.

D 3 For his Law is weak; it is unable to enclose
the great flow of His symbols in the small bosom[140]
of its kings and priests.

---

138. Ephrem puns on *šmš*, "sun," and *šmš*, "to serve." The "lamps" are the Old Testament types of Christ; their truth is overshadowed by the fullness of his truth.

139. A misprint [?] in Beck's text makes this plural, although the verb is singular.

140. The Syriac '*wb*' may designate any kind of hollow or recess. It occurs throughout this hymn in diverse senses, rendered variously as "bosom," "womb" or "gulf" depending on the immediate context.

W 4   If the blind say that the types and symbols of scripture
        are kept for the one to come, their disgrace is manifest
        for the Messiah has come.

W 5   The blind err, for this flow of symbols
        pours from the former ones to Him, [but] it cuts off the one to
            come
        for the Messiah has received it.

W 6   Since the bosoms of the just were too small, He poured out [the
            flow of symbols],
        and since the [messiah] to come is false,[141] [the flow] cuts off before
            him
        since it met Him in the sea.

W 7   This stream of symbols was unable to cleave
        the sea into which it fell and to flow toward another
        since the Sea of truth received it.

W 8   Since it is a wondrous gulf,[142] all creatures
        cannot fill it. It confines all of them
        but is not confined by them.

H 9   The prophets poured into it their glorious symbols.
        Priests and kings poured into it their wondrous types.
        All of them poured into all of it.[143]

Z 10   Christ[144] was victorious and rose up. By His explanations for
            symbols,
        by His interpretations for similes, He, like the sea, will receive
        into Himself all the streams.

H 11   Consider that if all the kings willed to turn aside
        all the rivers so that they would not come to the sea,
        [the rivers] would [still] come to it by force.

Y 12   Therefore, the sea is Christ Who is able to receive

---

141. In this and the following verses Ephrem argues against the Jewish argument that the Messiah, the Anointed One, the Christ, has not yet come.

142. The gulf is the sea, which is Christ; cf. str. 12, below. Greek Christian writers often use the philosophical formulae, "enclosing" and "not enclosed" to describe God; cf. W. R. Schoedel, "Enclosing, Not Enclosed: The Early Christian Doctrine of God," *Early Christian Literature and the Classical Intellectual Tradition*, ed. W. R. Schoedel and R. Wilken, Festschrift for Robert Grant, Théologie Historique 53, 75–86. Ephrem's expression here appears to be the equivalent of these formulae.

143. This strophe is out of order in the alphabetical arrangement and perhaps belongs before strophe 4.

144. Or "the Messiah," "the Anointed One."

the sources and springs and rivers and streams
that flow forth[145] from within scripture.

K 13   The gulf of every depth into which rivers incline
will be chagrined by [the sea], since it cannot receive
their streams into itself.

L 14   Again, toward whomever you wish to incline scripture,
he, too, will be proved unable to fulfill
its histories in himself.

M 15   For it is Christ who perfects its symbols by His cross,
its types by His body, its adornments by His beauty,
and all of it by all of Him!

---

145. The Syriac is more graphic, "belch forth."

10

This hymn is the completion of the acrostic begun in the ninth hymn. Here Ephrem argues that the principal symbol of the Jewish scripture, the Passover, must refer to something beyond itself, namely to Christ. The salvation of the Passover does not refer to Moses (str. 2), nor is it self-sufficient, referring to nothing beyond the historical events themselves (str. 5). Its true meaning is that Christ has saved all people from Satan and from sin (str. 3–4). The truth of this view has been confirmed by the destruction of Jerusalem (str. 6–7). Further, the words of David in Psalm 110 predict Christ (str. 8–12). He closes with the metaphor of Christ the sea (str. 13–17), thematically linking this hymn with the previous one.

10

The same melody

N 1   Experiment, my son, by applying some of the histories of the First-
         born
       to the glorious Moses, and see that he, being conquered,
       is unequal to their power.

   Refrain: Blessed is He Whom the prophets portrayed.

S 2   This [miracle] of Egypt greatly hinders Moses
       who saved the people by blood since it was not a symbol of himself
       he portrayed by the sprinkled blood.
‘ 3   For with [his] generation Moses died in the wilderness,
       but the custom of the symbol was living and came
       up to binding with the true Lamb.
P 4   By His blood He saved the peoples as the lamb [saved] the People.
       The evil one was conquered by Him instead of Pharaoh, the
                tyrant;
       and instead of Egypt [they are delivered from] sin.

P 5   It would be easy, therefore, to hold that it merely came to be,
this symbol in Egypt. But the truth would not go away
from which the symbol flowed.

P 6   Parables cry out that by a limit they are restrained.
Behold the revealed sign that with the beginning of the peoples
the end of the People came into being.

P 7   The priesthood passed away since there is no sacrifice or altar.
Kingship has ceased; there is no throne or diadem.
The People sits in a stupor.

S 8   Seek and be fulfilled in David and what he sang:
"Sit at my right hand,"[146] and see that [even] in his majesty
he is small in its presence.

Q 9   Read what he wrote, "The Lord said."
Son of Jesse, reveal to us to whom did the Lord speak,
to your son or to your Lord?[147]

Q 10   David cried out in the spirit, "The Lord said to my lord."
The king of the People is the servant of our King;
Lord and son He was to him.

R 11   Therefore, high is His nature, and inclined is His compassion.
Lord and son He was to him: Lord because of His nature,
and son because of His compassion.

R 12   Shepherds and kings arose in the People.
They came to an end, but the symbols did not pass away with
      them
until they reached our King.

S 13   I have omitted the histories of all the prophets
to retrain my mind, for it is a small gulf
insufficient for [all these] droplets.

S 14   Allow, my tongue, the histories of all scripture
and of all natures to come to the Sea
that is the limit of all of them.

T 15   Neither the abyss nor the sea is in need of the weak streams.
Those come into it that have been wearied everywhere.
In its gulf they rest.

T 16   Come to the prophets and see how they need

---

146. Ps. 110.1.
147. Ibid.

to come to Christ, Who was wearied by the People.
Among the peoples [the prophets] are at rest.

T 17   Give me by grace, O blessed Sea,
one droplet of compassion that I may invest it and come
by means of Your flow to You.

18   The symbols were silent in love for they saw that Truth was
coming.
Blessed is He Whose parables have fulfilled all scripture
that had drawn His pictures.[148]

---

148. This verse does not fit into the alphabetic acrostic. It begins with shin.

11

This hymn presents with stunning clarity Ephrem's understanding of the symbolic presence of Christ in the natural world. The theme is that, like Christ, Who suffered willingly for the benefit of those who tormented him, many things in the natural world suffer for the benefit of those who exploit them (str. 20). The images are drawn mainly from the world of the builder, the craftsman and the farmer. They include three of the four elements: the sea, air and the earth, exploited by divers, birds and farmers, respectively (str. 4, 15, 16). Raw materials worked by craftsmen are cut stone, wood, iron, gold and pearls (str. 5, 6, 7, 8, 9). Agricultural products suffering for human benefit include wheat, grapes, fruits and honey as well as sheep (str. 10, 11, 12, 13, 17, 18). Finally, incense thrown on the fire is like Christ and the martyrs (str. 14). In addition to the general theme of philanthropic suffering, several specific allusions to the gospels and sacraments are made: The pearl is like the One Who was pierced; the body of the fruit is eaten for our benefit; the sheared lamb is like "the Lamb who divided his garments for his crucifiers" (str. 9, 12, 17, and cf. 10).

11

To the melody, "Your flock dolefully"

1   It is very difficult for the evil one to gaze at his ugliness.
    Goodness, like a mirror,[149] comes toward him
    to refute by his ugliness one who thinks he is beautiful.

Refrain: Glories to Your grace!

2   Grace befalls even the oppressor
    that by one thing he might learn two: he is aware and understands
    that he himself is bitter, [but] his Lord is sweet.

---

149. This image is developed at greater length in Virg. 31.12 and especially in CH 32; cf. Beck, *Spiegel*.

3   Because of this He did not come in the generation of the just.
It is not that they would not be worthy but so that His sweetness
might rebuke the bitter who have held back His coming.

4   The sea belongs to the diver[150] who bursts in and descends in it.
Its gulf gives space to him; it shows him its treasure;
it gives and enriches him; it carries [him] and brings him up.

5   Cut stone becomes by its suffering
a bulwark for the human being.[151] In calamity and in battle
it stands before him and preserves his treasures.

6   Wood by means of its harsh treatment resembles the cross:
It carries in the sea; it bears on dry land;
it increases by its uses; and enriches by its helps.

7   Even strong iron is weak in the fire.
It is malleable and yields to human strength,
and when it has been well-beaten, it repays the one who struck it.

8   Noble gold is beaten without offense.
To all those who beat it, it gives its sides as a symbol of our Lord.
Its insult is for honor; its suffering is for glory.

9   Iron and a sharp stake, indeed, pierce the pearl
like that One Who was pierced by nails and on the cross.
It becomes by its suffering an adornment for humankind.[152]

10 And who will tell the suffering of the grain of wheat?[153]
Indeed, how many scourgings and afflictions it encounters!
By its torments it gives life to its tormentors.

11 The foot of its crusher also abuses the cluster of grapes.
By its blood [the foot's] filth is washed away;[154] with its must[155] it
        sweetens him;
and if it ages with him, it makes him merry with its wine.

12 When a fruit is eaten, by means of its suffering its taste

---

150. Or the one baptized; it is clear from the previous hymn and from the succeeding strophes of this hymn that Christ is the Sea.

151. Literally, "son of man." On Christ as stone or rock, cf. Murray, Symbols, 205–12.

152. Ephrem develops this image at length in his hymns on the pearl, HdF 81–85, esp. in 82.12. For French trans., cf. Graffin, OS 12 (1967), 129–49; for English, Gwynn, NPNF ser. 2, 13, 293–304, which is a reprint of Morris, 84–98; or for HdF 82 only, Brock, Harp, 31–33.

153. Cf. John 12.24.

154. Ephrem seems to have in mind the rather unappetizing thought that the dirty feet of the grape treader are washed by the juice of the grape! On the grape cluster as Christological symbol, cf. Murray, Symbols, 113–30.

155. The juice as it flows from the pressed grapes.

pours out in the mouth. This is a symbol of that Fruit
that brings to life His eaters when His body is eaten.

13 When the honey that sweetens all is extracted,
as it is worked, it softens its strength for those who eat it.
It delights health; it nourishes sickness.

14 Incenses are, like the victors,[156] cast into the fire.
Their scents rise up like their good Lord
Who by means of His death exhaled the scent of His vitality.

15 So also when the bird beats the air
with its wings as with arms, the back [of the air] is subjected to it,
and like a bride it is carried on high by the power [of the air].

16 So also the farmer by means of iron
rends and cleaves the earth, but she is not angered by her suffering;
her treasures and her womb she opens by her sufferings.

17 The sheep in its shame strips off its garment and cloak
and gives all of it to its shearers,
like the Lamb Who divided His garments for His crucifiers.[157]

18 Great is the symbol of the lamb who is quiet in his life
and sings in his death. His loins are for festivities
and the strings of his lyre for melodies and songs.

19 So old is the teaching that its time is not known.
It dwells in youth although it is scorned along with it.
It becomes small [and] makes it great to honor it very much.

20 All these things teach by their symbols:
they open by their sufferings the treasure of their riches,
and the suffering of the Son of the Gracious One is the key of His
treasures.[158]

---

156. That is, the martyrs.
157. Mark 15.24 et par.
158. Despite the postscript reading, "Completed are the four hymns that interpret the mysteries of our Lord," this hymn has no formal or thematic links with the three preceding.

12

The subject of this hymn is the temptation of Christ by Satan as recounted in the gospel of Matthew (Matt. 4.1–11). Each of the thirty strophes begins with the same letter, ain, the sixteenth letter of the Syriac alphabet. The hymn has been prefaced to the following large collection (Virg 13–32) apparently because its first two hymns also concern the temptation of Christ.

Throughout the hymn Ephrem shows an interest in the psychology of the tale. Examining the three temptations in turn (str. 1–5; 6–12; 13–16), he probes and then faults the reasoning of Satan. Finally, he imagines Satan's bewilderment in contrasting his relatively easy success in tempting Adam with his utter failure to lure Jesus into sin (str. 17–27, esp. 22–27). The language and imagery of the athletic contest or the debate is used throughout (esp. str. 1–2, 5, 9, 30). There are a few indications of an anti-Arian polemic: The divine and human are contrasted (str. 8, 10, 16, 22); investigation of the nature of Christ is identified with Satan (str. 19). These themes are more fully developed in the fourteenth hymn.

12

On the melody, "I shall sing if it is lawful"

1   Our Lord labored and went out to the contest
    not to use force
    but to be victorious in conflict.
    Therefore he hungered, and by fasting he conquered
    that one who is justified by eating.

Refrain: Blessed is He Who humbled the pride of Satan.

2   The evil one saw an opportunity in [His] hunger;
    he demanded that He make stones into bread.[159]

---

159. Cf. Matt. 4.2–4.

[Satan] became a stone among stones;[160]
His heart trembled when he saw that He was a craftsman
and [yet] He defeated him in a debate.[161]

3   This [thought] came upon the evil one,
"If He is divine and He is hungry,
how will he regard me if I say,
'Make the stones bread and be nourished'?
Why will he bear the burden of His hunger?"

4   Blind was the evil one in his pride and his question,
for if He were God, as he said,
it escaped his notice that God does not hunger.
He approached to make [Him] err, but erred himself,
for he did not discern what he said.

5   [Satan] remembered questioning the house of Adam;
by his inquiry he persuaded;
he leapt from the inquiry to the explanation;
he asked, disputed, explained and conquered.
Here he asks and fails.

6   He lifted Him up and stood Him on the pinnacle[162]
as a symbol of the height of pride,
as a type of the depth of the Fall.
He lifted Him up to pride as He ascended
to lower Him to the Fall as He descended.

7   He was blind in this again as in that:
for if the psalm is fulfilled concerning Him:
"With his pinions," it is written there, "that he might save you."[163]
Indeed, unable to fall is the bird
under whose pinions the air is like the earth.[164]

8   He sought a pretext by which to make Him fall
[to see] whether He was divine or human
to know which is the way to go,

---

160. That is, Satan was reduced to silence by Jesus' reply.
161. Although Jesus is a workman, a carpenter, he is able to defeat Satan in a battle of wits. In contrast to much of the Greco-Roman tradition of despising those who work with their hands, Ephrem delights in finding positive views of workers and their work, as in the previous hymn. Further, cf. Nat. 8.11 and note ad loc.
162. Matt. 4.5–7.
163. Ps. 91.
164. Cf. Virg. 11.1.

so that if He were God, he would find out,
and if human, he would lead Him astray.

9   This was the work of our Athlete
Who did not let him know there that He was God.
For if he had known He was God
from the beginning, he would have fled
and would have spoiled the completion.

10   While he was leading into error, error entered upon him.
For he was unable to know He was God,
nor again was he able to investigate His being human.
For not as God did He exalt Himself
nor as human did He lose His footing.

11   For upon the sanctuary he lifted Him up
to convince Him that a human could become
god from the house of Divinity,
as he convinced Adam a human could
become god from that tree.

12   He remembered that the foreparents listened to him;
his counsels were a trick for youth,[165]
but sagacity came to overpower him.
His temptations were like a coronation
for Wisdom Who came to humble him.

13   He lifted Him up and set Him on a mountain,[166]
yet he did not call Him by the name to make Him proud,[167]
as if he had become persuaded that He was needy.
He was startled and offered Him a gift
so that the gift would bring Him to worship.

14   With schemes He blinded the schemer,
and instead of being confused, He remained quiet[168]
like one who knows that [Satan] is deceitful.
Since One is worshipped by all, the Lord of all,
He showed that acts of worship are suitable [only] for Him.

15   Upon this foundation of the beginning

---

165. Ephrem evidently shared the view that Adam and Eve were children and hence more easily deceived by Satan. Cf. Nat. 7.11, 26.8 and notes ad loc.

166. Cf. Matt. 4.8–10.

167. Satan does not address Jesus as Son of God this time, cf. Matt. 4.

168. A pun on *blbl*, "to be confused," and *bhl*, "to remain quiet."

our Lord built and erected His triumphs.
For although the deceiver changed his opinion,
he did not alter truth with him
Truth was pleased, and deceit was dispersed.

16   Therefore the factions in the contest mocked him,
since in the beginning he made Him God,
but he made Him human in the end.
In the beginning he had made Him worshipped,
in the end he made Him a worshipper.

17   The evil one remembered that he asked Him for food,
and he thought He was impoverished since He did not give.
On the other hand, he gave Him a gift,
and he saw that, like a king, He did not take [it].
He began with the two [alternatives], but he was disappointed.

18   Blind in his pride is cunning[169]
to try to exchange his possessions for worship.
Since he considered Him poor, He showed His greatness,
Whose grace is more abundant than [the evil one's] wares,
Who by worship would purchase all He [already] possessed.

19   For all these things this was his punishment
that instead of his knowing, he was known.
Our Lord called him Satan,[170]
but he did not know what to call Him.
He was furious that he came to investigate, but was investigated.

20   Human labor in weariness
by discovery is turned to rest.
The evil one who labored and investigated was exhausted,
and the more he failed to attain, [the more] he was tormented.
In discovery would be peace of soul.

21   He labored to ask or give Him [a choice of] the two things
in order to know whether He was empty or full,
but not as one full did He give to him
nor as one empty did He take from him;
his confusion was worse for him than his failure.

---

169. The Syriac word meaning "cunning" is an abstract noun, which is feminine, but because it represents the devil, Ephrem changes to the masculine pronoun in the next line.
170. Matt. 4.1.

22   He answered, saying to himself,
     "I have spoiled it that I made Him proud
     that I have called Him the Son of God.
     To act as God He is not able;
     to sin as human He was ashamed.

23   "I should have remembered that even the first Adam,
     had I made him proud as a lord,
     in his pride would have scorned honor
     so that it would not seem that the tree was better than he;
     his pride would have become a protector.

24   "On account of this, I extolled the tree
     in order by it to diminish man.
     When he saw his smallness, he would hold [himself] in contempt
     and run like a child for shame
     and go toward the tree that was greater than he.

25   "[But] this one fled because of the praise.
     [Pride] brings the rebellious into subjection without a staff.
     The corrupt man puts on the bridle of modesty
     when praised by an upright man;
     his pride impedes the running of his course.

26   "This one fled because I made him proud,
     for neither was He capable of falling
     nor did He hold sinning in contempt.
     I called Him God, and He would have sinned
     Therefore He fled into the scriptures.

27   "Shame enters by praise
     so that if one calls a feeble man eminent,
     he is not able to make [himself] eminent;
     again, to make [himself] base he is ashamed.
     I cunningly forced Him to flee.

28   The Honored One made pleasant what is considered insignificant,
     nor . . . for them to see it,
     nor . . . for it to bend,
     nor for them to mock at Him . . .
     that He should be without the shame of His ignominy.

29   . . .

30   The evil one fled from Him for awhile.

HYMN 12

In the time of the crucifixion he arrived,
and by the hand of the crucifiers he killed Him
so that He fell in the contest with death
to conquer Satan and death.

13

This is the first in the sub-collection of eighteen hymns on the same melody, "Blessed are you, Ephrata!" Their subject is the presence of Christ in scripture and in nature, focussing especially on subjects drawn from the New Testament. The first two hymns concern the temptation of Christ, as recounted by Matthew.

At the beginning of the hymn Ephrem seeks to establish natural links not only between the sufferings of Christ and the defeat of Satan but also between the daily struggle of the individual Christian and the conquest of the evil one. To this end he portrays the ascetics as directly attacking Satan through their fasting (str. 1, 3–4). Whereas sinners delight him (str. 6) and heretical speculations and disputation among Christians give him pleasure (str. 8–9), virtuous behavior deprives him (str. 7). The sufferings of Christ at the instigation of Satan redound to his defeat in ironically suitable ways (str. 2–3, 5, 10–11).

Throughout the hymn Ephrem uses the image of the public debate, the *Agon*, to analyze the confrontation of Christ with Satan (cf. str. 2 and 16). By the three temptations Satan intends to discover whether Christ is divine or human (str. 17). His attempt fails. Not only does he not find out who Christ is, but he himself is easily identified (str. 19). Satan becomes confused (str. 21). In the Garden of Eden he was able to conquer by his powers of persuasion, but here he fails (str. 5). Whereas the youth of Adam and Eve was no match for his cunning, the divine Wisdom easily outwits him (str. 11–12). Ephrem faults Satan's logic: If Christ is divine and so able to change stones to bread, He would not really be hungry (str. 4). Furthermore, Satan does not realize that Christ already possesses all he is offering in exchange for worship (str. 18). Finally Ephrem imagines for us the flawed reasoning of Satan after the encounter: His mistake must have been in addressing Christ as Son of God (str. 22); Adam would also have fled temptation if he had made him feel proud of his humanity (str. 23–24); Satan's praise made Christ feel ashamed to sin and yet, not being divine, He had been unable to change the stones to bread; thus He fled (str. 22, 25–27). Only at the moment of the crucifixion will Satan

realize the divinity of Christ. If had known at this moment of the temptation, he would not have returned to kill Christ on the cross, thus being
conquered by Christ along with death according to the divine plan
(str. 30).

13

To the melody "Blessed are you, Ephrata!"

1   All temptations surround the tempter of all
who dared tempt You.
Fasts and . . . are his great downfall:
with long fasts youths rack him;
Anchorites surround him and tear him to bits;
apostles torment him with their bones.
Bound with prayers, he is cast
into Gehenna before Gehenna's time.

Refrain: Praise be to our Justice!

2   Cast down is he who lifted You up on the cross,
who mixed vinegar for You, by whom You were [slain].
Bitter in his mouth is the gall You drank;[171]
in his heart is the spear that struck You.[172]
At a thief's right hand he crucified You,[173] but he was defrauded:
the Slain One slayed him who had slain us.
In the Pharisees and scribes he mocked You,[174]
but he has been made a mockery in the whole world.

3   Afflicted with a great thirst is he who gave You
a reed with gall to drink.
He recalls his cakes and libations,
he who became fat and burst from corpulence.
He sees the captive departing;
he sees his life diminishing.

---

171. John 19.29f. Cf. Mark 15.36 et par.
172. John 19.34.
173. Mark 15.27 et par.
174. Mark 15.31 et par.

Abstainers from wine diminish his abundance,
and he approaches extinction.

4 Accursed is he! If someone abstain from meat,
[the Devil's] own flesh wastes away until he makes him stumble.
His blood, too, is drained when he is unable
to douse the faster with wine.
If he does not see our passion inflamed,
in an oven he is tormented and burned.
In a great stove [he is burned]
if he sees human desire tamed.

5 Our killer killed You and was killed.
With nails You fastened him, while he crucified You.
With the thorns that crowned You, he was mocked.[175]
With the rod that struck You, he was beaten.
When he spat, his spittle fell on his own face.
He spat at You to his own shame.
You stripped off his graven images in which he clothed himself,
the despicable one who stripped you of your garments.

6 If he finds one who is abusive,
he takes delight all day.
Again, if he hears the sound of quarreling,
he enters there as if to a wedding feast.
His daily repast is hatred;
his usual supper is spite;
jealousy is his drink;
murder is his butcher, envy his baker.

7 If he goes without hearing the sound of mockery,
he becomes deaf.
If he sees no licentious behavior,
he becomes blind.
If he sees the estranged in harmony,
he is like one who has lost his other half.
If he sees friends, sorrow rests upon him
that he saw love on earth.

8 His tambourines and cymbals by you were abolished,
and his dancing and lamentations faded.

---

175. Mark 15.16–20 et par.

HYMN 13

[So] he works on us and divides us by inquiry.
He made us like a lyre that he might be comforted by us.
He played his wishes on us to refresh himself,
his tales and inquiries to make himself glad
In the investigation of hidden things he sang with our tongue
the song of his pleasure.

9   The contentious were led astray, and the investigators rose up,
boisterous and contentious.
The idols have been overthrown, but behold the apostates
who have named and multiplied all the gods.
Freedom who sells her freedoms
serves a multitude of lords.
Blessed is he who blots out his promissory note
with his tears.

10   In the wilderness he tempted You, and his feasts and festivals
in the wilderness have disappeared.
On the mountain he tempted You, Lord, with worship,
and mountains are no longer places of his worship.
Since he stood You up on the top of the Temple,[176]
You have overthrown the top of his temples.
The hunter was fooled;
in the trap set for You he was caught unawares.

11   By the stone [with which] he tempted You[177] were broken
the stones that he carved for emptiness.
Since he dared to say to You, "Throw Yourself down!"[178]
because of You he fell down and perished.
The One falling down cast down
the one who had come to cast down the One from above.
Satan led Him up
unaware that the Lowly One Who went up would cast him down
        from the height.

---

176. Matt. 4.5 et par.
177. Matt. 4.3 et par.
178. Matt. 4.6 et par.

14

Ephrem frequently accuses the Arians of a love of disputation and divisiveness. The prominence of this idea here probably indicates an anti-Arian intent (esp. str. 1–5). Rather than theological argumentation, the weapon of choice for the Christian is the simple quotation of scripture, "the armor forged by Moses" (str. 1.7–8). Jesus Himself used this method not only against his Jewish adversaries (str. 5) but, more importantly, against Satan (str. 2). The themes of an athletic contest between Christ and Satan (str. 9) and the hunt (str. 10–14) are both prominent throughout the hymn. The latter is associated with scriptural argument through the metaphor of the bow of the Old Testament and the three arrows of scriptural quotations shot by Jesus in his answers to Satan (esp. 10, 11, 14). As in the previous hymn, Ephrem finds it ironic that Satan unwittingly chose symbols of the power of Christ—stones, bread and kingship—to tempt him (str. 6, 7, 9, 11).

14

The same melody

1   Blessed are you, wilderness, in which
the conqueror of all struggled with the captor of all.
One is [Christ] who deprived him of his armor and his treasure
and snatched his captives and bound and left him.
O his deceits that were exposed and defeated!
He put on simplicity and conquered and confused him.
He conquered him with the armor
forged by Moses for the simple and innocent.

Refrain: Glory be to Your victory!

2   Blessed is the one who sees that even the Omniscient One
conquered the crafty one by quotations [of scripture].

320

He merely quoted again and again, and the evil one wailed
to see that He took refuge in simplicity.
For as a fish is at ease in water,
so Satan is in the disputation of controversy.
If there is no controversy, and if strife fails,
he flickers and is extinguished.

3 For the One who gave simplicity in His Testaments
was not weak.
For He gave truth against error.
The evil one saw truth and was afraid.
So he formed strife, gave it to us, and over us prevailed
the inquiries that make hatred grow.
Our perverse generation should be ashamed of the harm
it increases by its inquiries.

4 The One who said that by light
darkness was defeated, and death by life,
taught that envy is conquered by love,
and by his scripture deceit is transformed into wisdom.
Blessed is one who arms the tongue with Your word,
who quotes from what is Yours to Your adversary.
Our Lord, let us gaze upon You,
Who from Moses quoted to the evil one in Your temptation.

5 You have questioned, my Lord, and You have also been questioned
in order to provide a type to the disputants.
Your reasoning conquered the Sadducees,
and your argument reduced even the Pharisees to silence.[179]
From scripture You quoted to the evil one.
to show how much strength is hidden in it.
Our pride is not able to put on
the armor of Your humility.

6 With stones Satan tempted
the Stone that gave drink to the people,[180]
the Stone that was living bread,[181]

---

179. Mark 12.28–34 et par.
180. 1 Cor. 10.4, cf. Num. 20.11. On Christ the Stone or Rock, cf. Nat. 24.19, and Murray, Symbols, 206–12.
181. John 6.25–59.

the Stone that shattered the great image.[182]
He set out to tempt it and feared not
since he is blind in understanding and senseless.
Instead of the image You shattered Satan,
the cause of all images.

7   Whoever looked saw You, Our Lord,
standing on the peak,
The perfect Stone that went up and stood
upon the Stone that fools rejected.[183]
Cunning Satan led You up;
without discerning, he made You stand on Your symbol.[184]
The wonder to see: the symbol and its prototype,
the truth and its shadow.[185]

8   Up onto the high mountain Satan led the lowly One;
upon the height he set Him up.[186]
There, as if in a balance, were weighed
humility and pride.
The proud one was justly overthrown;
the Lowly One, exalted, overthrew him.
For You, our Lord, Satan, who tempted You,
rendered Your symbols.

9   On the mountain Satan tempted Our Lord [with kingship].
and in mockery he gave Him [as king] to the Gentiles.
With the word the reality came to exist
for [Satan] returned [the Gentiles] to his conqueror.
In the contests of the public games, the crown
belongs to the one judged right to take it.
[Satan] was not constrained by force,
for our Lord took [the crown] justly.

10 Blessed is He who stood firm and put to shame
the enemy of the age even as He looked on.
His own traps lifted him up; his own snares and nooses caught him.

---

182. Dan. 2.34.
183. Ps. 118.22, Matt. 21.42, Luke 20.17, Acts 4.11, Rom. 9.33, 1 Pet. 2.7.
184. The Stone of Dan. 2.34 becomes a mountain, Dan. 2.35.
185. Syriac: *r'z' wtpnkh šrr' wtllh*. The phrase is chiastic; i.e., the symbol and shadow are equivalent, prototype and truth are equivalent. In this example, it is clear that the prototype, *tpnk'*, is superior to the symbols, despite its later place in time; cf. Beck, Bildtheologie, esp. 251f.
186. Literally, "led Him up and put Him."

His shafts, his loops, his nets bound him.
From the quiver of Moses You borrowed;
You took three arrows from Your servant.
His testament was the bow
by which You shot arrows at our murderer.

11   The arrow he shot at You was the bread for which he asked,
symbol of the greed of Adam.
With bread he tempted the Sustainer of all,
Who by His fasting healed gluttony.
. . . Satan . . .
His disciples . . . the bridegroom was reclining
He who did not want to change stones
changed water at Cana.[187]

12   The evil one thought that [Jesus], cast down from the height,
would fall and cease to exist.
He provoked Him to cast Himself down since he thought
that from fright He did not allow Himself
to fall from the top of the Temple.
But since He rejected him and did not fall,
the evil one fell from his height—unforced,
when he perceived the Lowly One.

13   That bitter one filled his bow and took his stand
against Our Lord, the Sweet One.
Seeing that He put on a weak body, an infirm nature,
[Satan] erred and was deceived about Him.
The evil one saw His armor and trusted
that it was the armor of the vanquished Adam.
Great is his disgrace that by the very armor by which he conquered
his pride was defeated.

14   The evil one who shot a blunt arrow at You
became a target for sharp arrows.
You shot at him the arrow of humility
and two others of self-possession.
These were holy arrows, driven
into his unclean, stopped-up ears.
Avenged were the corruptions

---

187. John 2.1–12.

of the corruptor of the simple obedience of the household of Adam.[188]

---

188. Cf. Virg 12.12. The manuscript adds, "The two hymns on the temptation and contention of Satan to the melody of 'Blessed are you, Ephrata,' are completed."

15

Although a postscript identifies the subject of this hymn as John the Baptist and "John the lesser," its content is broadly baptismal. It is a series of blessings addressed to John the Baptist (str. 1–2), the Jordan River (str. 3), John the Evangelist (str. 4–5), and Simon Peter (str. 6–7), followed by curses addressed to Caiaphas (str. 8) and Judas (str. 9–10). In addition to the attention given to the baptism of Jesus by John, the recognition of the titles and role of Jesus by the figures praised or blamed provides a confessional theme appropriate to baptism.[189]

John the Baptist acknowledged that the baptism to be offered by Jesus was greater than his own (str. 1–3). John the Evangelist, identified with the beloved disciple as well as with the apostle John, deserves recognition for identifying Jesus with the Word of God (str. 4–5). Because Peter, "tongue" of the apostles, called Jesus Messiah and Son of God (Matt. 16.17), he was assigned a special leadership among the apostles (str. 6–7). Even the sons of Zebedee are blessed for perceiving the role Jesus as future Judge, although their request is unfulfilled (str. 7). But Caiaphas who unwittingly stated that Jesus would suffer for the sake of all people, is cursed (str. 8). By his despair and ignominious death, Judas provides a negative example of a witness to Christ regardless of his own intentions (str. 9–10).

15

The third [hymn] on the same melody
1   Blessed are You, even You, a barren woman's son,[190]
    whose hand was made worthy to be placed upon His head.
    You baptized the Baptizer Who baptized the Gentiles

---

189. For a similar theme using the infancy narratives, cf. Nat. 6.
190. Luke 1.7.

with a flash of fire and the Holy Spirit.[191]
Blessed is your discernment that trembled and did not approach
and your intellect that was commanded and did not resist.
The heavens were divided,[192] the Watchers were amazed and gave
    glory
that the Purifier of all was baptized.

Refrain: Praise to your priesthood!

2   Blessed are you, the greatest of the prophets
all of whom desired him from a distance.[193]
They longed for but did not see the Messiah, the Son,
but you placed your hand on His head.
Clothed in the Law, you exhibited zeal;
arrayed in the Messiah, you showed mercy.[194]
In you descended and came Elijah, who has not come [otherwise],
whom you, in fact, represented.[195]

3   Blessed are you, little Jordan River,
into which the Flowing Sea descended and was baptized.
You are not equal to a drop of vapor
of the Living Flood that whitens sins.
Blessed are your torrents, cleansed by His descent.
For the Holy One, Who condescended to bathe in you,
descended to open by His baptism
the baptism for the pardoning of souls.[196]

4   Blessed are you, too, chaste youth,
whom your Lord held like a child.[197]
He loved and cherished the chaste youth
in whom was hidden the pearl.[198]

---

191. Matt. 3.11, Luke 3.16, cf. Mark 1.8.
192. Mark 1.10 et par.
193. Cf. Nat. 1.12f., 20–60.
194. For Ephrem, John the Baptist is the pivotal figure in the transition from the justice of the Old Testament and the mercy of the New, cf. Martikainen, Gerechtigkeit, 79–83; and for his related role as transmitter of the Old Testament priesthood to Jesus, cf. Saber, Theologie, 69–82.
195. Cf. John 1.19–28.
196. Rather than being cleansed by the water of John's baptism, Jesus cleanses the waters of the Jordan and transforms the baptism of John from type to reality by bringing the Spirit; cf. Saber, Theologie, 69–82, 92f.
197. John 13.23–25.
198. On virginity as the pearl of great price, cf. Virg. 2.4–5, 2.10, 3.12. For another symbolic use of the pearl, cf. Virg. 11.9.

O Virginity, He came down and lifted you up;
before the Watchers, upon his breast He exalted you.
Without effort the Watchers gave the gift,
but by struggle you gave it.

5   Blessed are you, enriched by love, the key
of the treasury you happened upon.
The treasury had never been opened;
silence was its seal, but your voice opened it.
Blessed is your mouth that composed for us, "He is the Word."[199]
You explained the mute [word] to restrain us.
"God is the Word" is reality for the diligent,
vexation for the inquirers.

6   Blessed are you, too, Simon Peter,
holder of the keys that the Spirit forged.[200]
Great is the word and inexpressible.
that above and below binds and looses.
Blessed are the flocks He gave you;[201] how much they have
      increased!
For you fastened the cross upon the water.[202]
The flock in its love gave birth to every sort of
virgins and chaste ones.

7   Blessed are you who became head
and tongue for the body of your brothers.
The body is a composite[203] made of the disciples.
The sons of Zebedee were its eyes;
blessed are those two who, seeing His judgment seat,
asked their Master for theirs.[204]
By Simon is heard the revelation from the Father—
[Simon], the unshakeable Rock.[205]

---

199. John 1.1.
200. Matt. 16.19. Simon Peter is also the recipient of priestly power transmitted to Jesus from Simeon the prophet as well as from John the Baptist, cf. Saber, Theologie, 51–55, 73–78, esp. 77f.
201. John 21.15–17.
202. Cf. Matt. 14.28–33 and John 21.7, and Saber, Theologie, 55.
203. *mrkbt'*, "composite," is the same as the word for "chariot," a subject of speculative interest in rabbinic Judaism and one known to Ephrem, cf. Virg. 21.10.
204. Mark 10.35–45 et par.; cf. Virg. 26.13.
205. Matt. 16.13–18. On Peter as Rock in Ephrem and Aphrahat, cf. Murray, Symbols, 212–18. Ephrem's treatment of Peter here relies almost entirely on Matthew and John. For a

8   But you, woe to you, Caiaphas,
whose mouth was the herald of truth.[206]
This is the worker who labored and became weary.
but instead of a wage he sustained a loss.
The paymaster cried out that he was rejected
who prophesied without being hired.
The fruit of the blessing has been plucked
from the accursed by the obedient.

9   But you, woe to you, cache of stolen goods,
false disciple, servant of silver!
You surrendered the treasure, the treasure of life,
hidden in the wealth of the Gentiles.
Woe to your eyes that looked at Him but were not ashamed,
and to your mouth that kissed Him and feared not![207]
Perfidy was in your mouth,
treachery in your greeting, the noose upon your neck.

10   Woe to the despicable chief of tares
rejected and expelled by the pure heap of grain.
As in a furnace the wheat bread
separated and ejected him from its presence.
A tree bore him a friendship;
the bitter one burst open with his hatred.
Oppressed by the burden of the stolen silver,
he burst open, fell and perished.[208]

---

discussion of these New Testament materials, cf. *Peter in the New Testament*, ed. R. E. Brown, K. P. Donfried, J. Reumann (New York, 1973), esp. 75–108, 129–48.

206. John 11. 49–52.

207. Mark 14.43–45 et par.

208. Ephrem has combined elements of Matt. 27.3–5 with Acts 1.18. A postscript adds, "Finished is one hymn on John the Baptist and John the lesser."

16

In this hymn Ephrem emphasizes the importance of recognizing Christ and enjoying his blessings, especially in the Eucharist, rather than engaging in speculative theological scrutiny of the nature of the Son (esp. str. 4–6). He has surrounded this characteristic anti-Arian theme with New Testament materials illustrative of the open confession of Christ. The hymn begins with blessings pronounced on the two towns associated with the start of Jesus' ministry: Nazareth, where he spent his childhood; and Cana, where his public ministry began (str. 1–2). New Testament personages are blessed apparently with a view toward the inscrutability of God's ways as in the case of Zacchaeus (str. 3) and the cured demoniac (str. 6). Or they are blessed for the boldness of their statements as in the case of the blind man at Jericho (str. 7) and Nathanael (str. 8–9). Finally, a second Adam typology is elaborated (str. 10).

16

1   Blessed are you, Nazareth, hated by the [Jewish] people,[209]
    by the name of our King your name is made beautiful.
    An Heir grew up Who by His name clothed Himself in you,
    for He was also called "Nazarene."[210]
    Blessed are your marketplaces that cultivated the body
    of Him who cultivated minds by His Word.
    A miracle in Nazareth—
    that the Cultivator of all came down and grew up with infants.

    Refrain: Glory to the One Who sent Him!

2   Blessed be you, Cana, for your bridegroom,
    whose wine ran out, invited the Heavenly Bridegroom.[211]

---

209. Cf. John 1.46.
210. Matt. 2.23.
211. John 2.1–12; cf. Nat. 4.195.

He invited the Inviter Who invited the Gentiles
to the new wedding feast and to life in Eden.
Blessed are your guests who exulted in His blessing,
and your vessels that were filled at His word.[212]
In you heavenly graces were first brought to bloom,
shining forth for the first time.[213]

3   Blessed are you, hidden little man,
for he came from on high to stay in your house.[214]
The treasure entered, the Holy Treasure,
and scattered the hoards gathered by injustice.[215]
Blessed is your wealth that He sowed so that it might be reaped,
and your possessions dispersed to be handed over [to the poor].
He had you come down from the tree you had gone up,[216]
and he saved you by His wood.

4   Blessed are you, O wilderness, for upon His tables
our Lord wove for you a crown of silence.
Who that wishes to scrutinize his Creator
is able to scrutinize the bread that multiplied?[217]
Blessed is the one who eats His blessing and does not scrutinize
      Him
and enjoys His delights and does not dispute about His begetting.[218]
Our hunger reproves us, for humans need bread
but not to scrutinize it.

5   Our Lord has become our living bread,[219]
and we shall delight in our new cup.
Come, let us then eat it without investigation,
and without scrutiny let us drink his cup.
Who disdains blessings and fruits
and sits down to investigate their nature?
A human being needs to live. Come let us live and not die
in the depth of investigation.

---

212. John 2.7.
213. John 2.11.
214. Luke 19.1–10.
215. Luke 19.7–8.
216. Luke 19.5.
217. Exod. 16.1–36 et par.
218. This is part of Ephrem's standard anti-Arian polemic.
219. Cf. John 6.48–51.

6　Blessed also are you, whoever you are
　　from whom our Lord made to emerge
　　a swarm of demons that had settled in you.[220]
　　Ask the scholars who scrutinize the Son
　　where in you the thousands of demons lived.
　　Blessed are your disorderly voices that have been silenced
　　and your shattered limbs that rest.
　　In you is portrayed the world, stripped and contemptible
　　but made chaste by the One Who makes all chaste.

7　Blessed are you, too, courageous blind man
　　whose great boldness enlightened you.[221]
　　For if you had been silent as you were admonished,
　　silence would have kept you in darkness.
　　Blessed is your boldness for in it you also offer a type,
　　that the sinner, if he be bold, will obtain mercy.
　　[God] entered and left ten thousand talents right away
　　[for] the petitioner's boldness.

8　Blessed are you too, son of Hebrews,
　　whom your Lord called Bar Israel—
　　a new man not clothed in the guile of the serpent,
　　a simple man in whom Adam was reproached.[222]
　　The sound of the gospel you heard in the garden,
　　while Adam in Eden heard the just voice.
　　From next to the fig tree Nathanael was called,
　　clothed in new [garments].

9　Blessed are you whom they told among the trees,
　　"We have found Him Who finds all,
　　Who came to find Adam who was lost,
　　and in the garment of light to return him to Eden."[223]
　　The world in the symbol of the shade of the fig tree
　　is belabored as if in heavy shadow.
　　From beneath the fig tree as a symbol of the world, you emerged
　　to meet our Savior.

---

220. Mark 5.1–20 et par.
221. Mark 10.46–52 et par.; cf. HdP 5.7.
222. John 1.43–51, esp. 47.
223. On Adam's garment of light and other original attributes, cf. Nat. 5.4 and Virg. 3.2 and notes ad loc.

10 Very sad was the Tree of Life
    that saw Adam hidden from him.
    Into the virgin earth he sank and was buried,
    but he arose and shone forth from Golgotha.[224]
    Humankind, like a bird pursued,
    took refuge on it so it would arrive at its home.
    The persecutor is persecuted,
    and the persecuted doves rejoice in paradise.[225]

---

224. Matt. 27.53; for Adam buried at Golgotha, cf. E. A. Wallis Badge, *The Book of the Cave of Treasures* (London, 1927), 224–25.

225. The manuscript adds, "Finished is one hymn on Nazareth."

17

In this hymn Ephrem sets forth the city of Shechem as the type of the creation as well as of the church of the Gentiles. Just as Shechem was destroyed for the sake of avenging the rape of Dinah, the creation was destroyed through the sin of Eve. All this is the work of justice. But the work of grace also has its place. Because of the Samaritan woman at the well, Jesus brought salvation to her city of Shechem. Although Ephrem does not state it explicitly here, it is clear elsewhere that the symmetry is completed in Mary, Mother of Jesus, the woman through whom the creation was restored to grace.

Just as the fallen creation is full of dead bodies, so also the city of Shechem and its surrounding hills contain the bones of leaders of the Israelites: Joshua, Joseph and Eleazar son of Aaron. These three variously represent Jesus and his threefold messiahship: of prophet, king and priest. Other parallels are their similar or identical names: Joshua's name is identical with Jesus; Jesus is Bar Joseph, son of Joseph. Just as Joshua and Eleazar distributed the inheritance of the land to the tribes of Israel, Jesus offers the inheritance of salvation, refreshment and rest to all.

Finally, Jesus is portrayed as if he were a fourth-century pilgrim visiting the graves of the three "just men" buried at Shechem. Because they, the dead, and the Samaritan woman, the living, longed for the salvation brought by Jesus, he came to their Gentile city and saved it. Around the well of Jacob, Ephrem informs us, is built a church on which the words of Jesus to the Samaritan woman are inscribed—a message for the entire church of the Gentiles.

17

On Shechem on the previous melody

1   Blessed are you, Shechem,[226] between grace
and justice wondrously set.
Because of Dinah, the daughter of Jacob, you were judged.
The circumcised destroyed you, made you a grave.[227]
Blessed is He who came to you, Son of the Gracious One, and
      consoled you,
for the sons of justice had drawn their swords against you,
Since on a woman's account they killed, buried and concealed you,
by a woman you were resuscitated.[228]

Refrain: Blessed is the One Who . . . Shechem.

2   Blessed are you, O Shechem,
in whom is portrayed all creation, for one who understands.
Through Eve the serpent began to destroy the earth,
full of corpses, as a type for you.
Blessed is the creation! He Who imprinted and portrayed
the two of you, one on the other, revived [creation] in your symbol.
You, O Shechem, are the beginning and the parable
of the church of the Gentiles.

3   Blessed are you, blessed [city], for on your mountain was
Joshua Bar Nun like a sweet spice.[229]
Therefore you were not defrauded of the fulfillment
of Jesus the true name.[230]
Blessed is your beauty that the names adorn,
the name of the servant and the name of his Lord.
Blessed are you, enviable one, for in your grave is Joshua,
and in your heart is our Lord.

4   Blessed are you, O Shechem, in whom is planted
even the pure tree of symbols.

---

226. Shechem, son of Hamor, could be addressed here, but the succeeding lines show that the city is meant.
227. Cf. Gen. 34.1–31.
228. The Samaritan woman at the well; cf. John 4.1–42.
229. Josh. 24.29f.
230. In Syriac, as in Hebrew, the names Joshua and Jesus are identical; cf. Nat. 1.31 and note ad loc.

Placed in you was Joseph,[231] who bore the types,
and upon his limbs were the symbols of his Lord.[232]
Blessed is your womb form which he peers out at us,
Joseph . . . Bar Joseph imprinted.
Who is able . . . to pluck from your branches
the symbols of our Savior?

5 Blessed are you, O Shechem, among whose tribe is placed
Eleazar, Son of Aaron.[233]
Aaron was prevented from crossing the river;
[Eleazar] entered, divided and distributed the inheritance.[234]
Blessed are you in whom dwell triple symbols:
even chiefs and prophets and priests.
From above came to you the Threefold One[235] in Whom
the bones of your glorious men rejoiced.

6 Blessed are you, whose entire land flourishes
with the bones of just men who portrayed the Son—
blossoms plaited with their symbols,
crowning the Son as He entered you.
With them you crowned the King Who came to you,
[the King] whom the mad one[236] crowned with a crown of thorns.
Who has ever seen symbols who from their graves
crowned the victor?

---

231. Josh. 24.32.

232. The textual lacuna makes it difficult to be certain of the precise typological relation understood by Ephrem here, but it is perhaps only the fact that Jesus is Bar Joseph, son of Joseph, but cf. also Virg. 18.6.

233. Josh. 24.33.

234. Josh. 14.1—19.51.

235. *tlyty'* should be read as "threefold" rather than "third," the reference being to the threefold messiahship of Jesus as priest, prophet and king, cf. Virg 19.9. This seems Ephrem's intention more than the suggestions of Beck, cf. Epiph. 8.6 and CNis. 1.11.

236. Ephrem portrays Jesus as if he were a fourth-century pilgrim coming to Shechem to visit the graves of Joshua, Joseph and Eleazar. The gravesites to which Josh. 24.29–33 testifies, as well as the church built around the well of Jacob (cf. str. 10), are attested as pilgrimage sites in two fourth-century sources, the accounts of the Bordeaux pilgrim and Jerome. Whereas Jerome and others, following the tradition of Gen. 50.13, locate the grave of Joseph at Hebron, the Bordeaux pilgrim situates it at Shechem, Bord. 588.1 and Hier. epis. 108, cf. Wilkenson, Pilgrims, 38, n.92 and 51. Jerome, in describing the travels of Paula, recounts her veneration of sites on Mount Ephrem reputed to be the tombs of Joshua and Eleazar and her visit to the church constructed around Jacob's well, Jer. Epis. 108, cf. Wilkenson, Pilgrims, 51. Jerome also relates the church and well to John 4. Egeria also mentions a church associated with Melchizedek, possibly at Shechem, Eger. Itin. 13, cf. G.E. Gingras, trans. *Egeria: Diary of a Pilgrimage*, ACW 38 (New York, 1970), 197f., n. 172.

7 Among your tribe weary men found rest:
Joseph, Joshua and Eleazar.
In you also the weary Gentle One found rest.
Although tireless He became tired to give you rest.
Blessed is your well at which He found rest
Whose rest announced rest to you.
Blessed are you, restful one, for whom refreshment multiplies
in our Lord Who pours forth all.

8 Blessed are you that happened to have the treasures of bones
that the Lord came to visit.[237]
Heavenly treasures were the graves
full of the bones of just men.
Blessed are the graves of your just men who exulted
and the gates of your palaces that were opened.
Blessed are you, O Shechem, for the dead and the living
in you long for our Savior.

9 Blessed are you, O Shechem, in which the True One
disavowed His own words for the sake of your life:
"Go not in the way of pagans,
nor into a Samaritan city."[238]
Blessed are you, like Nineveh, absolved
by the Just One; He passed judgment but He saved it.
Jonah grieved over Nineveh's repentance
but in you our Lord rejoiced.

10 Blessed are you, O Shechem, for upon your well
today is built a holy church:
For behold, "I baptize with living water
for which your mouth asked there.
Whoever drank from your well thirsted again and returned to it;
My baptism needs no repetition."[239]
Blessed are you, O Shechem, upon whose well and church
His exact words are portrayed.[240]

---

237. Matt. 10.5.
238. Cf. Jon. 3.10–4.11, cf. Virg. 42–50, esp. 50.
239. Cf. John 4.1–15.
240. Other sources of the late fourth century mention the church, but not the inscription, cf. str. 8, above.

18

Ephrem continues his typological exegesis of the Jewish scriptures touching on the city of Shechem, stressing not only the fulfillment of the types in Christ but also his superiority to them. Jacob watering his flocks at Shechem anticipates Christ bringing salvation to the Gentiles (str. 1). The duplicitous demand of Dinah's brothers serves to teach a lesson against circumcision itself; the violence of their retribution is contrasted with the love of the covenant of the "Gentle One" who was slain (str. 2–3). Animal imagery is used to evoke the two levels of the story: The dove betrayed by the serpent represents at once the Shechemites deceived by Dinah's brothers and humankind betrayed by Satan. The pagans, represented by wolves and wild animals, are saved by the Lamb, Christ, while the Jewish people, the ewe, rejects him (str. 4). Yet the gift of salvation is not given to unregenerate pagans: Bar Hamor, Shechem, was a licentious man who was ultimately responsible for the destruction of the city; and the Samaritan woman, reproached by Jesus, is implicitly contrasted with the consecrated virgins of the church (str. 5).

The hymn ends with a rehearsal of the typological interpretation of the three men buried at Shechem or its vicinity. Since both the sons of Jacob and the Egyptians received Pharoah's grain distributed by Joseph, and since Joseph was buried at Shechem, that city symbolizes the presence of both Jewish and Gentile Christians in the church (str. 6). When Joshua saved Rahab and her family, he anticipated Jesus' salvation of the Samaritan woman and her townspeople, which, in turn, represents the salvation of all the Gentiles (str. 7). Through a play on words, Eleazar and the Levitical priesthood are confirmed as the Jewish representatives of Jesus and his apostolic priesthood (str. 8). Finally, the burial at Shechem of these three Jewish antetypes of Jesus and Jesus' visit there are concrete evidence of the validity of Ephrem's typological exegesis, affirmed in principle by Matthew 13.52 (str. 9–10; cf. str. 6–8).

The same melody

1 Blessed are you, O Shechem, for from that well
Jacob had his mute flocks drink,
and from that church over the well
Christ had His flocks drink.
The flocks of Jacob have passed away and disappeared,
but the flock of Christ has grown and does grow.
The symbols were swallowed, and the shadows were completed;
by Jesus all is sealed.

Refrain: Blessed is He Who taught Shechem!

2 The deceitful brothers placed a condition on you,
a condition that became the cause of your death,
for they were unfaithful to their covenant.[241] Behold the True One
Who resembled Him and His promises.
Instead of the condition contrived by hatred,
behold the symbol devised by love.
Instead of slayers, behold the Slain One
Who was slain but gave you life by His death.

3 How much indeed the former generations were disturbed,
but by you, Gentle One, all was made peaceful.
Drunk with anger, they licked venom,
so that even the circumcised destroyed the circumcised.
O circumcision, put to shame by its advocates,
for this was not God's zeal crying out for it.
Its own sword reproved circumcision in Shechem
as a hater of humans.

4 O dove who trusted the serpent,
the Lamb has saved your simplicity,
for your wolves are represented by Him and were taught by Him.
They put on His humility and were reconciled with Him.
Woe to the Hebrew sheep[242] that butted Him;

---

241. Cf. Gen. 34.13–29.
242. Here and in the following line Ephrem plays on words via metathesis: *l'rb' 'bry'* and
pqrt . . wpwrqnh.

the ewe raved at Him and in Him she lost her salvation.
But the wild animal, forgetting her customary behavior,
was tamed by Him.

5 Blessed are you, O Shechem, town of Jacob!
Jacob gave you to Joseph the just.[243]
Bar Hamor, that licentious man, destroyed you;
Joseph, the glorious, inherited you.
Since Bar Hamor seduced the daughter of Jacob and raped her,
the Holy One taught your daughter and instructed her in modesty.
Because of the One who was victorious, the virgins of your church
have won their crowns.

6 Blessed are you, O Shechem . . . that proclaimed
symbols of . . . to the People and the peoples,
for even the proud circumcised men
came down to buy corn from the uncircumcised one.[244]
The symbol and its explanation are in your church
in which uncircumcised and circumcised dwell.
Indeed the Savior went to Joseph
to perfect his symbol in his city.[245]

7 He went again, to perfect the symbol hidden
in Joshua Bar Nun, who lived in your land.
For he saved Rahab the harlot
who had been the maelstrom of many men.[246]
Jesus the Most High freed your daughter
who had belonged to many men.[247]
Rahab saved only the household of her fathers,
but your daughter [saved] many.

8 He came, furthermore, to your land to perfect
the symbol hidden in Eleazar,
the priest who crossed over with Joshua[248]
and accompanied him as a symbol—

---

243. Cf. Gen. 33.19 and Josh. 24.32.
244. Pharaoh, cf. Gen. 42.
245. Jesus went to Shechem to Joseph's burial place as a sign that the church is for both Jews and Gentiles.
246. Josh. 2.1–21, 6.17–25.
247. Cf. John 4.16–18, but in the light of Virg. 22.12–13, perhaps the allusion here is to John 7.53–8.11.
248. Cf. Josh. 3.3–6 and 4.16–18.

the symbol of the apostles who accompanied Jesus,[249]
Like the Levites, they were priests in the world.
Blessed are you, desirable one; in your symbols
the truths shine forth and are resplendent.

9   Blessings multiply for you, blessed one,[250]
. . . blessings bear your dead.
Behold . . . their bones . . .
Instead of bones . . . symbols in your womb.
Types shine forth and even bones are revived in those
who by deeds are saved by their Lord.
Blessed are you, O Shechem, for symbols and bones
thunder in your womb.

10 Even if all the tribes were in need
as the poor, your tribe would still be rich.
For "from his treasure he brought out something new
and something old," as it is written.[251]
Blessed is your glorious crown! How enviable!
Precious jewels are on it and how fair they are!
Joseph and Joshua and the son of Aaron the priest,
our Lord and His heralds.

---

249. Depending on the vocalization, *lwy'* may mean either "companion" or "Levite."
250. The city of Shechem is addressed.
251. Cf. Matt. 13.52.

19

In this third hymn on the city of Shechem, Ephrem continues the theme of Shechem as the representation of the Gentile church, completing it with the introduction of bridal imagery. Rejected by Judah, Christ, the Light, has been joyfully accepted by Shechem (str. 1); the church of the Gentiles is the bride of Christ (str. 2). Expressing the intimate dwelling of God within the Gentile church in the language of the Pentateuch, Ephrem goes on to say that Jesus brought the Ark back to Shechem (str. 4–5). This adds a further dimension to his exegetical message for Semitic Christians like Ephrem who might trace their ancestry to one of the "lost tribes" of Israel, such as the tribe of Ephrem, more plausibly than to the tribe of Judah. He clearly has in mind the fact that Joshua was from the tribe of Ephrem. His brief allusion to Hosea makes it equally clear that he knows that Jereboam and Ahab were Ephremites, and that the prophet railed against the tribe of Ephrem as the worst of idolaters (str. 10). Regardless of all this and to the chagrin of the descendants of Judah, argues Ephrem, the threefold messianic promise has passed over to Shechem, to the church of the Gentiles, founded on the bones of Joseph, Joshua and Eleazar (str. 6–9).

19

The seventh on the same melody

1 Blessed are you, O Shechem, in which visited
the Light persecuted by the land of Judah.
Others approached and asked
the Fount of mercies to depart from their presence.[252]
Blessed are your children who entreated and surrounded
that treasure of glorious perfumes

---

252. Cf. Matt. 8.34.

that they might inhale and be sated, and that the power of His
    deeds
might permeate their senses.[253]

Refrain: Blessed is the city of Shechem!

2 Blessed are you, crowned Bride
into whom entered the Bridegroom Whom Zion hated.
The lame who had been cured rejoiced and danced in you;
the deaf shouted for joy; the mute sang praises.
Your inhabitants were numbered among those at the marriage
    feast.[254]
Cities sang praises with hosannas to Him.
Zion's ears were sickened at your joyful shout,
for your voice reached her presence.

3 She carved an idol . . .
  . . .
  . . .

4 Among your tribe the Ark was set up again.
The Gentiles saw, but frightened and angry were
the circumcised; they persecuted their king, and He went out
and came to Shechem, full of Gentiles.
Among the tribe of Joshua he made the Gentiles cry out.
Among the tribe they were consoled by our Savior.
Gentiles rejoiced, but the Jewish people grew angry and jealous.
Praise to the Omniscient One!

5 Among your tribe was pitched the meeting tent,[255]
and all its festivals resounded in your land.
Who will raise you to greater honor than this
that God Himself should dwell in you?
Israel was envious of how greatly you were magnified,
for the Ark was among your tribe.
. . . the people . . .
That was sustained . . .

6 This . . . eagle

---

253. Cf. John 4.30, 39–42.
254. Probably an allusion to Matt. 21.1–14, rather than to John 2.1–11.
255. Josh. 18.1.

and as a symbol he was solemnly borne.
Among your tribe Eleazar was buried,[256]
and inside your mountain, Joshua Bar Nun.[257]
A man . . . Ephrem . . .
Joshua Bar Nun . . . that glorified you . . .
Blessed are you, a standard with His legions.
His angels came down and surrounded him.[258]

7   Joshua Bar Nun gathered a congregation,
and came carrying Joseph with great pomp;
he placed him in you.[259] From his bones
wafted the smell of his victory.
A desirable blossom and a triumphant flower
struggled with fire and extinguished it.
Who has even seen a blossom that surrounded
itself with its glory?

8   O free [city] purchased for one hundred ewes[260]
even your number is significant.
Your crown was sealed and your type completed.
your symbol perfected, your measure filled.
Promised Land, promised to Abraham,
the just bought their own inheritance with their money.
In them is symbolized their Lord Who bought His flocks with His
      Blood;
with His sufferings [He bought] His own possessions.[261]

9   Who . . . you, O Shechem, among the tribe of Ephrem.
The blessed women carried your remedy.

. . .

The heads of tribes . . . Ephrem
Your kingdom cries out with Joseph,
and with Eleazar your priesthood shouts joyfully,
and with Joshua your prophecy. Blessed are you, the tribe
by which he clothes Himself in the three [offices].

---

256. Josh. 24.33.
257. Josh. 24.29f.
258. Like Jesus, cf. Mark 1.13 et par., Joshua was assisted by angels, cf. Josh. 5.13–15.
259. Exod. 13.19 and Josh. 24.32.
260. Gen. 33.19 and Josh. 24.32; Beck has noted that, like Ephrem, the Peshitta states the purchase price as one hundred ewes rather than one hundred pieces of gold.
261. Cf. Virg. 12.18.

10 That . . . Ephrem's wage is dissipated,
for I have adorned you with your own crowns.
Indeed, I have not magnified the treasure of sweet spices;
the odor of his fragrant herbs wafted over me,[262]
for the name I bear, is beloved by you.
Recall me in the prayer of your church.
Ephrem is my name, and when Hosea cries out against me,
console me with your help.[263]

---

262. Hos. 4.17–5.14 et passim.
263. A postscript reads, "The three hymns about Shechem are completed."

20

This is the first of two hymns on the city of Ephrem, in which, according to John's gospel, Jesus took refuge just before His final return to Jerusalem. Ephrem sets forth an elaborate typological interpretation of this event, working on several levels simultaneously. First he enumerates three Old Testament types for flight under persecution: Jacob, Moses and Elijah (str. 2). Then he elaborates the conditions of Jesus' withdrawal to Ephrem. He argues that both the human opponents of Jesus in Jerusalem and Satan, despite their determination to kill Jesus, wished to avoid doing so on Passover—not only because of the potential for popular unrest, but especially to disguise the typology of Christ as the Passover Lamb (cf. the Paschal theology of John's gospel) (str. 3–5). However, just as the flight into Egypt in the Matthean infancy narrative was designed to show the typological link of Jesus to the Exodus (cf. Matt. 2.15), the flight of Jesus to Ephrem at the end of the ministry shows another aspect of the same Paschal mystery (str. 6).

The flight to the city of Ephrem should remind us of Jacob's blessing of Ephrem in Egypt. That blessing is symbolic in two respects: First, the crossed arms of Jacob are a type of the cross of Christ; second, this same gesture, in elevating the younger son over the older, shows the substitution of the Gentiles for the Jews as the recipients of the promises of God (str. 7–11). By placing the Gentile acceptance of Jesus at the entry into Jerusalem (str. 9), Ephrem justifies the apparent change of divine preference as the timely choice of the Divine Gardener who plucks the fruit in season (str. 11). The final strophe is a statement of the hymnist's belief that the symbols of the Creator's truth are to be found throughout the creation as well as in scripture.

20

The eighth hymn to the same melody

1 Blessed are you, too, Ephrem, the city
in which the Lord of cities was hidden.[264]
On dry ground waves swelled against Him
Who silenced the waves on the sea.[265]
Blessed is your harbor that received with love
the persecuted ship of disciples.[266]
The sailor had seen your calm harbor
and enriched you with His discourses.[267]

Refrain: Glory to the One Who sent You!

2 Jacob, when pursued, turned aside to Haran;[268]
Moses, persecuted, turned aside to Midian;[269]
even Elijah fled to Zarephath;[270]
the uncircumcised received the circumcised.
But blessed are you who became worthy of the Lord,
Who was persecuted by His servants, the crucifiers.
The Just One Who hid His all-scourging sceptre
was persecuted in return.

3 The wolves heard long before from John
who called Christ the True Lamb,[271]
and they wanted to kill Him before the festival
that He might not become the Paschal Lamb
so they might forget the path forged

---

264. John 11.54.
265. Mark 6.45–52 et par.
266. Entry into the harbor is an image frequently found, along with other sailing imagery, in early Christian literature. For the Greek and Latin sources, cf. H. Rahner, *Symbole der Kirche, Die Ekklesiologie der Väter* (Salzburg, 1964), 243–48, 548–64; and J. Danielou, *Primitive Christian Symbols*, trans. D. Attwater (London, 1964), 58–70. In the Syriac environment this language is applied to Christ, to Mary and other saints, the church and the sacraments, especially baptism, cf. Murray, Symbols, 249–53, and E. Hambye, "The Symbol of the < < Coming to the Harbour>> in the Syriac Tradition," OCA 197, 401–11. For Mary as the harbor, cf. Nat. 9.4.
267. For another example of Christ as sailor, cf. Virg. 31.15.
268. Gen. 27.42—28.5.
269. Exod. 2.11–15.
270. 1 Kgs. 17.8–10.
271. John 1.36.

by the lamb that was slain in Egypt.[272]
But they handed down and bore the lambs with their symbols
to the True Lamb.

4 The evil one played a hidden trick on those
who were his visible harp:
"Let us not kill Him at the festival
lest there be a great clamor for Him."[273]
Satan saw the lamb and was alarmed,
and how greatly he feared His month and His day!
He hastened to kill Him before Nisan's moon
and its fourteenth day.

5 Our Lord, Who did not ever want to constrain
either our will or our freedom,[274]
kept His distance rather than oppose evil men.
When He had provided a place, he provided a type,
that when His day and month should arrive,
He might go to His glorious mystery.
To the city called . . .
. . .

6 Just as he went to Egypt as a child
to take His symbol from there,[275]
He set out in the end for the city of Ephrem
to go bearing His great symbol.
In Egypt He took refuge at the first;
in the city of the household of Ephrem at the last.
He began and ended: for Egypt the beginning,
for Ephrem the completion.

7 In Egypt were portrayed two symbols
when Jacob crossed his hands.[276]
How lovely the sight and how beloved the symbol,
how glorious the type and how clear the cross!
He crossed his arms and portrayed
the Crucified One and the glorious cross.

---

272. Cf. Exod. 12.
273. Mark 14.1–2 et par.
274. On the importance of free will, cf. Nat. 1.98, 4.140–42, Virg. 25.7 and notes ad loc.
275. Matt. 2.13–15.
276. Gen. 48.1–22, esp. 14. Cf. Murray, Symbols, 46.

Blessed is the child on whose head was portrayed
the all-life-giving cross.

8   That name was given to his town;
it was named Ephrem city,
so that the city also keeps Ephrem's name,
the symbol of its Lord entrusted to it,
so that to that blessed city
our Savior went to clothe Himself in
the great symbol portrayed in the name
of Ephrem in Egypt.

9   The cross portrayed gave the right of the first-born
to Ephrem, the symbol of the Gentiles,
those who went out to meet our Lord
when He returned from the city of Ephrem.[277]
Aramaeans glorified Him with their palm branches;
the circumcised were silent and [so] they were rejected.
The symbol has been revealed: The Gentiles have become the first-
      born;
they were first with their hosannas.

10   [The text of this verse is very fragmentary.]

11   See: He, being omniscient, served
all of them in their seasons.
Even the laborers pluck fruits
in their seasons and their months.
The symbols of the Wise Laborer, too,
go with His seasons.
O Laborer Whose symbols were gathered,
Who is a reservoir of all symbols!

12   In every place, if you look, His symbol is there,
and when you read, you will find His types.
For by Him were created all creatures,
and He engraved His symbols upon His possessions.[278]
When He created the world,

---

277. Cf. John 12.12–15. Ephrem's characterization of the crowds as Gentiles is noted by
Murray, Symbols, 46; For a suggestion of the thought process that leads him to this view, cf.
Hayman, Image, 429.

278. Ephrem refers to the ancient custom of marking one's belongings, cf. Nat. 1.99, 12.3,
28.7 and notes ad loc.

He gazed at it and adorned it with His images.[279]
Streams of His symbols opened, flowed and poured forth
His symbols on His members.

---

279. Here the "types" (*ṭwps'*) are in scripture, while the "symbols" (*r'z'*) and "images"(*ywqn'*) are in nature, but Ephrem is not consistent in this usage, cf. Beck, Bildtheologie, 244, where he cites Azym. 4.22 with its *dmwt'* in the Law, *ywqn'* in the prophets, and *r'z'* in nature.

21

This second hymn on the city of Ephrem develops further the themes of the previous hymn. As before, the starting point is the theme of Jesus' refuge in the city of Ephrem, dwelling this time on the peacefulness of that refuge and comparing it with the refuge of Christian ascetics in the desert (str. 1–2). Again, the flight into Egypt is invoked as a parallel, reinforced this time by comparison of Herod with Caiaphas, and the fact that Ephrem's mother was Egyptian (str. 3). Jesus took certain actions deliberately to fulfill the types: just as he went to Egypt and to Nazareth with typological intent, He went to Ephrem and to Bethany and, most of all, he died as the Passover Lamb on 14 Nisan (str. 4). The transfiguration, portrayed as another instance of taking refuge from Jewish persecution, provides another parallel to the flight to Ephrem (str. 5–6).

In the final strophes Ephrem seeks to demonstrate that Ephrem bar Joseph is an authentic type of Christ. Using the exegetical technique of gematria, he shows that the name of Ephrem is inherently related to the cross and to the Crucified One (str. 8). Further, his mother, Asenath, daughter of an Egyptian priest, represents the Gentile church; just as she loved her husband Joseph, the church of the Gentiles loves her husband, Jesus, the son of Joseph. Her numerous children, the Gentile Christians, are sealed with the cross at baptism (str. 9). Three crosses represent the mystical presence of Christ throughout the creation: in the heavenly chariot, in the human being, and in the earthly creation (str. 10). Ephrem is the recipient of a threefold blessing: Offered by his father Joseph to his grandfather, Jacob, he is blessed by Jacob and his city is crowned by Christ as His bride (str. 11).

21

The ninth on the same melody
1   Blessed are you, Ephrem, that in your city,

350

that distant one, neighbor of the desert, companion of solitude,
the Lord of cities found rest.[280]

. . .

Blessed are your gates, blessed by His entry,
and your streets sanctified by His footsteps.
[Ephrem's] desert is the symbol of the desert of the world,
for it gave peace to the One Who gives peace to all.

Refrain: Blessed is He Who gladdens all.

2   Blessed are you, in whom rested the weary Lord,
and the persecuted community lived in your peace.
. . . her companions . . .
fish . . . from the dragons . . .
His lambs were consoled that there was no
Caiaphas chief of the wolves, the Sodomites.
In you [God] portrays a type for the ascetics who love
the all-liberating desert.

3   Into Egypt Mary fled from that king
drunk with the blood of the tribes,[281]
and thus You fled to the city of Ephrem
from Caiaphas, drunk with rage.[282]
Zion slandered Him in the scribes;
Jerusalem persecuted Him in the priests.
In Egypt He was hidden, and he was concealed in Ephrem,
whose mother was an Egyptian.[283]

4   He went down to Egypt, fulfilled the symbol and returned.
He went to Nazareth for the sake of its symbol;[284]
likewise He went to create a symbol in Ephrem,
and in Bethany with a colt and the Gentiles.[285]
His symbols were passed down one to the next.
His prototypes received one from the other.

---

280. John 11.54.
281. Cf. Matt. 2.13–18.
282. Cf. John 11.49–53.
283. Gen. 41.45, 50–52.
284. Matt. 2.23.
285. Mark 11.1–11 et par., esp. Matt. 21.4f.

In Nisan He completed the measure of all symbols
on the fourteenth[286] day.
5   Simon, going up to Mt. Tabor,
lovely and undisturbed by the crucifiers,
persuaded the Lord, "It is good, my Lord,
for us to be here, without disturbers;
it is fitting for us with righteous men in tents;
it is peaceful for us with Moses and Elijah
rather than in the Temple full of the confusion
and the bitterness of the Jews."[287]
6 . . . Ephrem
    . . .
    . . . this city
is not among the cities of the Jews.
Where is the strife of the scribes?
Where are the threats of the priests?
Simon perhaps said, "The city is very quiet,
our Lord, let us stay."
7   For while all creatures gazed at Him,
they all gave Him their trust.
While the writings He read gazed at Him,
they gave Him books of their interpretations.
Again while Ephrem, that blessed city,
was looking at Him with joy,
he took from his head the symbol that crowned him
and offered it to the Conqueror.
8   If, moreover, you calculate the name of Ephrem,
it is three hundred thirty one.[288]
The cross is portrayed in its calculation;

---

286. Although the principal ms. reads "fifteenth," Beck has rightly altered his translation to correspond to the date of Passover.

287. Cf. Mark 9.2–8, esp. 5, et par. Cf. Virg. 20.2.2–3.

288. Here Ephrem uses the rabbinical exegetical device called *gematria;* cf. Nat. 27.2 and note ad loc. In ordinary usage each letter of the Hebrew or Syriac alphabet also represents a number. In one kind of *gematria* the numerical equivalents of each letter of a word are added together to achieve the numerical value of the word. Words which add up to the same value are assumed to be in mysterious relation to one another. Thus here when Ephrem compares the total for *'prym,* "Ephrem," (331) with the combined total for *ṣlyb',* "Crucified" (133), and *zqyp',* "cross" (198), and finds them identical, he is satisfied that he has proved his point once more: There is a mysterious relation between the blessing of Ephrem and the crucifixion.

the crucified too imprints His measurement,
the cross with the hands stretched out on it.
On "crucified" and "cross" his name depends.
How much I have wandered in you, child, that from all of you
crosses gaze at me.

9 You are the son of Asenath, the daughter of a pagan priest;[289]
she is a symbol of the church of the Gentiles.
She loved Joseph, and Joseph's son
in truth the holy church loved.
She had many children by the Crucified,
and on every member the cross is engraved.
By the symbol of Ephrem crosses are crowded into her,
by the birth from water.[290]

10 The cross is engraved on the chariot
to which are harnessed the living Cherubim.[291]
Again, the cross is engraved on the human being
in the symbol even his structure stands.[292]
A third cross is also engraved
on the bird[293] and on the earth and all that is on it.[294]
Three crosses encompass everything;
by you they are portrayed, O child.

11 Blessed are you on whose head
are symbolically placed three right hands.
Joseph offered you; Jacob marked you;
their right hands gave you the crown.
And the hidden heavenly right hand
wove a diadem for you in Samaria.[295]
Not everyone was able, child, [to understand]
the symbols portrayed in you.

---

289. Gen. 41.45, 50–52.

290. Ephrem's understanding of baptism is closely linked with the crucifixion; cf. Saber, Théologie, 51–55, 132–34.

291. Cf. Ezek. 1.4–25, and HdF 55.3.

292. Cf. HdF 18.12, also Just. I apol. 55.

293. Cf. HdF 18.2.

294. Cf. HdF 17.11, 24.8, also Just. apol. 60.

295. Beck suggests an allusion to Acts 8.12, but cf. also Virg. 19.2.

22

This first of two hymns on the Samaritan woman at the well is like the hymns that precede it in the collection in that Ephrem singles out for comment a Gentile from the New Testament, specifically from John's gospel, to argue her typological importance for his contemporaries. He begins with the assertion fundamental to Christian typological exegesis, that Jesus has fulfilled what Moses began; here the assertion is clothed in the language of farming and drawing water from a well (str. 1). This leads easily to the Samaritan woman who came to the well of Jacob seeking ordinary water and received instead the living water of Christ (str. 2). The promise that one who receives the living water will not thirst again is interpreted to mean that there is only one Messiah (str. 3).

At this point Ephrem launches into a surprising argument: It is not the case that this woman has been divorced and remarried five times and is therefore reproached by Jesus for immorality. Instead she is the victim of a plight like that of Sarah before her marriage to Tobias (str. 4–5). Because the deaths of five successive husbands made all fearful of marrying her and yet to be unmarried subjected her to reproach, she had devised a false marriage for the sake of appearances. Far from being virtually a harlot, as others assume, Ephrem argues that her secret revealed by Jesus is that she is living chastely in her marriage (str. 12–13). This is evident on three grounds: 1) the confidence of her manner of argument (str. 5–9); 2) Jesus' willingness to speak along with her (str. 5, 10–11); and 3) several typological precedents for her behavior for example, others, notably Elizabeth and Hannah were chagrined by their lack of husbands or children (str. 14–15); just as the unmasking of a deception by Abraham and Sarah about Sarah's marital status led to the respect of a Gentile king for God, the unveiling of this woman's deception led to the belief of a city of Gentiles (str. 16–18); just as Tamar disguised her marital status for the sake of continuing the messianic line, so the deception of the Samaritan woman led to the revelation of the Messiah to her people (str. 19–20). Finally, Ephrem asserts that the woman, led step by step in conversation with Jesus, "is a type of our humanity that he leads step by step" (str. 21).

22

On Samaria on the previous melody

1   Our Lord labored and He went like a farmer
to water the seed that Moses sowed.
Directly to the well He went to give
hidden and living water for the sake of the revelation.
Blessed is Moses, who, with the book he wrote, sowed
the symbols of the Messiah, still young;
by [Christ's] watering were the seeds of the house of Moses
        perfected,
and they were reaped by His disciples.

Refrain: Praises to your humility!

2   Blessed are you, drawer of ordinary water,
who turned out to be a drawer of living water.[296]
You found the treasure, another Source,
from Whom a flood of mercies flows.
The spring had dried up, but it broke through to you and gave you
        to drink.[297]
He was poor, but He asked in order to enrich you.
You left behind your pitcher, but you filled understanding
and gave your people to drink.

3   Blessed are you to whom He gave living water to drink,
and you did not thirst again, as you said.
For he called the truth "living water,"
since all who hear it will not thirst again.[298]
Blessed are you who learned the truth and did not thirst;
for one is the Messiah and there are no more.

---

296. Cf. John 4.1–42. The pericope is similarly treated in Comm. Diat. 12.6.16–20.
297. John 4.28–30.
298. John 4.13–15.

Your husbands are many, your Messiahs are not many,
for one is the Only-begotten.[299]

4 Blessed are you, woman, because you saw
that your husbands were dead, and your reproaches were many.
Other men were afraid to take you [in marriage],
lest they, like their counterparts, die.[300]
You took a pretended and bribed husband
to set aside your reproach but not to approach your body.
The contract and the oaths that you made secretly
He revealed to you, and you believed in Him.[301]

5 Blessed are you, who are slandered even by our people,
although by your people you were not reviled.
We have called you a harlot, but if you were,
your bad reputation would have wafted to Him.
Blessed is your perception that you disputed with your Lord.
Your dispute shows that your heart was not contemptible.
If you had been a harlot, your silence would have offered tears
    to the one who gives life to all.[302]

6 For she answered and spoke as a learned one,
as a disputant, yet modestly,
"Our fathers worshipped on this mountain."[303]
Since the heads of [her] people [were] of the house of Abraham,
it was not necessary for her to petition about her sins,
for her love had been bound in the presence of righteous men.
Since He revealed to her one thing, she prodded Him to teach her
reality without contention

7 She answered again, saying perceptively,
"Lord, I see that you are a prophet."[304]
If, indeed, our Lord revealed her shame to her,
compassion in judgment would be righteous for her

---

299. Ephrem contrasts Christian belief with Samaritan messianic expectations. Possibly he alludes here specifically to the followers of a Samaritan messianic figure named Dositheus; cf. Or. c. Cels. 1.57, 6.11; further, H. Chadwick, *Origen: Contra Celsum* (Cambridge, 1965), 325, n. 1. Jerome takes the woman's five husbands to be the books of the Pentateuch and the sixth to be Dositheus, Hier. epis. 108 (v322 13.3)
300. Cf. Tob. 3.7–15, 6.10–8.9.
301. Cf. John 4.16–19.
302. Cf. Luke 7.36–50.
303. John 4.20a.
304. John 4.19.

as for the sinful woman who sought forgiveness
with her head bowed and her mouth closed.
But she was modest yet her head was high
and her voice was authoritative.

8   She said, "I have no husband,"[305] to tell Him the truth
and to test Him in two respects:
what she had and what she did not have—to see if He
would be able to arrive at her secrets.
Our Lord revealed the two of them and amazed her,
who both had and did not have a husband.
She was astonished and convinced; she was amazed and believed,
and she acknowledged [Him] and worshipped Him.

9   Obey, my tongue, put to rest your labor
and run in silence to meet your rest.
Who, indeed, calls to you to become, without pay,
the advocate of words for the reviled woman?
Not out of malice have you been slandered, O woman;
our Lord will forgive even those who slandered you.
Scripture will console you, and we, too, will comfort you
commensurate with our weakness.

10   Since our Lord did not allow at all
even one of His [disciples] to remain with Him,
if you were a harlot, would not this Holy One
have given cause for calumny?
Into the presence of the daughter of Jairus, who was dead,
He brought three of His disciples and entered.[306]
The entire city was persuaded of your respectability.
Glory to the One Who set you free.

11   . . .
who slandered . . .
. . . the body, since . . .
The scriptures blushed to explain to them
in what manner and how much unclean men have slandered.
He alone labored with you and sanctified you,
in order to be like His glorious Father,

---

305. John 4.17a.
306. Mark 5.21–43, esp. 5.37, et par.

Who alone fashioned woman and sanctified her,
and led her to Adam.[307]

12   Therefore, since she concealed [her] secret
and she heard the saying about living water,
she tested with this sign, "If he reveals to me
the marriage contract that exists, then he is a god."
Our Lord revealed to her this secret of hers and gave her to drink,
and she thirsted not for worldly water.
She left the mortal man and did not seek his protection,
for the Living One espoused her.[308]

13   Rightly she said and our Lord confirmed
concerning that man, that he was not her husband.
Yet He revealed that he existed, and if he had been a wicked man,
[Jesus] would not have been able to conceal [this] utterly
since He was trusted by her.
Therefore she to whom He said, "He exists," witnesses
that he was either old or indigent and sat in her protection
as she in his shelter.

14   It is written, "Seven women will take
a single man" out of their shame,
but they seek nothing more than his name
"to make the reproach pass away" from their ears.[309]
For among Samaritans and Hebrews it is a curse
[to be] a widow or a barren or divorced woman.
[About] Elizabeth it is written that by means of her conception
the reproach of her barrenness passed away.[310]

15   The rival wife of Hannah also with this
annoyed her about her barrenness.[311]
How harsh is the reproach of her, who [has buried]
tree and fruit, husband and children.

---

307. Beck sees an anti-Marcionite or anti-Manichaean polemic here.

308. Ephrem infers that the woman now openly embraces celibacy. If this understanding antedates Ephrem, and if Vööbus is correct in arguing that celibacy was required of the baptisand of the early Syriac Church, then this might be a dimension of the iconographic significance of the Samaritan woman's portrayal at the Dura baptistery; Vööbus, Celibacy. Cf. C. H. Kraeling, with C. B. Welles, *The Christian Building, Excavations at Dura-Europos, Final Report*, 8.2, (New Haven, 1967), 67–69, 186–88, 207, n. 5, 210–12, Pl. XL.

309. Isa. 4.1.

310. Luke 1.25.

311. 1 Sam. 1.1–2.11, esp. 1.6.

She was called an accursed vine,
consumer of blossoms and destroyer of vinedressers,
the earth that destroyed the seeds and the sowers.
Glory to the One Who let her forget![312]

16   Let us read, for it is not hard for Abraham
to convince [us] about the daughter of Abraham.
Sarah and Abraham made a contract,
a secret that no one knew:
"Therefore, say of me that I am [your] brother."[313]
If Abraham and Sarah, the faithful ones,
deceived when they were compelled, so also when compelled,
she deceived the onlookers.

17   Just as when Sarah and Abraham affirmed
in this symbol as if for our benefit,
so also the daughter Abraham affirmed;
she as well as he [did so] for our advantage.[314]
Although she had a husband, Sarah denied [it]
but she made a husband for herself as a pretext.
Come let us marvel at the diverse deceits
of respectable women!

18   Just as God . . .
revealed that Sarah was the wife of a husband,
so also the Son of the Most High
revealed that this woman was without husband.
And just as by Sarah . . .
the house of Abimelech believed because of her,
so the Samaritans believed because of her
who received the One Who restores life for all.

19   Tamar saw that her consorts were dead,
and she sat down [as a prostitute at the gate] to great reproach.
Judah feared that he would die and Shelah too.[315]
. . . type, the Samaritans feared.
Tamar deceived and made her reproach pass away,

---

312. The Samaritan woman is once again the subject of the last lines of this strophe. The Syriac here should read *ld'nšy* rather than *ld'šy*.
313. Gen. 20.1–18, esp. 20.13; cf. Gen. 12.10–20, Gen. 26.6–11, and Nat. 20.4.
314. Ephrem puns on *'wdrn'*, "benefit," and *ywtrn'*, "advantage," here and in str. 19.7–8.
315. Gen. 38.6–30, esp. 38.11; cf. Comm. Diat. 12.6.19.

and the Samaritan woman concealed her reproach.
Tamar's deceit was revealed for our benefit,
and hers for our advantage.

20 Tamar trusted that from Judah
would arise the king whose symbol she stole.[316]
This woman, too, among the Samaritans expected
that perhaps the Messiah would arise from her.
Tamar's hope was not extinguished,
nor was this woman's expectation in vain,
as from her, therefore, our Lord arose in this town,
for by her He was revealed there.

21 Because she in her desire said, "The Messiah will come,"
He revealed to her with love, "I am He."
That He was a prophet she believed already;
soon after, that He was the Messiah.
O Wise One, Who appeared as a thirsty man,
[and] soon was called a prophet,
[and next] she understood He is Messiah; she is a type of our
      humanity
that He leads step by step.[317]

316. Cf. Nat. 9.12.
317. Comm. Diat. 12.6.18.

23

Here Ephrem portrays the Samaritan woman primarily as an apostle. Ephrem praises her for her readiness to share her insight into Jesus' messianic identity (str. 1). Also laudable is the immediacy of her response to one small sign, to be contrasted with the obstinacy of those who refused to accept even the greater evidence of miracles (str. 2). Yet it is Christ himself who determines the flow of his living water appropriate to each human being (str. 3). In her revelation to others of what she had heard, she is like Mary who conceived by her ear and thereby brought the Son to the world (str. 4–5). Like the words of the prophets, what she spoke became reality (str. 6). Even before the Twelve were permitted to do so, she preached the good news of salvation to the Gentiles (str. 7). The final strophes introduce themes of Eve and Adam, Christ as the Bread of Life, Shechem and Joshua, but the fragmentary state of the text makes it impossible to determine their relation to the previous strophes.

23

The eleventh on the same melody

1   Blessed are you, O woman, for not suppressing
your judgment about what you discovered.
The glorious Treasury was Himself present
for your need because of His love.
Your love was zealous
to share your treasure with your city.
Blessed woman, your discovery became
the Discoverer of the lost.

> *Refrain: Glory to the Discoverer of all!*[318]

2   Blessed are you, O woman, for not wearying
your Hunter[319] as has the daughter of Sion.

---

318. Or "Omnipotent One."
319. Cf. Comm. Diat. 12.6.16.

With that small sign He taught and caught you,
and, in turn, He showed His great wealth,
so that not [merely] by your word would there be faith in Him,
Who had shown signs that were mighty.
Small was the blessed sign for her
by comparison with miracles.

3 The glorious fount of Him who was sitting
at the well as Giver of drink to all,
flows to each according to His will:
Different springs according to those who drink.
From the well as single undifferentiated drink
came up each time for those who drank.
The Living Fount lets distinct blessings
flow to distinct people.[320]

4 O, to you, woman in whom I see
a wonder as great as in Mary!
For she from within her womb
in Bethlehem brought forth His body as a child,
but you by your mouth made Him manifest
as an adult in Shechem, the town of His father's household.
Blessed are you, woman, who brought forth by your mouth
light for those in darkness.

5 Mary, the thirsty land in Nazareth,
conceived our Lord by her ear.[321]
You, too, O woman thirsting for water,
conceived the Son by your hearing.
Blessed are your ears that drank the source
that gave drink to the world.
Mary planted him in the manger,
but you [planted him] in the ears of His hearers.

6 Your word, O woman, became a mirror
in which He might see your hidden heart.[322]

---

320. Cf. Virg. 22.21.

321. Elsewhere Ephrem uses this imagery to elaborate a much broader parallel between Eve and Mary, cf. Eccl. 35.17, 49.7, cited by Beck, Mariologie, 33f. Graef notes the same idea in Zeno, cf. Graef, Mary, 56–59.

322. Ephrem frequently uses the image of the mirror as the transmitter of "knowledge, insight into otherwise hidden and invisible things;" cf. Beck, Spiegel, 5.

"The Messiah," you had said, "will come,
and when He comes, He will give us everything."[323]
Behold the Messiah for Whom you waited, modest woman!
With your voice . . .

. . .

your prophecy was fulfilled.

7   Your voice, O woman, first brought forth fruit,
before even the apostles, with the *kerygma*.
The apostles were forbidden to announce Him
among pagans and Samaritans.[324]
Blessed is your mouth that He opened and confirmed.
The Storehouse of life took and gave you to sow.
Into a city that was as dead as Sheol
You entered and revived your dead [country].

8   Blessed are you, O woman, . . .

. . .

Eve . . . Adam

. . .

Cluster . . . blessing
. . . clusters . . .
As . . .
. . . all of them ran to swallow it.

9   Eve had become a vine of death;
the sprouts from her first brought forth pains.
By desire she plucked the fruit that also
was first-ripe . . .

. . .

. . . was desirable

. . .

He ate . . .

10 Blessed are you, O Shechem, into which the hungry entered
to buy bread for the Sustainer of all.[325]
But you entered and gave the Living Bread,
the Truth who freely disclosed Himself.

---

323. Cf. John 4.25.
324. Matt. 10.5.
325. John 4.8.

Blessed are your fields that in the parable were whitened
and attained the blessed harvest.[326]
Ears of grain are not ripened, [but] souls were perfected;
they became zealous, were whitened and resembled you.

11 Blessed are you, O Shechem, beloved of righteous men.
Treasure . . . and treasury of symbols

. . .

[Joshua] made laws and judgments on Shechem;
in you Jesus is also named.[327]
This . . . the wood of our Savior.
Indeed how many blessings and symbols you recall!
Blessed is He who magnified you, our native land![328]

---

326. John 4.35.
327. Cf. Josh. 24.1–28; and Virg. 17.3.
328. In calling Samaria "our native land" Ephrem not only alludes to the land of the patriarch whose name he bears, Ephrem the son of Joseph, but he also confirms his identification of the Samaritans and Canaanites with the Gentile church, cf. Virg. 17–23. A postscript reads, "The two hymns on the Samaritan woman are completed."

24

This hymn returns to the theme of the first three of the collection: virginity, theologically understood. Ephrem contrasts the freedom, peace and happiness of the virginal state with the transitory joys of marriage (esp. str. 1, 8, 11, 12). The pangs of childbirth, the transitoriness of youthful beauty, and the shortcomings of human bridegrooms are specifically invoked (str. 5, 11, 12, 13). Several distinctive images are interwoven to illustrate the meaning of virginity. The virgin is a tree, her womb a nest in which the sparrow of chastity makes its home (str. 1, 3). The virgin as a tree easily passes over into the image of a shoot grafted onto the Tree of Life (str. 4). Yet she is also bride and temple and castle (str. 8, 10, 11). She contemplates the lasting beauty of God, as did Mary Magdalen and the prophetess Anna (str. 7, 10). A complex array of bird imagery is linked to the trees as well as to the heavenly heights: Chastity, the bird who builds her nest high above the earth to protect her young, the virgins, from the serpent, Satan, is able to soar like the eagle upward to the heavenly bridal couch (str. 3). The virgin, or virginity or chastity—all grammatically feminine—is a dove that alights on the olive tree, symbol of Christ (str. 9).

24

On virginity, to the same melody
1 Blessed are you, virgin, with whom
the comely name of virginity grows old.
In your branches chastity[329] built a nest;
may your womb be a nest for her dwelling place.
May the power of mercy preserve your temple.[330]

---

329. "Holiness," *qdyšwt'*, acquires the meaning of "chastity" in early Syriac literature. For chastity as a bird, cf. Virg. 1.6 and 2.1.
330. From Greek ναός.

May the voice of the Mighty One restrain your enemy
that you may be a good incentive for onlookers
forever and ever.

Refrain: . . .

2   Blessed are you . . . pearl
. . .

3   Blessed are you, heavenly sparrow
whose nest was on the cross of light.[331]
You did not want to build a nest on earth
lest the serpent enter and destroy your offspring.[332]
Blessed are your wings that were able to fly.
May you come with the holy eagles[333]
that took flight and soared from the earth below
to the bridal couch of delights.[334]

4   Blessed are you, O shoot that Truth cultivated;
He engrafted your medicine into the Tree of Life.
Your fruit exults and rejoices at all times
to drink the drink of the Book of Life.
Blessed are your branches . . .
. . .
. . . and was spoken . . .
. . .

5   Blessed are you, O bride, espoused to the Living One,
You who do not long for a mortal man.
Foolish is the bride who is proud
of the ephemeral crown that will be gone tomorrow.
Blessed is your heart, captivated by the love
of a beauty portrayed in your mind.[335]
You have exchanged the transitory bridal couch for the bridal couch
whose blessings are unceasing.

---

331. The cross of light is a symbol of paradise, cf. CNis 69.21 and HdF 18.11.2.
332. Cf. Virg. 2.3.
333. Cf. Azym. 17.11.
334. Ephrem's use of heavenly bridal imagery is reminiscent of the song of Judas Thomas in the *Acts of Thomas* 6–7.
335. Like the image of the mirror, the image of a painting or drawing is frequently used by Ephrem to speak of hidden things made apparent to the mind; cf. Beck, Bildtheologie, 244–49, and idem. Spiegel, 5–8.

6 Blessed are you, O ewe lamb who offered yourself,
   . . .

7 Blessed are you if you will be a daughter to Mary[336]
   whose eye scorned all persons.
   She turned her face away from everything
   to gaze on one beauty alone.
   Blessed is her love that was intoxicated, not sober,[337]
   so that she sat at His feet to gaze at Him.
   Let you also portray the Messiah in your heart[338]
   and love Him in your mind.

8 Blessed are you, peaceful woman, who as if on high
   stood and considered humankind.
   You saw the world, weary and distressed
   and utterly burdened with a wearisome yoke.
   Blessed is your beauty—free and not laboring at
   the unending service of [your] Betrothed.
   You chose the Bridegroom Whose splendor would adorn you
   and Whose dew would refresh you.[339]

9 Blessed too is that dove[340] who scorned
   splendid cedars[341] and cypresses.
   She took shelter[342] in the love of the blessed Olive Tree[343]
   that was the King's Son, your Betrothed.
   . . .

10 Blessed also is that Anna who hated
   her house and loved the Temple of her Lord.[344]
   She gazed intently at hidden beauty
   for eighty years but was not sated.
   Blessed is her gaze that she concentrated on the One.

---

336. Luke 10. 38–42.

337. Contemplation was described as "sober inebriation" in a variety of philosophical and religious texts of Late Antiquity, cf. Lewy, Sobria ebrietas.

338. Again, the language of portraiture is invoked, cf. Virg. 2.15 and 24.5.

339. The Syriac includes word play not easily reproduced in English: *dhdrh mhdr lky / wtlh mtl' lky* = Whose splendor would adorn you/ and Whose dew would refresh you.

340. Cf. Virg. 2.8.

341. With a different vocalization *'arzê*, "cedars," would become *'râzê*, "mysteries, symbols."

342. Again, a different vocalization makes *tpas*, "take shelter," into *tapes*, the denominative verb from *twps'*, "type."

343. Cf. Virg. 4–7.

344. Luke 2.36f.; Ephrem's calculation of Anna's eighty years in the Temple does not correspond to the scriptural account. "Temple" here is *hykl'*.

Put to shame by her are inattentive, foolish women.
But, noble woman, be modest and preserve your beauty
from all for the Lord of all.

11   Blessed are you, O castle, castle of the King,[345]
whose gate is greater than mortal beings.
The glorious King dwelt within you.
Let His love be a bulwark for your beauty.
Your womb escaped from the pangs of the curse.
By the serpent the pains of the female entered.[346]
Let the defiled one[347] be put to shame, seeing that
his pangs were not in your womb.

12   Blessed are you who have abstained,
for merry is the beginning, morose the end of this life.
It begins joyfully as an adventure;
it ends mournfully as a deception.
Blessed is your heart that hated the world
that, while beginning, has passed away and ceased to exist.
Beauty blossoms for the foolish woman and makes her proud,
but it fades and makes her downcast.

13   Blessed are you, free woman, who sold yourself
to the Lord Who became a servant for your sake.
A free woman serves a husband who wanders
and wrongs her love . . .
Blessed . . .
. . .[348]

---

345. Mary, mother of Jesus, may be meant here. "Castle" is *byrt'*.
346. Gen. 3.16. If Mary is addressed here, Ephrem alludes to the notion of her painless childbirth in the following lines; cf. Od. Sol. 19.6–10, and Prot. 18–19.
347. Satan, cf. HdP 12.11.
348. The fourteenth strophe is too fragmentary to translate.

25

Although the manuscript identifies the subject of this hymn as "the very blessed disciple," it has as its broader concern the presence of Christ in all his followers. John, identified with the "beloved disciple" of the fourth gospel, and Mary, the mother of Jesus, are types through whom we are able to see Christ as in a mirror while they themselves saw him in one another (str. 9). After a brief plea to share in the love of Christ for the beauty of the beloved disciple (str. 1), Ephrem turns to the Johannine account of the crucifixion, where Jesus invites Mary and John to regard one another as mother and son. The love and care that flowed from Mary to her Son are echoed by the love of Jesus for John and repaid by entrusting her to his care (str. 2–3). John shows a special resemblance to Jesus, Ephrem assumes, because he takes Jesus' place as Mary's son. But a deeper ethical mystery is contained here: The love of John for his Lord led him to imitate him, thus bringing into higher relief the *imago dei* engraved on each human being (str. 4). Through John's resemblance to his Lord, Christ remains present to his mother, and similarly he makes himself present to all who seek him (str. 5–6).

The images of earthly rulers, in contrast to the rulers themselves, are without speech or reason. The situation is reversed for God and God's human images: The Divine Being is beyond speech and rational analysis, but humans speak; they are God's harps (str. 7). Scriptural examples, then, give us access to the inscrutable mysteries of God. Just as in one another Mary and John see the complementary mysteries of God's condescending love for us and the bold access to divine love now open to human beings, so also, through them, we may see this twofold mystery of our Savior (str. 8–9). Just as John and Joseph recognized that Mary was the temple and tabernacle in which God dwelt, we should recognize Christian virgins, betrothed to Christ, as his temples, symbols of the mystery of the incarnation (str. 10–11). The incarnation is an unfathomable mystery (str. 11–12): When Jesus healed Peter's mother-in-law and when as an infant he was presented to the prophetess, Anna, He was in reality the Creator of the world and the Source of prophecy (str. 13–16). King

Solomon with his thousand wives is a type of Christ, Who is spiritually betrothed to many thousands of virgins, the first of whom is Anna (str. 16–18).

25

On the very blessed disciple, thirteenth on the same melody

1 Gracious One, Who condescended to give Himself
even to the odious that they might be adorned by Him,
make me also worthy to be adorned
by the handsome beauty of Your disciple.
In this one You loved[349] let me take refuge to find mercy.
Let me praise the one You cherished that I may be pleasing.
Let me therefore sing his love that You might reward me
with mercy rather than [just] wages.

Refrain: Glory to the Omnipotent One!

2 Blessed are you, O woman, whose Lord and son
entrusted[350] you to one fashioned in His image.
The Son of your womb did not wrong your love,
but to the son of His bosom[351] He entrusted you.
Upon your bosom you caressed Him when He was small,
and upon His bosom He also caressed him,
so that when he was crucified He repaid all you had advanced to
    Him,
the debt of His upbringing.

3 For, the Crucified repaid debts;[352]
even yours was repaid by Him.[353]

---

349. John 13.23, 19.26, 20.2, 21.7, 21.20.
350. The Syriac redundantly adds "and gave." Cf. John 19.26.
351. "Womb" in the previous line and "bosom" here are both '*wb*', in contrast to *ḥdy*' in the next two lines. Cf. John 13.23, 21.20.
352. Cf. Col. 2.13–14.
353. Although the scriptural reference suggests that Mary's debt to God as a member of sinful humanity is meant, the last lines of the previous strophe indicate that the human debt of Jesus to his mother is meant.

He drank from your breast[354] visible milk,
but he [drank] from His bosom hidden mysteries.[355]
Confidently He approached your breast;
confidently he approached and lay upon His bosom.
Since you missed the sound of His voice, He gave you his harp
to be a consolation to you.

4 The youth who loved our Lord very much,
who portrayed [and] put Him on and resembled Him,
was zealous in all these matters to resemble Him:
in his speech, his aspect and his ways.
The creature put on his Creator,
and he resembled Him although indeed he did not resemble what
      He was.
It is amazing how much the clay is able to be imprinted
with the beauty of its sculptor.[356]

5 He left you yet did not leave you, since in His disciple
He returned and came to dwell with you.
Gracious is He who undertook sending Himself
to those far away although He was there.
His will descends to everyone;
He sends His love to every region.
Although He is hidden from all, to everyone who seeks Him
He is entirely present.[357]

6 Since He saw that you could not wean your love
from that infant whom you weaned,
He imprinted Himself, and the pure one represented the Innocent
      One
that in His disciple you might see
  . . .
  . . . that it is fitting the image is portrayed.

---

354. The Syriac is *tdky*.
355. That Judas was to be the betrayer, cf. John 13.21–30, cf. Azym. 14.11, Cruc. 3.15, as noted by Beck, but surely more is meant.
356. Virg. 2.15.
357. It is not clear whether the presence of Christ is mediated only through other human beings, like John, who resemble him, or whether it may be attained through a more general presence of God in the world, as this line seems to imply.

An articulate one stood for the Silent One
Who was judged and did not speak.[358]

7   All the images of kings are silenced
although their lords are very articulate.
The images of our Savior are a wonder
since their wills are their harps.[359]
The Word of that glorious Silence is
He whose manner of being cannot be spoken.[360]
The creature utters a sound, rather than the Father and the Son
Who dwell in one another and are Silent.[361]

8   The youth in the woman was seeing
how much that Exalted One was lowered,
how He entered [and] dwelt in a weak womb
and emerged [and] was suckled with weak milk.[362]
The woman also wondered at how much He grew
that He went up and lay upon the bosom of God.
The two of them were amazed at one another, how much they were
      able
to grow by grace.

9   You, Lord, Whom they saw in . . .
while observing one another:
Your mother saw You in Your disciple;
And he saw You in Your mother.
Oh, the seers who at every moment
see You, Lord, in a mirror[363]
manifest a type so that we, too, in one another
may see You, our Savior.

10   With awe and tenderness the youth honored
the Temple in which You dwelt, to teach us
that today the King's Son dwells

---

358. Mark 14.61 et par.

359. For the free will as virtually the *imago dei*, cf. Beck, Reden, 64–74, esp. 65, n.2; but for other aspects of the *imago dei*, cf. Kronholm, Motifs, 45–51.

360. In Syriac as in Greek, reason and speech are synonymous, as are rationality and the capacity to speak; the capacity to speak of the God's manner of being would imply the capacity to comprehend the divine essence.

361. HdF 11.6.

362. Nat. 4.146–213, Nat. 5.19–24.

363. Those who see Christ are like mirrors, reflecting his image to others; cf. Beck, Spiegel, and idem, Bildtheologie, 268–73.

in holy virgins.[364]

The discerning person who perceives she is a temple
is terrified of dishonoring Your betrothed.
Oh, how grievous to dare
to dishonor the King in His Temple!

11 Joseph and also John honored
Your mother's womb as a symbol.[365]
It is the symbol of the Tabernacle, the temporal Tabernacle,
in which Emmanuel was dwelling.[366]
Both of them persist in admonishing us
not to belittle God in His temples.
A dispute! How frightful that by our investigation
we should measure that immeasurable Height![367]

12 A depth unable to be fathomed by inquirers!
A height too high for mortals!
A length unable to be gauged in cubits!
A breadth not measurable in handspans!
If you had the wings of seraphim,
you would by no means be able to measure
the Infant in his crib—contemptible in His appearance
but great in His secret reality.

13 Blessed are you, sick mother-in-law of Simon,
whom the Physician on high came down to visit.[368]
Although He approached, it was not to touch your hand,[369]
for He is the One Who stretched out all the veins.
He buried the fever in them.
The source of perspiration partook of their[370] fire.
By the glance of their Lord the two of them
both conquered and were conquered in the one body.

14 In your sick body dwelt a fever,

---

364. Cf. Nat. 17.5–6. Christ is also present in male virgins, CNis 46.1, cf. Beck, Mariologie, 37.

365. Cf. Nat. 16.16.

366. For Mary as the Ark of the covenant, cf. Nat. 4.113, and 16.16.

367. As Beck notes, this is an anti-Arian polemic; cf. HdF 4.17.

368. Mark 1.29–31 et par.

369. Mark 1.30 and Matt. 8.15, but cf. Luke 4.39, where Jesus does not touch her hand.

370. I.e., the veins' fire. Perspiration was seen as a cure for fever, as Beck notes, cf. Epiph. 7.16.

hidden, invisible fire.
In your Physician's body [dwelt] the fire of the height,[371]
visible only to spiritual beings.
This is a wonder, and who is able to speak of it?—
that the fervor of mercy entered, cooled and healed you.
The listeners were amazed at the perfection that allayed
the intensity of her fever.

15 Blessed are you, fair old Anna,
whom the silent Infant made a prophetess,[372]
for His hidden silence roared in your mind
so that in you He might sing of His exploits.
In you He interpreted His deeds as a child,
but He will complete them Himself as an adult—
the Infant Who, although silent, sang in every tongue,
Who is the Lord of all mouths.

16 Blessed are you, old woman, treasure of perception,[373]
whom this ancient Babe met.
You, therefore, old woman, he espoused first of all,
the Babe Who came to espouse souls.[374]
He made you the first of all of them,
and by your old age he put childishness in its proper place.
He polished a mirror [and] set it up for children
to learn modesty.

17 King Solomon took fully a thousand
wives—a very licentious thing![375]
Our glorious Lord made disciples of myriads of myriads
Of virgins—a powerful, splendid thing!
In this son of David was seen a singular thing,
But in You, Son of David, took place a miraculous thing!
O, Son of Isaiah, from whose seed two sons[376]
. . .

---

371. Christ as a fiery coal, cf. Nat. 6.13. 9.15, 11.5 and HdF 10.10.
372. Luke 2.36–38; cf. Nat. 6.13–14.
373. Cf. Virg. 22.5.
374. For Christ as the Bridegroom of souls, cf. CH 17.5.
375. 1 Kgs. 11.3.
376. For Isaiah's two sons and their symbolic names, cf. Isa. 7.3–4 and 8.1–4; a lacuna in the manuscript leaves Ephrem's thought incomplete.

18   Solomon was unruly as to his will,[377]
a fruit of the earth as to his root.
The will of the unsullied Child is pure,
and His nature is as pure as His Begetter.[378]
The flock of the pure Lamb is also chaste,
The herd of the licentious one is unruly.
The daughters of Tyre led him astray,[379] but, as it is written,
a daughter of Tyre worshipped You.[380]

---

377. On the importance of the will, cf. Nat. 1.98, Virg. 20.5, 25.7 and notes ad loc.

378. Ephrem does not distinguish the divine from the human will in Christ. This in conjunction with his bold kenotic imagery made his hymns especially open to the interpretation of later so-called Monophysite thinkers such as Philoxenus, cf. Beck, Reden, 89–91.

379. 1 Kgs. 11.1–8, esp. 11.1, where only Sidon is mentioned, not Tyre.

380. Mark 7.25–26. A postscript reads, "Completed is one hymn on the disciple whose blessedness was great."

26

Resuming the theme of spiritual marriage to Christ that ends the previous hymn, Ephrem looks at a series of women in the New Testament whom he characterizes as spiritual brides of Christ. From him as Creator and Lord they had received all; out of his gift each of them gave to him as a human being (str. 16.5–6). This relationship is symbolic of marital intimacy (str. 16). In addition each woman teaches a particular lesson. In Mary, mother of Jesus, are portrayed "the childlike daughters of the innocent Eve," the Christian virgins (str. 1). Martha, Mary and Lazarus, respectively, are remembered for having fed Jesus, having received his teaching and having been restored to life by him (str. 2). But Martha herself is praised for her outspokenness as well as for her service (str. 3). The anointing of Jesus by the sinful woman, perhaps to be identified here with Mary, sister of Martha, is placed in a line with priestly and royal messiahship, as well as being a model of forgiveness (str. 4). The woman who cried out to Jesus, "Blessed is the womb that bore you" is the means for encouraging all to pursue God's blessing (str. 5). The healing of the woman with the hemorrhage is a model of the healing of hidden anger (str. 6). The parable of the widow's mite warns us against greed disguised as prudence (str. 7–8). The Syro-Phoenician woman represents the faith of the Gentiles (str. 9). The widow whose son was resurrected without her request reminds us that the Son saved the creation by his free act, not in response to our entreaties (str. 10). The girl raised by Jesus is a model of simplicity (str. 11). The mother of James and John is praised for her foresight in anticipating the role of Jesus as judge (str. 12–13). Finally, the wife of Pilate, who judged Jesus, is another model of Gentile faith (str. 14–15).

Clearly Ephrem has sought out women from the New Testament as models for Christian behavior. Surprisingly, in cases where the gospel account seems to imply a reproach from Jesus to the woman, Ephrem seems unaware or ignores this feature (str. 3, 5, 9, 12–13). Further, several times he praises the woman for her boldness in speaking, even in the case of the Syro-Phoenician woman, whom he perceives as correcting Jesus' overly narrow view of salvation only for the Jews (str. 2, 9, 12–13).

26

Fourteenth on the same melody

1 The Gracious One Who coaxed me to speak the blessings
that His mouth announced . . .
. . . opened [my] mouth
not to investigate but to confess
that One Who sprang forth from Mary to portray by her
the childlike daughters of Eve, the innocent Eve.[381]
I shall sing for Your advent the blessings of chaste women
that I may be worthy of association with You.

Refrain: To You be praises from all!

2 Blessed are you, Martha, who without fear
served the One feared by all.[382]
You nourished the Storehouse Who freely gives
living bread to humankind,
Blessed is your sister whom He made tranquil and taught,[383]
and your brother who was strengthened and revived.[384]
By you[385] He stirred up the divided, the disunited,
to be united in one love.

3 Blessed are you, Martha, to whom love gave
the confidence that opened your mouth.[386]
By the fruit Eve's mouth was closed
while she was hidden among the trees.[387]
Blessed is your mouth that sounded forth with love

---

381. Mary is so strongly portrayed as the second Eve that she is simply called "the innocent Eve." Cf. Beck, *Mariologie*, passim.
382. Luke 10.38–42.
383. Luke 10.39.
384. John 11.1–44.
385. Martha, Mary and John. The Syriac is plural.
386. Luke 10.40.
387. Gen. 3.8.

at the table at which God reclined.
You are greater than Sarah who served the servants,[388]
for you [served] the Lord of all.

4 Blessed are you, woman, most enviable of women,
who kissed the holy feet![389]
Your hands anointed the holy Anointed
Whose horn priests and kings had anointed.
Blessed are your sufferings that were healed by the Word
and your sins that were forgiven by a kiss.[390]
He taught His church to kiss in purity
[His] all-sanctifying body.[391]

5 Blessed are you, woman, whose voice became
a trumpet . . . among the silent.
A blessing you gave to the pure womb
that carried the Lord of blessings.[392]
Blessed are you to whom as the representative of others
He handed over the blessing He gave you in conversation.[393]
The blessing that He gave you He made a part of the whole
so that all would pursue it.

6 Blessed are you, woman! The flow of mercy
met you and healed the flow of your blood.[394]
That Sun Who dispelled from souls
the frost of the hidden death—
its hidden flash radiated and dried up
every fresh anger the mind perceives.[395]
With the tip of your finger, you tasted the healing of the springs
of the Sea of benefits.

7 Blessed are you, woman, living in poverty,
who put two treasures on High.[396]

---

388. Gen. 18.6.
389. Luke 7.38, 45; the parallel versions all lack this detail.
390. Luke 7.45–48. Although the anointing is in all four gospels, only Luke identifies the woman as a sinner and includes this detail.
391. This might refer to sacramental practice.
392. Luke 11.27.
393. Luke 11.28.
394. Mark 5.25–34 et par.
395. The flow of blood represents hidden anger.
396. Mark 12.41–44; cf. Luke 21.1–4.

It is a wonder on which Greatness gazed.
His eye reached out to the contemptible thing.
The two obols were weighed and they surpassed
a talent on God's scale.
Her life depended on the obols she lent,[397]
and, impoverished, she stood [there].

8 Who is not reproved by greed?
And in whom is not hidden a foul manner of life?
Who has not stored up and set [aside] too much,
so that it reproaches him that he has not been purified?
Let one who resembles you, O widow, praise you,
for my mind is too poor[398] to gaze at you.
By your poverty is convicted and exposed
the provision of our greed.

9 You, too, daughter of Canaan, for righteousness
conquered the Unconquerable One by boldness.[399]
The Just One set a boundary on the land of the Gentiles
that the gospel might not cross over.[400]
Blessed are you who broke through the obstacle fearlessly.
The Lord[401] of boundaries praised you for the strength
of your faith.[402] From afar He healed
your daughter in your house[403]

10 Blessed are you, too, O widow,
for the world was dead, and your son was dead.[404]
But your son revived without entreaty,
and without prayer the creation was saved.
Your wailing did not summon the Physician,
nor did our prayer make our Savior bend down.

---

397. As Beck has suggested, she "lent" them since she put them "on High"; cf. Virg. 26.7.2, just above.

398. Here Ephrem puns on "reproved," *bsyr* (in the first line of the strophe), and "poor," *bsyr*.

399. Matt. 15.21–28, cf. Mark 7.24–30. Ephrem also praises the woman at the well of Shechem for her boldness, cf. Virg. 22.5–9.

400. Matt. 10.5f.

401. Beck's Syriac text has plural here, apparently a misprint.

402. Matt. 15.28.

403. Mark 7.30.

404. Luke 7.11–17.

Mercy made Him condescend—the One Who came down and gave
    life
to the world and to the youth.[405]

11 Blessed are you, too, young girl,[406]
[you] who are like a mirror of simplicity.
He brought you to life and nourished you,[407]
for childhood is in need of learning.
The girl who was dead is a symbol of the innocent flock.
Our Lord brought to life from the dead [Jewish] people
a sleeping corpse as a symbol of the youthful soul.
He summoned them and she was revived.[408]

12 Blessed are you, woman, who, seeing
  . the Son seated, did not hesitate.
Doubtless His seat was contemptible and insignificant,
but you were not confused as the daughter of a woman.[409]
Blessed are you who saw in your understanding the glorious
    judgment seat
and you saw places for your beloved [sons].[410]
Like you are the mothers who join
their sons to our Savior.

13 Blessed are you, woman, who while our Lord
was on earth, saw Him on high.
Your love was exalted and broke through heaven
and saw the Son on the right hand.
Blessed is your gaze! How great its range
that it measured that immeasurable mountain.
From within His smallness your faith
saw His greatness.

14 That woman also, wife of the just man
who sat in judgment of the Judge of all—

---

405. Ephrem puns on *'lm'*, "world," and *'lym'*, "youth."
406. Mark 5.21–43 et par.
407. Luke 8.55. The other accounts lack this detail.
408. The verb must be read as 3 sg. fem. with one ms., since the girl, her corpse and her soul are all grammatically feminine.
409. I.e., as a human being; the expression is the feminine counterpart to the more common and supposedly generic "son of man."
410. Matt. 20.20–28; cf. Mark 10.35–45, where James and John make their own request.

dreams tormented her, visions upset her.[411]
A beckoning Watcher[412] in her dream took pity on her;
he found faith in her and increased it.
To the shame of the [Jewish] people the daughter of Gentiles
        shouted out.
Jerusalem cried out against the Good One, "Let Him be
        crucified!"[413]
But she [cried out], "Let Him be spared!"[414]

15   A wonder are you, woman, and also your spouse,
who washed his hands upon his judgment seat.[415]
Waves . . . of a pure dream
purified and cleansed you, too, in sleep.
The Gentiles were gleaming and purified and cleansed,
but the [Jewish] people were blackened and defiled by that
blood . . . the lamb put on light,
but the kid [put on] darkness.

16   Blessed, then, are all of you, O chaste women,
the church that was joined [in marriage] to the Son.[416]
It is a wonder how much the Holy One condescended
so that women might be joined [in marriage] with honor.
They received from His bounty, and they gave to Him and
        nourished Him.[417]
From His gift they reached out to Him and satisfied Him.
He gave us a refined symbol in His intimacy.
Glory to His purity![418]

---

411. Matt. 27.19.
412. An angel; cf. Nat. 1.61, 4.199.
413. Matt. 27.22f.; cf. Mark 15.13f., et par.
414. Cf. Matt. 27.19.
415. Acts of Pilate 4.
416. Ephrem puns on *nkpt'*, "chaste women," and *nqyp'*, "joined."
417. For a similar idea relative to Mary's care of Jesus in the womb and as an infant, cf. Nat. 4.182–86.
418. A postscript reads, "Completed is the one hymn about the women disciples, those who were joined (in marriage) to our Lord."

27

Just as the twenty-fifth hymn of this collection ended by contrasting the "sons of David," Solomon and Jesus as bridegrooms, this hymn begins by contrasting these two as musicians. Whereas Solomon's music is associated with false worship, Jesus' music brings joy to the entire creation (str. 1–2). In the fourth strophe Ephrem introduces the central theme of this hymn and of the three which follow: The music of Christ is played on three harps—the Old and New Testaments and nature (str. 4.4–6). Whereas Jews, heretics and pagans play only one harp or choose inappropriate musical instruments, the church plays the three harps of Christ (str. 3–4). Just as Christian baptism in three names is a touchstone of orthodoxy, so is the playing of the three harps, meaning a theology that teaches a God who is at once the God of the Jewish scripture, Father of Jesus Christ and Creator of the universe (str. 4). Ephrem identifies himself as one who qualifies both with respect to his baptism and his playing of the three harps (str. 5). At the end of time three groups will praise God with music: the resurrected, the elect who have not died, and the angels. Evil will be silenced (str. 6).

27

Fifteenth on the same melody
1   Solomon in his wisdom made harps
    by which the Queen of Sheba was amazed.[419]
    She heard that he had been led into sin, and she scoffed;[420]
    he delighted the demons with his songs.[421]

---

419. Cf. 1 Kgs 10.12f.; cf. Ginzberg, Legends, IV, 143–49, 152, 300.
420. According to the biblical account Solomon was led into sin by his wives, cf. 1 Kgs. 11.1–8, but Ephrem may mean by the music of the pagan cults. Cf. HdF 83.6, where he says that Solomon became a pagan.
421. Cf. 1 Sam. 16.14–23, where, by contrast, David's playing drives away the demons.

The faithful son of David Himself came,
and He made glorious harps.
The creation listened, heard and was overjoyed
by the sound of His promises.

Refrain: Blessed is the One Who makes all wise.

2 Solomon sinned . . .
Our Lord condescended to the foolish one,
the soul intoxicated with idolatry.[422]
The demon made it drunk with his song,
with trumpet and flute and cymbal.[423]
The Son of David came . . .

. . .

3 [The Jews and others played][424]
on harps in various ways.
The circumcised chose for themselves the harp of Moses,
and the others each [chose] his harp.
The unclean stole[425] and took numerous stringed [instruments].
Droning they took to be equal to song.
As bees in their hives they droned
as a symbol of blasphemy.[426]

4 Blessed are you, O church, whose congregation
sings with three glorious harps.
Your finger plucks the harp of Moses
and [the harp] of our Savior and [the harp] of nature.
Your faith plays the three [harps],
for three names baptized you.
You were not able to be baptized in one name nor
to play on one harp.

5 I, who have believed that they are as one
and also from One and by means of One,

---

422. Since the soul is grammatically feminine, Ephrem continues to play on the bridal imagery of Virg. 25.17–18 and Virg. 26.
423. An allusion to pagan cult as per Beck, Virg. 13.8, CJ 1.16.
424. The text is absent, but the following lines make this the probable sense of the missing line, as per Beck.
425. The Syriac adds "and took."
426. Beck has noted similar expressions in polemics against Mani, Marcion and Bardaisan in CH 1.11, 1.17 and 52.3.

I have honored Moses, I have worshipped the Son
and I have professed that nature is pure.[427]
You have baptized me in the faithful names,
and you have handed me the glorious harps.
By them I have been made worthy of your coming, O Bridegroom,
You Who have been revealed . . .

6   The dead who came out of their graves[428]
will sing glory on their kitharas.
The living who fly up in their chariots[429]
will sing glory with their harps.
The watchers will blow their horns.
The evil ones will inherit a shutting of the mouth.
Since I have no [more] voice, sing in me that I may sing for you.
Glory to your advent.[430]

---

427. Against Mani and Marcion, as per Beck, CH 28.7 and 10, CH 45.9.

428. 1 Thess. 4.16.

429. 1 Thess. 4.17, where the living fly up in or with the clouds; for the clouds as chariots, cf. HdP 1.7 as per Beck.

430. A postscript adds, "Completed is the one hymn on the Queen of Sheba and on Solomon."

28

This is the first of three hymns developing the theme introduced in the previous hymn: the three harps of God. Here more fully than anywhere else, Ephrem has elaborated the essential features of his symbolic theology.[431] This first hymn is addressed to Christ, who is portrayed first as the musician sounding the varied strings of the three harps (str. 1). But the imagery shifts quickly to the visual arts and especially to imperial portraiture. The symbols of the Torah, the prototypes of the gospels, and the powers and signs of nature are like pigments mixed by Christ, the Painter, to portray not only himself but also his Father (str. 2). The types and prophecies of the Old Testament are like preliminary drawings, which are covered over by the paints (str. 3–4). He is the Light illuminating the shadows (str. 5). Like the king entering a distant region of his realm, his images pale beside his actual presence; yet, in contrast to his enemies, the faithful subjects of the king would never destroy those images (str. 6, 10). Even when a new image of the king is sculpted to replace the obsolete images made in earlier years, the old image is not destroyed (str. 10.4–8). These are lessons for the Jews and for the Marcionites. Because the former misunderstood and abused the kingship, they no longer have a king (str. 7–9). The latter mistakenly view the images of the king as rivals for the king and thus want to destroy his images when they realize they are inferior to the king himself or obsolete (str. 5–6, 10–12). The church recognizes the differences between the unchanging name and nature of God, on the one hand, and the names of the divine virtues and the transformations undergone for the sake of love in the incarnation, on the other hand (str. 11, 13).

---

431. Beck, Bildtheologie, 256; for analysis of these three hymns, cf. ibid. 248–54.

28

The sixteenth on the same melody

1 Who has ever sung the wonder and the miracle
and sounded altogether myriads of strings,
and mixed into wisdom the old
and new with the natural?[432]
The image of the Creator was hidden in them;
upon them openly You portrayed Him.
From all of them[433] appeared the Lord of all
and the Son of the Lord of all.

Refrain: Glory to Your hiddenness!

2 The scattered symbols You have gathered
from the Torah toward Your beauty,
and You set forth the prototypes in Your gospel
and powers and signs from nature.[434]
You mixed pigments for Your portrait.
You were observed by Yourself and You portray Yourself,[435]
O Painter Who also portrayed His Father in Himself!
The Two portray One Another.

3 Prophets, kings and priests, all of them created,
have portrayed You, though they were unlike You.
Created servants are not at all sufficient,
for You alone are sufficient to portray Yourself.
Your portrait has been fully drawn.[436]
You perfected it by Your advent.
The drawings were swallowed up by the strength of the pigments,
resplendent in all colors.

4 Faded is the drawing of the temporal lamb.

---

432. The strings played are on the harps of the Old and New Testaments and of nature; cf. Virg. 27.4, 29.4–5, the colophon to Virg. 30, CH 40 and Beck, Bildtheologie, 248f.
433. *'(y)k* is otiose here and in Virg. 30.1, according to Beck.
434. That is, the *r'z* of the Torah, the *tpnk'* of the gospels, and the *ḥyl'* and *rwšm'* nature, cf. Beck, Bildtheologie, 249–54, but for different arrangements, cf. Virg. 20.12 and 30.1. Unlike the other terms, *tpnk'*, "original" or "prototype" is not used interchangeably with "type," "symbol" or "image," cf. ibid. 250–52 and Virg. 14.7.
435. The imagery of the mirror is added to the painting imagery, cf. Virg. 25.4–11, CH 32.17, and Beck, Bildtheologie, 249.
436. The root *ršm*, "to draw, engrave," is introduced here; cf. Beck, Bildtheologie, 256–59.

Resplendent is the glory of the True Lamb.
Very weak too is the drawing of the staff
. . . the cross of light
. . . and the fixed serpent:
in the wilderness it portrayed the crucified body.[437]
The transitory symbols have been completed and swallowed up
by the truth that does not pass away.

5   The daybreak that is from You, the dawn that is from You
confined and swallowed . . .
By the shining forth of Your advent the shadows have been
        illuminated.
The types have come to an end, but the allusions persist.
The flash of the symbols has been swallowed up by Your rays.
Your symbols have passed away, but Your prophets have not passed
        away.
The [Jewish] people have erred in their reading of the prophets,
and they maintained that You were not You.

6   For You, Lord, it is easy to make a symbol;
even scripture has an image and a table.[438]
The images of kings do not pass away
when the king comes to his region.
Kings who slaughter kings
also efface and destroy their images.
Since our King is exalted, His images are in His Temples
and His images are among His possessions.

7   The scribes killed the Son of the King.
. . . another king
. . .
But they were unable [to make] another king.
They wanted to but could not make Him king.[439]
Oh, that they might know Who did not allow it!

---

437. Cf. Num. 21.8–9. The brazen serpent was seen by many early Christian writers as a type of Christ crucified; Tertullian, especially, invokes the image in the context of anti-Marcionite polemics, cf. Tert. adv. Marc. 2.22, 3.18, and de idol. 5.

438. The Syriac *dp'* may mean "board, tablet, leaf of a diptych" or "table, wooden altar," the former meaning continues the artistic imagery, the latter introduces an allusion to the Eucharist, Margoliouth, 96a.

439. John 6.15.

How harsh is the necessity of our silent Lamb,
Who was slain and did not cry out for help![440]

8   They sought a king for themselves without a [divine] command.[441]
By force they wanted to lead God.
How often they have killed kings and made others,
and even others after them.
In seven days they killed two kings,[442]
and they have remained a long time without making another king.
Behold, Daniel taught, "He is killed and [the people]
had no other king again."[443]

9   The sword of Jezebel cut down prophets,[444]
but the sword of Jehu cut down her sons.[445]
The prophets of the Lord were massacred and discarded,
but the sons of the king were massacred and heaped up.
The prophets followed in order and did not cease;
the kings were generated and were not diminished.
What a disgraceful sight! that the source of those
who crucified our Fount has dried up.

10   When the king of a region enters it,
he adds a new image there,
the images that stood for him having been [merely] a shadow.
His lifestages pass away, but his images remain.
An image is sculpted for his maturity.
The prophets remain; His images do not pass away.
By the Spirit [the image] is sculpted for the maturity of that One
Who is portrayed in all the prototypes.

11   He is the glorious, immutable nature,
but because of His love, He acquired changes.[446]
Colors were put on: the symbols and types,
and also all the prototypes and all the lifestages.

---

440. Cf. Isa. 53.7 and Virg. 11.18.
441. Cf. 1 Sam. 10.19.
442. The allusion is unclear; possibly as in the Book of Daniel where a "week" is to be taken as seven years.
443. Cf. Dan. 9.26.
444. 1 Kgs. 18.4.
445. 2 Kgs. 10.7–11.
446. Cf. de Halleux, Mar Ephrem, esp. 45–47; and Beck, Reden, 77–95, esp. 87f.

The crucifiers saw Him and dishonored Him.[447]
The tares saw Him and made Him alien.[448]
The church has seen Him and, while knowing His nature,
worships His changes.

12 [God] saw, therefore, and dishonored that teaching
that refutes its [own] words of its own accord,
For the "Good" it called the "Alien,"
a name that is [to be taken] as opposed to His creature.
[These are] perceptions Marcion propounded for us—
[Marcion] by whom "Just" and "Good" and "Evil" are denied.
Let Your scripture confute him,
for the names of the Alien are not in Your book.

13 If He has no alien name,
He also has no impulse to alienation.
But if He had no name for His substance,
neither would He have a nature proper to Himself.
Our God has a name and a nature.
His names indicate His virtues:
Just by His word and God by His gifts
And Lord in His possessions.

14 Names are the simplest of all
But . . .

        . . .

        . . .

Our Lord's deeds and His names
that demand worship . . .
. . . necessarily depends
on the name of our God.

---

447. The Jews are meant.
448. The Marcionites are meant, as the following strophe makes clear.

29

Once again, the theme of this hymn is the three harps—this time with the emphasis on the harp of nature and the consistency of its song with the music of the two harps of scripture (str. 1–2). Anti-Marcionite polemics play an especially prominent role here. The raising of Lazarus shows, for example, that the Father of Jesus is not "Alien" but is the same as the Creator, since the resurrected human nature is essentially the same as created human nature (str. 2–3). Although the "temporal harp" of the Old Testament is inferior to the "true harp" of the New Testament, they play many of the same themes. Ephrem shows that some themes characteristic of the supposedly inferior God of the Old Testament are echoed in the New Testament: God's regret and the language of sacrifice (str. 4–7). In addition, the harps of the Old Testament and nature proclaim the same Lord (str. 9). All three harps agree that some animals are despicable and that only the human being is universally honored (str. 11). Yet because the harp of Moses and the Law were too old and weak to restrain human licentiousness, God replaced Moses with Jesus (str. 10, 12, 13).

29

Seventeenth [on the same melody]
1 The Word[449] of the Most High came down and put on
a weak body with hands,
and He took two harps
in His right and left hands.
The third He set up before Himself
to be a witness to the [other] two,

---

449. Although "word," *mlt'*, is grammatically feminine, Ephrem sometimes treats it as masculine; cf. Beck, translation ad loc.

for the middle harp taught
that their Lord is playing them.

Refrain: Glory to Your wise [decrees]!

2   He played, and that third harp
was harmonious and completed the [other] two.
When He awakened and revived Lazarus,[450]
the former nature was not changed.
If it were an imperfect nature,
why did He not perfect it and [then] awaken it?
It would have been very simple to perfect
in its restoration what was corrupt and ruined.

3   See, therefore, that here too the "Alien"[451]
who awakened the dead was like the Creator.
It suffices that He did not fight against and change life,
but [rather] He changed the one who was awakened.
By one awakening He taught us three things:
of the Creator, of His servant . . .
   . . .
   . . .

4   Therefore our Savior played on that harp,
the old one of Moses and propounded its symbols.
   . . .

5   Your hands, our Savior, have two harps:
the temporal harp and the true harp.[452]
   . . .

He played new and old [songs].
How are symbolic mouths able to distinguish
wondrous tastes of every sort?
Whoever was sick was reproved, whoever was healthy was
      overjoyed
by the sound of succor.

6   But the harp of Moses also sang
that the Lord regretted having made humankind.[453]

---

450. John 11.
451. The Marcionite term for the Father of Jesus.
452. The Old and New Testaments, respectively.
453. Gen. 6.6.

The children of the left hand heard this and were perplexed.
They held that His nature was susceptible to regret.[454]
Likewise our Savior played the harp
that from Him the cup might pass away—[455]
[The cup] in which earlier He had rejoiced—and He clothed in a
      hated name
Simon who [said], "Far be it from me!"[456]

7   The harp of Moses played and sang,
"God loves sacrifices."[457]
The apostle sang about the Son
that He had been a sacrifice to the Father[458]
. . .

8   . . .

9   Who has ever seen two harps,
one silent and one endowed with speech?[459]
But the silence of that one, its preaching,
was not heard by rational [creatures].
For the silent one persuaded by deed,
but the one endowed with speech [persuaded] by sound.
By words and by deeds both,
they proclaimed the Lord of all.

10   . . .

. . .

Few understood their power.
The harp was weary, and its hearers did not perceive
the power of the parables.

11   Moses wrote that the serpent was hateful,[460]
and our Lord came and set a seal on this.[461]
Nature agreed with them since it hated [the serpent].

---

454. A Marcionite philosophical critique of the God of the Jewish scripture as anthropo-morphic.

455. Cf. Mark 14.36 et par.

456. Cf. Matt. 16.22.

457. Cf. Gen. 8.21 and the same issue against the Marcionites in CH 30.2 and 36.13, as noted by Beck.

458. Eph. 5.2 and the same citation and argument in CH 36.7, again noted by Beck.

459. The former is nature, the latter the Old Testament.

460. Gen. 3.14; as in str. 7 above, Beck has noted the same argument and counter argument in CH 43.4f.

461. Luke 10.19, and cf. CH 43.5, as per Beck.

The three voices agreed with one another.
To the Creator this animal was despicable,
but pigs were despicable to our Savior.[462]
Nature agreed with them that the human being alone is chosen
to be honored by all.

12   Error also constructed harps
that sweetly played [feigned] temperance,[463]
and they heard and were overjoyed like babes
whose wills are unbridled
and whose inner impulses were loosed
and whose untamed senses were overcome.
The voice of the Law became for them
the droning of a harp.[464]

13   [God] saw that the old man Moses could not
play this harp any more.
He put to rest and thrust out the obsolete old man
and He gazed at Jesus whose name was [new,
and all of the prophets] . . .
   . . .

---

462. Mark 5.13 et par.; cf. CH 43.6 as per Beck.
463. The allusion is to the teachings of Bardaisan, cf. Beck ad loc. CH 1.11 and 1.17.
464. Cf. Virg. 27.3.

30

Christ plays the three harps together blending their music into a harmony pleasing to healthy ears but unpleasant to the unhealthy (str. 1–3). Just as Saul could not endure the music of David, the Marcionites and Jews dislike the music of Christ, the Son of David (str. 2). But, in reality, the three voices are harmonious; by the miracles of the New Testament nature attests its unity with both Testaments (str. 4). The miracles of the New Testament teach a further lesson about human freedom: Specifically the taming of the sea, the incident with the Gadarene swine, and the cursing of the fig tree, in contrast to the treatment of the beloved disciple, teach us to appreciate our unique position in the creation as recipients of grace and freedom (str. 5–9). The hymn ends with an eloquent and paradoxical meditation on the incarnation: Christ is son of both the dead Adam and the living God; by being bound, he released those bound by sin; having lost the garment of his body in death, he sought and found it among the dead (str. 11–12).

30

1 But who has seen our Lord and admired
His playing on three harps?
He blends their counterpoint wisely
lest their hearers be alienated:
signs, symbols and prototypes,[465]
so that nature and scripture may convince.
With the one creation He bound together two Testaments
to put the doubters to shame.

---

465. For "prototype," cf. Virg. 14.7 and note ad loc. and Virg. 28.2.

HYMN 30

Refrain: Praise to the Omniscient!

2   Already drawn on the harp of David
was also the harp of the Son of David,
for while he played and sang,
Saul's melancholy ears could not endure [it];[466]
by the spirit within him Saul was saddened.
As Saul against David, therefore,
the ears of tares and scribes[467]
stood on end against the Son of David.

3   They heard, therefore, that the Lord of all was coming,
and they were confused as weak men.
How much the healthy melodies multiplied
for the healthy ear . . .

    . . .

but both new and old annoyed [the sick ear].
It therefore escaped and rejected all things of the Law
and most of the things of the Savior.[468]

4   If what makes you wander is the voice of Moses,
the voice of our Lord will gather you.
But if the two voices trouble you,
nature, with which they are bound together, will testify:
The sea and the wind and even death that has been conquered,[469]
the bread that is multiplied that persuaded those who ate it,[470]
so that dust might be the bread of doubters
who alienate the Judge of all.

5   Free human beings are not, then, more difficult
than that great sea that obeyed.
He dammed up with a Word the mouth that cried out
against sailors and ships.
He coerced the sea, the nature of which is subject.

---

466. 1 Sam. 19.9–10.

467. The tares are heretics, here the Marcionites; cf. Beck, Bildtheologie, 249f. The scribes are singled out as they are the ancestors of the leaders of rabbinic Judaism. Both Marcionites and Ephrem's Jewish contemporaries reject the Christological reading of the Old Testament.

468. The Marcionites rejected the Old Testament and most of the New Testament, retaining only a modified form of Luke's gospel and the Pauline epistles.

469. Mark 6.45–52 et par.

470. Mark 6.30–44 et par.

He did not coerce the generation whose will rules.
By the two of them[471] He taught compulsion and freedom,
nature and will.

6   Whatever is coerced, the force that coerces it
shows that its nature is to be commanded.
Whatever is contested, its contesting
teaches that it is entirely concerned with freedom.
He compelled the herd of swine and sent it,[472]
but He did not compel freedom to learn.
With demons and swine He taught us how much He loves
the human race.

7   He permitted the legion [of demons] as requested,[473]
to be dishonored in that herd of swine.
Our race He made great, and in John
He even caressed and put us on his breast.[474]
Although the evil one has freedom,
with a means that is not his He coerced him,[475]
for in himself[476] the defiled one rules
by the impulse of his freedom.

8   Let the synagogue learn that she is not more difficult
than the wind that is on the sea.
A fearful [wind] blew, but He coerced and bound it,[477]
[He] Who rebuked unrestrained freedom.
The substance[478] of the fig tree was fresh green;
He cursed the fig tree gratuitously to let us know;[479]
as a harsh Judge He encountered the fig tree to teach us
that toward us He is gentle.

9   Therefore while He is just, to us He is gracious,

---

471. The sea, on the one hand, free human beings, on the other. On human freedom, cf.
Nat. 1.98, Virg. 20.5, 25.7, and notes ad loc.
472. Mark 5.8 et par.
473. Mark 5.9–13, et par. "Legion" is normally feminine in Syriac, but here it is treated as
masculine.
474. John 13.25; cf. Virg. 25.
475. The "means" of coercing Satan is apparently the swine, as Beck suggests.
476. Or in his actual existence, his reality, his *qnwm'*. Since the apparent compulsion of
Satan in the expulsion of the demons from the swine is inconsistent with the free will that
Ephrem attributes to him, the incident is treated here as an exception.
477. Mark 6.45–52 et par.
478. Or "nature," *kyn'*.
479. Mark 11.20–25 et par.

and although He is indeed harsh, for us He is humble.
With respect to this fig tree He dealt
neither with grace nor with justice.
Let the oppressed cry then how much He oppresses.
. . . did not give

. . .

the Physician of His crucifiers.
10 With nails they fastened You, but You made them
like medicines for their pains.
They pierced You with a lance and water flowed forth,[480]
as the blotting out of their sins.
Water and blood came out to make them fearful
and to wash their hands with Your blood.
The Slain One gave water from His blood to His slayers
[so that] they would be purified [and] at rest.[481]
11 You are also the son of the dead and bound father,[482]
whom the Son of the Living Father released.
The Good One Who was bound released the bad.

. . .

The bound were released by One bound;
the crucifiers were saved by the Crucified.
For the crops that were stored up by sinners
there are springs of assistance.
12 The result of Your death is full of life.
You released the captives of Your captivity.
Your body You stripped off, my Lord, and as you lost it,
among the dead You descended and sought it.
Death was amazed at You in Sheol,
that You sought Your garment and found [it].[483]
O Wise One Who lost what was found
in order to find the lost![484]

---

480. John 19.34.
481. An allusion to baptism.
482. Adam.
483. On the imagery of garments, cf. Nat. 3.9, 28.7, Virg. 37.6 and notes ad loc.
484. The postscript reads, "Completed are the three hymn on our Lord's symbols that are seen in the Old and New [Testaments] and [in] nature."

31

Although the manuscript entitles this hymn, "On the Birth of Our Lord,"
it is more properly on the births of our Lord, which is to say, on baptism!
In his sermon on our Lord, Ephrem enumerates four births of Christ: the
generation from the Father, the birth from Mary in the incarnation, the
baptism by John, and the emergence from Sheol at the resurrection. Thus
the entire economy of salvation is encompassed by the notions of birth,
and conversely, baptism becomes symbolic of each of the stages of the
divine plan.[485] This hymn elaborates some of these ideas while arguing
the superiority of Christian baptism to the Jewish understandings of forgiveness. Beginning with the double birth of Christ, from the Father and
from Mary (str. 1), Ephrem proceeds to portray Christ as Good Steward,
High Priest, Hyssop, Sacrificial Lamb, Treasure, Rock, Balance, Justifying Wall, Levelling Gate, Yoke, Mirror, Cluster of Mercy, Staff of Wheat
and Skilled Sailor (str. 2–15). Throughout, he stresses the superiority of
grace to the Law (esp. str. 6), while still emphasizing the rigor of the final
judgment (esp. str. 9). He ends on a personal note with a paean to the
beauties of everyday life and a lament to the inadequacy of his hymns to
express due gratitude (str. 16–17).

31

ON THE BIRTH OF OUR LORD

To the melody, "I fear to chant glory"

1   Christ, You have given life to the creation by Your birth
that took place openly from a womb of flesh.
Christ, you dazzled understanding by Your birth
that shone forth from eternity from the hidden womb.[486]

---

485. Cf. Saber, Theologie, 98–101.
486. That is, the generation by God the Father; cf. Nat. 13.7, 21.7–8, 27.15 and 19.

I am amazed by You in two [ways]: The wandering find life in You,
but investigators[487] go astray in You.

Refrain: Glory to You, my Lord, and to Your Father!

2 Good Steward of Your merciful Father
in Your hand is the key of the treasury of His mercy.
You open [it] and make enter the offerings of all.
You open [it] and make emerge pardon for all.
Blessed is the one who put his offering into Your hand
and takes mercy in its place.

3 By You, then, Being Itself is served in the Holy of holies.
You took up the sacrifice and sprinkled the libation.
Do not reject our sacrifice due to flaws in it.
Our prayer is a sacrifice, and our libation is weeping.
Blessed is the one who sends up his sacrifices in Your hand
and the smell of whose incense is sweetened by You.

4 Purifying Sprinkling, Pardoning Hyssop,
Who pardons all their sins in a baptism of water!
All the sprinklings of the Levites are unable
to pardon one People with their weak hyssops.
Blessed are the peoples [whose] hyssop was the Merciful One,
Who purified them with mercy.[488]

5 Desirable Offering offered for us!
Sanctified Sacrifice which He offered: Himself!
Libation Who made the blood of calves and sheep pass away!
Lamb Who was the offering Priest for Himself!
Blessed is the One Whose intercession became a censer
and was offered by You to Your Father!

6 The Law of the People rejects outward blemishes;
the grace He chose for the peoples tolerates their blemishes.
Blemishes are not chosen by [grace]; it receives penitents.
Your beauty, Lord, without blemish will not espouse our blemishes,

487. That is, the Arians. This is Ephrem's usual designation of them; cf. Beck, Reden, 111–18.

488. Cf. Saber, Theologie, 46, 108.

Blessed is the one who cleanses his stains by Your hand
and makes himself entirely pleasing by You.[489]

7 Rich Treasure Who came to the needy!
Streaming Font Who flowed to the thirsty!
Wise Instruction Who came to the simple!
Memory Who chased error from the creation!
Blessed is the one who knows Who You are, O Christ,
and acquires You and was purchased by You.

8 Blessed are You upon Whom rests hope that was cut off.
You are the Rock on which is built the building of the peoples,
the Balance into which is gathered a distracted mind.
the Justifying Wall that stands before the weak.
Blessed is the one who perceives how and how much You have loved
   him
and who has wept and blushed that he has rejected You.

9 Levelling Gate that separates.
Therefore in this world everyone enters by it into truth,
but in the other world it separates and gives entry to life.
In this world His mercy equalizes; in the next He will separate by
   His judgment.
Blessed is the one who remembers His expulsion in every moment
and increases the provisions for his way.

10 The Reproving Furnace, Who does not receive the peoples
in the presence of the household of the People,
investigates, tests and separates.
The fraud of the People entered and was unmasked and rejected.
The truth of the peoples entered and was believed and chosen.
Blessed is the one who became judge for himself
and in You he reproved himself!

11 O Yoke Who set free the subjected freedmen,
deceased while performing a hidden service.
They hated the yoke of open service.
They sold their freedom, and they sold their service.
Blessed is the one who seized his captivity with Your help
and by You took captive his captivity.

---

489. In this strophe Jewish Law is strongly contrasted with the grace of Christ; for a thorough study of this issue in Ephrem's works, cf. Martikainern, Gerechtigkeit.

12 Clear Mirror[490] constituted for the peoples.
    They acquired a hidden eye, approached and contemplated it.
    They saw their hatred; they reproached them[selves].
    Their faults they scoured in it; their ornaments they beautified in it.
    Blessed is the one who confuted his hatred by Your beauty,
    and Your resemblance was imprinted on him.[491]

13 The Cluster of mercy, glorified in the vineyard,
    Who refused labor but seized [its] fruits
    for the one who gave Him gall, shared His sweetness.
    He was trampled and gave the medicine of life to the peoples.
    Blessed is the One Who gave drink from the sober grape[492]
    and was not despised in secret.

14 The beautiful Staff that grew among the ugly tares
    gave the bread of life without toil to the hungry.[493]
    He released the curse that held Him captive in Adam
    to eat by sweat the bread of pains and thorns.
    Blessed is he who eats from His blessed bread
    and makes pass away from him the curse.

15 Skilled Sailor Who has conquered the raging sea,[494]
    Your glorious wood is a standard; it has become the rudder of life.
    Your wind[495] of mercy blew; the ships set straight out
    from the raging sea to the harbor of peace.
    Blessed is he who has become a sailor for himself,[496]
    has preserved and brought forth his treasure [on dry land].

16 But remaining are all those things the Gracious One made in His
            mercy.
    Let us see those things that He does for us every day!
    How many tastes for the mouth! How many beauties for the eye!
    How many melodies for the ear! How many scents for the nostrils!

---

490. For the image of the mirror as a means to self-knowledge and moral improvement, cf. Beck, Spiegel, and idem, Bildtheologie, esp. 268–73.

491. Cf. Nat. 1.99, 12.3, 28.7 and notes ad loc.

492. On vineyard imagery, cf. Murray, Symbols, 95–130, and on sober inebriation, cf. Virg. 24.7 and note ad loc.

493. Cf. Nat. 4.31.

494. For the nautical imagery, cf. Virg. 20.1 and note ad loc.; for translation and comment on this strophe, cf. Murray, Symbols, 251f.

495. Or "Your Spirit of mercy."

496. Or "for his soul."

Who is sufficient in comparison to the goodness
of these little things?

17 Who is able to make thousands of remunerations in a day?
[Even] if there dwell in him a great spring of words,
he will be unable by words and melodies to make
the great remuneration of every hour,
O Gracious Cheated One, Who, although cheated daily,
does not cease to do good![497]

---

497. The postscript reads, "Completed is one hymn on the birthday of our Lord."

32

This hymn is a series of thanksgivings by persons and places related to the beginning of the synoptic gospels. Two theological themes appear consistently here: the wonder of the incarnation and the fulfillment of Old Testament types in Jesus. Nazareth, birthplace of Jesus, attests his divinity and humanity (str. 1). As remarkable as the fact that Simeon, "the old priest," is able to carry the divine Infant, is our ability to hold him in the Eucharist (str. 2). Egypt witnesses the fulfillment of the types of Joseph and Moses by Jesus (str. 4). John the Baptist passes on the priesthood to him (str. 5). Christ's victory over Satan's temptations is definitive (str. 6–7). The town of Bethsaida has given over her fishermen to Christ, the fisher of all (str. 8–9).

32

On the melody, "The heavenly assembly"

1 Nazareth thanks You that she was worthy of Your birth.
O Nazarene, she offers Your childhood a crown,
and she offers another crown to Your hiddenness.[498]
By Your conception in the womb, she was first aware
of Your pure woven garment
and Your pleasing plaited crown:
the name and the body that completed You.

---

498. Here Ephrem expresses poetically the divine and human aspects of Christ [without the technical terminology of post-Chalcedonian theology, of course]. Childhood, body and garment represent the humanity; hiddenness, the name and the crown represent the divinity.

HYMNS ON VIRGINITY

Refrain: Our Lord, make me worthy to send up praise
with the righteous on the day of Your coming.

2   O the old high priest,[499] ordered to bear Your strength.
Bearer, One borne Who resembles His bearers.
Infant Who adorns the arms of old age,
permit me, too, my Lord, to lift You up in Your bread.[500]
O Mountain Who [so] willed and was borne
that by handfuls Your sea might be contained
and Your fire embraced in the bosom.

3   With all infants I confess that He dwells in me.
With the blessed name of Nazareth He called a people.[501]
Into His kingdom and His glory may He have me enter with the
      just,
and among the fearful Watchers . . .
. . .
. . .
and with the children . . . He exulted.

4   Egypt thanks Him for He has made her worthy—
[she] who lifted Joseph the just into the chariot.
Behold the Lord of Joseph on a humble lap.
Moses the persecuted babe! Our Lord the persecuted infant!
Put to shame was Pharaoh who had threatened Moses,
and [put to shame were] Herod who plotted against our Lord
and Satan who by his instruments was mocked.[502]

5   Levitical lamp sent before the sun!
Servant who was ordered to baptize his Lord
but who waited for the Holy Spirit to descend
to dwell upon the Great One Who had become small!

---

499. The Syriac word used here, *kwmr'*, usually designates a pagan priest in contrast to a priest of Israel. Here Ephrem refers to Simeon, who is not a priest, but a prophet; cf. Luke 2.25–35. Nevertheless, he is seen by Ephrem as a transmitter of the Jewish priesthood to Christ; cf. Nat. 9.3, Virg. 15.7 and notes ad loc.

500. Ephrem refers to the eucharistic bread. Beck takes this as evidence that Ephrem's contemporaries received the bread in their hands. This is probable, cf. Virg. 33.7, but it is also possible that Ephrem speaks here as a deacon.

501. Ephrem seems to imply that Christians are known as Nazarenes or Nazoreans. This was generally true at an earlier time, but in this late fourth-century context probably constitutes evidence of the Jewish-Christian features of Syrian Christianity; on "Nazorean," cf. Brown, Messiah, 208–19, 223–25.

502. Cf. Matt. 2.

Let this persuade [us] that John who baptized Him was exalted,
and pardoned was the servant who bathed[503] Him;
sanctified [was] the river that received Him.[504]

6 The aspects of His temptations increase His crownings,
and three crowns will rejoice greatly three times
from the wilderness and the mountain and the pinnacle of the
    Temple:
The crown of His victory ascended to the Father Who sent Him
for the sake of our spirit that wandered and returned,
for the sake of our soul that was lost and was found,
for the sake of our body that sinned and was pardoned.[505]

7 It is sad and harsh for the evil one over whom You were victorious.
He went back and donned enticement in his humiliation,
and the perversity of his rebellious mouth was rebuked.
In the disciple, his instrument, he came to conquer but was
    conquered.
In the thief who betrayed You and was hanged
and that mouth that watered You and was shut off
and that lap that gathered and scattered.

8 Bethsaida offers a crown to the Fisher of all.[506]
The Fisher of all caught her to fish with her fishermen.
[Then] they made a catch for the belly but [now] for the kingdom.
Twelve fishermen went out; they caught the world.
They fished for kings from the sea of bile
and freemen from the abyss of desire
and servants from the trickle of evil.

9 City of fishermen, you who are [merely] a handful,
in the net you have gathered the inhabited earth by your fishermen
so that you kindled the fire of our Lord in the world.
You devoured and wiped away the handful of interwoven thorns;
you devoured the idols that did not breathe

---

503. A pun on ḥs', "pardoned," and sḥ', "bathed." John the Baptist is portrayed by Ephrem as a transmitter of the Levitical priesthood to Jesus, cf. Virg. 15.1–2.

504. Cf. Virg. 15.3 and note ad loc.

505. Ephrem uses the threefold temptation of Christ as an occasion to present his tripartite anthropology. Human beings consist of spirit, soul and body, and all three are redeemed through Christ. On Ephrem's anthropology, cf. Nat. 22.40 and note ad loc.

506. In this strophe Ephrem plays on various words formed from the root, ṣwd, "to catch" or "to fish." Further, cf. Nat. 4.35 and note ad loc.

and the sorcerors and diviners so they did not chant
the soothsayers and familiar spirits so they did not murmur.[507]

---

507. The postscript reads, "The end of one hymn on Nazareth."

The subject of this hymn is the so-called nature miracles, as opposed to healing miracles of Jesus. While these stories in themselves stress the dominion of Christ over nature, the hymn's emphasis on nuptial and royal imagery intensifies the triumphant eschatological tone. The initial strophes (str. 1–3) describing the wedding feast at Cana and the miracle of the changing of water into wine, introduce not only the theme of the Son's power over Nature but also the nuptial and *adventus* themes: The church is the bride of Christ and "in her magnificence she portrays [his] advent." His sovereignty over death and Sheol is illustrated by the raising of the widow's son in Nain (str. 4–5). The multiplication of loaves and the miraculous catches of fish show the abundance of His blessings as well as His might (str. 6–8). Finally, the walking on water is presented in conjunction with the triumphal entry into Jerusalem and the rout of the demons as a royal *adventus*, a victorious procession of the ruler of the sea and the land and the height and the depth (str. 9–10).

33

The second on the same melody
1 Let Cana thank You for gladdening her banquet!
The bridegroom's crown exalted You for exalting it,
and the bride's crown belonged to Your victory.
In her mirror allegories are expounded and traced,[508]
for You portrayed Your church in the bride,
and in her guests, Yours[509] are traced,
and in her magnificence she portrays Your advent.[510]

---

508. The mirror brings hidden and symbolic truths into visibility; further on "mirror," *mḥzyt'*, and "allegory," *pl't'*, cf. Virg. 11.1, 25.9 and 31.12 and Beck, Bildtheologie, esp. 264–73.
509. Ephrem uses two different words for guest here, *ḥrp* and *zmn*.
510. For the language of painting and drawing here, based on the roots *ṣwr* and *ršm*, cf. Nat. 8.2, Virg. 2.15, 24.5,7, 25.4–11, 31.12, and notes ad loc.

HYMNS ON VIRGINITY

Refrain: Make even me worthy that by Your garments I may enter, our Lord, Your glorious bridal chamber!

2 Let the feast thank Him for in multiplying His wine.
Six miracles were beheld there:
the six wine jugs set aside for water
into which they invited the King to pour His wine.
Blessed is the guest
who ignored the bride's beauty
to contemplate You, our Lord, [and] how fair You are.

3 "I am grateful to be found worthy to invite him among my guests—
that Heavenly Bridegroom Who descended and invited all.[511]
To enter His pure feast I am invited.
Among the generations I shall confess that He is the Bridegroom
      and there is no other,
and His bridal chamber is prior to the ages,
and His feast is rich and not wanting—
unlike my banquet that was lacking and He filled it."

4 Nain, may you worship Him; may you offer Him a crown.
With that dead man who lives may you crown life.[512]
The deed of our Lord is the crown of his crowning.
Death was crowned as it conquered the youth
who marched with his crowns into Sheol;
he completed the victory when he returned it
to that Voice Who summoned him and revived him.

5 Even dusty city walls were polished by the All-conquering.
Even the dark gates were gladdened by the All-smiting.
Even the mourning crowds were rejoicing in the All-merciful,
and those who had wept for the dead man, lifted up and carried[513]
      the living man.
He consoled the widow and made her rejoice,
and He gladdened the city and enlightened it,
but He made Sheol gloomy and sorrowful.

6 Let the field in which bread multiplied thank Him.[514]

---

511. Cana, personified as a woman, or possibly the bride, speaks. For nuptial themes in Ephrem and other early Syriac literature, cf. Murray, *Symbols*, 131–58.

512. Cf. Luke 7.11–17.

513. The Syriac reverses the order of these verbs.

514. Cf. Mark 6.30–44 and 8.1–10 et par.

The hungry were satisfied and had provisions left over; they took
   them up and went away.
Their provisions that they received announced You in their cities.
Your bread of barleys was more desirable than the king's table.
Blessed is the one who was worthy to eat it.
Blessed is the one who wondered and did not eat
to contemplate You, our Lord, with awe.

7   The two ships[515] were filled with allegories
as a symbol of hands and feet and ears and eyes,
that ears might be filled [with] truth at every moment
and eyes might be filled with modesty at all times,
and hands might take Your body,[516]
and feet trample a path to Your house,
and all of them might exist for Your glory.

8   The sea crowns You by the catch it offers You.
Like blossoms it mingled all sorts and offered [them] to You.
It filled two ships as a symbol: it gathered and heaped
the net of the apostles with a symbol of one hundred fifty fish.[517]
It emulates the harp of the prophets
who wove a varied crown
of one hundred fifty psalms.

9   The sea became calm, an expanse without disruption.
The Pure One went down to walk into this calm [expanse].
The sea wove its waves [into] a crown for God.[518]
It saw Him walking on the water and hastened to crown Him;
He entered its currents, it bore Him in state and lifted Him up,
and to the land, its neighbor, it held Him out.
The land emulated the sea and exalted Him.

10   For You a desirable way was made smooth in the sea,
and a clear way was adorned on dry land.
Before the feet of our Lord the sea smoothed its waves,[519]

---

515. Cf. Luke 5.7.
516. This is a better confirmation of Beck's surmise that the Eucharist was received in the hand than Virg. 32.2, q.v.
517. Cf. John 21.11.
518. From this point on, the *adventus* imagery becomes increasingly prominent; further on this subject, cf. Sabine G. MacCormack, *Art and Ceremony in Late Antiquity*. The Transformation of the Classical Heritage I (Berkeley, 1981), esp. 4–73.
519. Cf. Mark 6.45–52 et par.

the land carried [Him] and before Him it took and spread out
    garments.
The waves saw You and were calmed,
and the garments saw You and were spread out.
[Both] waves and garments honored You.[520]

11 By You sea and land were subjugated, and they carried You—
a powerful chariot harnessed without a yoke.
A herd of demons roaming on the land saw [this];
into hogs they fled, entered [and] hid, but they did not escape.[521]
The land rejoiced to see their humiliation.
The sea danced for joy . . . at their disgrace.
The height and the depth saw their ruin.

---

520. Cf. Mark 11.1–11, esp. 7–8, et par.
521. Cf. Mark 5.1–20 et par. They fled from the man to the hogs, which then rushed into
the sea and drowned.

34

In this hymn Ephrem explores the familiar theme of Judaism, Christianity and the call of the Gentiles, this time relating it to authority and martyrdom. First he introduces some women and cities representative of the ethnic and religious groups. The woman with the hemorrhage and the daughter of Jairus are types of the Old and New Testaments, respectively (str. 1–3). Then a series of cities populated by Gentiles are portrayed offering homage to Christ: The city of Ephrem, was a place of refuge for Him (str. 4); Through the Samaritan woman, Shechem was brought from error to truth (str. 5–6); Tyre, Sidon and the cities of the Decapolis are favorably contrasted with Capharnaum and Jerusalem (str. 7). In an apparent change of direction, Ephrem turns to the rebuff of the request of the sons of Zebedee (str. 8). The connection is possibly the statement he has omitted—that Jesus reproaches them for wanting to rule over their fellows as if they were Gentiles.[522] Instead Ephrem substitutes other models for the same lesson: children and angels (str. 9). Rather than promotion from above, the will is the proper means for attaining true greatness (str. 10), and martyrdom is the greatest exaltation, as James and John learned (str. 11). But Ephrem ends with a reproach to his congregation: Far from being ready for martyrdom, they are doubtful and contentious and have fallen prey to Arian beliefs (str. 12).

34

The same melody

1 The woman with the hemorrhage feared to approach the Lord of
        all.[523]
   She was encouraged by the One Who encouraged sinners.

---

522. Cf. Mark 10.42 et par.
523. Cf. Mark 5.25–34 et par.

In her wish He perceived that she wanted to delight in Him.[524]
He happened upon her faith [but] He was present since He willed
    it.
Her blood flowed, but her love was restrained.
As to her blood, she rejoiced that He dried it up,
but as to the font of her love, [she rejoiced] that He made it flow.

2   Let the daughter of Jairus give thanks, let her offer the crown.[525]
Young women extend their crowns to kings,
   and in images Victory is portrayed by a maiden.[526]
You have conquered the death of Eve in the daughter of Eve.[527]
Instead of Eve she crowns You.
Receive the glorious crown that she has offered,
   and by You let it ascend to Your Father with our praises.

3   A great wonder has met me if I will be able to tell it:
that the maiden who lay dead before You
and the woman whom You healed behind You [constitute] a type.
From behind You and before You they offer crowns.
The allegories that crown You
are the two Testaments that adorn You,
the Old and the New that praise You.

4   The inheritance of the house of Ephrem thanks You
for visiting the distant city of Ephrem.[528]
It was a city far removed from the crucifiers.
So that Your multitude might escape from the wolves and be
      refreshed,
the city became a peaceful harbor for Your ship.
For the sake of allowing Your persecuted flock to rest,
may You bring it to the harbor of life.

5   And let Shechem worship Him; let her offer Him a crown,
for upon the well He sat;[529] from the deep He lifted her up.
A hidden whirlpool swallowed her but she was silent,
for the mouth of the well had secretly seized her daughter.

---

524. In this line Ephrem puns on words with the root *ṣb'*, "to will or wish."
525. Cf. Mark 5.21–43 et par.
526. Ephrem refers to the portrayal of Nike, frequent on coins and other imperial art.
527. That is, by raising the daughter of Jairus from the dead.
528. Cf. John 11.54, and Virg. 20.1, for the same scriptural allusion paired with the image of the harbor.
529. Cf. John 4.1–42, esp. 6.

From the depth of error He silenced her.

Without a bucket, since she had none, he gave her to drink

teaching from the depth of His wisdom.

6 He revealed to her the structure of her pretenses, and she was
amazed.[530]

A Ploughman, Who was pleased not to sow, chose

that field of reproaches that stood without a worker.

The shame of five ploughmen [of whom] she was bereft[531] passed
away.

She did not force [the sixth husband] lest he should die,

and this man feared to take her.

Our Lord is the One Who revealed their secret.

7 Daughter of Tyre, worship Him, and Sidon that He did not
enter.[532]

Crowns came to Him from the ten cities.[533]

Capharnaum renounced Him, and He renounced it in all the
woes.[534]

In Sodom and in Tyre He reproached the haughty land.[535]

Our Lord put to shame the Canaanite woman

whose love bellowed out so that she asked Him.[536]

To Jerusalem that cried out to crucify Him [be shame].

8 Let the place thank Him where the sons of Zebedee asked.[537]

What they were seeking He sought; what they were asking He took.

He plundered their treasures and showed their treasure.

The astute innocent believed about Him not as they saw.

They called the Persecuted One "the Word,"

---

530. We, too, may be amazed at Ephrem's innovative interpretation of Jesus' words to the woman at the well, cf. Virg. 22.4–15.

531. The Syriac is active.

532. Jesus did not enter the city of Sidon to heal the Syro-Phoenician woman's daughter; cf. Mark 7.24–30 et par.

533. The Decapolis, a commercial and political league of ten independent cities of Transjordan; the participant cities are variously enumerated in ancient sources, cf. J. Finegan, *The Archeology of the New Testament: The Life of Jesus and the Beginning of the Early Church* (Princeton, 1969), 61–70. For Jesus' healing there, cf. Mark 7.31–37 et par.

534. Ephrem puns on *kpr*, "to renounce", and the name of the city of Capharnaum, which he then uses as a symbol of Jewish rejection of Jesus. For Jesus' curse of Capharnaum, cf. Matt. 11.20–24 et par.

535. As Beck suggests, probably Sidon and Tyre are meant here, cf. Matt. 11.20–22.

536. She asked Him to cure her daughter, cf. Matt. 15.21–28, esp. 24f.

537. Mark 10.35–45 et par.

and also the Judged One [they called] "Lord" and "Son,"
and the Crucified One "God" and "man."

9   When the disciples hastened to the throne of the ruler,
He showed them a child who receives orders without becoming
     angry
and [who], like the Watchers, serves without murmuring.
Since the Watchers do not have thrones,[538]
our Lord refused [to bestow] apparent majesty,
and to true majesty He counseled them:
to look at children and become great.[539]

10   The treasure of freedom exceeds a gift,
and the treasury of [free] will [exceeds] the gift of grace.[540]
"You have in you [the capacity] to be greater," our Lord said.
Who will measure how much the great will may increase?[541]
Our Lord restrains; His [will] holds them.
lest He bury His [will] by theirs.[542]
They acquired His, but they were exalted by theirs.

11   Those who received majesty but did not assume it, were greatly
     exalted,
for complete love is reproved but is not turned aside.
He Who refused their request increased their love.
He had refused majesty, but He gave them what is great.
He shut the gate to show their steadfastness.
When they pressed, they did not receive;
by their death they opened it and entered alive.

12   But we, on the other hand, have seen His majesty.
If our eye had seen Him beaten, we would be sickened.
The disciples loved Him in the mocking of Herod.
In our time kings have worshipped Him,[543] but we have been
     doubtful and suspicious.

---

538. Only God is enthroned in heaven, not the "Watchers," angels, who stand attentively in his presence, cf. Cramer, Engelvorstellungen, 126–28. On the larger question whether the distinct groups of angels are hierarchically arranged among themselves or whether they are merely functionally distinguished among themselves and hierarchically ranked with respect to God and humans, cf. ibid. 81–108, and Beck, Reden, 107–110.

539. Cf. Matt. 18.1–4, 19.13–15 et par.

540. Cf. Nat. 1.98, Virg. 20.5, 25.7, 30.5–8 and notes ad loc.

541. On the power of the will, cf. Nat. 4.140–42.

542. Although humans have freedom, this does not negate Divine Providence.

543. Constantine and his sons.

HYMN 34

Contentious generation![544] How much you have gone astray
that you proclaim a creature as Creator
and preach the Lord as a fellow servant![545]

---

544. The Syriac has two nouns rather than a noun with adjective. Ephrem reproaches the Arians, as the following lines indicate clearly.

545. The postscript, "Completed is one hymn on Cana," should have followed the previous hymn.

35

This hymn begins with three scriptural personalities associated with the city of Jericho: Zacchaeus, the blind Bar Timaeus, and Rahab (str. 1). Although Zacchaeus climbed a sycamore tree, Ephrem associates him with the subsequent pericope of the cursing of the fig tree and contrasts the fig tree with the branches of palm waved by the crowd upon Jesus' entry into Jerusalem (str. 2). Returning to the idea of Bar Timaeus, the third strophe introduces the Johannine account of the healing of a blind man. Consideration of the reaction of the Jewish leadership to this incident leads him to attack the Pharisees and justify Jesus' abrogation of the sabbath as a means of saving the weak and sinful, such as the penitent woman of Luke's gospel. Through association of this incident with the anointing at Bethany, Ephrem is led to Martha, Mary and Lazarus. Finally, focusing on the Mount of Olives and the triumphal entry into Jerusalem, Ephrem plays on the contrast between those who recognize Jesus as Christ and the Jewish authorities who did not.

35

The same melody

1   Jericho, worship him; offer him a crown.
By the mouth of the short Zacchaeus,[546] extend praise,
and by the voice of Bar Timaeus[547] extend thanksgiving,
and with the splendid thread of Rahab[548] gird on his crown.
By means of Rahab who was saved, sing his praise;

---

546. Cf. Luke 19.1–10.
547. Cf. Mark 10.46–52; Matthew has two men, cf. Matt. 20.29–34; in Luke he is unnamed, Luke 18.35–43.
548. Josh. 2.

by Bar Timaeus, who saw, glorify him,
and in Zacchaeus who conquered,[549] crown him.

2   The fig tree that he climbed deserved curses,
for the leaves of scorn stretched out to the guilty.[550]
The children did not take from its branches for [their] praise,[551]
since the leaves of the fig tree were not suitable for a conqueror's
     praise.
The guilty who were acquitted ran to it,
and exiles who were stripped took refuge in it,
and the agitated who stumbled hid in it.

3   A wonder sprouted in the place where He spat
that from clay He made salves for the eyes.[552]
He took and cast dust on the eyes, and they were opened.
O Healer Who opened [the eyes of] the blind man with a speck!
The priests were jealous that he abrogated the sabbath,
for its abrogation bound them.[553]
[Those] who disputed, were bound and stifled.

4   He sanctifies sabbaths to sanctify the unclean,
and He confines the day to gather the wandering.
In the binding of sabbaths they are released to provoke to anger
that the idle might breathe [and] sin [and] provoke to anger.
Therefore our Lord abrogated the sabbath,
since their tongue was bound by dispute
and their idleness was released for work.

5   Let the sinner give thanks—the unclean woman, who was not
     ashamed
to enter the banquet of the pure and holy.[554]
With what boldness she made her way through the crowd [and]
     entered.
Instead of wine, love intoxicated her, the friend of wine.[555]

---

549. Ephrem puns here on "Zacchaeus," *zky*, and "conquered," *zk'*.
550. Zacchaeus climed a sycamore, Syriac *t'nt' pkyht'*, not a fig tree, simply *t'nt'*. Ephrem takes advantage of the similarity to evoke other associations; cf. Mark 11.12–14 et par. Here, too, he alludes to the notion that Adam and Eve were received hospitably by the fig tree, found elsewhere in Ephrem as well as in some rabbinic traditions; cf. Cruc. 5.15 and Kronholm, Motifs, 219.
551. Cf. Mark 11.1–10 et par.
552. Cf. John 9, esp. 9.6–7.
553. Cf. John 9.16ff.
554. Cf. Luke 7.36–50 et par.
555. On sober inebriation, cf. Virg. 24.7 and note ad loc., also Virg. 31.13, 37.3.

For each one who has put on the love of the Most High,
who is girt with the armor that is unforged,
despises the sword that has been forged.

6   By her hair she took a blessing from His sweat.
The impurity from Your body cleansed her mind.
And she who had been made an occasion of death for everyone
became an occasion of repentance for sinners.
The unclean who saw her glorified You,
and sinners saw her and praised You,
and the holy wondered at her and crowned You [with praise].

7   Her adornments and her plaits that had caused onlookers to sin
were a towel for You that wiped Your feet.[556]
Iskariot whom You washed, wronged Your towel.[557]
By that thing by which she was lost, she was found, since she
        believed,
so that triumphant was the oil that had condemned her,
and sanctified was her mouth that had defiled her,
and purified was her beauty that had debased her.

8   Let Mary give thanks to you, the chaste one who was not ashamed
to enter the glorious, resplendent and sanctified banquet.[558]
Without embarrassment let us approach the fearful one without fear.
People who fear are proud, but God is plain to all.
It is good that we have a King who is not fearful,
and the Son of the King Who is mingled but not proud,
and a Judge who chastises but is not angry.

9   Let Martha thank You. Let her bring a crown to You—
and the sister who did not serve and the brother, all three.[559]
Together they have crowned you with one . . . crown of siblings,
. . . he lifted up to the head . . .
By her service Martha became famous;[560]
Mary You made famous by her love;[561]
and Lazarus because of his resurrection.[562]

---

556. Cf. Luke 7.38.
557. Cf. John 13.1–30.
558. Here Luke 7.36–50 is conflated with John 12, thanks to John 11.2.
559. Cf. John 12.2.
560. Cf. Luke 10.38–42.
561. Cf. Matt. 26.13 and Luke 7.47.
562. Cf. John 11, esp. 45–53.

10   Let the Mount, the Mount of Olives, give thanks to Him Who sat
       on it,
    and the disciples who simply asked Him there.[563]
    In the furnace of truth He purified the question
    from the filth of controversy and the strife of the scribes.
    The question and the answer He weighed and gave.[564]
    The stones neither outweighed nor were outweighed,
    so that mouths would neither harm nor be harmed.

11   "With the branches of my children I give thanks that you made me
    a new way for You, made smooth by cloaks.[565]
    And that a colt was fitting for you to ride, I remember.
    Instead of elders who deny You glory and do not cry out,
    let the horn summon, my Lord, the dead.
    Let the elders glorify you at last
    when they have seen the stones crying out."[566]

12   The former priests desired your beauty but did not see [it][567]
    The middle priests hated your beauty and displeased you.
    The priests of the churches grasp you in their hands,
    the Bread of life that came down and was mingled with the
       senses.[568]
    Because they hated You, hateful are Your persecutors,
    but Your lovers are handsome because they earnestly desire You,
    and Your heirs are rich because they acquire you.

13   The land that hated You is worthy of curses,
    and the city that crucified You, as Sodom was its habitation,
    the holy town in which an owl hoots.
    Zion has her barrenness, but Your church has her fruitfulness
    by the trumpet of your peace that resounds in her
    and the kithara of Moses that is played by her
    and the harp of David that is played by her.[569]

---

563. Mark 13.3–4 et par.
564. Cf. Mark 13, esp. 5–37, et par.
565. Cf. Mark 11.1–10 et par. The common notion that children waved the palm branches is based in a conflation of Matt. 21.14–17 with the entry into the city in Matt. 21.1–11. The speaker is the Mount of Olives.
566. Cf. Luke 19.40.
567. For the idea that the righteous of the Old Testament were awaiting Christ, cf. Nat. 1.12f, and 20–60.
568. Cf. Nat. 22.14.
569. The postscript reads, "Completed is one hymn on Jericho."

36

In this hymn Ephrem vividly evokes, sometimes through personification, a sequence of places associated with the passion, resurrection and ascension of Jesus: the Upper Room (str. 1), Gethsemane (str. 2), Golgotha (str. 3), Emmaus (str. 4), the Lake of Tiberias (str. 5–8), and the Mount of Olives (str. 9–10). Like some of the earlier hymns of this collection, this hymn may have some relation to the development of Christian pilgrimage to the Holy Land in the fourth century. Alternatively, it may be seen as commentary on a continuous gospel account, drawing especially on materials from Luke and John. Since this hymn, with the other hymns in this group on the same melody, emphasizes ascension themes, they may even have been written for an early ascension liturgy.[570] In any case, the hymn ends on a stirring eschatological note.

36

The fifth on the same melody

1   In the mouth of my just ones I give thanks that He broke in me
that Living Bread that was broken for His disciples,
and I remember that in the basin of water they have been washed.
Instead of the Twelve for whom He stood and became a servant
are myriads of Watchers who will stand
before His throne at the End.
Judas they will menace [saying] how much he disbelieved.[571]

---

570. This feast entered the Western liturgical calendar from Jerusalem through fourth-century pilgrims like Egeria; cf. *Egeria: Diary of a Pilgrimage*, trans. and annotated by George E. Gingras, ACW 38 (New York, 1970), ch. 42, pp. 117f., 244f. The combination of themes in the present hymns seems to indicate a similar sequence in the Syriac-speaking environment.

571. The angels form a sort of chorus, commenting on the drama of salvation, cf. Cramer, *Engelvorstellungen*, 148–52.

HYMN 36

Refrain: Glory to the mercy that sent You to us to give us Your body, a living sacrifice!

2   Let the place in which He sweated [blood] offer Him a crown.
Let His sweat[572] in disputation make the doubter sweat.
For, although everyone sweats to a degree,
the one whom He slayed without measure sweated without
     measure.
. . . put on
. . . that at the right moment
. . . sweat of toil . . .

3   To You again Golgotha gives thanks that she was made equal
to that great mountain that was erected higher than her,[573]
and she is waiting for Your great procession to be consoled,
to see You, the Judge of all, on the terrible judgment-seat,
and the crucifiers hanging[574] for vengeance,
and Caiaphas[575] standing in disgrace,
and the thief dwelling in the Garden.[576]

4   Let a town[577] so give thanks to You, a traveler who entered and fled.
You deceived Cleophas in order to educate by Your explanation,
that you might not alarm the weak children by Your resurrection.
To make them perfect, My Lord, you tore the veil with the bread.[578]
Your brightness will be revealed completely at the End
when the veil will be lifted from all,
so that the crucifiers may see that it is You.

5   Three trophies were arranged in a mystery:
bread, fish and inextinguishable fire.[579]
It was not the bread baked by the sweat of the house of Adam.
Who, indeed, has ever had a table set out of Himself:

---

572. Ephrem puns on place, *dwkt'*, and sweat, *dw't'*.
573. Mount Sinai. With clear allusion to a Moses-Christ typology, Ephrem plays on the relative heights of Mount Sinai and Golgotha, a little hill outside the city of Jerusalem. Here, too, he puns on the root, *zqp*, here meaning "to erect" but most often meaning "to crucify."
574. Or "crucified," Syriac *tl'*.
575. The high priest is named only in Matthew and in John, cf. Mt. 26.57, and John 18.24.
576. Luke 23.43.
577. The reference to Cleophas in the next line indicates that the town is Emmaus, cf. Luke 24.13–35.
578. Luke 24.30f.
579. John 21.9, though there is only one fish here according to both the Greek and the Peshitta.

Fish caught without water,[580]
Bread baked without hands,[581]
Coals heaped up without sticks?

6 The Lord of the flock who ate[582] with the disciples,
took and entrusted His flock to Simon who hears Him.[583]
He repeated the command three times to increase the admonition.
Three pledges he took from the shepherd
that with love[584] he would tend His lambs
and care for His sheep with affection
[and] keep His ewes with respect.

7 They saw that they were weak, needy, small and ignorant
and the land was full of learned men[585] and rulers.
Behold, by the fire and the fish and the bread He persuaded them.
By the revealed banquet He revealed the future [banquet]—
He Who heaped up abundance without work,
that Teacher of the Gentiles without money
by ignorant men, the vessels of His wisdom.

8 A gesture and a command served Him Who commands all,
and the rich will rules over all treasures.
It took abundance and heaped it up before the All-sustainer.
This banquet was pure, brief and suitable
for our God Who ate without being hungry,
Who ate salt[586] with humans[587] in His affection
that we might remain in His truth and love.

9 They accompanied Lazarus who departed into the grave.

---

580. On Christ and the apostles as fishermen, cf. Nat. 4.35, Virg. 32.8 and notes ad loc. The fish is a Christological and eucharistic symbol in the inscription of Aberkios; cf. Introduction n. 12, above.
581. The later notion of icons made without hands is foreshadowed in the present allusion to the eucharistic bread; further, cf. McVey, Microcosm, 100f.
582. Literally "to eat salt," hence to be a companion; cf. John 21.15–17.
583. A pun on the name, Simon, *šm'wn*, and "to hear, obey," *šm'*.
584. Syriac, *ḥwb'*, as opposed to *rḥmt'*, translated "affection" in the next line.
585. Or scribes.
586. As above in stanza 6.1.
587. The Syriac is singular.

The Great One departed for the height, and the Galileans[588]
    accompanied Him.
[He is] far and near and hidden in His revealing.
Lazarus died and revived and mingled and sat down to eat.
Our Lord descended to Sheol and returned.
He ascended to His heavens and behold He is mingled with the
    lower [world].
Again He mingles with [and] has those who love Him sit down to
    eat.
10 "More than all who rejoice, I[589] rejoice to have seen Him
Who has made my lands rejoice and has been lifted up. I escorted
    Him,
and I am going to hear His living voice
when He calls the dead, as He called our dead, 'Come out!'[590]
They will all answer Him and emerge,
and not a bone will remain in Sheol
where [as yet] Lazarus alone has answered Him."[591]

---

588. Possibly instead of "Galileans," *glyly'*, the text should read *gygl'*, "Wheels," the group
of angels associated especially with ascension, along with the Cherubim. Although they are not
well-known in Christian literature, they are mentioned in a similar context by Ephrem himself;
cf. CJ 3.17, where he also puns on the two words, and Cramer, Engelvorstellungen, 73–75.
589. The speaker is the Mount of Olives, personified.
590. Cf. John 11.43.
591. The postscript reads, "Completed is one hymn on the church."

37

Ephrem's basic concern in this hymn is soteriological. The serpent, Satan, who had conquered humans and caused them to age and die, was himself conquered by Christ (str. 1). Through the incarnation and the Eucharist, human nature has been recreated by the infusion of Christ's body (str. 2). To ailing human nature he came as a physician with three medicines: bread, wine and chrism (str. 3). By giving his own body to death, the destroyer of human bodies, Christ both sated and destroyed death itself (str. 5). On behalf of the soul, who by free will had stained her garment, the body with sins, Christ washed that garment in his blood (str. 6). Contrary to both the Jewish and the Marcionite views, Jesus completed the Jewish scripture and restored the work of the Creator in the incarnation and salvation (str. 7–8). Even his perfect body, ascended into heaven, has the same nature as ours (str. 9). In the final strophe, an important witness to Ephrem's Christian upbringing, he explicitly sets his orthodox Christian faith over against Judaism, idolatry and heresy.

37

The seventh on the same melody

1   The serpent wounded Eve[592] and she became old;[593] he rebelled
        against all—
against kings and priests,[594] prophets and saviors.
The Root of Isaiah wearied the dragon.[595]
By the early Root from Mary he was conquered,

---

592. Ephrem probably chooses to mention Eve rather than Adam here for the sake of the pun on "Eve" and "serpent"—*ḥw'* and *ḥwy'*.
593. Beck takes the serpent as subject of this verb, but his text indicates that the reading of these first few words is uncertain. Eve as subject makes better sense, cf. Nat. 7.11.
594. Pagan priests, *kwmr'*, rather than Jewish priests, but cf. Nat. 9.3 and Virg. 32.2.
595. Isa. 11.10; further on the "dragon," cf. Nat. 8.3 and note ad loc.

Prayer murmured, and he was enfeebled.

The Signet[596] blew on him and dried him up

Adam's bones leapt for joy in Sheol.

2   His body was newly mixed with our bodies,

and His pure blood has been poured out into our veins,

and His voice into our ears, and His brightness[597] into our eyes.

All of Him has been mixed into all of us by His compassion,

and since He loves His church very much,

He did not give her the manna of her rival.[598]

He had living bread for her to eat.[599]

3   Wheat, the olive and grapes, created for our use—

the three of them serve You symbolically in three ways.

With three medicines You healed our disease.

Humankind had become weak and sorrowful and was failing.

You strengthened her with Your blessed bread,

and You consoled her with Your sober wine,

and You made her joyful with Your holy chrism.

4   The sheep and also the ewe, who were created for our use—

a cloak from the wool of sheep He wore . . .

Instead of . . . His four symbols . . .

Behold the Source . . . from the hem of Whose garment[600]

. . . our help . . .

And [to] each one according to the capacity of his understanding[601]

Your spring gives without jealousy.

5   The body thanks You that it was saved by Your abasement—

the sheep that had strayed, while the lion lay in ambush to
        dismember it:

sin in secret is a wild animal that tears it to pieces.[602]

David preserved himself while he saved the lamb.[603]

Instead of our body You gave Your body

---

596. Syriac *ḥtm'*, cf. Nat. 1.99, 12.3, 28.7, Virg. 20.12, 31.12, and notes ad loc.

597. Or "manifestation, epiphany," Syriac *dnḥ'*.

598. A rival wife in a polygamous society. Israel is, of course, meant. The word here, *'rt'*, provides a pun with *'dt'*, church.

599. John 6.35.

600. Cf. Mark 5.25–34, 6.56 et par.

601. Cf. Nat. 4.197–200, Virg. 22.21, 23.3.

602. Sin "in secret," Syriac *bksy'*, could mean either "secret sin" or that in a symbolic sense sin is a wild animal.

603. Cf. 1 Sam. 17.34–37, and Nat. 7.8.

to that Death that consumed us but was not sated.
By You alone it was sated and burst.

6   Let the soul thank You—that filthy thing that You wiped clean
of the stains of debts she incurred by her freedom.[604]
For her whose will wove her a stained garment,
the Merciful One wove a garment of light, and He clothed her.
Whereas priests cleansed with a bird at daybreak,[605]
You cleansed the soul that had acted foolishly.
You bathed it in Your blood, bleached [it] and made it gleam.[606]

7   With the scribes our Lord debated.
Clothed in their scripture, He cast [them] down in controversy.
With the breastplate of truth, the psalms, He was girded.
He questioned them and was questioned, and victorious was He
Whose shield [was] the Torah
and Isaiah His sword and spear
and the prophets the arrows for His bow.[607]

8   His names silently renounce the Stranger,[608]
for Jesus is Messiah and our Lord and our God.
From the full treasures of the Creator He stole [and] became rich.
Justice He stretched out like a bow in the Temple:
He shot fearful warnings at the scribes.
He shot an arrow at a demon and silenced him,[609]
and another at a legion and punished it.[610]

9   The body from Mary rebuked that one who said
that with another body the Heavenly One dwelled in her.
Perfect is the body, but how did it grow with our bread?
It has sweat and spit and tears and even blood.
And if the ascended body is unsullied,
still it resembles our body since it died.

---

604. Cf. Beck, Reden, 89–91.

605. Cf. Lev. 14.1–7.

606. Not only the crucifixion but also Christian baptism are the means of this superior priestly cleansing, cf. Saber, Theologie, 46, 108, 123.

607. Cf. Virg. 14.4–5, 10–11, 13–14.

608. Marcion's name for the True God as opposed to the false deity of the Jewish scripture.

609. Cf. Mark 1.23–26 et par.

610. Cf. Mark 5.1–20 et par.

Renounce [error] and confess that their nature is one.[611]

10 Your truth [was] in my youth; Your verity [is] in my old age.
I rejected and expelled the party of the crucifiers;
I scorned graven images and the metal of strange [gods]
and the new fraud that would be contrived to deceive us.
The old and new [frauds] I deny, my Lord;
by the Old and New [Testaments] that I have believed
I have taken the measure of my hymns.[612]

---

611. That is, renounce the heresy of Marcionism and confess that the nature of Christ's body and ours is the same. This translation differs significantly from Beck's. For a similar anti-Marcionite polemic concerning the unity of the created and resurrected human nature, cf. Nat. 17.18.

612. The postscript adds, "Completed is one hymn on the faith."

38

Here Ephrem seems to be looking for a suitable explanation of the behavior of Lot and his daughters. He excuses Lot on the grounds that he needed consolation and the daughters on the grounds that they thought they must be the only people left on earth after the destruction of Sodom and Gomorrah. Ephrem's explanation of the daughters' behavior is found also in Jewish haggadic traditions.[613]

38

The same melody as "God Whom you [men] loved"

1   O Lot's daughters, who made the simple man drink a foul drink.[614]
They gave [it] for marriage, but he drank for consolation.

Refrain: To You be glory, Judge of all!

2   He drank to assuage his sorrow and by the wine to forget his terror.
By the wine he summoned sleep, since sleep fled from fear.

3   He drank to forget the terror of the devastating lightning bolts that
consumed [Sodom and Gomorrah].
He became drunk to make pass away from his heart the avenging
thunderclaps.

4   He drank to settle his heart that the sound of horrors had uprooted.
His ears suffered, and his heart raved with the bellowing [from]
Sodom.

5   Broken was the heart of his daughters since voices were confused
with voices,
mouths bellowed from the depth, roars and thunderclaps from the
height.

---

613. Cf. Ginzberg, Legends, V, 243, n. 188, and idem. Haggada, 110f.
614. Cf. Gen. 19.30–38.

6 Even this earth bellowed since the wrath [of God] can make it
     bellow.
  The four cities that burned suddenly gave one bellow.

7 Grace restrained the foolish girls,
  and if [it had] not, who would be able to live with those sounds?

8 Even the sea bellowed there . . . became a deaf-mute . . .
  . . . wrath of the Divinity . . . the sea and the land.

9 The sounds made the foolish girls think the entire creation was
     perishing
  since the smoke spread and did not allow them to see.

10 A fog spread there and gave no opportunity for the eye.
  [Only] at a short distance was one able to see anything.

11 The outsider could enter from [outside] the fumes and the fog.
  Lot could not go out; he was afraid to leave his house of refuge.

12 From all these things, they surmised the entire creation had
     perished.
  The old man was alarmed, being an old man, and the foolish girls,
     [too], being girls.

13 But if the old man was terrified, how much indeed would youth
     fear!
  He saw that his daughters were alarmed and that his wife had
     become a pillar [of salt].[615]

14 The old man and his daughters thought the wine would console
     [them]
  and make them forget the terrors that surrounded them on all sides.

15 The foolish girls went out from the inhabited earth; the desert
     mocked them.
  . . . that mocked very much, and the desert asked the inhabited
     earth . . .

16 They thought[616] . . .

17 . . . Wine consoles old age; conception consoles youth.[617]

---

615. Gen. 19.26.
616. The remainder of this strophe and much of the following one is illegible.
617. A postscript reads, "Completed is one hymn on Lot and his daughters."

39

This hymn is an alphabetical acrostic, using the letters of the first half of the alphabet. Instructions for the melody are illegible. Despite the fragmentary state of the text, some themes may be discerned. The coming of Christ has freed us to work (str. 1). When we were without hope beyond death, God planted truth, love and hope in our hearts, minds and souls, the promise of eternal life and the way to attain it (str. 11–12). Like a shipwrecked sailor, Adam could not rise from the depths, even with the help of angels and prophets, until Jesus came to conquer the evil one and to bring grace (str. 2, 7, 15,16).

39

' 1   I shall confess that I am freed, and ask to be enriched.
I shall work to earn wages, and scatter seed to be fully supplied.
For our Lord came down and gave silver for merchants
and seed for farmers, truth for preachers
and ears for hearers.

   Refrain: Praise to Him Who sent You to enrich us by Your coming!

' 2   Ships of souls in the waves of evils!
Lost treasures in the sea of crimes!
You came down . . .
. . . it was suitable for their waves
. . . their paths.
[Strophes 3–6 are illegible.]

7   . . .
Who was exalted . . . they escaped from him.
You humbled the evil one in the contest.
Weakness conquered him; infirmity subdued him,

for in You he was conquered by all.

[Strophes 8–10 are illegible.]

W 11 And since the inhabited earth had become a stem without fruits,
the Vine from Egypt brought forth early . . .[618]
You came down and planted Your truth in our heart,
Your love in our mind, Your affection in our generation
and Your hope in our souls.

Z 12 Everyone was preparing provisions for Gehenna.
Everyone was providing an abundance for loss.
You came down and became the Guide to the House of life,
the Way to discipline, the smooth [Way] to the kingdom,
and the Gate of entry.

Ḥ 13 Wine . . . was . . .
. . . tastes.
You . . . and You were . . . all.
and truth made all wise, and the thread . . . all,
and the goal . . . all.

Ṭ 14 . . .
Falsehood . . . fruit.
You came down [and] reproved . . . in Your furnace
. . . by Your mortality
and death by Your life.

Ṭ 15 Adam had sunken down. Spiritual angels came down
to help, but he did not come up. Prophets [came], but he did not
rise.
By You he who had sunken like iron turned and came up.
You made the heavy one fly, and You sank the light one
like iron and wood.[619]

Y 16 O Jesus, for Whose exploits the mouth does not suffice,
nor the voice for His helps, nor a measure for His abundance,
to Your Father in You be glory, for You came down from His
[place]
and went up from ours. His grace came down to us in You,
and glory goes up by means of You.

Y 17 It is fitting . . . my Lord for a handful of Your worshippers,

---

618. Cf. Ps. 80.8f.
619. Cf. Virg. 11.4 and Saber, Theologie, 120f.

HYMNS ON VIRGINITY

. . . His guide . . . in wombs . . .
. . . a wonder . . . His smallness
. . . in the desert . . . a storehouse from this
Guide of our learning.[620]

---

620. A postscript reads, "Completed is one hymn of thanksgiving."

40

Although this hymn completes the alphabetical acrostic started in the previous hymn, its themes are different. The emphasis on truth against error and peace against contentiousness identifies it as an anti-Arian work. Whereas the righteous people of old yearned for the Messiah, we, who have received his benefits, are ungrateful and contentious (str. 1–3) The synoptic parable of the talents, loosely recalled, provides illustrations for these faults (str. 4–6). Truth is more important than fasting, as even the martyrs illustrate (str. 7). The story of the tower of Babel is interpreted as a lesson against contentiousness rather than against pride (str. 11–12).

40

The same melody

K 1 My Lord, in all ages the righteous hunger for Your coming.[621]
They all lie down and go to sleep thirsting for Your revelation.
You come down and made their great remembrance,
for You revealed their desire and showed their longing
to rebuke our satiety.

Refrain: Blessed is He for Whom the righteous long!

L 2 We are led [to wonder] at them and at us: How much the people of
   old hungered;
they departed without murmuring; they praised, lay down and
   were silent.
You came down and opened Your treasure for the poor,
but, having become rich, they went astray, cheated and trampled
   the seals
and treasures of the kingdom.[622]

---

621. Cf. John 8.56, Nat. 1.12f., 20–60, Virg. 35.12.
622. Cf. Matt. 7.6.

M 3   From Your treasure-house they took the obols,[623]
and by them the just inherited talents of wealth.
You came down and gave silver to our poverty
and talents for our laxity, but we acquired debts[624]
from the treasures.

N 4   Let us wonder at that first man who brought ten talents.[625]
His treasury was full of wealth, but his mouth was full of
     silence.[626]
The wretched man . . .
. . . he said with You.

S 5   He makes himself very distant from that first man
who worked, grew rich and was silent and fearful, although rich.
Blessed is he whom You praise![627] Stamped on us are the signs
of the wretched one who contended with You.[628] His ingratitude is
     in our mouth,
his dispute on our tongue.

'6   The first one doubled his talents,[629] but the lazy one doubled
the sounds of his complaints. A second Nabal,
found [to be] a son of David, the wretched one kept the silver.[630]
Let us wonder at the disputers[631] who do not even keep
the capital, faith, for her[632] Lord.

P 7   The mouth of the confessors, my Lord, will be struck and will
     confess.
[If] their tongue has been cut out, mutilated, it will sing His praise.
The mouth of the faithless eats and disputes, my Lord,
and drinks and contends again. It carries in sweet things
and takes out bitter things.

S 8   Let our fasts be truth and our vigils also verity,
since fast and also vigil error defiles.
Since You came down to teach that food does not defile

---

623. Cf. Mark 7.42.
624. Or "sins."
625. Cf. Matt. 25.14–30 and Luke 19.11–27, but the details do not match the hymn.
626. But cf. Matt. 25.20, where he speaks.
627. Cf. Matt. 25.21,23.
628. Cf. Matt. 25.24f.
629. Matt. 25.16, but not Luke.
630. Cf. 1 Sam. 25.1–42.
631. That is, the Arians.
632. That is, faith's Lord.

and drink does not make unclean; filth from the heart
makes a human being unclean.[633]
[Strophes 9, 10 are illegible.]

R 11 The High One came down [and] confused voices and tongues[634]
that were made capable of harm and He taught . . :
and He gave the disciples a multitude of tongues
that their verity might be as a type . . .

Š 12 . . .
Since He saw the confusion in His age for that people,
He destroyed the tower [of Babel] . . . for the disputers.
They divided . . . that truth might not be built—
[truth], the tower of our redemption.

T 13 Let Your justice give thanks by which was separated the straw
and the dust of learning, just as also chaff
is separated from wheat[635] and the dregs from the clarified [wine].
Thus was separated . . . the true church
. . . false . . .
[The fourteenth strophe is illegible.]

---

633. Cf. Mark 7.14–23 et par., Matt. 15.10–20.
634. Cf. Gen. 11.1–9.
635. Cf. Matt. 13.30.

41

This short alphabetical acrostic is in the personal style of some of the Old Testament psalms, presuming boldly on God's grace and mercy. Notable themes are the portrayal of Christ as a bird and as a Levitical priest (str. 2).

41

To the melody, "Who will not stir up his mind?"

' 1   I shall ask with every mouth and take by every means.
I shall increase on every occasion and sing in every melody
glory in every song.

Refrain: Glory to the All-merciful!

B 2   I give heed to Your mercy; in Your wings I take shelter.[636]
Of my foolish deeds I am ashamed; by You may my sins be blotted out.
With Your hyssop, You cleanse all.[637]

G 3   It is revealed that You are gentle; it is revealed that You are merciful.
Revealed is Your goodness; hidden is Your majesty.
Perfected is Your favor.

D 4   Miserable is our mind; it resembles a tree
that needs to be watered each day.
It is easy for us to profess You.

H 5   Grant me what I ask. I have believed that I shall receive.
These things that were sought my senses were seeking.

---

636. For Christ portrayed as a bird, cf. Nat. 17.1, 26.13 and notes ad loc.
637. For hyssop, symbol of Christ's Levitical priesthood and his power to forgive sins, cf. Nat. 1.25, 9.3, Virg. 8.10 and 21, notes ad loc., and Saber, Theologie, 45–49.

So Your mercy willed.

[Strophe 6 is illegible.]

Z 7   You purchased me to belong to You; justify me[638] that I may give
           You thanks.

It is the age when the pure will sing with their voices
divine songs.

---

638. The Syriac must be changed from *zkny* to *zkyny*. Beck's translation does not match his text, which gives the 3 sg. m. perfect rather than the imperative.

42

This is the first in a set of nine hymns on Jonah.[639] After a brief statement of the story (str. 1–5), Ephrem begins a more imaginative meditation. The language of weather and agriculture (str. 6–9) quickly gives way to the language of childbirth (str. 10–28). Here Jonah's two conceptions are the center of attention: the first being a natural conception by his mother; the second an unnatural one by the whale. Since the faculty of speech or reason is what distinguishes humans from animals, Ephrem enjoys the paradox that a rational creature, Jonah's mother, conceived him as an irrational, speechless fetus, while an irrational animal, the whale, conceived him as a rational adult. A single strophe alludes to the Christological symbolism established in the gospels, which is central to Ephrem's own poetry (str. 29). This is followed by consideration of Jonah's priestly qualities (str. 30–33).

42
ON JONAH AND NINEVEH

1 Jonah hired a ship and went down [to sea].[640]
   With silver he bought a watery drowning.
2 A bare voice entered Nineveh.
   A hundred thousand souls were engaged in business there.[641]
3 The naked voice that sowed—
   its harvest [was] a hundred-twenty-thousandfold.

---

639. Although he presents the texts as if there were nine hymns, Beck argues convincingly that the last four (Virg. 47–48 and 49–50) are actually two hymns split in half. Hence there are actually only seven hymns in this set, cf. CSCO 223, vii. I have followed the numbering of Beck's text here, so it appears here as if there are nine hymns, Virg. 42–50.
640. Jon. 1.3.
641. Cf. Jon. 4.11.

4 On the boat human mouths tore him in pieces.[642]
In the deep the whale's mouth swallowed him up.[643]

5 In Nineveh that He healed, thousands without limit
poured upon Him all praises.

6 By means of one good man He healed them,
and the cloud of mouths poured forth His glory.

7 Therefore twenty-two myriads of mouths
from below to above rained glory.

8 The boughs that have been exposed to hail[644] are bereft and ugly,
since the hail has stripped the leaves and fruits.

9 By the hail of his sayings Jonah beat down [Nineveh],
and her boughs shed [their] splendid fruits.

10 By the birthpangs of his sayings[645] he hastened the community
of Nineveh to bring forth voices of glory.

11 Instead of a living creature the prophet generated
the barren one [Nineveh] who brought forth fruits of glory.

12 A whale in the sea swallowed him too.
It conceived and brought him forth instead of females.

13 In the sea it conceived him; on land it brought him forth.
It delivered him to the all-suckling land.

14 He was conceived and born as in nature,
once more conceived and born unnaturally.

15 A woman conceived as usual,
and in addition she brought forth as in nature.

16 A fish conceived him unnaturally,
and in addition he brought him forth not in the usual way.

17 When a woman endowed with speech[646] conceived him,
he took his beginning in her as a speechless one.

18 But again when a speechless whale conceived him,
inside him [the whale] had an advocate endowed with speech.

19 When a woman on land conceived him,
he was not aware of her prayers.

---

642. Cf. Jon. 1.8–11.
643. Jon. 1.17.
644. The Syriac *'tbrd* must be a denominative verb formed from *brd*, "hail."
645. In this and the following strophe substantial changes in word order are necessary to attain a smooth English translation.
646. Or "rational."

20 But when the fish in the sea had conceived him,
    the fish was not aware of his prayers!

21 But when he was conceived within a human woman
    he resembled an animal that was speechless.

22 An animal conceived him in the womb of the sea;
    that silent one became endowed with speech.

23 Within one endowed with speech he was quiet;
    within a silent one he became endowed with speech.

24 The womb on land brought forth in months.
    The womb in the sea brought him forth in days.

25 When his mother brought him forth, he grew;
    She swore a vow for her infant.

26 When the fish brought him forth in the sea,
    the infant in the womb swore a vow.

27 Who has seen an infant in the womb
    that swore a vow upon his birth?

28 Who has seen an infant that becomes a fetus?
    Who has seen a fetus delivered from the mouth?

29 The servant bore the symbols of his Lord
    in his conception and his birth and in his raising to life.[647]

30 Who has seen a priest in a fish
    who offered a prayer to his God?

31 A pure temple the fish became for him,
    and the mouth of Jonah [became] a censer.

32 The smell of incense rose up from within the abyss
    to the High One Who sits in the highest heaven.

33 His Savior came down; He became the key of the mouth.
    Silence delivered the Herald of words.

---

647. Cf. Matt. 12.38–41 and Luke 11.29–32.

43

In this hymn Peter is contrasted with Jonah (str. 1–2). Unlike Jonah, the reluctant prophet sent to the Gentiles, he went willingly to be their apostle. He, rather than Paul, is here portrayed as the apostle to the Gentiles. Although this might be due to some remaining aversion to Paul, traceable to early Jewish Christianity in this area, it is more probably for the sake of Ephrem's extensive use of the image of Peter as a fisherman. The main theme here is the contrast between Peter's acceptance when he caught fish for their death and his censure when he caught sinners for life (esp. 3–15). Finally, the theme is brought to cosmic dimensions as a contrast between death and the Living One (str. 16–17).

43

The same melody

1 Simon rejoiced when he cast his net
and gathered in it living fish for death.

2 Jonah was distressed when he cast his net
and gathered in it thousands of dead [people] for life.

3 Simon obeyed the One Who said to him,
"You have caught for death, [now] make disciples for life."[648]

4 O the one who caught fish to be consumed,
come catch the peoples lest they be consumed!
[Strophe 5 is illegible.]

6 [Simon] put to death the living and brought to life the dead.
He was loved when he put to death; he was hated when he brought
to life.

---

648. Cf. Mark 1.17 and Matt. 4.19. For the same contrast with regard to all the apostles, cf. Virg. 32.8.

7   Although he was catching fish for death,
    when he caught abundantly, he was praised.

8   But although he was catching people⁶⁴⁹ for life,
    when he caught abundantly he was insulted.

9   In that [time] when he brought to life, he was a helper,
    but in the [time] when he put to death, he was not harmful.

10 For this belongs to the existence of fish,
    that after life they arrive at death.

11 But [it belongs] to the existence of sinners,
    that after death they return to life.

12 Indeed he caught and gave fish for food,
    but he delivered the peoples from the Devourer.⁶⁵⁰

14 His net made human mouths rejoice;
    His gospel made the mouth of death mourn.

14 What was given for food fed its eater.
    What was not given for food tore apart its Devourer.

15 He held his net so it would confine the fish.⁶⁵¹
    He tore apart sin that swallowed the peoples.

16 Death brought up to the land
    fish that lived in the belly of the sea.

17 The Living One raised up to the height
    the peoples who were dead in the belly of sin.

18 By the catching of fish hunger decreased.
    By the catching of the peoples . . .
    [Strophes 19, 20, 21 are illegible.]

---

649. The Syriac is singular, "son of man," meaning human being.
650. Death. Ephrem puns here on food ('*wkl*') and Devourer or eater ('*kwl*').
651. Cf. Luke 5.6 and Matt. 4.21.

44

In this hymn Jonah is contrasted with Abraham and Moses, always to his disadvantage. In both cases the invidious comparison is taken as typical of Jews and Gentiles as well. Whereas Abraham prayed for mercy for the city of Sodom, Jonah prayed for the punishment of Nineveh (str. 1–2). Ephrem claims this is typical of the circumcised, who expect to be chosen purely for their name, whereas the uncircumcised, such as the Gentiles of Nineveh did the deeds of repentance (str. 3–14). Likewise Moses is better than Jonah since he was a righteous man struggling with an unruly congregation (str. 15). Jonah's complaint, on the other hand, is that the people listened to him (str. 16). Again, Ephrem takes this behavior as typical of "inward" vs. "outward" circumcision (str. 17–20). The names of individuals and groups are less important than their deeds, as Cain, Abel and the Assyrians demonstrate (str. 21–23).

44

The same melody

1 That Sodom not be overthrown Abraham prayed.[652]
That Nineveh be overthrown Jonah hoped.[653]

2 That man prayed for [a city that] abused Watchers.[654]
This man was angry at [a city that] made the Watchers rejoice.[655]

3 Although I sent you,[656] you have not gone from me.
When you preached, they ran [and] believed in you.[657]

---

652. Cf. Gen. 18.22–33.
653. Cf. Jon. 4.1–5.
654. Cf. Gen. 19.1–11.
655. Cf. Cramer, Engelvorstellungen, 148–52.
656. Christ, as Logos and thus the Divine Presence in the Old Testament, speaks to Jonah.
657. Cf. Jon. 3.1–9.

4 You who are downtrodden broke the yoke,
   but those rebels rush to the yoke.

5 You, son of the People who showed [what] your people [is],
   but the peoples showed this of their brothers.

6 Discernment showed you [were one] of the circumcised,
   but they showed the acceptableness of the uncircumcised.

7 Although you are quite suitable by virtue of your lineage,[658]
   and although they are rejected,[659] their election is in them.

8 I chose the circumcised, but they have rejected themselves.
   I rejected the uncircumcised, but they have dedicated themselves.

9 Election, therefore, is not [a matter] of names,
   for deeds enter and dismiss the names.

10 The furnace of testing of the name is the deed.
    In it is tested whether it is the true name.

11 For there is fruit that is very splendid,
    but its taste is the opposite of its beauty.

12 Even the despicability of the bee,
    the most despised of all, is a spring of sweetness.

13 Splendid names—the house of the Hebrews—
    are sweet names that make bitter things flow.

14 The mention of their name is sweet to the ear.
    The taste of their fruit ravages your mouth.

15 Moses who sweetened the water with wood—[660]
    his congregation was made bitter by the molten calf.[661]

16 And you, who by your flight made the sea bitter,[662]
    sweetened Nineveh by the sound of your trumpet.[663]

17 He whose body is circumcised but whose heart is uncircumcised
    is circumcised outwardly but uncircumcised in secret.

18 But he whose heart is circumcised but whose flesh is uncircumcised
    is circumcised for the Spirit but uncircumcised for the eye.

19 In the name of his circumcision the circumcised fornicates.
    With the cup of his purity he drinks mire.

---

658. Literally, "you in whom is your lineage."
659. Probably due to a misprint, Beck's text lacks the seyame to indicate this is the Afel pl. masc. participle.
660. Cf. Exod. 17.1–7.
661. Cf. Exod. 30.
662. Cf. Jon. 1.4.
663. Cf. Jon. 3.3–10.

20 By a circumcised heart the uncircumcised becomes holy.[664]
In the bridal chamber of his heart dwells his Creator.

21 It was not his name [that] made Abel fair.
Because he desired innocence, his name was desirable.[665]

22 Eve chose the name of Cain,
but since he hated his brother, his name was hated by all,

23 The Assyrians! Inflammatory names!
They gave fruits of desirable tastes![666]

---

664. Or "chaste."
665. On Cain and Abel here and in the following strophe, cf. Kronholm, Motifs, 220.
666. Cf. Nat. 19.3–6.

45

Here Ephrem dwells on a series of paradoxes. First, rather than willing the destruction of the repentant people of Nineveh, Jonah ought first to look for the destruction of the disobedient Jewish people (str. 1–9). Next, playing on ideas of awakening and calming, he presents a series of images to show that Jonah aroused when he should have assuaged and vice versa (str. 10–16). This leads to the next paradox, swallowing and disgorging (str. 17–22). Finally, the lot cast against Jonah tended toward death, while the sackcloth of the Ninevites led them toward life (str. 23–31).

45

The same melody

1 O son of Mattai,[667] how has the city of Nineveh
offended you that you awaited its dying?

2 If you are a zealous man, go uproot first
the city that I made pleasant, that gave withered [fruits].[668]

3 But if you are merciful with the faithless,
why is your anger poured out upon penitents?

4 The vine as a bride I led out from Egypt.[669]
Instead of blossoms she bore sins.

5 Nineveh as clusters [of grapes] bore fasts
and as bunches [of grapes] all just deeds.[670]

6 Instead of clusters arrayed in leaves
her children put on sackcloth.

7 And instead of watering that makes fruits flourish
milk was withheld from the mouths of her children.

---

667. Cf. Jon. 1.1, Pes.
668. Cf. Isa. 5.1–7.
669. Ps. 80.8.
670. On the vineyard imagery, cf. Virg. 31.13 and note ad loc.

8 The swine that loved the calf
ate the vine of Jacob under its shade.[671]

9 Nineveh that acquired graven images by Error
overthrew her idols lest she be overthrown.

10 He sent him to land; he fled to sea.
He sent him to Nineveh; he boarded a ship.

11 To Nineveh He sent him to awaken the peoples.
He slept on the ship; the peoples awakened him![672]

12 Instead of assuaging the sins of land
he went to awaken the waves on the sea.

13 He abandoned silencing the iniquity of the city.
He went to stir up a storm of the sea.

14 Instead of sanctifying the wicked city
he went to overturn a ship of the sea.

15 [Instead of] keeping watch on land and putting wickedness to sleep
he went to sleep at sea and awakened the water.

16 One who was quiet on the ship made the water cry out.
One who cried out on land silenced wickedness.

17 A fish swallowed him who had not gone to set free
the city that the greedy mouth[673] swallowed.

18 The visible mouth disgorged him.
The hidden mouth disgorged the city.

19 Disgorged, the swallowed one became a preacher
to the city that swallowed him on land and disgorged him.[674]

20 When he fell into the sea, he sated the fish.
When he preached on land, he annihilated the greedy one.

21 On the ship they asked him, "Who are you and whose?"[675]
In Nineveh they believed him without questioning.

22 On the ship all the sailors buried him [in the sea].
In Nineveh all the sinners healed him.

23 By his entering the ship the lots[676] fell on it.
By his entering Nineveh sackcloth spread on it.

---

671. Cf. Ps. 80.13.
672. Cf. Jon. 1.5f.
673. Sin and death, as Beck has suggested.
674. That is, he entered the city, preached and then left the city, cf. Jon. 3–4.
675. Jon. 1.8.
676. Or "sentence." Cf. Jon. 1.7–16.

24 Scripture was scattered on all the lots.
Ashes were scattered on all the sackcloth.
25 The lots that fell [were] as for death.
The sackcloth that was spread [was] as for life.
26 The lot caught the servant who had fled,
but the sackcloth put down the city that had rebelled.
27 The lot incited the many against one,
but the sackcloth revived many by one.
28 By this [lot] were opened mouths to blame.
By this [sackcloth] was opened a mouth of supplication.
29 The lot accused the one to kill him,
but the sackcloth had mercy on and saved the many.
30 This [lot] became the cause of judgment to kill,
but this [sackcloth] became the treasure of life to save,
31 The lot wrote names in the deep.
The sackcloth wrote names in the height.

46

The hymn begins with a consideration of the symbolic significance of the judgment of Jonah, which was in reality mercy for the Ninevites (str. 1–9). It represents baptism, on the one hand (esp. str. 3–5), and Christ's condemnation to death, which saved all people, on the other (str. 6–9). But there is still a judgment to come for us (str. 10–16). This leads him to a consideration of sins after baptism, which are to be atoned by a combination of ablutions (or anointing?) for the sick (str. 17f.), God's mercy (str. 19f.), repentance (str. 22) and good works (str. 23–26).

46

The same melody

1 Jonah intended to go down to the sea
to flee on a ship from God.

2 But waves rolled him about like avengers.
A lot seized him and gave him to the waves.

3 The lot caught him for the name of fugitive,
but not immediately and at once did it judge him.

4 It submerged and brought [him] up and then judged him.
That he would sink and emerge, it prophesied to him.

5 It portrayed a symbol even of our sins
that after the resurrection will rebuke us.

6 The lot portrays him who would come to save
Nineveh since it resulted in delivering her [from] death.[677]

7 The lot that resulted as if for death[678]
saved one hundred twenty thousand.

---

677. Ephrem plays on the meanings of *pṣ'* "lot or judgment" and "to deliver." No doubt he alludes to Christ as well as to Jonah as the one "who would come to save Nineveh;" cf. str. 10–12, below.

678. Jonah's death—and Jesus' too.

8 One judgment that took place at sea
   annulled the judgments of thousands on land.

9 The writ[679] that judged the one
   tore up twelve myriad letters of bondage.

10 Therefore the letter of bondage of sins that is hidden within us
   is well-silenced now so that it may cry out at the End.

11 With us it is buried; with us it rises.
   When the judgment seat is established it will cry out to rebuke.

12 Insofar as tears are found in our eyes,
   we will blot out with our tears the letter of bondage of our sins.

13 Insofar as just deeds are in [our] hands,
   we will close up with our just deeds all the breaches.

14 Who will give us [the possibility] that visible tears
   will blot out concealed sins?

15 Who gives us [the possibility] that by visible things
   an invisible wound may be healed?

16 Insofar as free water is found,
   give to drink a valuable cup.

17 The baptized washed the feet of the holy ones,
   so that there is no baptism [but] there is sprinkling.[680]

18 The spattering of sins after you have been baptized
   can be washed with the washing of the sick.

19 Justice encompassed and confined us.
   There is a chance for us again—grace.

20 Lest we be ravished, justice confined us.
   Lest we succumb, grace had mercy on us.

21 Since there is no baptizing again, there [should be] no sinning again,
   but since there is spattering, there is sprinkling.

22 He Who gave hope in baptism
   gave repentance lest hope be cut off by Him.

23 But harsher is the work after you have been baptized
   than that work before you have been baptized.

24 Sins before baptism
   by simple work are able to be atoned.

---

679. Greek, πιττάκιον.
680. Ephrem seems to present Jesus' washing of the apostles' feet, in John 13.4–17, as a precedent for the washing of the sick—or the anointing of the sick. The enigmatic statement that "there is no baptism" is best explained as Beck suggests, that there is no second baptism.

25 And if the imprint of scars sullies [the Christian],
baptism whitens and wipes clean.

26 But sins after baptism
with double works are able to be overturned.

27 When works and mercy have truly healed,
the imprint of scars will call for a miracle.

47

This hymn is an alphabetical acrostic in reverse order, although the aleph strophe is missing and a few others are repeated. It continues into the following hymn. The hymn begins with the repentance of the Ninevites (str. 1–5) and God's desire for the fruits of that repentance (str. 6–10). The exchange of repentance and mercy results in their mutual joy (str. 11–15), but in the discontent of sin and justice (str. 16–18). Since sins are like waves, the ship of Nineveh needs the rudder of fasting to stay afloat (str. 19–20). Jonah was a poor sailor since he did not wish to keep his ship, Nineveh, afloat (str. 21–24).

47

The same melody

1. The Ninevites repented to give offerings:
   a pure fast of pure babes.
2. Flowing breasts they withheld from babes,
   that they might suck floods of mercy.
3. In [Nineveh] flowed tears of repentance,
   and her land shed forth all exploits.
4. For easy is the growth of the fruits
   of this land of repentance.
5. Tears moistened her; mercy shone on her;
   weeping rained in her; pity sprouted in her.
6. The King of the height saw and desired
   the fruits that Nineveh grew in the depth.
7. The Heavenly One desired the delicious fruit,
   the fruit that a flow of tears grew.
8. The High One hungered very much for her tears,
   since He tasted remorse in her fruits.[681]

---

681. On the "hunger" of God, cf. Nat. 13.13f. and Virg. 4.1.

9   He came down and opened the treasury of mercy
to purchase by His mercy the fruits of His servants.

10   When mercy was consumed and He took fruits,
the avenger rejoiced that it was demanded.

11   Who has seen servants exchanging
with their master fruits for mercy?

12   Indeed what measure served there
that sufficed to measure [both] tears and mercy?

13   It is a measure that two weighed and stamped:
repentance and grace.[682]

14   By it repentance gave fruits.
By it grace gave mercy.

15   The two tasted of the two.
In giving and taking the two rejoiced.

16   The two rejoiced but [another] two were discontented:
sin below, justice above.

17   Sin was discontented that evil had cooled,
and justice was discontented that love had cooled.

18   The shedding of tears conquered the shedding of anger,
and the sentence of fasting released the sentence of judgment.

19   And since sins became waves and submerged [sinners],
fasts became a rudder and rescued [them].

20   For Nineveh had become a ship.
Anger shook[683] it; pity steadied it.

21   Every sailor rescues his ship.
Jonah expected to sink his ship.

22   They threw him over into the sea so he would learn[684]
not to overthrow the city on land.

23   A man sank; by mercy he came up.
The one whom [mercy] rescued, expected to sink.

24   By mercy he came up, but he forgot mercy.
What he learned at sea, he rejected on land.

---

682. Here and in the following strophe Ephrem puns on *tybwt'* and *ṭbtwt'*, "repentance" and "grace." In this strophe reference is made to the official stamp on certified weights used in trade.

683. Apparently the Afel of *mwṭ*, otherwise attested only in P'al and Ethp. as Beck notes.

684. A pun on *ylp*, "learn," and *'lp'*, "ship."

48

This portion of the alphabetical acrostic of the previous hymn dwells on God's merciful propensity to correct the imbalances wrought by human perversity, rooted in the free will. The judgment of Jonah overturned the natural order of things; he became food for a fish and Nineveh became food for death (str. 1–5). God's mercy set this disarray into order again, as he had created it (str. 6–12). Our freedom is the source of the problem for us as for Adam (str. 13–15). But God rescues us and makes an adornment of our flaw (str. 16–22).

48

1 A judgment took place on the ship of Jonah.
There has not been one like it in all the houses of judgment.

2 The lot became for him like a judgment seat.
The fish snuffed him in like a judge.

3 He shut him in [his] belly, a prison,
so he could not escape from the Creator of all.

4 The great sea to the great fish
handed over the miserable one [who] fled from the Great One.

5 Since he fled, he became food for a fish,
and he gave Nineveh [as] food for death.

6 The Gracious One Who makes straight all perversities
set in order Jonah's contradictions.

7 For him He returned from within the fish.
Nineveh He snatched from the mouth of the greedy one.

8 He saw the man the fish swallowed.
He created [the fish] for eating, [the fish] swallowed its [intended]
eater.

9 Again, He saw Nineveh that the coward had captured.

He created [Satan] for captivity, [Satan] captured his [intended]
    captors.

10 Mercy rushed to straighten the perversities,
and contradictions were set in order.

11 He ordered the fish to spit out the man
and to return to being food for us.

12 He chided the evil one, and he released Nineveh.
The captured one recaptured her captor.

13 What is overturned[685] and perverted is from freedom.
What sets in order and is made straight is from grace.

14 Our freedom does not cease to prevert.
His grace does not cease to make straight.

15 Freedom made hateful the beauty of Adam
that he might be god . . . human.

16 But grace adorned its flaws,
and God came to be human.

17 Divinity flew down
to rescue and lift up humanity.

18 Behold the Son adorned the servant's flaw,
so that he became god as he had desired.

19 To You be glory, Straightener of every fault!
To You I give thanks, Adorner of all flaws!

20 Since our freedom ceases not to break through,
Majesty wearies not to repair.

21 Your grace accompanies our evil—
the spring of peace for a raging fire.

22 Since wherever the fire kindles its flame,
the light of Your mercy presses hard to extinguish [it].

---

685. This should be *hpyk* rather than *hpky*.

49

This hymn together with the following one is an alphabetic acrostic. Many letters are repeated; some are out of order. Here as in a previous hymn, Ephrem contrasts the behavior of Jonah with that of other models from the Old Testament. Joshua (str. 1–3), Moses (str. 4–10, 13) and Isaac (str. 11–12) all dealt better with their people and their God. Yet Jonah, because he is a type of Christ, par excellence, was the most successful (str. 15–21): In spite of him, his is the most effective Medicine of life (str. 15–17, 21); his oarsmen and God have rescued the sunken ship of Nineveh (str. 18–20).

49

The same melody

1   The High One sent a circumcised healer
to circumcise the heart of the uncircumcised people.

2   By the sword of Joshua the Hebrews were circumcised.
By the voice of Jonah the Ninevites were circumcised.

3   The circumcised Jonah was ashamed of the circumcised,
since he saw the uncircumcised had circumcised [their] heart.

4   When Moses delayed, he exposed the circumcised
since they showed by the calf the uncircumcision of [their] heart.

5   In the contest of forty days
the circumcised were put to shame; the uncircumcised triumphed.

6   The Ninevites conquered in forty days.
Instead of their bodies they circumcised their hearts.

7   The leaven of Egypt was hidden among the People.
It overthrew their heart for strangeness.[686]

---

686. I.e., the leaven of Egypt overthrew true faith from the heart of the Israelites and led them to the worship of strange gods.

8 The leaven of Abraham was hidden among the peoples.
   It overthrew their idol for faith.

9 The people of Moses tasted the sweetness.
   but for forty days they vomited up bitter [words] to him.

10 Jonah gave Nineveh bitter [words] to drink,
   but for forty days her fruits were sweet.

11 Isaac with words and mournful sounds
   for forty days persuaded his father.

12 Jonah lifted Nineveh up as if at the judgment seat,
   and for forty days he tortured it with his words.

13 Moses taught; the People apostatized.
   The healer was irritated that his remedy did not avail.

14 Nineveh repented; it grieved Jonah.
   The healer was irritated that his medicine triumphed.

15 The medicine of which one of the healers
   has healed ten myriads of the sick?

16 The Medicine of penitents came down from the height.
   He scattered pardon among the sins.

17 As much as you are irritated, Jonah, rejoice
   that of all the prophets your medicines are most triumphant.

18 As much as you are irritated, be joyful, sailor,
   that your oarsmen have rescued the sunken ship.

19 The High One answered the sunken ship,
   for the sunken ship was all of the penitents.

20 He answered at sea; He answers on land.
   He rescued on land as at sea.

21 Jonah's voice became a medicine of life.
   He sowed death with it, but life sprouted.

50

This continuation of the previous hymn commences with a description of the effectiveness of the Ninevites' fast (str. 1–12). Jonah's words of judgment really belong to God, who was more pleased with the Ninevites than with the Israelites (str. 13–17). God's manner of exchange is to begin with anger, but then to show mercy if the fruits of repentance are forthcoming (str. 20–23). Since Jonah failed to understand God's ways with human beings, he needed the symbol of the gourd plant (str. 18f. and 24–27).

50

The same melody

1 "The generations that you saved, blessed you, Jonah.
You bore blessings instead of curses.[687]

2 "They made crowns of repentance.
They crowned Me through you since they lived through you.

3 "They wove blossoms that did not fade.
Instead of flowers they wove an ascetic life.

4 "Prayers they wove like lilies
that flourished in the flowing of tears.

5 "Fasts they mingled with humiliation
and prayers by means of just deeds.

6 "In ashes and sackcloth that make beauty fade
the crown of the saints rejoiced.

7 "Ashes and weeping that blind the eyes
enlightened the eyes of the Ninevites.

8 "Ashes and sackcloth she offered [as] blood money.
She conquered the injustice of her adversary at law.

---

687. God addresses Jonah, as becomes apparent in the second strophe.

9   "She who spread ashes passed by suspicion.
She who put on sackcloth lessened anger.[688]

10   "Ashes and tears were the offering.
At the gate of heaven they made reconciliation.

11   "Flowing were tears hidden in eyes.
Flowing was mercy hidden in heaven.

12   "Flowing were tears, and they saddened faces.
Flowing was mercy, and it made them rejoice.

13   "O Jonah, you lifted [and] brought forth woes
and bore and brought enviable blessings.

14   "For they heard from you sounds of anger,
and they made Me hear [what is] Mine: sounds of praise.

15   "You took a hoe and went to uproot.
Your hoe belonged to the Fruit Grower.

16   "The vineyard that put to shame the vineyard of My beloved[689]
bore blessings instead of husks."

17   The fruits of the hateful vineyard ripened.
its fruits moistened its vineshoots.

18   Jonah rejoiced at the young gourd plant,
but he grieved over the vine bearing exploits.

19   The young plant was cut off; Jonah was irritated.
The fruits of the vineyard made the Watchers rejoice.

20   Give thanks to the One Who sent His anger to Nineveh
that His anger might be a merchant of mercy.

21   For two treasures His anger opens:
the treasure of the deep and the treasure of the height.

22   Urgently the fruit went up from below to the height.
Urgently mercy rained from above to the deep.

23   Urgently the blood money went up from below to the height.
Urgently pity came down from above to the deep.

24   The fig tree had reached the time of its cutting.
With the tranquil fruit[690] her worker pledged.

---

688. Here are puns on *qṭmʾ*, "ashes," and *qnṭʾ*, "suspicion," and on *mkt*, "put on," and *mkkt*, "lessened."

689. The beloved of God is Israel. Israel's vineyard is put to shame by the vineyard of the Gentiles, here the people of Nineveh who repent.

690. Or the dead fruit.

25   Jonah lifted his axe to uproot
      the fig tree that suddenly had acquired health.
26   Since he wanted to cut down the beloved of the King,[691]
      the worm cut down his beloved young plant.
27   Since he did not rejoice in peace as a son of peace,
      he was poured into the sea as a contentious man.[692]

---

691. The city of Nineveh, cf. Jon. 4.5–11.

692. Although a postscript reads, "Completed are the nine hymns on Jonah and Nineveh," there are only seven hymns in this set since 47–48 and 49–50 are each a single alphabetic acrostic.

51

This hymn has themes common to Middle Platonic philosophy, for example, the theme of light as representative of the presence of God and the *epinoiai* or manifestations of God appropriate to the spiritual level of the seeker.

51

On the melody: My brothers and my fathers and my sons, be persuaded by my instruction

1   On Sunday the light conquered and was exalted as a parable.[693]
Each one of the six days approached him and crowned him,
and also the creatures that were pleasing to him.
The new males rejoiced to see the new females:
the sheep, flocks and herds that were created,
doves with all the flying creatures,[694] fish in their varieties.
He was exalted and also exalted [them].
Blossoms they wove only recently into a symbol of our Lord,
a crown that conquered the darkness.

Refrain: Praise to the One Whose truth confuted the liars!

2   For three days the light served and was hidden.
For three years our Light served and was exalted.
Of all cities He was manifested[695] in Judea alone.
A second symbol is the sun that as its Lord

---

693. The light at the beginning of time is a symbol of Christ, who conquered sin and death on Sunday, the day of the resurrection.

694. Literally, bodies.

695. The Syriac *dnḥ* means "shine forth" or "manifest." The related noun *dnḥ'* means "dawn," "manifestation," or "epiphany." Ephrem plays on the nuances of these words, especially in the context of his major symbol here, Christ, the Sun, the Light; cf. also Nat. 1.6 and 4.69.

was manifest in every place.
On the fourth day[696] it shone forth.
By four books[697] our Sun shone forth.
The primal darkness abated.
He returned a second time with His rays and blotted it out.[698]

3   In a symbol our Lord distributes light without a fee.
He opened His treasury as grace and He scatters it.
To each who meets Him He gives and He makes him rich.
For to all eyes
His gift is equal without jealousy.
Even to the weak eye in His wisdom
He gives from His blessings; He reaches out to it with His beams.
Since [the weak eye] is not sufficient for His radiance,
His energy moderated by His love He manifests to it.[699]

4   Bare faces are clothed with light and become beautiful.
For light is the garment of the bare eye.
When the eye had put [it] on, it did not sense that [light] clove to it,
but only that [the light] shone forth,
and although it is scattered and is cast into the eyes,
[light] is not felt there and sensed.
[It is] the symbol of our Savior, Who surpasses investigation:
the soul in the symbol of the eye
is filled but not able to contemplate His generation.

5   All creatures are endued with their beauties and varieties.
One that is not garbed in the color of light is unsightly,
for it is the most beautiful and pleasing of all garments.
The eye that is naked is garbed in darkness, without argument,
and it is endued with an unsightly color,
and the one who strips off our Savior willingly,
puts on black Satan,
and with the color of gloomy Error
the miserable one is endued again.

6   When there is no road at sea or on land, it is disturbing.
In You are paths made plain and clear,

---

696. Cf. Gen. 1.14–19.
697. The gospels.
698. Word play on '*ṭp*, "returned," and '*ṭ*', "blotted out."
699. Cf. Thphl. Ant. Autol. I.2.

and even all our stumbling blocks are reproved by Your coming.
Reptiles and wild animals revere You freely.[700]
They go away to their dens when they have seen You.
Your manifestation to the robber persuades him without a rod,
and without the sword's being taken up,
[Your manifestation] withholds [and] hides the murderer's sword.

7   Adam and Eve newly met You.
They saw their manifestations[701] in You, the Light, and rejoiced.
They saw again in You their leaves and were saddened.
The true Light came.
The sinful woman garbed herself in modesty.
Even the thief entered the blessed garden.[702]
Darkness kissed him . . .
. . . his flaws
but the darkness rushed to take refuge
in the dark.[703]

8   Satan and death with the serpent, their companion,
immediately desired the Bloom [and] choked it in their assembly.
Gloomy hot blasts surrounded it in their perfidy
The Blossom, troubled by[704]
gloom and darkness and night,
sprouted [into] a flower in Sheol.
It became the Tree of Life that saved creation.
It ascended for coronation,
and [God] magnified the coronation of Him Who conquers the
       conquerors.[705]

9   Animals saw You, the Light, and rejoiced.
Souls saw the true Light and were cleansed.
By a symbol of flocks, herds and sheep that met You,
resounding rational congregations came to meet our Lord,

---

700. Literally, "without force."
701. Or "brightnesses."
702. *spr* has been omitted in this translation. However, Beck notes that his text is uncertain here. The word order is unusual. Cf. Luke 23.43.
703. Beck suggests, presumably on the basis of "darkness kissed him," that in addition to the cosmic struggle between light and darkness, Ephrem alludes to Judas and Jesus.
704. The Syriac is active.
705. Christ is the Blossom who becomes the Tree of Life and conquers the conquerors, Satan and death.

and they went out with hosannas to receive Him.
Instead of the primal silence that came to meet the light,
later the mouths of the heavenly ones
came to meet our Light with glory.

10 Behold a wonder, my beloved ones, a Light sufficient for all they
    wish:
Who opened even stopped up ears and mouths,
Who made straight withered hands, Who in His love fed the
    hungry.
Hands He made straight give glory,
and mouths He opened chant praises,
and feet He made straight dance for joy,
and the couches whose dead He revived come to meet Him
and the hungry with their food and the debtors with their release.
"Blessed is Your coming!" they cry out.

11 Instead of light that wearies the living by its coming[706]
the true Light gives rests to the weary.
The fishermen He freed from the hard work of their fishing,
and He spares all from all.
"Leave the flock bleating in the sheepfold
and the herds[707] bellowing in their mountains
and the herds[708] neighing in their meadows too
and the mountains that are quarried.
Despise [and] leave these and save yourselves."

12 If the visible light is intangible,
how can the hidden Light be comprehended?
But if He is not able to be touched by thought,
how did they seize Him [and] crucify Him?
The light was awakened out of darkness.
In Your symbol He also emerged from the grave.
Instead of six days that came out to [the light] and were adorned,
the height and the depth and the four directions,
[these] six worship You.

---

706. That is, the light of morning.
707. Of cows.
708. Of horses.

52

The first few strophes of this hymn, to the same melody as the previous one, continue the Middle and Neo-Platonic and anti-Manichaean themes of light and darkness as symbols of Christ and of Satan and death, respectively. In the fourth strophe, however, Ephrem uses the idea of the blinding brightness of the Light to begin a polemic against the Arians, whom he typically brands as disputers, searchers and investigators who lack humility and a sense of the limitations of their creaturely knowledge.

52

The same melody

1   Darkness was made king and conquered and was conquered,
    but since it was not a being,[709] it was overcome and reproved.
    The evil one conquered Adam and expected not to succumb.
    Although our Light was hidden,
    by that light nearby He was portrayed.
    Since it conquers the darkness, it was prophesied
    that by the advent of our Lord Satan would succumb.
    In the beginning darkness succumbed and announced that the evil
        one, too,
    would succumb in the End.
2   Therefore from before this hateful victory of his
    while he had not yet conquered that Adam and been exalted,
    he was first portrayed in the humiliation of the conquered darkness,
    the prophet that resembles him.[710]
    The dark proclaimed about the Darkness,
    and the brightness instructed about our Light.

---

709. A common neo-Platonic argument against Manichaeism.
710. That is, the darkness is the prophet of Satan, foreshadowing his victory over Adam.

O the proclaimed who resemble their proclaimers!
On Sunday the Light conquered,
and it portrayed our Savior, His day and His victory.

3 The sun proclaimed three symbols in the world:
that few are able to gaze at it in its strength,
for the healthy one are its rays, for the sick one are its beams.
Our Sun supplies three symbols:
that His perfect commandment is for the perfect,
and the gentle[711] commandments for the average.[712]
The perfect one is able to catch Christ by His humility.[713]
Pride is sick and is unable
to consider the strength of humility.

4 The source of the rays is that bringing forth of our Savior.[714]
Our mind is much too weak to investigate it.[715]
If one hopes to investigate it,
it is revealed that he is not sufficient to the Source
Whose streams push on him and resist going out.
They eject him, cast him out and hurl him by their rushing.
If you are able, gaze at the sun's disc
that, while flying, is still.
It is wonder in its course and a wonder in its stillness!

5 The visible light is intangible.
The hidden Light is too fine to be touched
like a ray whose investigation slips away at all times.
If our eyes close to hold the light in them,
it fades and darkens them by its departure,
and all our minds that investigate
You, our Light, become blind,
for Your bringing forth is unsearchable,
for Your wealth is incomprehensible and Your treasure is unable to
    be investigated.

---

711. Or "abstinent."
712. Or "the middle ones."
713. The Syriac word is the equivalent, but not a cognate, of the Greek *kenosis*.
714. The word here translated as "bringing forth" normally refers to a mother giving birth,
but here the allusion is to the Father's "bringing forth" of the Son; for similar references to the
"womb" of God. cf. Nat. 13.7, 21.7–8, 27.15 and 27.19.
715. Either the "bringing forth" or the Savior might be meant here.

6   You have humbled the pride of[716] those bold disputers.
    You have humbled the voice of the assailing searchers.
    You have confused the faction of the attacking investigators.
    They hoped to investigate Your Light,
    but Your extent could not be grasped to be investigated,
    Your manifestation could not be cut off to be grasped,
    Your flow could not be stayed to measure Your source.
    You have hidden in Your Parent.
    If His womb can be investigated, its Offspring can also be
          comprehended.

7   Your bringing forth confuses us and is incomprehensible,
    and Your inquiry overtakes us and is unsearchable.
    Your Light fills us but is unable to be grasped.
    Who has searched out our Sun?
    Your extent is unable to be seized that we should know it.
    Your manifestation is ungraspable that we should measure it.
    If the [Divine] Being were comprehensible, His bringing forth
          would be investigable.
    If the Parent had been interpreted,
    it would be easy for His Offspring[717] to be explained.

8   Let us take the gnat, smallest of all creatures.
    Its body is great but not able to be weighed
    by this inquiry, the rational balance.
    O gnat, where are your viscera,
    your eye and your ear that we may touch you?
    What hand[718] constructed your limbs?
    You are the proclaimer of your Creator.[719]
    In his substance the gnat became a mountain:
    Although his body is quite small, his investigation is great.

---

716. Literally, "for."

717. Or "his bringing forth."

718. An alliterative pun, *[a]'yd' [i]'yd'*.

719. It is perhaps an anti-Marcionite polemic that led Ephrem to choose the gnat here to proclaim the Creator, since Marcion adduced fleas, snakes and other noxious creatures to argue that the Creator was not good. But Arius also contributed to the discipline of insect theology, since he argued that every creature, even the worm, since it is created by God, is in the image of God. Ephrem begins with a point more pertinent to anti-Marcionite polemic, that the little gnat proclaims its Creator, but then he turns it to his anti-Arian polemic. Since even the little gnat is not easily investigated, how much less can we investigate the Logos who created both us and the gnat?

9   Therefore, let all the mighty creatures be left out
     and more than these, the splendid human being,
     and more than the human, the distant heavenly [beings].
     What is left then is
     for us to contemplate in silence how hidden is
     this Offspring whom we despised but Who sustained us.
     Let us bring our thank offering to the Awesome One
     Whom they have angered by questions
     and abased by investigations and limited by controversies.

10   Every thing has quantity and weight and measurements.
     Mute and quiet and silent is their nature.
     As if endowed with speech, they extend persuasion by their silence
               to us
     who have weighed and measured and quantified.
     You, our Lord, Mind and Intellect,
     have never been measured, weighed and quantified.
     Rational measures cry out in the creation
     that Your generation cannot be weighed
     nor Your depth quantified nor Your height measured![720]

---

720. Ephrem plays on the irony that although we human beings are rational, articulate
creatures who should emulate the Logos, the word and mind of God, we must be taught by the
irrational and speechless things of the creation to respect the inscrutability of the Logos. A
postscript adds, "Completed is the writing of the hymns on virginity and on the symbols of our
Lord that are fifty-one [or, according to one manuscript, "fifty-two"] in number, that blessed
Mar Ephrem composed."

Index

INDEX

INDEX

and Peter, 441–442; words of judgment of, 458–460
Joseph, 77–79, 105, 108, 337, 339–341, 343, 350, 353
Joshua bar Nun, 67–68, 337, 339, 343
Jovian, Emperor, 22
Judah, 81, 299
Judaism, 10–12, 14–15, 411–415
Judas, 72, 271–272
Julian, Emperor, 16, 19, 21, 35 (*See also Hymns Against Julian*)

Kaleb, 67
Kenosis, 106, 118, 131, 133, 158, 187

Lamech, 70
Lazarus, 390–391
Leah, 285
Letters, 210–213
Levi, 299, 300
Light, 281–286, 465–468
Liturgical festivals, 199–204
Logos, 187–189
Lot, 67, 428–429
Lot's daughters, 428–429
Love, 261, 264–265
Lucian of Samosata, 24

Magi, 110, 112, 145–147, 166–167, 181, 191–196, 199–200
Mari, 7
Mariology, 33–34
Marriage, spiritual, 376–381
Martha, 376–377
Mary: and addressing Jesus, 110–112; and birth of Jesus, 99–100, 102; blessedness of, 118, 122, 203; God's presence in, 148–152; and incarnation, 44–45; on incarnation, 105, 108–109; and letters, 211–212; as mouthpiece of Jesus, 145–146; as new Eve, 153–154; and relationship with Jesus, 77–78, 80, 131–134; types of, Ephrem's, 33–34; uniqueness of, 124–125; virginity of, 140–144, 148, 151, 214–217
Medicine of Life (*See* Jesus)
Melchizedek, 66, 124–125, 300
Mesopotamia, 5–8, 13, 16
Messiah, 211–212 (*See also* Jesus)

Methuselah, 69–70
Micah, 64, 77, 202
Michael, house of, 158, 160
Michal, 140, 142–143
Middle Platonic philosophy, 461, 465
Midian, 346
Miracles, nature, 407–410
Modesty, 271–274
Monimos, 24
Mosaic laws, 140
Moses, 67–68, 77, 79, 115–116, 140, 144, 299, 320–324, 346, 391, 443–445, 456–457
Myrrh, 179, 183–184

Nain, 407–408
Narses of Persia, 7
Nathanael, 329, 331
Nativity (*See also Hymns on the Nativity*): and Caesar Augustus, 158–159; feast of, 105, 107; liturgical theme of, 89; praise of, 115, 117; singer at, 173–175; vigil on, 173
Nature miracles, 407–410
Nebo, 24
New Testament, 42–43, 63–64, 82, 87, 166, 169, 276–278
Nicene orthodoxy, 3–4
Nisibis: Christians in, 5–8; church of, 8; defenses of, 233, 241; Ephrem the Syrian's last years in, 17–23; Jews in, 14; under siege, 12–17
Noah, 66, 70, 115–116, 299
Noah's ark, 214
Numbers, 210–213

Oil and ointment: and baptismal themes, 292–296; for fuel, 281–286; and Jesus, symbolism of, 287–291; restorative properties of, 275, 278–279; symbolism of, 275–280
Old Testament, 32–33, 66–68, 76, 140, 144, 275–278, 345–346, 403–406
On the Church (Ephrem), 221–226
On the Syrian Goddess (Lucian of Samosata), 24

Pagan deities, 5–6, 24, 243, 245–246
Pagan oracles, 233, 236–239

INDEX

Other Volumes in this Series